Register for Free Membership to

solutions@syngress.com

Over the last few years, Syngress has published many best-selling and critically acclaimed books, including Tom Shinder's *Configuring ISA Server 2000*, Brian Caswell and Jay Beale's *Snort 2.0 Intrusion Detection*, and Angela Orebaugh and Gilbert Ramirez's *Ethereal Packet Sniffing*. One of the reasons for the success of these books has been our unique **solutions@syngress.com** program. Through this site, we've been able to provide readers a real time extension to the printed book.

As a registered owner of this book, you will qualify for free access to our members-only solutions@syngress.com program. Once you have registered, you will enjoy several benefits, including:

- Four downloadable e-booklets on topics related to the book. Each booklet is approximately 20-30 pages in Adobe PDF format. They have been selected by our editors from other best-selling Syngress books as providing topic coverage that is directly related to the coverage in this book.

- A comprehensive FAQ page that consolidates all of the key points of this book into an easy to search web page, providing you with the concise, easy to access data you need to perform your job.

- A "From the Author" Forum that allows the authors of this book to post timely updates links to related sites, or additional topic coverage that may have been requested by readers.

Just visit us at **www.syngress.com/solutions** and follow the simple registration process. You will need to have this book with you when you register.

Thank you for giving us the opportunity to serve your needs. And be sure to let us know if there is anything else we can do to make your job easier.

SYNGRESS®

YNGRESS®

Nessus
Network Auditing

Renaud Deraison

Haroon Meer

Roelof Temmingh

Charl van der Walt

Raven Alder

Jimmy Alderson

Andy Johnston

George A. Theall

Jay Beale   Series Editor

HD Moore   Technical Editor

Noam Rathaus   Technical Editor

KEY	SERIAL NUMBER
001	HV764GHVB7
002	POFGBN329M
003	HJWWQV734M
004	CVPLQ6CC73
005	239KMWH5T2
006	VBP95BNBBB
007	H863EBN643
008	29MKVB5487
009	69874FRVFG
010	BNWQ6233BH

PUBLISHED BY
Syngress Publishing, Inc.
800 Hingham Street
Rockland, MA 02370

Nessus Network Auditing

Publisher: Andrew Williams
Acquisitions Editor: Christine Kloiber
Technical Editor: Jay Beale, HD Moore,
 and Noam Rathaus

Page Layout and Art: Patricia Lupien
Copy Editor: Beth Roberts
Indexer: Nara Wood
Cover Designer: Michael Kavish

Distributed by O'Reilly Media, Inc. in the United States and Canada.
For information on rights and translations, contact Matt Pedersen, Director of Sales and Rights, at Syngress Publishing; email matt@syngress.com or fax to 781-681-3585.

Acknowledgments

We would like to acknowledge the following people for their kindness and support in making this book possible.

Syngress books are now distributed in the United States and Canada by O'Reilly Media, Inc. The enthusiasm and work ethic at O'Reilly is incredible and we would like to thank everyone there for their time and efforts to bring Syngress books to market: Tim O'Reilly, Laura Baldwin, Mark Brokering, Mike Leonard, Donna Selenko, Bonnie Sheehan, Cindy Davis, Grant Kikkert, Opol Matsutaro, Steve Hazelwood, Mark Wilson, Rick Brown, Leslie Becker, Jill Lothrop, Tim Hinton, Kyle Hart, Sara Winge, C. J. Rayhill, Peter Pardo, Leslie Crandell, Valerie Dow, Regina Aggio, Pascal Honscher, Preston Paull, Susan Thompson, Bruce Stewart, Laura Schmier, Sue Willing, Mark Jacobsen, Betsy Waliszewski, Dawn Mann, Kathryn Barrett, John Chodacki, and Rob Bullington.

The incredibly hard working team at Elsevier Science, including Jonathan Bunkell, Ian Seager, Duncan Enright, David Burton, Rosanna Ramacciotti, Robert Fairbrother, Miguel Sanchez, Klaus Beran, Emma Wyatt, Rosie Moss, Chris Hossack, Mark Hunt, and Krista Leppiko, for making certain that our vision remains worldwide in scope.

David Buckland, Marie Chieng, Lucy Chong, Leslie Lim, Audrey Gan, Pang Ai Hua, and Joseph Chan of STP Distributors for the enthusiasm with which they receive our books.

Kwon Sung June at Acorn Publishing for his support.

David Scott, Tricia Wilden, Marilla Burgess, Annette Scott, Andrew Swaffer, Stephen O'Donoghue, Bec Lowe, and Mark Langley of Woodslane for distributing our books throughout Australia, New Zealand, Papua New Guinea, Fiji Tonga, Solomon Islands, and the Cook Islands.

Winston Lim of Global Publishing for his help and support with distribution of Syngress books in the Philippines.

Series Editor, Technical Editor

Jay Beale is a security specialist focused on host lockdown and security audits. He is the lead developer of the Bastille project, which creates a hardening script for Linux, HP-UX, and Mac OS X; a member of the Honeynet Project; and the Linux technical lead in the Center for Internet Security. A frequent conference speaker and trainer, Jay speaks and trains at the Black Hat and LinuxWorld conferences, among others. Jay is a senior research scientist with the George Washington University Cyber Security Policy and Research Institute and makes his living as a security consultant through the MD-based firm Intelguardians, LLC, where he works on security architecture reviews, threat mitigation, and penetration tests against Unix and Windows targets.

Jay wrote the Center for Internet Security's Unix host security tool, currently in use worldwide by organizations from the Fortune 500 to the Department of Defense. He leads the Center's Linux Security benchmark team and, as a core participant in the non-profit Center's Unix teams, is working with private enterprises and US agencies to develop Unix security standards for industry and government.

Jay has written a number of articles and book chapters on operating system security. He is a columnist for Information Security Magazine and previously wrote a number of articles for SecurityPortal.com and SecurityFocus.com. He co-authored the Syngress international best-seller *Snort 2.0 Intrusion Detection* (ISBN: 1-931836-74-4) and serves as the series and technical editor of the Syngress Open Source Security series, which includes *Snort 2.1 Intrusion Detection, Second Edition* (ISBN 1-931836-04-3) and *Ethereal Packet Sniffing* (ISBN 1-932266-82-8). Jay's long-term writing goals include finishing a Linux hardening book focused on Bastille called, *Locking Down Linux*. Formerly, Jay served as the Security Team Director for MandrakeSoft, helping set company strategy, design security products, and pushing security into the third largest retail Linux distribution.

Technical Editors and Contributors

HD Moore is one of the founding members of Digital Defense, a security firm that was created in 1999 to provide network risk assessment services. In the last four years, Digital Defense has become one of the leading security service providers for the financial industry, with over 200 clients across 43 states. Service offerings range from automated vulnerability assessments to customized security consulting and penetration testing. HD developed and maintains the assessment engine, performs application code reviews, develops exploits, and conducts vulnerability research.

Noam Rathaus is the co-founder and CTO of Beyond Security, a company specializing in the development of enterprise-wide security assessment technologies, vulnerability assessment-based SOCs (security operation centers) and related products. He holds an electrical engineering degree from Ben Gurion University, and has been checking the security of computer systems from the age of 13. Noam is also the editor-in-chief of SecuriTeam.com, one of the largest vulnerability databases and security portals on the Internet. He has contributed to several security-related open-source projects including an active role in the Nessus security scanner project. He has written over 150 security tests to the open source tool's vulnerability database, and also developed the first Nessus client for the Windows operating system. Noam is apparently on the hit list of several software giants after being responsible for uncovering security holes in products by vendors such as Microsoft, Macromedia, Trend Micro, and Palm. This keeps him on the run using his Nacra Catamaran, capable of speeds exceeding 14 knots for a quick getaway. He would like to dedicate his contribution to the memory of Haim Finkel.

Contributors

Renaud Deraison is the Founder and the primary author of the open-source Nessus vulnerability scanner project. He has worked for SolSoft, and founded his own computing security consulting company, Nessus Consulting. Nessus has won numerous awards, most notably, is the 2002 Network Computing 'Well Connected' award. Mr. Deraison also is an editorial board member of Common Vulnerabilities and Exposures Organization. He has presented at a variety of security conferences including the Black Hat Briefings and CanSecWest.

Raven Alder is a Senior Security Engineer for True North Solutions, a consulting firm specializing in network security design and implementation. She specializes in scalable enterprise-level security, with an emphasis on defense in depth. She designs large-scale firewall and IDS systems, and then performs vulnerability assessments and penetration tests to make sure they are performing optimally. In her copious spare time, she teaches network security for LinuxChix.org and checks cryptographic vulnerabilities for the Open Source Vulnerability Database. Raven lives in the Washington, DC area.

Jimmy Alderson is the Technical Product Manager at Atlanta-based GuardedNet, a leader in Security Information Management, as well as a Founding member of DC-based firm Intelguardians Network Intelligence. He is a member of the CVE Editorial board and a founding member of the Behavioral Computational Neuroscience Group which specializes in applications of stratification theory. Jimmy was the author of the first Security Information Management system as well as the original pioneer on the use of Taps for performing intrusion detection on switched networks. He has been an active member of the security community since 1992 specializing in vulnerability assessments, penetration tests, intrusion detection, architecture design/review, policy compliance and product design. As a manager, consultant, trainer, coder, and businessman, Jimmy lives a nomadic life from one area of expertise to another, as well as one geographic area to the next. Jimmy currently resides in Atlanta, GA where he spends most of the summer months indoors.

Andy Johnston co-author of *Unix Unleashed v4*, supports IT security at the University of Maryland, Baltimore County (UMBC). He specializes in intrusion detection, incident response, and computer Forensics. Andy's background includes twelve years with Computer Sciences Corporation, primarily on NASA contracts. He has been active in local SAGE groups and has presented at SANS conferences.

Andy holds a bachelor's degree in biology from Princeton University and a master's degree in math from UMBC. He currently resides in Baltimore.

Haroon Meer (B.Com [Info. Systems], CNA, CNE, MCSE, CISSP, CCSA, CCSE) is the Director of Development at SensePost. He completed his studies at the University of Natal with majors in information systems, marketing, and information systems technology. He began working for the University's Computer Services Division during his first year of study and stayed on as a Systems Consultant, specializing in inter-network connectivity and Internet related systems. He joined SensePost in 2001 as part of the technical team, where he spends most of his time in the development of additional security related tools and proof of concept code. He has released several tools/papers on subject matters relating to Network / Web Application security and is a regular presenter at conferences like Black Hat and DefCon.

Roelof Temmingh is the Technical Director and a founding member of SensePost - a South African IT security assessment company. After completing his degree in electronic engineering he worked for four years at a leading software engineering company specializing in encryption devices and firewalls. In 2000 he started SensePost along with some of the country's leaders in IT security. Roelof heads SensePost's external security analysis team, and in his "spare time" plays with interesting concepts such as footprint and web application automation, worm propagation techniques, covert channels/Trojans and cyber warfare. Roelof is a regular speaker/trainer at international conferences including the Black Hat Briefings, DefCon, RSA, FIRST and Summercon. Roelof gets his kicks from innovative thoughts, tea, dreaming, lots of bandwidth, learning cool new stuff, Camels, UNIX, fine food, 3am creativity, and big screens. He dislikes conformists, papaya, suits, animal cruelty, arrogance, track changes, and dishonest people or programs.

George A. Theall is a frequent contributor to the Nessus mailing lists, is the author of several popular Nessus-related tools and has also contributed rewrites of several of the supplemental scripts and associated documentation in Nessus, to be distributed starting with version 2.2. He has authored many Perl scripts including: update-nessusrc, update-nessus-plugins, describe-nessus-plugin, and sd2nbe. George has worked as a systems developer and systems administrator for a major hospital in Philadelphia.

Charl van der Walt is a founder and director of SensePost Information Security, a South Africa-based Infosec services company. Having studied computer science in South Africa and then mathematics in Germany, Charl started his career as a programmer, before moving on to technical support and later to technical design of security technologies like firewalls, VPNs, PKI and file encryption systems, and finally to security analysis, assessments, and penetration testing. As a CISSP and BS7799 Lead Auditor, Charl's combination of technical and theoretical skills are applied to developing systems and methodologies for understanding, evaluating and managing risk at all levels of the enterprise. He regularly releases work on both technical and theoretical issues and can often be see teaching or speaking at academic institutions and security conferences like Black Hat and DefCon.

Appendix Contributors

Michel Arboi is a Computer Security Consultant in the Algoriel ISO15408 evaluation laboratory. Over the course of his career, Michel has had extensive experience writing software (in C, mostly under UNIX), and is known for his work with Nessus. He has written about a hundred test plugins, has implemented OpenSSL support and wrote the second version of the Nessus Attack Scripting Language (NASL) interpreter - the scripting language designed specifically for Nessus. Michel received his Master's Degree in engineering from ENSTA, and is currently trying desperately to decrypt several languages: English, Arabic, and Greek.

Ty Gast (CISSP) is a Senior Security Engineer at Betrusted, a premier global provider of security, identity and trust solutions to the world's leading organizations. With 11 years of experience, he specializes in many facets of information assurance, including security assessments (network-based, wardialing, and wireless), secure network architecture development, computer forensics analysis, and managed security solutions. He was instrumental in constructing a large-scale Dragon IDS monitoring system monitoring hundreds of clients and thousands of devices, to include creating customized programs to handle alerts automatically without human intervention. He has also designed and taught computing courses for the U.S. Government. Ty currently resides in the Baltimore, MD area.

About the CD

The CD-ROM accompanying this book includes the successful open-source tools: Snort, Ethereal and, of course, Nessus. Most files are included as a gzip-compressed tar archive, but in some cases .zip compressed files for use on Windows systems are included. Although the latest version of each piece of software at the time of this writing was placed on the CD-ROM, it should be noted that open source projects have active development cycles and so newer software versions may have been released since publication. An excellent place to find links to the latest releases of each piece of software is by checking each tool's homepage (i.e. www.snort.org and www.ethereal.com).

For Nessus, we've included two versions: version 2.0.10a, which is currently the most stable version at the time of this writing for UNIX-compatible systems only; and version 2.1.1, the current development version also for UNIX-compatible systems only. This version is in beta and may not be stable yet, but it has the ability to perform local security checks in addition to remote tests. For any updates or newer versions, please visit the www.nessus.org site.

We've also included NeWT v2.0, a stand-alone security scanner made available by Tenable Network Security. NeWT (Nessus Windows Technology) is a native port of Nessus under Windows and is very easy to use and install. It runs the same vulnerability checks as the Nessus vulnerability scanner and also supports custom NASL checks.

Contents

Chapter 8 Under the Hood 239

Chapter 9 The Nessus Knowledge Base 271

Foreword

Every now and then, people ask me why I created *Nessus*, and more importantly why I chose this name. In Greek mythology, Nessus is a centaur whose blood-stained robe killed Hercules, while in Larry Niven's "Ringworld", Nessus is an alien from a paranoid and more evolved civilization than ours. Some people have even asked me if "Nessus" was an acronym (as in "NEtwork Security Scanner for US" or something similar). However, none of these guesses are correct, and so here is the story behind Nessus.

In 1996, at the age of 16, I finally got fed up with the constant crashes of Mac OS 7, and installed a very eclectic version of Linux on my Power Macintosh called 'MkLinux'. I basically switched from Mac OS, a fully graphical environment with Netscape, to MkLinux, which was running the twm window manager and Lynx as a web browser. I still have fond memories of that transition, where every day would bring its own share of joy and satisfaction: configuring my modem to get Internet access, getting the sound card to work, recompiling the kernel, recompiling the micro-kernel (MkLinux was Linux running on top of the MACH kernel), or getting the new releases of the kernel(s) by modem. But, the two things that struck me the most on this system was the loopback interface and the fact that multiple users could be logged in at the same time.

The multi-user approach of Linux sounded like a great invention from the perspective of a MacOS user, and a good Samaritan. The second UNIX account I created was the *guest* account, with no password. This account was created so that I could invite friends to log into my new powerful UNIX workstation and they would be able to test it without having to install it on their system.

The loopback interface was also great as it meant I could program network-enabled applications without having to connect to the Internet to test them. Under MacOS 7, you had to have a real network connection (modem or Ethernet) to actually test your applications. Under UNIX, I did not have to establish a phone connection to test my various programs, and that was exactly what I was looking for. In addition to this, network programming under UNIX was surprisingly easy compared to MacOS, so I started to write small applications (like a text-based email client because I could not figure out how to configure sendmail to send mail thru my ISP).

By mid-1997, I was very familiar with my now-tamed UNIX system, and I routinely went on IRC to chat with friends. One day I realized that someone had logged in using the *guest* account I had created and forgotten about, and attempted to wipe my whole hard drive (this attempt fortunately failed thanks to the user permissions), and so I decided that it was time to do a little checkup of my system with a tool which would tell me what an "attacker" could see from the point of view of the network. And therefore I installed SATAN, which was popular at the time.

Getting SATAN to install on a MkLinux system was no fun—MkLinux was missing a lot of the basic utilities SATAN required to work properly—like 'showmount'—so I had to wrestle for a couple of days before I could get a version which was somehow working. I ran it and I was disappointed by the results: half of the tests had not worked properly due to missing utilities, the GUI was quite confusing and the report was not as strict as I wanted it to be (it should have told me to disable more services). At the time, I was also very interested in the IT security field, so I decided that writing a new network security scanner could be a good idea. I exchanged design ideas with two friends—Jan Roudot and Philippe Langlois (who later on co-founded Qualys)—and in late 1997, I started to code a new scanner which would: be plugin based, not use any of the local Unix commands to do its job and be written in C. I also set up a real network at home with an old Sun3 workstation, and even got access to a university network to do my testing. When confronted with the need to name this program, I took a mythology encyclopedia, and decided to pick a name at random. And this is how I picked the name "Nessus". Just luck (and good luck too—had I named the project "Hephaestus", it might have been slightly less popular).

In 1998, on April 4th, I announced the availability of the initial "alpha" version of Nessus on the bugtraq mailing list, with its 50 different remote security checks. The volume of feedback I received was really unexpected. Dozens of people had downloaded Nessus, tested it and came up with improvement suggestions, and basically the project started to snowball from there. I decided to maintain and continue improving it—thus becoming some kind of monomaniac—until I got bored with it. Fortunately, Nessus is a very interesting project to work on, as its internals cover a wide range of areas—from networking issues to software parallelism. It also made me discover a wide range of software, since I had to write a plugin every time a flaw would be found. So, over six years after the initial release, I'm still not yet bored with the project—quite the opposite actually.

The only problem with Nessus is the lack of documentation—writing code is fun, documenting how it works is much less. Fortunately, this book now fills that gap and will help you to get familiar with the tool, to get the most out of it, but also to know its limitations and how to deal with them. When I read the list of authors for this book, I was thrilled to recognize so many familiar names, and I could not be happier with it. This book will not only teach you how to use Nessus, but also how Nessus works internally—why its design is done the way it is, and why that makes it both powerful and flexible to perform a wide range of network-based operations.

Enjoy the read!

—Renaud Deraison
Founder of the Nessus Project
September, 2004

## Chapter 1

Vulnerability Assessment

Solutions in this Chapter:

- **What Is a Vulnerability Assessment?**
- **Automated Assessments**
- **Two Approaches**
- **Realistic Expectations**

☑ **Summary**

☑ **Solutions Fast Track**

☑ **Frequently Asked Questions**

Introduction

In the war zone that is the modern Internet, manually reviewing each networked system for security flaws is no longer feasible. Operating systems, applications, and network protocols have grown so complex over the last decade that it takes a dedicated security administrator to keep even a relatively small network shielded from attack.

Each technical advance brings wave after wave of security holes. A new protocol might result in dozens of actual implementations, each of which could contain exploitable programming errors. Logic errors, vendor-installed backdoors, and default configurations plague everything from modern operating systems to the simplest print server. Yesterday's viruses seem positively tame compared to the highly optimized Internet worms that continuously assault every system attached to the global Internet.

To combat these attacks, a network administrator needs the appropriate tools and knowledge to identify vulnerable systems and resolve their security problems before they can be exploited. One of the most powerful tools available today is the vulnerability assessment, and this chapter describes what it is, what it can provide you, and why you should be performing them as often as possible. Following this is an analysis of the different types of solutions available, the advantages of each, and the actual steps used by most tools during the assessment process. The next section describes two distinct approaches used by the current generation of assessment tools and how choosing the right tool can make a significant impact on the security of your network. Finally, the chapter closes with the issues and limitations that you can expect when using any of the available assessment tools.

What Is a Vulnerability Assessment?

To explain vulnerability assessments, we first need to define what a vulnerability is. For the purposes of this book, *vulnerability* refers to any programming error or misconfiguration that could allow an intruder to gain unauthorized access. This includes anything from a weak password on a router to an unpatched programming flaw in an exposed network service. Vulnerabilities are no longer just the realm of system crackers and security consultants; they have become the enabling factor behind most network worms, spyware applications, and e-mail viruses.

Spammers are increasingly relying on software vulnerabilities to hide their tracks; the open mail relays of the 1990s have been replaced by compromised "zombie" proxies of today, created through the mass exploitation of common vulnerabilities. A question often asked is, "Why would someone target my system?" The answer is that most exploited systems were not targeted; they were simply one more address in a network range being scanned by an attacker. They were targets of opportunity, not choice. Spammers do not care whether a system belongs to an international bank or your grandmother Edna; as long as they can install their relay software, it makes no difference to them.

Vulnerability assessments are simply the process of locating and reporting vulnerabilities. They provide you with a way to detect and resolve security problems before someone or something can exploit them. One of the most common uses for vulnerability assessments is their capability to validate security measures. If you recently installed a new intrusion detection system (IDS), a vulnerability assessment allows you to determine how well that solution works. If the assessment completes and your IDS didn't fire off a single alert, it might be time to have a chat with the vendor.

The actual process for vulnerability identification varies widely between solutions; however, they all focus on a single output—the report. This report provides a snapshot of all the identified vulnerabilities on the network at a given time. Components of this report usually include a list detailing each identified vulnerability, where it was found, what the potential risk is, and how it can be resolved. Figure 1.1 shows a sample Nessus Security Scanner report for a network of only five systems; the number of vulnerabilities is already over 100!

Figure 1.1 Sample Nessus Report

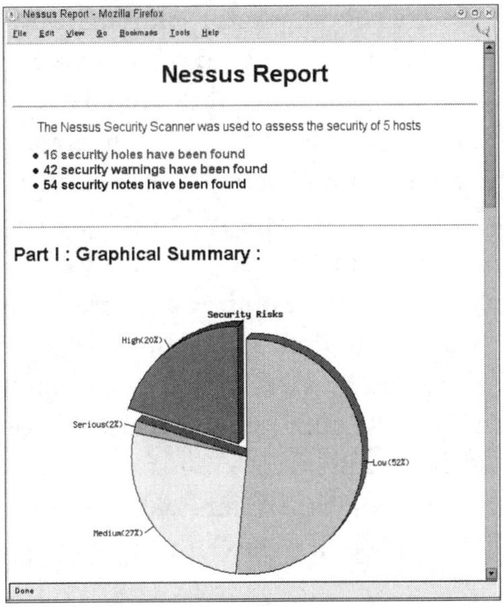

Why a Vulnerability Assessment?

Vulnerability assessments have become a critical component of many organizations' security infrastructures; the ability to perform a networkwide security snapshot supports a number of security vulnerability and administrative processes. When a new vulnerability is discovered, the network administrator can perform an assessment, discover which systems are vulnerable, and start the patch installation process. After the fixes are in place, another assessment can be run to verify that the vulnerabilities were actually resolved. This cycle of assess, patch, and re-assess has become the standard method for many organizations to manage their security issues.

Many organizations have integrated vulnerability assessments into their system rollout process. Before a new server is installed, it first must go through a vulnerability assessment and pass with flying colors. This process is especially important for organizations that use a standard build image for each system; all too often, a new server can be imaged, configured, and installed without the administrator remembering to install the latest system patches. Additionally, many vulnerabilities can only be resolved through manual configuration changes; even an automated patch installation might not be enough to secure a newly imaged system. It's much easier to find these problems at build time when configuration changes are simple and risk-free than when that system is deployed in the field. We strongly recommend performing a vulnerability assessment against any new system before deploying it.

While many security solutions complicate system administration, vulnerability assessments can actually assist an administrator. Although the primary purpose of an assessment is to detect vulnerabilities, the assessment report can also be used as an inventory of the systems on the network and the services they expose. Since enumerating hosts and services is the first part of any vulnerability assessment, regular assessments can give you a current and very useful understanding of the services offered on your network. Assessments assist in crises: when a new worm is released, assessment reports are often used to generate task lists for the system administration staff, allowing them to prevent a worm outbreak before it reaches critical mass.

Asset classification is one of the most common nonsecurity uses for vulnerability assessment tools. Knowing how many and what types of printers are in use will help resource planning. Determining how many Windows 95 systems still need to be upgraded can be as easy as looking at your latest report. The ability to glance quickly at a document and determine what network resources might be overtaxed or underutilized can be invaluable to topology planning.

Assessment tools are also capable of detecting corporate policy violations; many tools will report peer-to-peer services, shared directories full of illegally-shared copyrighted materials, and unauthorized remote access tools. If a long-time system administrator leaves the company, an assessment tool can be used to detect that a backdoor was left in the firewall. If bandwidth use suddenly spikes, a vulnerability assessment can be used to locate workstations that have installed file-sharing software.

One of the most important uses for vulnerability assessment data is event correlation; if an intrusion does occur, a recent assessment report allows the security administrator to determine how it occurred, and what other assets might have been compromised. If the intruder gained access to a network consisting of unpatched Web servers, it is safe to assume that he gained access to those systems as well.

Notes from the Underground…

Intrusion Detection Systems

The difference between vulnerability assessments and an IDS is not always immediately clear. To understand the differences between these complimentary security systems, you will also need to understand how an IDS works. When people speak of IDSs, they are often referring to what is more specifically called a network intrusion detection system (NIDS). A NIDS' role is to monitor all network traffic, pick out malicious attacks from the normal data, and send out alerts when an attack is detected. This type of defense is known as a *reactive security measure* as it can only provide you with information after an attack has occurred. In contrast, a vulnerability assessment can provide you with the data about a vulnerability before it is used to compromise a system, allowing you to fix the problem and prevent the intrusion. For this reason, vulnerability assessments are considered a *proactive security measure*.

Assessment Types

The term *vulnerability assessment* is used to refer to many different types and levels of service. A host assessment normally refers to a security analysis against a single system, from that system, often using specialized tools and an administrative user account. In contrast, a network assessment is used to test an entire network of systems at once.

Host Assessments

Host assessment tools were one of the first proactive security measures available to system administrators and are still in use today. These tools require that the assessment software be installed on each system you want to assess. This software can either be run stand-alone or be linked to a central system on the network. A host assessment looks for system-level vulnerabilities such as insecure file permissions, missing software patches, noncompliant security policies, and outright backdoors and Trojan horse installations.

The depth of the testing performed by host assessment tools makes it the preferred method of monitoring the security of critical systems. The downside of host assessments is that they require a set of specialized tools for the operating system and software packages being used, in addition to administrative access to each system that should be tested. Combined with the substantial time investment required to perform the testing and the limited scalability, host assessments are often reserved for a few critical systems.

The number of available and up-to-date host assessment solutions has been decreasing over the last few years. Tools like COPS and Tiger that were used religiously by system administrators just a few years ago have now fallen so far behind as to be nearly useless. Many of the stand-alone tools have been replaced by agent-based systems that use a centralized reporting and management system. This transition has been fueled by a demand for scalable systems that can be deployed across larger server farms with a minimum of administrative effort. At the time of this publication the only stand-alone host assessment tools used with any frequency are those targeting nontechnical home users and part-time administrators for small business systems.

Although stand-alone tools have started to decline, the number of "enterprise security management" systems that include a host assessment component is still increasing dramatically. The dual requirements of scalability and ease of deployment have resulted in host assessments becoming a component of larger management systems. A number of established software companies offer commercial products in this space, including, but not limited to, Internet Security System's System Scanner, Computer Associates eTrust Access Control product line, and BindView's bvControl software.

Network Assessments

Network assessments have been around almost as long as host assessments, starting with the Security Administrator Tool for Analyzing Networks (SATAN), released by Dan Farmer and Wietse Venema in 1995. SATAN provided a new perspective to administrators who were used to host assessment and hardening tools. Instead of analyzing the local system for problems, it allowed you to look for common problems on any system connected to the network. This opened the gates for a still-expanding market of both open-source and commercial network-based assessment systems.

A network vulnerability assessment locates all live systems on a network, determines what network services are in use, and then analyzes those services for potential vulnerabilities. Unlike the host assessment solutions, this process does not require any configuration changes on the systems being assessed. Network assessments can be both scalable and efficient in terms of administrative requirements and are the only feasible method of gauging the security of large, complex networks of heterogeneous systems.

Although network assessments are very effective for identifying vulnerabilities, they do suffer from certain limitations. These include: not being able to detect certain types of backdoors, complications with firewalls, and the inability to test for certain vulnerabilities due to the testing process itself being dangerous. Network assessments can disrupt normal operations, interfere with many devices (especially printers), use large amounts of bandwidth, and create fill-up disks with log files on the systems being assessed. Additionally, many vulnerabilities are exploitable by an authorized but unprivileged user account and cannot be identified through a network assessment.

Automated Assessments

The first experience that many people have with vulnerability assessments is using a security consulting firm to provide a network audit. This type of audit is normally comprised of both manual and automated components; the auditors will use automated tools for much of the initial legwork and follow it up with manual system inspection. While this process can provide thorough results, it is often much more expensive than simply using an automated assessment tool to perform the process in-house.

The need for automated assessment tools has resulted in a number of advanced solutions being developed. These solutions range from simple graphical user interface (GUI) software products to stand-alone appliances that are capable of being linked into massive distributed assessment architectures. Due to the overwhelming number of vulnerability tests needed to build even a simple tool, the commercial market is easily divided between a few well-funded independent products and literally hundreds of solutions built on the open-source Nessus Security Scanner. These automated assessment tools can be further broken into two types of products: those that are actually obtained, through either purchase or download, and those that are provided through a subscription service.

Stand-Alone vs. Subscription

The stand-alone category of products includes most open-source projects and about half of the serious commercial contenders. Some examples include the Nessus Security Scanner, eEye's Retina, Tenable Security's Lightning Proxy, and Microsoft's Security Baseline Scanner. These products are either provided as a software package that is installed on a workstation, or a hardware appliance that you simply plug in and access over the network.

The subscription service solutions take a slightly different approach; instead of requiring the user to perform the actual installation and deployment, the vendor handles the basic configuration and simply provides a Web interface to the client. This is primarily used to offer assessments for Internet-facing assets (external assessments), but can also be combined with an appliance to provided assessments for an organization's internal network. Examples of products that are provided as a subscription service include Qualys' QualysGuard, BeyondSecurity's Automated Scan, and Digital Defense's Frontline product.

The advantages of using a stand-alone product are obvious: all of your data stays in-house, and you decide exactly when, where, and how the product is used. One disadvantage, however, is that these products require the user to perform an update before every use to avoid an out-of-date vulnerability check set, potentially missing recent vulnerabilities. The advantages of a subscription service model are twofold: the updates are handled for you, and since the external assessment originates from the vendor's network, you are provided with a real-world view of how your network looks from the Internet.

The disadvantages to a subscription solution are the lack of control you have over the configuration of the device, and the potential storage of vulnerability data on the vendor's systems. Some hybrid subscription service solutions have emerged that resolve both of these issues through leased appliances in conjunction with user-provided storage media for the assessment data. One product that implements this approach is nCircles' IP360 system, which uses multiple dedicated appliances that store all sensitive data on a removable flash storage device.

The Assessment Process

Regardless of what automated assessment solution is used, it will more than likely follow the same general process. Each assessment begins with the user specifying what address or address ranges should be tested. This is often implemented as either a drop-down list of predefined ranges or a simple text widget where the network address and mask can be entered. Once the addresses are specified, the interface will often present the user with a set of configuration options for the assessment; this could include the port ranges to scan, the bandwidth settings to use, or any product-specific features. After all of this information is entered, the actual assessment phase starts. Figure 1.2 shows the assessment configuration screen for the Nessus Security Scanner.

Figure 1.2 Nessus Scan Options

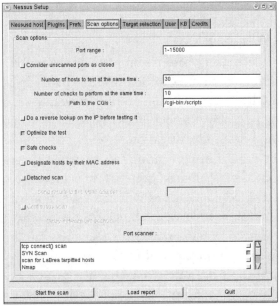

Detecting Live Systems

The first stage of a network vulnerability assessment determines which Internet Protocol (IP) addresses specified in the target range actually map to online and accessible systems. For each address specified by the user, one or more probes are sent to elicit a response. If a response is received, the system will place that address in a list of valid hosts. In the case of heavily firewalled networks, most products have an option to force scan all addresses, regardless of whether a response is received during this stage.

These types of probes sent during this stage differ wildly between assessment tools; although almost all of them use Internet Control Message Protocol (ICMP) "ping" requests, the techniques beyond this are rarely similar between two products. The Nessus Security Scanner has the capability to use a series of TCP connection requests to a set of common ports to identify systems that might be blocking ICMP messages. This allows the scanner to identify systems behind firewalls or those specifically configured to ignore ICMP traffic. After a connection request is sent, any response received from that system will cause it to be added to the list of tested hosts. Many commercial tools include the capability to probe specific User Datagram Protocol (UDP) services in addition to the standard ICMP and TCP tests. This technique is useful for detecting systems that only allow specific UDP application requests through, as is commonly the case with external DNS and RADIUS servers.

Identifying Live Systems

After the initial host detection phase is complete, many products will use a variety of fingerprinting techniques to determine what type of system was found at each address in the live system list. These fingerprinting techniques range from Simple Network Management Protocol (SNMP) queries to complex TCP/IP stack-based operating system identification.

This stage can be crucial in preventing the assessment from interfering with the normal operation of the network; quite a few print servers, older UNIX systems, and network-enabled applications will crash when a vulnerability assessment is performed on them. Indeed, the biggest problem that most administrators encounter with automated assessment tools is that they can disrupt network operations. Often, the administrator will have to spend time rebooting devices, retrieving garbage printouts from network-attached print servers, and debugging user problems with network applications. This identification stage can often be used to detect and avoid problematic systems before the following stages can cause problems.

Enumerating Services

Once the host detection and identification steps are complete, the next stage is normally a port scan. A port scan is the process of determining what TCP and

UDP services are open on a given system. TCP port scans are conducted by sending connection requests to a configured list of port numbers on each system. If the system responds with a message indicating that the port is open, the port number is logged and stored for later use. UDP port scanning can often provide inconsistent results, since the nature of the protocol makes obtaining consistent results difficult on most networks.

There are 65,536 available TCP ports; however, most assessment tools will only perform a port scan against a limited set of these. Limiting the scan to a subset of the available ports reduces the amount of time it takes to perform the assessment and substantially decreases the bandwidth required by the assessment (in terms of packets per second, not the total number of bytes). The downside of not scanning all available ports is that services that are bound to nonstandard, high port numbers are often completely ignored by the assessment. The Nessus Security Scanner provides an option that allows the user to define how these ports are treated. The default is to consider all nonscanned TCP ports open, which can take quite a bit of time during the assessment, especially in cases where heavy packet filters or firewalls are in place. Figure 1.3 shows the Nessus Security Scanner performing the service enumeration phase of the assessment.

Figure 1.3 Nessus Enumerating Services

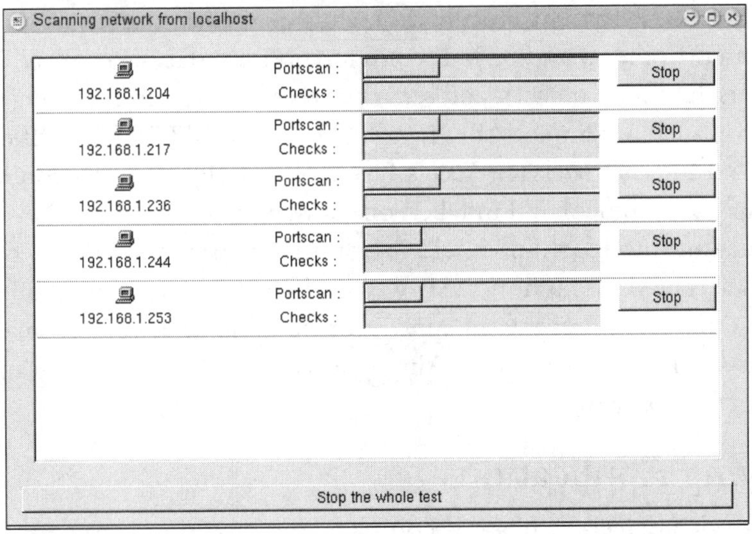

Identifying Services

After the port scan phase, many assessment tools will try to perform service identification on each open port. This process starts with sending some common application requests and analyzing the responses against a set of signatures. When a signature matches a known application, this information is stored for the later use and the next service is tested. Although not all assessment tools perform this stage, the ones that do can provide much more accurate results, simply by knowing which vulnerabilities to check for on what ports.

The Nessus Security Scanner includes a robust service identification engine, capable of detecting more than 90 different application protocols. This engine uses a set of application probes to elicit responses from each service. After each probe is sent, the result is matched against a list of known application signatures. When a matching signature is found, the port number and protocol are stored for future use and the engine continues with the next service. If the Secure Sockets Layer (SSL) transport protocol is detected, the engine will automatically negotiate SSL on the service before sending the application probes. This combination of transport-level and service-level identification allows the system to accurately detect vulnerabilities even when the affected service is on a nonstandard port.

The HyperText Transfer Protocol (HTTP) is a great example of a service that is often found on a port other than the default. Although almost all standard Web servers will use TCP port 80, literally thousands of applications install an HTTP service on a port other than 80. Web configuration interfaces for many Web application servers, hardware devices, and security tools will use nonstandard ports. E-mail protocols such as Simple Mail Transfer Protocol (SMTP), Post Office Protocol 3 (POP3), and Internet Message Access Protocol (IMAP) are often configured with the SSL transport protocol and installed on nonstandard ports as well. A common misconfiguration is to block spam relaying on the primary SMTP service, but trust all messages accepted through the SSL-wrapped SMTP service on a different port. Additionally, this phase prevents an application running on a port normally reserved for another protocol from being ignored completely by the scan or resulting in false positives.

Identifying Applications

Once the service detection phase is complete, the next step is to determine the actual application in use for each detected service. The goal of this stage is to identify the vendor, type, and version of every service detected in the previous stage. This information is critical, as the vulnerability tests for one application can actually cause another application to crash. An example of this is if a Web server is vulnerable to a long pathname overflow. If any other vulnerability tests send a request longer than what is expected by this system, the application will crash. To accurately detect this vulnerability on the Web server instead of crashing it, the system must first identify that specific application and then prevent any of the problematic vulnerability tests from running against it.

One of the most common problems with most assessment tools is that of the *false positive* where the tool reports a vulnerability that does not actually exist on the tested systems. False positives can produce a huge amount of verification work for the assessment engineer. When application identification information is either missing or incomplete, test results will often include false positives. When the developers of these assessment tools write the vulnerability tests, they often assume that the system they are interacting with is always going to be the product in which the vulnerability was discovered. Different applications that offer the same service will often respond to a probe in such a way that the vulnerability test logic registers a vulnerability. For this reason, application identification has become one of the most critical components of modern assessment tools.

Identifying Vulnerabilities

After every online host has been identified, each open port has been mapped to a known service, and the known services have been mapped to specific applications, the system is finally ready to begin testing for vulnerabilities. This process often starts with basic information-gathering techniques, followed by active configuration probes, and finally a set of custom attacks that can identify whether a particular vulnerability exists on the tested system.

The vulnerability identification process can vary from simple banner matching and version tests, to complete exploitation of the tested flaw. When version detection and banner matching are used to identify a vulnerability, false positives often result due to application vendors providing updated software that still displays the banner of the vulnerable version. For this reason, version numbers are often consulted only when there is no other way to safely verify whether the vulnerability exists.

Many common vulnerabilities can only be identified by attempting to exploit the flaw. This often means using the vulnerability to execute a command, display a system file, or otherwise verify that the system is indeed vulnerable to an attack by a remote intruder. Many buffer overflow and input manipulation vulnerabilities can be detected by triggering just enough of the flaw to indicate that the system has not been patched, but not enough to actually take down the service. The assessment tool has to walk a fine line between reliable vulnerability identification and destructive side effects.

Vulnerability tests that use banner checks will encounter problems when the tested service has been patched, either by the vendor or system administrator, but the version number displayed to the network has not been updated, or at least when it has not been updated in the way the vulnerability test expects. This is a relatively common practice with open-source UNIX-based platforms and certain Linux distributions.

Reporting Vulnerabilities

After the analysis is finished, the final stage of the assessment process is reporting. Each product has a unique perspective on how reports should be generated, what they should include, and in what formats to provide them. Regardless of the product, the assessment report will list the systems discovered during the assessment and any vulnerabilities that were identified on them. Many products offer different levels of reporting depending on the audience; it is useful to provide a high-level summary to management giving a system administrator a report that tells him or her what systems need to be fixed and how to do so. One of the popular features in many assessment tools is the capability to show trend reports of how a given network fared over time. Figure 1.4 shows the Nessus Security Scanner's HTML report summary.

Figure 1.4 Nessus Report Summary

Two Approaches

When performing an automated vulnerability assessment, the actual perspective of the test can have a huge impact on the depth and quality of the results. Essentially, there are two different approaches to vulnerability testing: administrative and outsider. Each has distinct advantages and disadvantages, such that many of the better assessment tools have migrated to a hybrid model that combines the best features of both approaches. Understanding these different approaches can provide insight into why two different assessment tools can provide such completely different results when used to test the same network.

Administrative Approach

The administrative approach performs the assessment from the perspective of a normal, authenticated system administrator. The assessment tool might require that it be launched by an authenticated administrative user or provided with a user account and password. These credentials can be used to detect missing patches, insecure configuration settings, and potentially vulnerable client-side software (such as e-mail clients and Web browsers).

This is a powerful approach for networks that consist of mostly Windows-based systems that all authenticate against the same domain. It combines much of the deep analysis of a host assessment with the network assessment's scalability advantages. Since almost all of the vulnerability tests are performed using either remote registry or remote file system access, there is little chance that an assessment tool using this method can adversely affect the tested systems. This allows assessments to be conducted during the day, while the systems are actively being used, without fear of disrupting a business activity.

The administrative approach is especially useful when trying to detect and resolve client-side vulnerabilities on a network of workstations. Many worms, Trojans, and viruses propagate by exploiting vulnerabilities in e-mail clients and Web browser software. An assessment tool using this approach can access the registry of each system and determine whether the latest patches have been installed, whether the proper security settings have been applied, and often whether the system has already been successfully attacked. Client-side security is one of the most overlooked entry points on most corporate networks; there have been numerous cases of a network with a well-secured perimeter being overtaken by a network simply because a user visited the wrong Web site with an outdated Web browser.

Unfortunately, these products often have some severe limitations as well. Since the testing process uses the standard Windows administrative channels—namely, the NetBIOS services and an administrative user account—anything preventing this channel from being accessed will result in inaccurate scan results. Any system on the network that is configured with a different authentication source (running in stand-alone mode, on a different domain, or authenticating to a Novell server) will not be correctly assessed. Additionally, these products may have issues similar to the issues of host-based assessment tools, network devices, UNIX-based servers, and IP-enabled phone systems may also be completely missed or return incomplete results.

Network and host-based firewalls can also interfere with the assessment. This interference is a common occurrence when performing assessments against a system hosted on a different network segment, such as a demilitarized zone (DMZ) or external segment behind a dedicated firewall. Additionally, network devices, UNIX-based servers, and IP-enabled phone systems might also be either completely missed or have only minimal results returned. An example of this is a certain Windows-based commercial assessment tool that will report missing Internet Information Server (IIS) patches even when the Web server has not been enabled or configured.

This type of testing is very helpful to verify a networkwide patch deployment, but should not be relied upon as the only method of security testing. Microsoft's Security Baseline Scanner is the best example of an assessment tool that uses this approach alone. Many of the commercial assessment tool offerings were originally based on this approach and have only recently started to integrate different techniques into their vulnerability tests. The differences between administrative and hybrid solutions is discussed at length in the section *The Hybrid Approach*.

The Outsider Approach

The outsider approach takes the perspective of the unauthenticated malicious intruder who is trying to break into the network. The assessment process is able to make decisions about the security of a system only through a combination of application fingerprinting, version identification, and actual exploitation attempts. Assessment tools built on this approach are often capable of detecting vulnerabilities across a much wider range of operating systems and devices than their administrative approach counterparts can.

When conducting a large-scale assessment against a network consisting of many different operating systems and network devices, the outsider approach is the only technique that has a chance of returning accurate, consistent results about each discovered system. If a system is behind a firewall, only the exposed services will be tested, providing you with the same information that an intruder would see in a real-life attack. The reports provided by tools that use this hybrid approach are geared to prevent common attacks; this is in contrast to those tools using the administrative approach that often focus on missing patches and insecure configuration settings. In essence, the outsider approach presents a much more targeted list of problems for remediation, allowing the administrator to focus on the issues that would be the first choices for a potential intruder.

Although this approach is the only plausible method of conducting a vulnerability assessment on a heterogeneous network, it also suffers from a significant set of drawbacks. Many vulnerabilities simply cannot be tested without crashing the application, device, or operating system. The result is that any assessment tools that test for these types of vulnerabilities either provide an option for "intrusive" testing, or always trigger a warning when a potentially vulnerable service is discovered. Since the outsider approach can only detect what is visible from the point in the network where the assessment was launched, it might not report a vulnerable service bound to a different interface on the same system. This is an issue with reporting more than anything else, as someone reviewing the assessment report might not consider the network perspective when creating a list of remediation tasks for that system.

The Hybrid Approach

Over the last few years, more and more tools have switched to a hybrid approach for network assessments. They use administrative credentials when possible, but fall back to remote fingerprinting techniques if an account is either not available or not accepted on the tested system. The quality of these hybrid solutions varies greatly; the products were originally designed with only the administrative approach in mind have a difficult time when administrative credentials are not available, whereas the products based on the outsider approach often contain glitches when using an administrative account for tests. It seems that the latter has better chances at overcoming its hurdles without requiring a re-write. Overall, though, these products provide results that are often superior to those using a single approach. The Nessus Security Scanner and eEye's Retina product are examples of tools that use this approach.

One of the greatest advantages of tools using the outsider approach is that they are often able to determine whether a given vulnerability exists, regardless of whether a patch was applied. As many Windows network administrators know, installing an operating system patch does not actually guarantee that the vulnerability has been removed. A recent vulnerability in the Microsoft Windows Network Messenger service allowed a remote attacker to execute arbitrary code on a vulnerable system. Public exploits for the vulnerability started circulating, and companies were frantically trying to install the patch on all their internal workstations. Something that was overlooked was that for the patch to take effect, the system had to be rebooted after it was applied. Many sites used automated patch installation tools to update all their vulnerable systems, but completely forgot about the reboot requirement.

The result was that when an assessment was run using a tool that took the administrative approach, it reported the systems as patched. However, when an assessment was run using the Nessus Security Scanner, it reported these systems as vulnerable. The tool using the administrative approach simply checked the registry of each system to determine whether the patch had been applied, whereas the Nessus scan actually probed the vulnerability to determine if it was still vulnerable. Without this second assessment, the organization would have left hundreds of workstations exposed, even though the patches had been applied. The registry analysis used by many tools that take the administrative approach can miss vulnerabilities for a number of other reasons as well. The most common occurrence is when a hotfix has been applied to resolve a vulnerability, and then an older service pack is reapplied over the entire system. The changes installed by the hotfix were overwritten, but the registry entry stating that the patch was applied still exists. This problem primarily affects Windows operating systems; however, a number of commercial UNIX vendors have had similar issues with tracking installed patches and determining which ones still need to be applied.

Recently, many of the administrative and hybrid tools have developed new techniques for verifying that an installed patch actually exists. Shavlik Technology's HFNetChk Pro will actually check the last reboot time and compare it to the hotfix install date. The Nessus Security Scanner actually accesses the affected executables across the network and verifies the embedded version numbers.

The drawbacks to the hybrid approach are normally not apparent until the results of a few large scans are observed; because the administrative approach is used opportunistically, vulnerabilities that are reported on a system that accepts the provided user account might not be reported on a similar system that uses a different authentication realm. If the administrator does not realize that the other system might be vulnerable as well, it could lead to a false sense of security. These missed vulnerabilities can be difficult to track down and can fall under the radar of the administrator. Because there is a higher chance of these systems not being patched, the hybrid approach can actually result in more damage during an intrusion or worm outbreak. Although the administrative approach suffers from the same issue, tools using the administrative approach take it for granted that systems outside of the authentication realm will not be tested.

Realistic Expectations

When the first commercial vulnerability assessment tools started becoming popular, they were advertised as being able to magically identify every security hole on your network. A few years ago, this might have been close to the truth. The number of publicly documented vulnerabilities was still quite small, and tracking vulnerability information was an obscure hobby. These days, the scenario is much different, whereas there were a few hundred well-documented vulnerabilities before, there are literally thousands of them now, and they don't even begin to scratch the surface when it comes to the number of flaws that can be used to penetrate a corporate network.

In addition to the avalanche of vulnerabilities, the number and type of devices found on an average corporate network has exploded. Some of these devices will crash, misbehave, or slow to a crawl during a network vulnerability assessment. A vulnerability test designed for one system might cause another application or device to stop functioning altogether, annoying the users of those systems and potentially interrupting the work flow. Assessment tools have a tough job; they have to identify as many vulnerabilities as possible on systems that must be analyzed and categorized on the fly, without reporting false positives, and at the same time avoid crashing devices and applications that simply weren't designed with security in mind. Some tools fare better than others; however, all current assessment tools exhibit this problem in one form or another.

When someone first starts to use a vulnerability assessment system, he or she often notices that the results between subsequent scans can differ significantly. This issue is encountered more frequently on larger networks that are connected through slower links. There are quite a few different reasons for this, but the core issue is that unlike most software processes, remote vulnerability testing is more of an art form than a science. Many assessment tools define a hard timeout for establishing connections to a service or receiving the result of a query. If an extra second or two of latency occurs on the network, the test could miss a valid response. These types of timing issues are common among assessment tools; however, many other factors can play into the consistency of scan results.

Many network devices provide a Telnet console that allows an administrator to reconfigure the system remotely. These devices will often set a hard limit on the number of concurrent network connections allowed to this service. When a vulnerability assessment is launched, it might perform multiple tests on a given port at the same time; this can cause one check to receive a valid response, while another gets an error message indicating that all available connections are being used. If that second check was responsible for testing for a default password on this particular device, it might completely miss the vulnerability. If the same scan was run later, but the default password test ran before one of the others, it would accurately detect the vulnerability at the expense of the other tests. This type of timing problem is much more common on network devices and older UNIX systems than on most modern workstations and servers, but can ultimately lead to inconsistent assessment results.

Tools & Traps…

Assessing Print Servers

Almost all vulnerability assessment tools have one thing in common; they are capable of eating a print server alive. The problem stems from the fact that many print servers offer a variety of network services that can be used to spool documents directly to the attached printer. The most problematic of these services is the Direct Print Protocol, which is a TCP service. This can cause problems with automated assessment tools, as the service identification phase can often cause reams of paper to printed out, covered in what appears to be garbage. Another common issue relates to the custom FTP service that many print servers run. This service will allow authentications using any username and password combination and simply prints out any files that are uploaded. If the assessment tool is looking for insecure FTP configurations, it might end up printing out a test file when running against a print server. To compound matters, quite a few print servers have such shoddy TCP/IP implementations that a simple port scan can take them offline, and a full power cycle is required to return them to service.

Dynamic systems are the bane of the vulnerability assessment tools. If an assessment is in full swing and a user decides to reboot his workstation, the assessment tool will start receiving connection timeouts for the vulnerability tests. Once the system comes back online, any subsequent tests will run normally; however, all tests launched during the period of downtime will result in missing vulnerability results for that system. This type of problem is incredibly difficult to detect when wading through a massive assessment report, and at this time only a handful of commercial systems offer the capability to detect and rescan systems that restart during the assessment process.

Despite the extraordinary amount of refinement and testing that most assessment tools have undergone, false positives continue to annoy network administrators and security consultants alike. As we discussed earlier in the chapter, a false positive is simply a vulnerability that is reported, but does not actually exist on the tested system. These annoyances can build to quite a bit of verification work—before you throw out Nessus or any vulnerability assessment application for the false positive load, take the time to tune it as we show you later in this book. Nonstandard Web servers, backported software packages, and permissive match strings inside vulnerability test scripts are the top causes for false positives.

The Web server software that provides a configuration console for many network devices is notorious for causing false positives; instead of returning a standard "404" error response for nonexistent files, these systems will often return a success message for any file that is requested from the system. In response, almost all of the popular assessment tools have developed some form of Web server fingerprinting that allows their system to work around these strange Web servers. These solutions range from incredibly robust, such as the one found in the recent versions of the Nessus Security Scanner, to almost not worth the bother, as in certain commercial products.

The Limitations of Automation

Vulnerability assessment tools are still no replacement for a manual security audit by a team of trained security experts. Although many assessment tools will do their best to find common vulnerabilities in all exposed services, relatively simple vulnerabilities are often missed. Custom web applications, written under tight deadlines and for small user bases, often perform inadequate security checks on user input, but automated assessment systems may not find these flaws. Although the chances of an automated assessment tool being able to find a vulnerability in this software are slim, a security analyst experienced with Web application testing could easily pinpoint a number of security issues in a short period of time. Just because an automated assessment does not find any vulnerabilities does not mean that none exist.

Summary

As the number of discovered vulnerabilities increases every day, networks are becoming increasingly difficult to keep secure. Vulnerability assessments have become the preferred method of managing security flaws for many organizations. The ability to quickly identify misconfigured and unpatched systems, combined with the ease of use and accuracy of many assessment tools, has changed the way many administrators manage their systems. Network vulnerability assessments provide the wide view of security weaknesses on a given network, supplemented by host assessment solutions that provide granular hardening steps for critical systems.

The traditional process of system hardening and patch application has been left in the dust; as the sheer quantity of vulnerabilities is more than most administrator teams can keep track of, especially for diverse networks. Automated assessment solutions have come to the rescue, with both stand-alone and subscription-based options. The average administrator no longer needs to become a security savant simply to keep his or her systems secure. The same repeatable process allows administrators to track, resolve, and verify vulnerabilities.

Although almost all assessment tools advertise their capability to detect and report all critical vulnerabilities, the way these systems are designed and the techniques they use for vulnerability tests vary widely. Not all assessment solutions are created equal; tools using the administrative approach are almost useful when it comes to identifying vulnerabilities in network devices and across large networks. At the same time, tools using the outsider approach are restricted by the technical limitations of the vulnerabilities themselves, often ignoring vulnerabilities that they simply are unable to test. Fortunately, many of the more popular solutions have solidified around a hybrid approach for vulnerability testing, allowing for unprecedented levels of accuracy and depth.

Vulnerability assessments are not a security panacea; although they excel at detecting vulnerabilities in widely deployed products, even relatively simply flaws can be missed. The current market of assessment tools can often cause problems with network devices, slow internetwork links, and custom applications. No matter what tool you use, false positives will always be a significant problem; although many solutions have made huge steps in reducing these, backported patches and vague version identifiers will guarantee that these never entirely disappear. The depth and flexibility of a manual security assessment will always be better than any automated solution; there is no replacement for a skilled analyst manually reviewing your systems, network architecture, and in-house applications.

Solutions Fast Track

What Is a Vulnerability Assessment?

☑ A vulnerability is any flaw that an attacker can use to gain access to a system or network.

☑ Vulnerability assessments provide a snapshot of the security posture of your network.

☑ Host assessments provide detailed information about the weaknesses on a system.

☑ Network assessments pinpoint flaws that a remote attacker can use to gain access.

Automated Assessments

☑ Manual assessments are no longer feasible for entire networks due to the sheer number of vulnerabilities that exist.

☑ Stand-alone and subscription assessment models each have distinct advantages.

☑ Automated assessments tend to follow the same process regardless of the tool.

☑ The assessment process is essentially staged information gathering.

Two Approaches

☑ Two assessment tools can provide very different results depending on their approach.

☑ The administrative approach is often safest, but might not be reliable.

☑ The outsider approach provides the same information an attacker would have.

☑ Robust assessment tools use a hybrid approach for maximum vulnerability coverage.

Realistic Expectations

☑ Assessments can cause a myriad of side effects on an average corporate network.

☑ Consecutive between assessments is often less than ideal.

☑ False positives will always be an issue, but recent tools are making progress.

☑ Manual security audits still provide better results than any assessment tool can.

☑ Penetration testing can provide a deeper, if not wider, view of your network, from the perspective of an attacker.

Frequently Asked Questions

The following Frequently Asked Questions, answered by the authors of this book, are designed to both measure your understanding of the concepts presented in this chapter and to assist you with real-life implementation of these concepts. To have your questions about this chapter answered by the author, browse to **www.syngress.com/solutions** and click on the **"Ask the Author"** form. You will also gain access to thousands of other FAQs at ITFAQnet.com.

Q: I am planning to use a vulnerability assessment tool at my organization. Is there any reason to assess the internal networks as well as the external?

A: While systems exposed to the Internet should always be incorporated into a vulnerability assessment plan, internal assessments can actually reduce the risk to the organization even more. When a new worm appears that exploits one or more known vulnerabilities, the first step an organization should take is to secure all external and internal systems. An internal assessment can be used to verify that internal assets are not at risk to an automated attack. Internal networks are vulnerable to infection through users who are compromised through their e-mail clients and Web browsers; a worm infection on an internal network segment can result in the inability for the business to function. Additionally, unethical consultants, disgruntled employees, and visitors using the network can leverage insecure systems to gain access to sensitive information.

Q: What is the difference between a vulnerability assessment and a penetration test?

A: One of the biggest problems with the security industry is consistent naming of services. A strong contributing fact is that many near dishonest security firms are selling "penetration tests" that are nothing more than a vulnerability assessment using automated tools. A vulnerability assessment is the process of identifying vulnerabilities on a network, whereas a penetration test is focused on actually gaining unauthorized access to the tested systems and using that access to the network or data, as directed by the client. A penetration test is a great way to determine how well your security measures respond to a real-life attack and what an attacker could accomplish or compromise, but may not result in a detailed analysis of every system on your network.

Q: Can a vulnerability assessment find users with weak passwords?

A: Although manual vulnerability assessments can include password auditing, automated vulnerability assessment tools are rarely able to detect common or weak passwords. The reason behind this is not that the tool is not technically able to perform the check, but that the process of testing each user could result in an account lockout. This is primarily the case with Windows domains; however, it can also apply to many commercial UNIX systems. While some automated assessment tools will test for accounts with a default or blank password, they would still not be able to detect an account with a simple one-character password. Finally, automatic tools might slow the application or network being tested. This is a part of the security assessment process that needs to be very carefully coordinated with administrators to achieve maximum success while causing a minimum of negative effects for users.

Q: My organization uses an intrusion prevention system (IPS). What complications will this cause with a vulnerability assessment?

A: The goal of an IPS is to block hostile traffic before it reaches a potentially vulnerable system. Many automated assessment solutions depend on being able to send a specially crafted attack probe and to determine whether the system is vulnerable by analyzing the response. If the IPS blocks the initial probe, the vulnerability assessment will not be able to accurately detect that vulnerability. The solution to this is either to configure the IPS to specifically ignore traffic originating from the vulnerability assessment tool, or only run the tool from the protected side of the IPS. Most assessment tools are not designed to bypass these systems; however, an advanced intruder could easily detect the IPS and find a way to exploit a vulnerability while avoiding the IPS's block. Evading intrusion detection and prevention could easily be a book of its own; however, sufficient it to say that what the IPS is looking for might not be what the intruder uses to successfully exploit the vulnerability.

## Chapter 2

Introducing Nessus

Solutions in this Chapter:

- **What Is It?**
- **The** *De Facto* **Standard**
- **History**
- **Basic Components**

- ☑ **Summary**
- ☑ **Solutions Fast Track**
- ☑ **Frequently Asked Questions**

Introduction

"At first, hapless one, he prayed with serene soul, rejoicing in his comely garb. But when the blood-fed flame began to blaze from the holy offerings and from the resinous pine, a sweat broke forth upon his flesh, and the tunic clung to his sides, at every joint, close-glued, as if by a craftsman's hand; there came a biting pain that racked his bones; and then the venom, as of some deadly, cruel viper, begain to devour him."

—Sophocles (440-430 BCE)

Nessus was a centaur in Sophocles' ancient manuscript, "The Death of Heracles." This beastly creature dupes the wife of Heracles into giving her husband a garment that has been poisoned, thus bringing an end to the mighty Heracles. One could speculate for quite a while on how this ancient and mythological tale might have inspired the name of the most widespread open-source vulnerability scanner in use today. However, speculation is all that it would be, as according to Renaud Deraison, he has "no special reason" for dubbing his project Nessus.

Renaud does, however, have a special reason to be proud. The Nessus Project is one of the many successful security-centric open-source projects today. It finds its place as a tool of the unfunded security researcher, and of the highly funded security consultant. Nessus enjoys accolades from many years of competitive product reviews and was recently picked as one of *PC Magazine*'s "best products of 2003." Moreover, the Nessus project is now defined by an active community of about 1,500 outspoken participants and many more yet to be heard from.

In this chapter, we explore the myriad reasons why so many people use Nessus. We discuss the history of the Nessus project and detail its basic components. We also spend some time looking at the effect it has had on the best practices of today.

What Is It?

Nessus is not the world's first free open-source vulnerability scanner. However, it is the most ubiquitous Open Source scanner in use today, and has been for many years. The Nessus Project was conceived early in 1998. At the time, open-source vulnerability scanners had fallen behind the well-funded commercial products of the same ilk. It was then that Renaud Deraison decided to start the project that would become known as Nessus.

Nessus is a robust vulnerability scanner that is well suited for large enterprise networks. The fact that it is free makes it well suited for the security budget, too. Its extensibility allows its users to leverage their own expertise in developing vulnerability checks without having to be a part of the development project. This same feature allows for quick updates of current vulnerabilities from the large community of users who keep the project alive and up to date.

The *De Facto* Standard

The fact that Nessus now finds itself as a high-ranking contender in traditional product testing is a testament to its rapid adoption and continued use, as well as its ability to compete with the best the commercial world has to offer. In 2001, Greg Shipley performed a product review of vulnerability scanners for *Network Computing Magazine*. Although this review discovered that at the time, no scanner detected all of the 17 vulnerabilities tested, it did show Nessus as the leader, detecting 15 of the 17 vulnerabilities in the review.

A couple of years later, in 2003, *Information Security Magazine* of TechTarget performed a review of the top-five vulnerability scanners. In their review, they tested for 10 known vulnerabilities. Of the products tested, Nessus came in second place, detecting 6 of the 10, with the first-place winner detecting 9.

What do these reviews tell us about Nessus? There is more data here than meets the eye. First, the very placement of a completely open-source product in reviews with the industry leaders of commercial vulnerability scanners tells us that Nessus is a contender in this realm. Next, the fact that Nessus came in first place in the first review explains one reason why so many security service providers use Nessus. A free product that outperforms commercial products in competitive reviews is always a good thing to have. Combined with in-house code improvements or signature checks often added by service providers, Nessus often becomes an amazingly strong tool.

The second-place showing in the second review could have been caused by many factors typically solved by the advocacy of the product's company during the review process. It is common for reviewers to have product representatives assist them during initial configuration of the software being reviewed. Nessus, however, relies on the user base to be the advocates, and thus does not share the same product review advantages that commercial scanners do.

Nessus is a must-have in the security consultant's cadre of tools. The fact that it is free (and we really can't stress this enough) is cause enough to use it. However, its flexible architecture provides yet another reason. The client/server architecture of Nessus makes scans more scaleable, manageable, and even more precise. Many users set up a nessusd server, which performs scans at the request of a client running on another machine. Employing this configuration provides the consultant many ways to build a business model around Nessus, as we'll explore throughout the book.

Many commercial providers of security services use Nessus, and a few of them provide periodic internal scans on a subscription basis by taking advantage of the Nessus client/server architecture. Quite often, they will ship a Nessus appliance, loaded with the current Nessus plugins as well as their very own custom checks, to a client site where it performs the scanning. This allows the service provider to scan from any point within the client's network without sending consultants on-site. Some businesses even go so far as to write all of the plugins they use from scratch, using none of the Nessus community's checks. Regardless of how commercial security providers apply Nessus to their business model, the vast majority of security services firms use Nessus to some extent.

The security consultant for hire is not the only beneficiary of the free and flexible nature of Nessus. In-house security teams throughout the IT industry employ Nessus internally. They use the client/server model to a different end, however. The in-house security team will often deploy nessusd servers throughout their network, allowing the remote execution of timely scans without the bandwidth spikes caused by using a traditional scanner to scan the entire network from a single point. This also allows the practitioner to scan each machine from an optimal point, so that internal firewalling rules don't interfere with the test. Additionally, this added ability to write custom plugins for Nessus allows the in-house security engineer to mold Nessus to the unique environmental factors of her enterprise network, from custom or otherwise rare third-party applications to particular filtering mechanisms in place.

The commercial software product space is also leveraging Nessus. Many software suites available today that focus on general security workflow and management, such as the Security Information Management (SIM) space, provide tight "low-level" integration to Nessus. Sometimes, these products will simply consume the XML output of a Nessus scan; other times, they might scan a host whenever a specific network event occurs. Whether used alone or in conjunction with other software, due to its free, flexible, and extensible foundations, Nessus remains the *de facto* standard for many different security experts with many different security needs.

Notes from the Underground...

The Dark Side of Security Consultants

The myriad of reasons that make Nessus such a great tool for security consultants also enable a dark phenomenon in the world of network security. All too often, consulting firms claim to have expertise in network security yet add minimal value to the output of their tools. For example, "Alice" performs vulnerability assessments for her firm, Yet Another Security Group (YASG). Her routine for performing vulnerability assessments begins by executing a free Nessus scan, and exporting the resultant report to the portable document format (PDF). Alice then prints out the report and places it in a $5.00 binder with her company logo on it. Alice finishes the process by delivering her report to the customer and referring them to the Nessus reference links for any further assistance they might need with remediation. She then receives her check for $20,000 as her customer reluctantly hands over the payment.

The issue here is not that Alice has used Nessus; in fact, this same issue haunts customers of consulting groups who use commercial scanners. Nay, the dark side of Alice's process lies in the fact that Alice provided zero value-add to what the customer could have easily done for free. Alice should have used Nessus as a starting point, and further examined each of the vulnerable hosts, not only to verify the vulnerability detections to be true, but to determine what level of risk these vulnerabilities posed for the customer. Is that CHARGEN-ECHO denial-of-service (DoS) vulnerability on the printer, or is it on the "old-but-still-in-use" VMS financials system? Is there a matching vulnerable host that can complete the requisite pair for the attack? What's the risk of such an attack occurring, and what effect could it have on the organization? This level of contextualization and vulnerability prioritization is not just a "nice-to-have" differentiator of an assessment; it should be a requirement for any customer who falls under regulatory compliance.

Further more, Alice should have been using other tools as well, both commercial and open source. If you are responsible for in-house security and decide to have a third party provide a different perspective of your

Continued

network security posture, request a sample report as part of the proposal process. In the case that they have no sanitized reports to provide, ask them to describe their method. If they won't provide either, find another security firm to provide the assessment.

History

It was 1998, and the network security industry was just getting into full swing as it rode on the tails of the dot-com era. Bugtraq, a mailing list that tracks security flaws, had yet to evolve into a full database and was a strictly underground effort run on a shoestring budget. Vulnerability scanners were being sold commercially for large sums of money to corporate IT departments with the cost rising in direct proportion to the number of devices being examined. The last remaining open-source scanner, the Security Administrator Tool for Analyzing Networks (SATAN), had been surpassed by commercial scanners, which proved to be more comprehensive. Network security was quickly rising in cost as the Internet moved out of the hands of the National Science Foundation and into the hands of private industry. Soon, the growth of the Internet skyrocketed as dot-com financial trends brought increasingly more "eyeballs" to the Internet, leading to a subsequent increase in cyber interlopers testing the limits of this growing frontier.

It was in this environment that Renaud Deraison created the project known as Nessus. It was an answer to the ever-increasing prices of commercial vulnerability scanners, and the relative stagnation of the SATAN project. Nessus was a framework, but it would require a community of knowledgeable security researchers working for free to bring Nessus up to the level of a full-fledged product.

Ever since Nessus first came on the scene in 1998, the community has grown by leaps and bounds. At the time of this book's publication, the general Nessus mailing list had over 1,357 participants with around 50 active posters. The Nessus Development mailing list consisted of 149 participants with approximately 15 active posters, and the Plugins Writers mailing list had 114 active users with 15 active posters. Figure 2.1 shows the growth rate of users on each of the active Nessus mailing lists, while Figure 2.2 shows the number of posts per month on each of these same mailing lists.

Figure 2.1 Growth Rate of Users on Active Nessus Mailing Lists

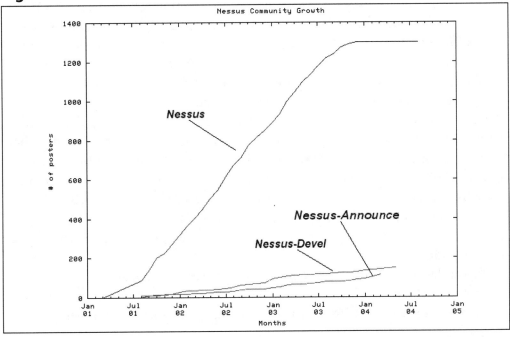

Figure 2.2 Posts per Month on Active Nessus Mailing Lists

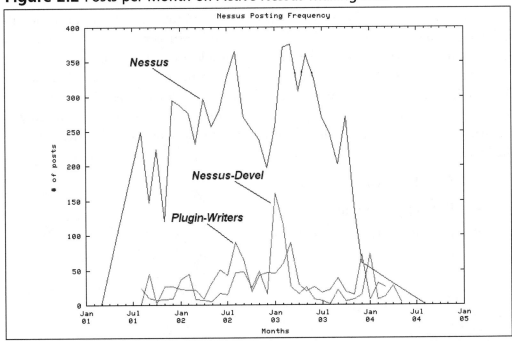

As these two charts make abundantly clear, with ~1,500 users on the general Nessus mailing list, Nessus has attracted a bit of attention. Of course, this is not a scientific poll of the entire Nessus community. Many folks have been using Nessus for several years and have yet to post to any of these lists, so there is no telling how many folks actually form the Nessus contingent.

These trends speak volumes about the past and the future of Nessus. Each month, more people are introduced to Nessus, and each month the community grows even stronger. Security researchers learn of the existence, popularity, and strength of Nessus in many ways. Some of them stumble across it after using their favorite search engine to find "Free Security Scanner." Others find out by word of mouth. Still others learn about Nessus in security training such as that found at the Sysadmin, Audit, Network, Security Institute (SANS Institute). SANS offers a week-long class detailing the tools of the security trade, and spends a good deal of time introducing students to Nessus and conducting a workshop on its installation and use.

Regardless of how people become aware of Nessus, the obvious trend is that the community surrounding the Nessus Project will continue to grow and continue to support the tradition of a free, up-to-date, vulnerability scanner.

Basic Components

What makes Nessus such a wonderful tool is the unique architecture on which it is built. The flexibility and resourcefulness of the Nessus architecture has taken every element of the security lifecycle into consideration. From the large-scale batch execution of vulnerability scans that capture the data, to the graphical and hyperlinked reports that represent the data, to the fix descriptions that are invaluable in patch remediation, all of these aspects create the foundation of a healthy security posture. We will touch on several of the components of this architecture, including:

- The Nessus Client and Server
- The Nessus Plugins
- The Nessus Knowledge Base

Client and Server

Originally, vulnerability scanners were all client based. A consultant would bring his or her laptop into a customer's site and plug in at the best possible location in the network to execute a scan. A scan on any network address space would take anywhere from an entire afternoon to a few days, depending on the breadth of the network and the depth of the scan parameters. This would render the laptop unusable for the amount of time the scan required.

The Nessus Project took this aspect of vulnerability assessments into strong consideration from its inception. To conquer this problem and many others, the Nessus Project adopted a client/server model for its foundation. This allows the security analyst to "detach" from the vulnerability scan and use his resources for other items while Nessus continues to do what it does best. This is just one benefit of leveraging the client/server model of Nessus. There are, in fact, many innovative ways to build a business model around this architecture, or to streamline the in-house vulnerability assessment process.

For example, let's say a security-consulting firm receives a contract to perform an on-site vulnerability assessment. Once the consultant arrives and obtains access to the customer network, he can fire up his Nessus client and securely connect to his firm's nessusd server. Once our sharp consultant initiates the external assessment, he can then detach his client from the server, knowing that the data will be ready for him later. Meanwhile, he can then begin his scan of the internal network using whatever equipment he brought along for the engagement.

Another more obvious benefit of this architecture is scalability. A machine with more memory and processing power, but especially memory, can run more tests at once, decreasing the scanning time. This results in a scan that finishes more quickly and leaves the consultant's laptop free, allowing him to interact with the network, providing context for findings. He'll take this opportunity to identify the roles of machines found during the scan, interviewing the organization's personnel as necessary. He can also perform manual verification of any findings, which is critically important to a high-quality vulnerability assessment. Every vulnerability scanner generates "false positives," or inaccurate statements of vulnerability. It's the engineer's job to confirm each vulnerability manually, so the on-site staff isn't left with both inaccurate vulnerability reporting and increased risk of ulcer.

From the perspective of in-house security teams, this architecture can be leveraged in a much different way. One of the problems that plague the in-house vulnerability assessment team is the internal firewall. Internal firewalls often have address translation tables, and the rapid-fire connections caused by vulnerability scanners quickly fill these tables, causing some firewalls to drop older connections. This adverse phenomenon affects both the users of the network and the assessment team's own scan. This effect, underscored by the overall bandwidth use of network scanners in general, can cause enough impact on the network to discourage frequent vulnerability scans altogether. By distributing nessusd servers throughout the enterprise network, the in-house security assessment team can bypass the traditional network issues caused by vulnerability scanners and easily automate frequent and periodic scans, ensuring a stronger overall security posture (see Figure 2.3).

Figure 2.3 In-House Network with Nessus Servers

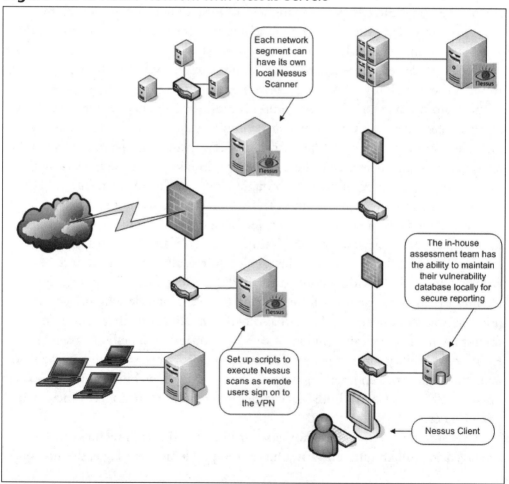

The Nessus client can connect to the nessusd server in many ways that employ both encryption and authentication. Which way would suit your network interests best? The first thing to consider is whether the nessusd server is located on the local loopback. If the nesssud server you want to connect to is in fact listening only on 127.0.0.1, then using the unencrypted scheme will be sufficient. This is the only case where you should ever use the "unencrypted" option. While there might be safe configurations where you can rely on unencrypted traffic with a certain amount of confidence, the only fully safe configuration is where no unencrypted traffic touches the physical network. This warning against unencrypted traffic, of course, becomes even more critical when the Nessus server is authenticating to various hosts or network components—the client must pass the relevant passwords to the server across its control connection. Use the encryption—it's much better than being embarrassed by your network administrator or an attacker on your network, each of whom can redirect and sniff traffic.

When using encryption, you can choose from Transmission Layer Security (TLS) or one of three versions of Secure Sockets Layer (SSL). SSL was created by Netscape as they created their first commercial browser, while TLS is an IETF standard based on SSL. These levels of encryption can be enforced by the nessusd server based on your encryption policy.

The next item you will want to consider when deciding which method of connection bests suits your network is related to the authentication scheme. At the time of this writing, Nessus supports both password-based and certificate-based authentication. This allows the security team to integrate Nessus with its current public key infrastructure (PKI) if desired. It also adds an additional layer of security in the defense of a set of data that could potentially allow any unauthorized viewer administrative control over network resources. This follows from the security principle of "Defense in Depth," the idea that multiple layers of defenses allow the defense to stand when an attacker is able to compromise one or more layers. Which authentication scheme and encryption method should you choose? This question should involve at least one meeting of the in-house security team before it is answered.

Damage & Defense...

Nessus and MySQL

The flexible Nessus architecture also has a feature that allows logging of the vulnerabilities found to a MySQL database. This database can be located on the same system as nessusd, or it can be located remotely in a much more centralized and protected location within the security infrastructure. One post to the Nessus list in early 2001 from the creator of the MySQL addition for Nessus pointed out that this data could be used for cross-correlation with alerts from intrusion detection systems (IDSs) in an effort to escalate those issues when the system is indeed vulnerable to such an attack. In his scenario, he would allow certain IDS events to execute a Nessus scan on the host for that specific vulnerability and, if subsequently found vulnerable, automatically notify the appropriate personnel.

The MySQL component of the Nessus architecture provides many uses. Some shops have homebrew scripts that comb their Nessus vulnerability database for all of the actions required for the respective system administrator of each of these systems. They then provide weekly reports to the other work centers of matters that need attention. This also allows for the possibility of trending over time. Reporting on vulnerability trends over time can provide management with the requisite metrics for obtaining an increased security budget in either time or money. They can also be used to show proof of compliance for many regulatory compliance initiatives such as British Standard 7799 and Sarbanes-Oxley.

If your company's networks are not being reviewed with a tool like Nessus with any frequency, then maybe the company should start this process. You can be sure that someone is indeed scanning the network, whether authorized or not.

The Plugins

Another aspect of Nessus that really sets it apart from other scanners is the power of the Nessus Attack Scripting Language (NASL, pronounced naz–ul). NASL allows security analysts to quickly create their own plugins for vulnerability checks. The result is that teams can easily add their security expertise to their Nessus scans by creating custom vulnerability tests. It also allows the in-house security team to create vulnerability checks for the protocols and services that are unique to their networks.

NASL most closely resembles C. It is specifically designed with security in mind, as it will only communicate with the host it is passed as an argument, and it will not execute any local commands. With this sandbox snug around the NASL interface, it is unlikely that a plugin can perform unexpected operations. NASL is also built to share information between security tests. This is achieved through use of the "Knowledge Base."

The Knowledge Base

The Knowledge Base allows today's plugins to leverage the data gleaned by earlier plugins. Consider a security check that tests for the existence of a Web server, and, if one is found, attempts to discern which implementation of HTTP is actually running. The plugin has the capability to set the value of a variable in the Nessus Knowledge Base for that host. Let's say that in one specific instance, our NASL script executes and finds Apache running on the remote host. The plugin then sets the host-specific Knowledge Base variable of "www/banner/80" to "Apache/1.3.29 (Unix) PHP/4.3.4 mod_ssl/2.8.16 OpenSSL/0.9.7a."

This allows all subsequent plugins the capability to read the value of "www/banner/80." Now, let's assume our next plugin reads this value. If it finds the string "OpenSSL/0.9.7a" in the returned value, it reports that this host is vulnerable due to an outdated version of OpenSSL. In this way, every plugin uses information already derived by more primitive plugins. Renaud suggests that plugins writers use the Knowledge Base as much as possible. This will serve to extend the capabilities of Nessus and speed up the performance of future plugins, which can search the Knowledge Base for data instead of having to traverse the network for it.

Summary

Ever since its beginnings in early 1998, the Nessus Project has been attracting security researchers from all walks of life. It continues this growth today. It has been adopted as a *de facto* standard by the security industry, vendor, and practitioner alike, many of whom rely on Nessus as the foundation to their security practices.

Nessus employs many security features that allow for an easy fit into any security infrastructure. The encryption and authentication mechanisms are robust. The sandbox-like feature of the NASL interface keeps the plugins focused and behaving as expected.

Because of its ease of deployment and its extensible scripting language, Nessus enjoys a full community of developers and users who continue to push the envelope of innovation.

Solutions Fast Track

What Is It?

- ☑ Nessus is a free and up-to-date vulnerability scanner.

- ☑ It is feature rich and has a flexible/extensible architecture.

- ☑ The Nessus Project has a large community of volunteers.

The *De Facto* Standard

- ☑ Nessus is a high-ranking contender in traditional product testing.

- ☑ Many commercial providers of security services use Nessus.

- ☑ In-house security teams throughout the IT industry employ Nessus.

- ☑ Many software suites available today provide low-level integration to Nessus.

History

☑ The Nessus Project was started in 1998 by Renaud Deraison.

☑ Nessus was conceived amidst stagnation of other open-source scanners and the rise in cost of commercial scanners.

☑ The Nessus general mailing list has over 1,350 participants and around 50 active posters.

☑ The Nessus community continues to grow at an exponential rate.

Basic Components

☑ The Nessus Project adopted a client/server model for its foundation. This client/server model allows the security analyst to "detach" from the vulnerability scan and use his resources for other items while Nessus continues to do what it does best.

☑ The Nessus client can connect to the nessusd server in many ways that employ both encryption and authentication.

☑ The Nessus Attack Scripting Language (NASL) allows security analysts to quickly create their own plugins for vulnerability checks.

☑ The Knowledge Base allows Nessus to share data gleaned from one plugin with the processes of another plugin. In this way, each plugin builds upon previously executed plugins.

Frequently Asked Questions

The following Frequently Asked Questions, answered by the authors of this book, are designed to both measure your understanding of the concepts presented in this chapter and to assist you with real-life implementation of these concepts. To have your questions about this chapter answered by the author, browse to **www.syngress.com/solutions** and click on the **"Ask the Author"** form. You will also gain access to thousands of other FAQs at ITFAQnet.com.

Q: How can I subscribe to the Nessus mailing lists?

A: Point your browser to lists.nessus.org. All of the archives and instructions to subscribe can be found there.

Q: If I use a centralized MySQL server for a backend database, won't the MySQL authentication credentials be sent unencrypted? How can I leverage a centralized database in a safe and secure manner?

A: Yes, that is true! The best thing to do is to get smart on SSH port forwarding. Using this will allow you to point each nessusd server at 127.0.0.1 as the MySQL database's IP address. This port accepts data and forwards it across an encrypted tunnel to the real MySQL database, thus marshalling your database entries over an encrypted tunnel to the actual database.

Q: Management won't let us use open-source software of any kind unless we can purchase support. Do any companies provide support for Nessus?

A: Yes. In fact, Tenable Security, which is listed on the Nessus home page, has positioned much of its business model around offering commercial support and services for Nessus. Tenable was actually begun by Ron Gula, developer of the Dragon IDS, and Renaud Deraisson, Nessus' creator. Tenable can be found via www.tenablesecurity.com.

Q: If Nessus is completely open source, who pays for the basic resources such as Web space and so forth?

A: Nessus is open source, and is supported by the efforts of many volunteers. However, it is also greatly funded by Tenable Security. Actually, though, the Web and FTP servers are provided by the U.S. Department of Commerce's National Technical Information Service. The mail and CVS servers are provided by the U.S. Treasury's Inspector General for Tax Administration's

Strategic Enforcement Division. A number of volunteer parties have provided resources for the Nessus Project, as can be found on the Nessus "Thanks" page at www.nessus.org/thanks.html. They include Guardent, James Leutri, CCNP (Security Consultant), Ayamura Kikuchi, David Lott from Pinkerton Netsecurity, Mike Gleason from NcFTP Software, Antonio Stano from securityinfos.com, Rain Forrest Puppy, The Turkish LUG, NASA Ames Research Center, Denis Ducamp, Karl Wieland, and more.

Q: How do I install Nessus?

A: Read the next chapter!

## Chapter 3

Installing Nessus

Solutions in this Chapter:

- **Quick Start Guide**
- **Picking a Server**
- **Source or Binary**
- **Installation from Source**
- **Configuring Nessus**
- **Installing a Client**
- **Updating to the Latest Plugins**

- ☑ **Summary**
- ☑ **Solutions Fast Track**
- ☑ **Frequently Asked Questions**

Introduction

Nessus is quite possibly one of the easiest packages to install. The myriad ways available to security analysts to deploy Nessus in their environment makes it a perfect match for the security organization that wants to control every aspect of an application. For this reason, there are many issues to consider when provisioning Nessus for your environment:

- Will you use many servers or just one?

- Will users be authenticated by password or client-side certification?

- Will this installation update and maintain itself, or will you perform this maintenance manually?

This chapter examines these types of questions, including the different methods of installation and their requisite skill sets. You can then choose your installation method based on your operating system preference, deployment process, skill level, and desired level of configurability. The members of the Nessus community have gone to great lengths to be inclusive in their installation methods—a side effect of having a community that spans many different operating systems and many different network environments.

Quick Start Guide

There are several ways to install Nessus in a quick manner. Of course, compiling from source is always recommended, but it is not always required and not always the quickest. Linux vendors and other UNIX vendors have made great progress toward offering quick and easy methods to install packages that quite often save time and do not require knowledge of compilers to get up and running.

There are three unique ways to install Nessus:

- nessus-installer.sh (least recommended)

- UNIX-specific package installation

- Compile from source

In the beginning of this chapter, we focus on the first two, those being the quickest. The remaining method, compiling from source, is covered in detail toward the end of the chapter.

The quickest method, and the least recommended, is to execute the following command as a user other than root:

```
lynx -source http://install.nessus.org | sh
```

This method is not recommended because you are in effect executing commands pulled from a shell script on a Web server via cleartext HTTP. There are three easy attack scenarios by which an attacker could control the shell script that you automatically execute. In the first scenario, an attacker uses a tool like hunt or ettercap to modify your HTTP session with the server. These tools can allow an attacker to modify any cleartext TCP session, taking it over or simply injecting data. To understand these attacks better, read the article "Taking Over Cleartext Protocol on Switched Networks" at www.bastille-linux.org/jay/taking-over-cleartext-protocols-switched.html. In the second scenario, an attacker simply compromises a Nessus Web or FTP server, or one of the mirrors, and modifies this script. Unlike in the download case where you can check the PGP signature on the files you're downloading, this method allows for no integrity check whatsoever. In the third scenario, an attacker poisons your DNS data, so that you pull this data from the wrong machine altogether. He could do that by compromising Nessus' DNS server, a root DNS server, or your DNS server. He could also use one of the many DNS poisoning tools, like dnsspoof or zodiac.

If an attacker uses one of these attacks when you're installing Nessus, you will unwillingly execute commands from a malicious site, probably backdooring your own machine. If you feel the odds of these attacks are negligible, then this method is available to you. This method will install everything in an automated fashion.

If you still want to use the automated script but are too cautious to install using this method, there is another avenue for you. Navigate to one of the following mirror sites shown in Table 3.1 and download `nessus-installer.sh`.

Table 3.1 List of Mirror Sites

Location	Server
United States (East Coast, via HTTP)	http://ftp.nessus.org/nessus/nessus-2.0.10a/nessus-installer/
United States (East Coast)	ftp://ftp.nessus.org/pub/nessus/nessus-2.0.10a/nessus-installer/
Germany	ftp://ftp.gwdg.de/pub/linux/misc/nessus/nessus-2.0.10a/nessus-installer/

Continued

Table 3.1 List of Mirror Sites

Location	Server
Germany	http://ftp.gwdg.de/pub/linux/misc/ nessus/nessus-2.0.10a/nessus-installer/
Switzerland	ftp://sunsite.cnlab-switch.ch/mirror/ nessus/nessus-2.0.10a/nessus-installer/
Russia	ftp://ftp.chg.ru/pub/security/nessus/ nessus-2.0.10a/nessus-installer/
Sweden	ftp://ftp.sekure.net/pub/nessus/ nessus-2.0.10a/nessus-installer/
Thailand	ftp://ftp.nectec.or.th/pub/mirrors/ nessus/nessus-2.0.10a/nessus-installer/
Australia	ftp://ftp.au.nessus.org/pub/nessus/ nessus-2.0.10a/nessus-installer/
Austria	ftp://ftp.at.nessus.org/pub/nessus/ nessus-2.0.10a/nessus-installer/
Turkey	ftp://ftp.linux.org.tr/pub/mirrors/nessus/ nessus-2.0.10a/nessus-installer/
Japan	ftp://ftp.ayamura.org/pub/nessus/ nessus-2.0.10a/nessus-installer/

(source: nessus.org)

After downloading nessus-installer.sh from one of these mirror sites, read the script, and make sure you understand what each command does. Finally, execute:

```
sh nessus-installer.sh
```

Again, understand that these automated methods introduce risk that most security-conscious engineers will choose to avoid. It is likely that the Nessus team introduced this method to cut down on the number of e-mails they received from new users requesting installation support. We strongly advise that you use the instructions in this chapter to install in a more secure way.

Nessus on Linux (suse/redhat/mandrake/gentoo/debian)

Given the propensity for proponents of open source to use Linux, a good bit of Nessus installations currently run on Linux. However, not all Linux flavors taste the same. Some Linux variants like Red Hat, SUSE, and Mandrake typically use

Red Hat's Package Manager (RPM) files, while others have their own unique methods of install, such as "emerge" within gentoo and "apt-get" within Debian. Although each flavor has a way to install Nessus natively, if you encounter any problems as you venture down the path of package purity, remember that you can always compile from source.

Please note the following additional considerations when installing Nessus on a SUSE Linux system. Installation on SUSE requires the following packages be in place prior to installation:

- bison.rpm
- flex.rpm
- gtkdev.rpm
- glibdev.rpm

RPM Installation

Several Nessus RPMs are maintained by different Linux vendors. These are not maintained anywhere within the Nessus.org Web site, and thus if you feel certain about your need for an RPM-based installation there are two choices available. The first choice, if your Linux distribution is covered under a support agreement, is to acquire it from your vendor. If your vendor does not maintain an RPM of Nessus, or does not maintain an RPM for the current version of Nessus, the best thing to do is to obtain your RPM from a public site dedicated to maintaining RPM integrity. An example of such a site is the somewhat well-known ATrpms collection found at www.atrpms.net. Sites like this, founded by Axel Thimm, work closely with the development teams of the projects they support to ensure the integrity of the source, and the integrity of the subsequent RPMs.

Before installing any RPM you find from a trusted repository, it is of the utmost importance to verify the authenticity of the RPM. Even though many sites offer MD5 signatures as a method of verifying the authenticity of a file, this method is weak and subject to attack as discussed in the accompanying sidebar. The safest method of authenticating the RPM is to leverage the digital signature verification method of the rpm tool.

Any trusted repository worth downloading RPMs from will have a public key available for download from a key server like pgp.mit.edu and often from their site as well. In the case of ATrpms, their key is located at http://ATrpms.net/RPM-GPG-KEY.atrpms. Do not use keys provided anywhere else than explicitly stated by the repository you have chosen. Once the public key has been acquired, it can be imported via the command line by first switching user to root and executing:

```
rpm --import  <keyfile>
```

After importing the public key of the trusted repository, any RPMs acquired from the site can be verified for authenticity by executing:

```
rpm --checksig  <file.rpm>
```

This should result in output that verifies the signature is OK:

```
nessus-server-2.0.12-16.rh9.at.i386.rpm: (sha1) dsa sha1 md5 gpg OK
```

Keep in mind that some distributions of Linux might have prerequisites that you will need to locate first. Once you find and authenticate your RPMs, you can install them by simply switching user to root and executing:

```
rpm -i <name_of_rpm>.rpm
```

Notes from the Underground…

MD5 Weakness

When it comes to verifying the authenticity of a file, many people have historically relied on the MD5 one-way hashing algorithm developed in 1991 by Ron Rivest of RSA Data Security while at MIT. One-way hashes have many uses, only one of which is an attempt to verify file integrity.

The problem with relying on MD5 hashes as a method of ensuring file authenticity is the ease in which this method is circumvented. For example, let's say Alice decides to maintain an RPM of Nessus on her Apache Web site. Eventually, Alice's Web site becomes very popular among users who rely on her up-to-date RPMs. Her users adapt an automatic process of installing these RPMs automatically via custom scripts, which also check the MD5 hash to be safe. One day, Bob discovers a new vulnerability in the Apache Web server version that Alice uses to host her Web site. Bob then replaces the RPM with a version laden with a Trojan that sends all scan data back to him. Bob notices that Alice's users are recommended to verify each package based on the MD5 hash that accom-

Continued

panies each RPM, so he simply runs his evil RPM through the MD5 hash algorithm and places the result on the site as well.

Now, all of Alice's users will verify the RPM based on the MD5 and find that it appears to be authentic. They will feel safe to install it and subsequently be sending all of their scan data back to Bob, who is an eager receiver. This form of a Man-In-The-Middle attack is a common occurrence, making the reliance on a private-public key combination imperative. Following the practice of verifying file authenticity based on digital signatures is part of defense-in-depth and removes the possibility of a Web site compromise affecting the authenticity of the files located there.

See the sidebar titled "Asymmetric Encryption" later in this chapter for a detailed description of the strength of digital signatures.

Gentoo Installation

Gentoo has an interesting tool available to its users when it comes to updating software packages. When working within the Gentoo environment, loading software is typically quick, easy, and by some accounts, actually enjoyable. To install Nessus using the Gentoo native package, installers simply execute the following command as root:

```
emerge nessus
```

Debian Installation

Debian users are familiar with .deb package files and the *apt-get* command. Assuming that your *apt-get* configuration files are up to date and correct, the following two commands are all you need execute (as root) to have a full install of Nessus:

```
apt-get install nessusd
apt-get install nessus
```

Nessus on Solaris

If you happen to be a Solaris user and want to install Nessus in a Quick-Start fashion too, you are in luck. Point your browser at www.sunfreeware.com, select your architecture and OS version combination from the right-hand side of the page, and you will find the Nessus binary and source packages. These will be tar'd and gzip'd. After downloading these files, unzip and untar them, at which point you should have a resultant .pkg file. To install this, simply type the following as root:

```
pkgadd -d <name of file>.pkg
```

The method of file verification that Sunfreeware uses is a bit different from most, and works well for the large amount of files they maintain. The MD5s for every PKG file are listed on one page. That page in turn is digitally signed with PGP. The public key required for this is located at www.sunfreeware.com/gpgsig.

After importing the public key into your key ring, the next step is to download the file www.sunfreeware.com/md5.html.asc and use *gpg* to verify its authenticity using the following *gpg* command sequence:

```
gpg --verify < mg5.html.asc
```

Picking a Server

The first item of business when preparing for the installation of a nessusd server is provisioning the system that will be home to your Nessus installation. The factors that go into deciding what OS, platform, network location, and so forth will all vary depending on the purpose and duties of the server. First, ensure that your system will not be performing double duty. Many times, the security organization requests a server and the first thing IT wants to do is to install a network management system on it. Quite frequently, someone will ask to put yet another arbitrary application on the system, thinking that perhaps the security organization might just have some spare cycles to share with the rest of the organization. No matter what the reason, the security organization should never allow another application to invade the Nessus installation unless it is a process that runs directly in tandem with the security process.

The sensitivity of the data that Nessus will be collecting, mixed with the amount of resources required while running a scan, creates a justification for the security organization to be greedy with its resources in this case. It is also often tempting to allow other members of the security organization to have shell access to systems that sit deep in the organization as a jumping-off point to other resources. Many times, a security analyst might want to leverage a system in a specific location to sniff traffic on that segment, or perhaps test some other theory relative to the security posture. Ensure that a process is in place to allow these activities in a limited fashion if necessary, without detracting from the resources required to perform the scheduled and nonscheduled vulnerability scans.

Supported Operating Systems

After determining what the scope of the system will be in conjunction with the Nessus process, the next step is to determine which operating system best suits your organization's needs. When considering which operating system to use, the security organization has a wide variety of choices. Nessus will install on just about any Linux distribution or UNIX operating system, from the BSD UNIX family to Solaris to even Mac OS X. The only obviously missing operating system for a server installation of Nessus is Windows. Although a Windows client is available in both free and commercial forms, the server component is strictly UNIX based, at least in the free Nessus program. There is actually a Windows Nessus server, in the form of Tenable Security's commercial product, Nevo, but this product is beyond the scope of this book.

Minimal Hardware Specifications

The next step in provisioning a system upon which to load Nessus is specifying the hardware required. This is going to depend heavily on the environment that Nessus will be scanning. If you will be scanning a class C address space (~255 hosts) and you expect to perform a scan like this very quickly, then you will want to ensure more than one processor (as Nessus is multithreaded) and between 1GB to 2GB of RAM. For a general scan that might take a few hours to perform, this is obviously overkill. However, for an internal scanning machine, time will be of the essence. There will be a limit to what your network can handle, but its capacity will grow over time, and thus it is better to ensure that the network continues as the bottleneck and not the system itself.

If your budget or choice of hardware is more limited, here are a few tips. First and foremost, memory is the greatest factor limiting how many hosts you can scan at once and how many tests you can run simultaneously. Increase processing power only after you've installed as much memory as is financially feasible. Second, make sure to scan multiple machines at the same time—this will make sure that your scan isn't entirely halted by a single odd machine. Third, make sure to run several tests/plugins at time, so that a single high-latency plugin doesn't slow your entire test. For example, if you have one plugin that takes 40 seconds while the next four take 10, with the delay solely due to latency, running two plugins at a time should take 40 seconds, while one at a time will take 80. To sum this up, here's a data point from Renaud Deraisson, creator of Nessus and co-author of this book. With 128 megabytes of *free* memory, you can achieve the best speed scanning 10 targets at once with five tests at a time. On a system with 256 megabytes of free memory, you would scan 20 targets with 10 tests. Remember, these estimates are based on *free* memory. A Linux machine with 256 megabytes of RAM will probably only have 128 to 192 megabytes of free memory.

Network Location

Since we've been making sure that the network provides the bottleneck, the last item to consider during the provisioning of the Nessus server will be the location of this system on the network. Once again, size matters. If your network is small enough, say around 255–512 hosts, then one Nessus server might do the trick for you and thus network location becomes much simpler to determine. In the case of the small network, find the location that has the fewest number of routing devices between the Nessus server and the majority of the targets to be scanned. If possible, ensure that no firewall exists between the Nessus server and its target selection. This will reduce the computational and bandwidth-related load on the routing devices produced by the scans.

If you're deploying Nessus on a large network, a bit more thought is required. You can deploy multiple nessusd servers throughout the network all waiting for the cue to scan their targets. Once triggered, these Nessus servers will then execute this scan simultaneously. The sweet spot you are trying to find here is the 24-hour window. If your entire network can be scanned inside one 24-hour window, then you are on the right path to having an extremely useful vulnerability assessment process. The process in this situation becomes divided into two phases. The first phase involves deploying multiple Nessus servers according to the same process and using the same concepts as when deploying only one. For example, ensure that there are a minimum number of network routing devices between the Nessus server and the targets of the scan. The second phase involves attempting to scan and potentially shifting scanning machines based on your results. You might find that some areas of your network take longer to scan than others due to greater numbers of targets located in those areas or targets with more open ports or other sources of latency. In those situations, you can add another server, move an existing server from one position to another, or simply configure one server to scan hosts for which another was previously responsible. At this point, you can try again for that temporal sweet spot: the 24-hour scan.

Source or Binary

The question of whether you will install Nessus using source compilation or a precompiled binary is best answered by defining what your process will be during initial installation and how you will update Nessus as new versions are released. You will need to decide whether you can trust the available precompiled binary packages—this section's sidebar "Trusting Binary Packages" discusses why you might not. You should also consider whether you desire any custom compilation options—if you need any, you'll need to compile from scratch.

For instance, let's say that you don't want to have to install GTK in order to run Nessus on your system. The client uses the Gimp Toolkit (GTK), but you want a command-line version, as you don't want to install any of the X libraries or have to handle securing it in the future. To support this installation you will be required to install from the source, while passing a compile option:

```
./configure –disable-gtk
```

Obviously, if you want to do any modification to base source code, you will require the Nessus source. Keeping Nessus up to date is actually easiest when you're compiling from source. Automated solutions even exist to make this easier—for instance, the Nessus FAQ lists a shell script that can be used to do just that. The script assumes you are installing from CVS with the development version and is located at http://hvdkooij.xs4all.nl/NessusFAQ/index.php?sid= 85621&aktion=artikel&rubrik=002&id=12&lang=en.

However, it is definitely easier to use binary packages. RPMs and .deb packages are maintained for the Red Hat and Debian distributions, as well as several others. Sunfreeware.com also maintains Solaris PKG files for the most current stable version. There are a few major disadvantages to using binary packages of Nessus, though. First, as we discuss in the next sidebar, "Trusting Binary Packages," you have to be careful whose binary packages you install—they could carry hostile code. Second, binary packages for most open-source software are rarely as current as the most recent release, at least if a third-party creates the packages. The packaging volunteer generally packages many different pieces of software and tends to update their packages with some delay, based on their available time and backlog. This is even more of an issue with a Linux distribution, which tends to release packages only once per distribution release, like every six months. These delays can be critical with software like Nessus or Nmap, each of which can see major functionality improvements in the course of six months. Binary packages are not really the best path when you're using

Nessus in an enterprise environment where keeping up to date can be critical in doing comprehensive vulnerability assessment. Third and finally, using binary packages often results in slightly slower performance. Most binary packages are compiled for 386s, to ensure that they can be used on any Intel hardware. This eliminates any code efficiencies that are normally introduced by the compiler as it chooses machine code specific to your processor. Code compiled specifically for today's high-end processors runs 5% to 10% faster than code compiled for the 386 running on that same high-end processor. As the 64-bit AMD and Intel chips gain ground, this speed-up should be greatly amplified. While AMD's 64-bit chips can run 32-bit compiled code, the same code runs much faster in native 64-bit mode.

Tools & Traps...

Trusting Binary Packages

The problem with using binary packages is that a third party is often introduced: the packager. Very often, this packager is completely unrelated to and not vetted at all by the developers—he's often just some guy who volunteered to create binary packages. The developers generally accept the offer so that they won't have to learn how to create packages for the given packaging system—they rarely check him or even the packages he creates. This leaves an untrustworthy party very capable of adding a crafty surprise to the source code before compiling or, often worse, to the installation scripts.

Remember, if an untrustworthy party creates the binaries from source, he can modify the installation contents or process to do anything he wants. Since your installer runs as root, the package creator has the ability to completely compromise your system! Most packaging solutions, including RPM, allow the package creator to include shell commands to be executed with root privilege before or after the file installation. If you don't know the person or organization creating them, or at least trust a party that's vetted the creator, you might want to compile the code yourself!

If you have found a trustworthy packager, do not need to issue compile-time options, do not require the 5% to 10% speed increase, and do not need to keep your Nessus install quite as up to date, then you could install Nessus from a binary package. Obviously, this book's authors do not recommend this route—compiling from source is simply a better solution.

Installation from Source

After determining that installing from source is the right choice for you and your organization, you will want to decide just how up-to-date your Nessus installation needs to be. For instance, you could install and update directly from the CVS server while you use the up-to-the-minute most recent version. However, this is not recommended unless you are an active participant in the Nessus development cycle and plan on being one of the first to encounter bugs. If instead you would classify your organization's use of Nessus as more of a consumer and less of a developer role, then you will want to download the latest tarballs from one of the twelve mirrors around the globe.

Software Prerequisites

Prior to downloading and installing Nessus, a few software packages need to be installed:

- **GTK** The Gimp Toolkit, version 1.2 (used for the nessus client)
  - ftp://ftp.gimp.org/pub/gtk/v1.2
  - The GTK can be omitted if desired. Remember to add the **–disable-gtk** option to the ./configure options when installing nessus-core.
- **OpenSSL** (used for client/server communication and the testing of SSL-based services)
  - www.openssl.org

Obtaining the Latest Version

As of this writing, nine different countries contain an updated mirror of the source files required for installation. They can be found at www.nessus.org/nessus_2_0.html and are listed in Table 3.2.

Table 3.2 Mirror Sites

Location	Server
United States (East Coast, via HTTP)	http://ftp.nessus.org/nessus/nessus-2.0.10a/src/
United States (East Coast, via FTP)	ftp://ftp.nessus.org/pub/nessus/nessus-2.0.10a/src/
Germany	ftp://ftp.gwdg.de/pub/linux/misc/nessus/nessus-2.0.10a/src/
Germany	http://ftp.gwdg.de/pub/linux/misc/nessus/nessus-2.0.10a/src/
Switzerland	ftp://sunsite.cnlab-switch.ch/mirror/nessus/nessus-2.0.10a/src/
Russia	ftp://ftp.chg.ru/pub/security/nessus/nessus-2.0.10a/src/
Sweden	ftp://ftp.sekure.net/pub/nessus/nessus-2.0.10a/src/
Thailand	ftp://ftp.nectec.or.th/pub/mirrors/nessus/nessus-2.0.10a/src/
Australia	ftp://ftp.au.nessus.org/pub/nessus/nessus-2.0.10a/src/
Austria	ftp://ftp.at.nessus.org/pub/nessus/nessus-2.0.10a/src/
Turkey	ftp://ftp.linux.org.tr/pub/mirrors/nessus/nessus-2.0.10a/src/
Japan	ftp://ftp.ayamura.org/pub/nessus/nessus-2.0.10a/src/

Nessus Mirrors (source: nessus.org)

The Four Components

At each of the mirror sites listed in Table 3.2 you will find at least four files that are required for a source installation (as seen in Figure 3.1). They should be downloaded and installed in the following order:

1. nessus-libraries
2. libnasl

3. nessus–core

4. nessus–plugins

Figure 3.1 Download of Files for Source Configuration

```
jsquared:~# ftp ftp.nessus.org
Connected to ftp.nessus.org.
220 ftp.nessus.org NcFTPd Server (licensed copy) ready.
Name (ftp.nessus.org:root): anonymous
331 Guest login ok, send your complete e-mail address as password.
Password:
230-You are user #4 of 50 simultaneous users allowed.
230-
230 Logged in anonymously.
Remote system type is UNIX.
Using binary mode to transfer files.
ftp> cd /pub/nessus/nessus-2.0.10a/src
250 "/pub/nessus/nessus-2.0.10a/src" is new cwd.
ftp> ls
200 PORT command successful.
150 Opening ASCII mode data connection for /bin/ls.
-rw-r--r--   1 ftpuser  ftpusers        509 Jan 22 11:27 MD5
-rw-r--r--   1 ftpuser  ftpusers     343047 Jan 22 11:24 libnasl-2.0.10a.tar.gz
-rw-r--r--   1 ftpuser  ftpusers     649493 Jan 22 11:24 nessus-core-2.0.10a.tar.gz
-rw-r--r--   1 ftpuser  ftpusers     418370 Jan 22 11:24 nessus-libraries-2.0.10a.tar.gz
-rw-r--r--   1 ftpuser  ftpusers    1443420 Jan 22 11:24 nessus-plugins-2.0.10a.tar.gz
226 Listing completed.
ftp> prompt
Interactive mode off.
ftp> mget *gz
```

For this example, we connected directly via FTP to **ftp.nessus.org**. We entered **anonymous** as our username and used **someone@syngress.com** as our password. A short directory listing displays the gzipped tarballs that we will download.

Once we've downloaded the tar balls, we execute `**tar xzf**` on each of these files (as seen in Figure 3.2). Each tar command creates a directory for each of the four components.

Figure 3.2 Executing tar-xzf on Each File

```
jsquared:~/nessus$ ls -al
total 2810
drwxr-xr-x    2 root     root        1024 Jun  1 00:32 .
drwxr-xr-x   16 root     root        2048 Jun  1 00:30 ..
-rw-r--r--    1 root     root      343047 Jun  1 00:22 libnasl-2.0.10a.tar.gz
-rw-r--r--    1 root     root      649493 Jun  1 00:22 nessus-core-2.0.10a.tar.gz
-rw-r--r--    1 root     root      418370 Jun  1 00:22 nessus-libraries-2.0.10a.tar.gz
-rw-r--r--    1 root     root     1443420 Jun  1 00:32 nessus-plugins-2.0.10a.tar.gz
jsquared:~/nessus$ tar xzf nessus-libraries-2.0.10a.tar.gz
jsquared:~/nessus$ tar xzf libnasl-2.0.10a.tar.gz
jsquared:~/nessus$ tar xzf nessus-core-2.0.10a.tar.gz
jsquared:~/nessus$ tar xzf nessus-plugins-2.0.10a.tar.gz
jsquared:~/nessus$ ls -al
total 2814
drwxr-xr-x    6 root     root        1024 Jun  1 00:33 .
drwxr-xr-x   16 root     root        2048 Jun  1 00:30 ..
drwxr-xr-x    5 root     502         1024 Jan 22 06:24 libnasl
-rw-r--r--    1 root     root      343047 Jun  1 00:22 libnasl-2.0.10a.tar.gz
drwxr-xr-x    8 root     502         1024 Jan 22 06:24 nessus-core
-rw-r--r--    1 root     root      649493 Jun  1 00:22 nessus-core-2.0.10a.tar.gz
drwxr-xr-x    6 root     502         1024 Jan 22 06:24 nessus-libraries
-rw-r--r--    1 root     root      418370 Jun  1 00:22 nessus-libraries-2.0.10a.tar.gz
drwxr-xr-x    8 root     502         1024 Jan 22 06:24 nessus-plugins
-rw-r--r--    1 root     root     1443420 Jun  1 00:32 nessus-plugins-2.0.10a.tar.gz
jsquared:~/nessus$
```

./configure

After each of the tar files has been extracted into its respective directory, it's time
to begin the configuration and compilation steps. The order in which this is done
is extremely important. First, we will make sure that we are the root user, and
then switch to the *nessus-libraries* directory and execute the following command:

```
$ ./configure
```

This will check our system for the required libraries and tools and prepare
the makefile used to set compilation options and installation paths for Nessus on
our system. It also creates a script titled *uninstall-nessus* that we will use to unin-
stall our old version without losing our old configuration (see Figure 3.3).

If we have an older version of Nessus installed that we're replacing, we must
run the following command as root before continuing:

```
# ./uninstall-nessus
```

Figure 3.3 Uninstallation of Nessus

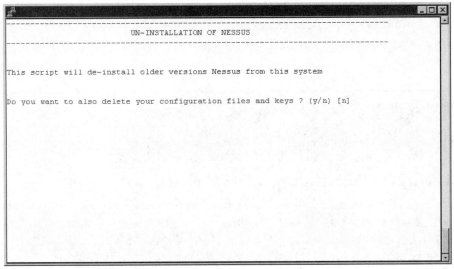

```
--------------------------------------------------------------------------
                      UN-INSTALLATION OF NESSUS
--------------------------------------------------------------------------


This script will de-install older versions Nessus from this system


Do you want to also delete your configuration files and keys ? (y/n) [n]
```

The script will prompt us as to whether we want to delete our older configuration files and keys. Unless we're simply removing Nessus from the system, we want to choose "n" for "no" here. Now, since we are simply upgrading the Nessus application and do not want to start from scratch, we choose "n." This will remove any files installed during our previous Nessus installations, leaving us ready to compile the Nessus-libraries.

The next step is to execute the **make** command. We simply type **make** on a line by itself and press the **Enter** key. The make program will begin compiling object files and linking them together, sending all sorts of output to the screen. This will take some time. Once this is done, we must switch user (su) to root, so that we can install the newly compiled files.

To install the compiled files, we first switch user to root with the **su** command:

```
$ su
```

We will be given a prompt at which to enter the root password, like so:

```
Password: <enter root password>
```

After typing the root password and getting our root prompt, we now run the following command:

```
# make install
```

This command installs all compiled files from the nessus–libraries tarball into their target directories, which are subdirectories of /usr/local by default. Now, this destination directory, or "prefix," can be changed by passing the command-line argument **--prefix=/some/other/directory** to the configure script.

Tools & Traps…

Do Not Run Configure or Make as Root

You may have noticed that the process shown for compiling Nessus doesn't run either **configure** or **make** as the root user. An important concept in security is the principle of Least Privilege, which dictates that you give any program (or user) only what privilege it actually requires to do its task. This decreases the damage that a hostile or compromised program (or user) can do.

As is the case when compiling most UNIX programs, these two compilation commands don't require root privilege to run—they simply compile the software. Only the **make install** step actually requires root privilege, as it needs to install software outside of the user's home directory. We use su, the UNIX switch-user command, to use root privilege only when necessary.

This might seem like an academic point, but it was vitally important when an attacker compromised a major distribution server for the massively popular tool tcpdump. The attacker didn't actually Trojan the tcpdump code; instead, he modified the configure script. The configure script installed a Trojan, which sent a shell back to the attacker whenever an administrator compiled the code on a system. Administrators who ran the configure script as root gave the attacker root access on their system, while every other administrator only gave the attacker access as a normal user. You can read more about this incident at: www.us-cert.gov/ federal/archive/advisories/FA-2002-30.html

It's also worth noting that users who check PGP signatures of any software, source or otherwise that they download seldom are caught by Trojaned software.

Upon completion of the file installation from our **make install** command, the output will give you a few additional items to examine or modify. First, it states that /usr/local/bin should be in your path. To determine this, execute the following command:

```
echo $PATH
```

You should see something similar to the following output:

```
/usr/local/sbin:/usr/local/bin:/usr/sbin:/usr/bin:/sbin:/bin:/usr/bin/X11
```

In our scenario, we do in fact have /usr/local/bin in our path. If we did not, we would simply execute the following command to remedy the situation:

```
export PATH=$PATH:/usr/local/bin
```

To place this directory in our path more permanently, along with every other user's path, we should add it to the command that sets the PATH in the global system files specific to the shell in use. For instance, the primary user shell on most Linux distributions is bash, which reads /etc/profile on a new user login. We can add the relevant line to the end of /etc/profile by executing this command as root:

```
# echo "export PATH=$PATH:/usr/local/bin" >>/etc/profile
```

The last file that the post-compilation notes exhort us to modify is the /etc/ld.so.conf file. It asks us to ensure that /usr/local/lib is in that file, and then to execute **ldconfig** after adding it. To verify that /usr/local/lib is found in this file on our Linux system, we simply execute the following command:

```
# grep /usr/local/lib /etc/ld.so.conf
```

If this returns a line that reads exactly "/usr/local/lib" then we have nothing to do. Otherwise, we'll need to add it to this file, running ldconfig afterward. We accomplish this via the command sequence:

```
# echo "/usr/local/lib" >> /etc/ld.so.conf
# ldconfig
```

On Solaris, we'd execute this command instead:

```
# export LD_LIBRARY_PATH=$LD_LIBRARY_PATH:/usr/local/lib
```

Now we are ready to change to the libnasl directory and perform the same **./configure** and **make** sequences. Remember to switch down to your regular user account until you need root for the final step. First, exit the root shell:

```
# exit
```

Now compile libnasl:

```
$ cd ../libnasl
$ ./configure
$ make
$ su
Password: <enter root password>
# make install
```

Nessus-core is next on our compilation path. It is here that the option of removing the dependency on GTK is performed, if you desire. Our command sequence looks very similar to that of the last package, with the simple addition of our configuration option. Of course, we will omit this option if we want to use the GTK graphical user interface (GUI) for Nessus:

```
# exit
$ cd ../nessus-core
$ ./configure --disable-gtk
$ make
$ su
Password: <enter root password>
# make install
```

After installing nessus-core, we are asked to ensure that /usr/local/sbin is in our path. As with nessus-libraries, we first check to see if /usr/local/sbin is in our path by executing:

```
# echo $PATH
```

If our path lacks the required directory, we can run:

```
# export PATH=$PATH:/usr/local/sbin
```

Our final compilation to perform is for the nessus-plugins. Much like the prior three packages we had to compile, we now execute the following commands:

```
# exit
$ cd ../nessus-plugins
$ ./configure
$ make
$ su
```

```
Password: <enter root password>
# make install
```

After this last step, our installation is complete. All required software has been compiled and installed in the required directories on the system. While this might seem complicated versus the one-line binary package install, it truly is simple. This command sequence becomes second nature to you as you compile and install Nessus, or even other open-source software, a few times. Our next step will be to perform the initial configuration of the Nessus server.

Configuring Nessus

For a **nessusd** Nessus server to communicate properly with a Nessus client, the administrator must execute a few more steps before running the client. The first of these involves the creation of the Nessus server certificate (as seen in Figure 3.4). To create the certificates required for secure communication between the client and the server, execute the following command on the server:

```
# nessus-mkcert
```

If OpenSSL is installed, then executing this command will initiate a Curses-based interface that will query you for a few configuration items. (Curses is a kind of text-based GUI language.) These are items common to certificate identification such as shelf life of the certificates and location information to be associated with the certificate.

Figure 3.4 Creation of the Nessus Server Certificate

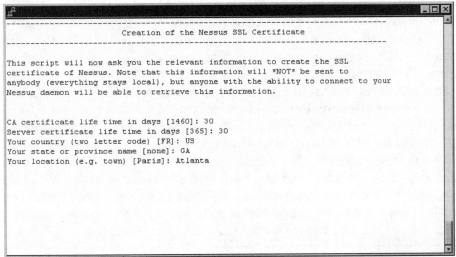

Once this information is entered, the script creates the following files:

- Certificate authority:
  - Certificate = /usr/local/com/nessus/CA/cacert.pem
  - Private key = /usr/local/var/nessus/CA/cakey.pem
- Nessus server:
  - Certificate = /usr/local/com/nessus/CA/servercert.pem
  - Private key = /usr/local/var/nessus/CA/serverkey.pem

These files contain the public and private keys used for the encryption of the session.

Tools & Traps...

Asymmetric Encryption

One of the fundamental elements of encryption is the requirement of a key. When a user encrypts a file, a key is used to provide a high enough degree of randomness in the resultant cipher text. The cipher text also requires a key to decrypt it back into the original plaintext. These key pairs come in two varieties. The first variety is termed *symmetric* and includes the use of two identical keys. Although this method has been used for many years, primarily where communication is limited to two parties, it is extremely vulnerable to crypto attacks. If any side of the communication is compromised, then any future communications are assumed compromised as well. Today, many protocols still use symmetric encryption in a limited fashion where keys are only valid for the length of one session. Even still, the key is stored in memory on either side of the connection.

Asymmetric encryption employs the use of two completely different keys. First, there is the public key associated with a person, or sometimes an organization, which is often used to encrypt any message anyone would want to send to this person in a secure fashion. The private key, kept safe from compromise by the intended recipient of the encrypted message, is then used to reveal the plaintext from the cipher text. In this fashion, anyone can encrypt a message to anyone else; however, only the recipient can decrypt the message. The public key is usually available from

Continued

key servers, Web servers, or other places accessible by users expected to send messages to the recipient. A common searchable repository of keys is located at pgp.mit.edu.

Another function of the asymmetric key pair applied in Public Key Cryptography is the *digital signature*. Whenever someone wants to send a document that is verifiably authentic, he can encrypt it with his secret private key. This document can then be decrypted with the user's public key located in the public domain. Sometimes, merely an MD5 or SHA-1 hash of the document is encrypted and then placed in the plaintext document in an attempt at brevity.

Creating the User Account

Once the server certificates have been created, the next step in setting up a nessusd server is the creation of users. To add a user, execute the following command:

```
# nessus-adduser
```

You will immediately be asked for a username—in this case, we used "centaur." The next order of business is to specify the type of authentication to use with this user. You can choose "pass" or "cert." If "cert" is selected, then nessus-adduser will ask you for follow-on certificate-related information. If you select "pass," please note that the password will be seen on the screen as it is typed.

Typically, it is best to be able to authenticate users based on what is known as *two-factor authentication*. This is where users are tested for something they know and something they have. In this case, these would be the password and the client certificate, respectively. Unfortunately, nessus-adduser does not leverage the defense-in-depth of two factor authentication at this time.

The nessus-adduser utility will ask for any rules that you might want to specify to limit the access of the user you're creating. This is a very robust feature of Nessus and should not be underutilized. Any number of rules can be specified per user, including none at all. Each rule consists of one line and follows this syntax:

```
accept|deny ip/mask
      and
default accept|deny
```

If, for example, you want to allow this user the ability to scan only hosts between 192.168.0.1 and 192.168.0.255, you would use the following rules:

```
accept 192.168.0.0/24
default deny
```

The first rule specifies which address space this user is allowed to scan. The second rule, or default rule, stipulates that this user is not allowed to scan any other address. Using these rules, a well-defined sandbox can be established for each user, ensuring that the users will only be able to leverage the power of Nessus over a well-defined subset of hosts that they have authorization to scan—often, each administrator is only allowed to scan hosts for which she is responsible.

After detailing each of the desired rules for this user, you must hold down **Ctrl** and press the **D** key. You will then be presented with the information you have provided thus far, accompanied by a query for confirmation:

```
Login           : centaur
Password        : n355u5_rUl3z!
DN              :
Rules           :
accept 192.168.0.0/24
default deny


Is that ok ? (y/n) [y]
```

Simply press **y** and **Enter** and the addition of our new user is complete.

Tools & Traps...

Individual Account-ability

Nessus can be configured to allow different users access to different areas of the network. This enables an entire litany of imaginative uses. For example, the security organization might set up the Nessus server in such a way that it becomes part of the system administration workflow. After granting scanning authorization to each area of the network only to those system administrators responsible for it, the frequency of scans can be monitored by the Nessus administrator. This allows the security organization to determine how proactive each department within the organization is in regard to risk mitigation. Followed up with some corporate

Continued

security awareness training for the newly anointed system administrators allows for a more involved security process that can be monitored as it progresses.

Many times, the security team ends up in an adversarial relationship with other areas of the organization. The security team can have the difficult job of delivering bad news about current problems, which can end up making someone in the organization look bad. In other cases, the problem is one of uncertainty. System and network administrators know the security team is looking at the environment, but doesn't know either the focus of the inspection or what results will be revealed. While this kind of problem can often be corrected socially within the organization by senior management, there are technical measures that the security team can take. One is that of giving each administrator the ability to view his own security vulnerability report. This takes the security organization out of the messenger-to-be-shot or stick-wielding role and empowers the responsible administrators to take greater ownership of their vulnerabilities. The most motivated administrators will often fix many of the simpler vulnerabilities on their own this way, thus gaining the opportunity to reduce the problem list before they meet with the security team. This tends to mitigate whatever ill will might be felt by most administrators toward the security organization. For some reason, people tend to take criticism better from a machine than from a potentially aloof security analyst. It's important to still keep records of some periodic audits, to provide both good internal knowledge and external motivation, but site security definitely improves when administrators have vulnerability data before those audits.

The final step to configuring your Nessus server is to make any modifications required to the /etc/nessus/nessusd.conf file. To modify this file, view it using your favorite text editor. For example:

```
vi /etc/nessus/nessud.conf
```

Several different items can be tweaked in this configuration file; however, we are only going to focus on a few. The first item specifies how much Nessus can impact the network during scans. This item is **max_threads**, which controls how many total simultaneous tests Nessus will run at once. For example, to scan five hosts with four tests each, this number would need to be at least 20.

```
# Maximum number of threads, i.e. simultaneous tests
max_threads = 15
```

By default, this is set to 15. When setting this, you will want to test it at different levels to see how it impacts the performance of the network. On one hand, you want to ensure that this is set high enough as to allow a full scan in a timely fashion. On the other hand, you have to balance this requirement with the load placed on the network. For a network that is not commonly busy, this number can be set rather high for the first couple of tests; for example, 25. If scans begin to impact network performance, or perhaps even the performance of the scan itself, scale this number back a bit.

Many of these items become default settings that can be modified later for each scan via the client. The following two items, for example, become default settings for the way Nessus leverages Nmap:

```
# Range of the ports that Nmap will scan
port_range = 1-15000
# Ping hosts before scanning them?
ping_hosts = yes
```

port_range sets the default range of ports that Nessus will scan. For the most comprehensive scans, we'll obviously want to set this to 0–65535. **ping_hosts** tells Nessus whether it should scan only hosts that respond to pings. Again, for comprehensive scans, we'd want to set this to "no," as many hosts that are well firewalled do not respond to pings even though their applications will interact with the network. Now, both of these settings can and probably should be set primarily through the client when you're using Nessus with only one user. When you have multiple users around the site using Nessus, you'll want to set extremely well thought-out defaults in this file, ensuring that less knowledgeable users get the best defaults possible.

Now, once all of the modifications are complete, save this file and exit your text editor. For a complete list of all of the directives used in the nessusd.conf file, please refer to the man page for nessusd.

Tools & Traps...

The man Page

The man page for nessusd lists all of the options used for configuring the nessusd server. Pay close attention to **checks_read_timeout**, which covers performing scans over slow links; **use_mac_addr** for scanning DHCP enabled networks; and **safe_checks**, which is used for disabling checks that might cause a denial of service (DoS) on important network resources. That said, if the network resource is important enough to turn off denial-of-service checks during normal frequent scans, then the resource is important enough to schedule an outage to ensure your systems are not vulnerable to these. Many of the most important configuration options are listed in Table 3.3 with their corresponding functions.

Table 3.3 Configuration Options

Configure Options	Corresponding Functions
plugins_folder	Contains the location of the plugins folder. This is usually /usr/local/lib/nessus/plugins/.
logfile	Path to the logfile. You can enter **syslog** if you want the nessusd messages to be logged via syslogd. You can also enter **stderr** if you want the nessusd logs to be written on stderr. Because nessusd is a sensitive program, you should keep your logs. Therefore, entering syslog is usually not a good idea and should be done only for debugging purposes.
max_checks	The number of plugins that will run against each host being tested. Note that the total number of processes will be max_checks x max_hosts, so you need to find a balance between these two options. Note that launching too many plugins at the same time might disable the remote host, either temporarily (for example, inetd closes its ports) or definitely (the remote host crashes because it is asked to do too many things at the same time), so be careful.

Continued

Table 3.3 Configuration Options

Configure Options	Corresponding Functions
be_nice	If this option is set to "yes," then each child forked by nessusd will nice(2) itself to a very low priority. This might speed up your scan, as the main nessusd process will be able to continue to spew processes, and this guarantees that nessusd does not deprive other important processes from their resources.
log_whole_attack	If this option is set to "yes," nessusd will store the name, pid, date, and target of each plugin launched. This is helpful for monitoring and debugging purposes; however, this option might make nessusd fill your disk rather quickly.
log_plugins_name_at_load	If this option is set to "yes," nessusd will store the name, pid, date, and target of each plugin launched. This is helpful for monitoring and debugging purposes; however, this option might make nessusd fill your disk rather quickly.
dumpfile	Some plugins might issue messages, most of the time to inform you that something went wrong. If you want to read these messages, set this value to a given filename. If you want to save space, set this option value to /dev/null.
cgi_path	By default, nessusd looks for default CGIs in /cgi-bin and /scripts. You can change these to something else to reflect the policy of your site. The syntax of this option is the same as the shell $PATH variable: path1:path2:...
port_range	The default range of ports that the scanner plugins will probe. The syntax of this option is flexible; it can be a single range ("1–1500"), several ports ("21, 23, 80"), or several ranges of ports ("1–1500, 32000–33000"). Note that you can specify UDP and TCP ports by prefixing each range by T or U. For instance, the following range will make nessusd scan UDP ports 1 to 1024 and TCP ports 1 to 65535 : "T:1-65535,U:1-1024".

Continued

Table 3.3 Configuration Options

Configure Options	Corresponding Functions
optimize_test	By default, nessusd does not trust the remote host banners. This means that it will check a Web server claiming to be IIS for Apache flaws, and so on. This behavior might generate false positives and will slow the scan somehow. If you are sure the banners of the remote host have not been tampered with, you can safely enable this option, which will force the plugins to perform their job only against the services they have been designed to check.
checks_read_timeout	Number of seconds that the security checks will wait when doing a recv(). You should increase this value if you are running nessusd across a slow network link (testing a host via a dial-up connection, for example).
non_simult_ports	Some services (in particular, SMB) do not appreciate multiple connections at the same time coming from the same host. This option allows you to prevent nessusd to make two connections on the same given ports at the same time. The syntax of this option is "port1[, port2....]". Note that you can use the KB notation of nessusd to designate a service formally. For example, "139, Services/www" will prevent nessusd from making two connections at the same time on port 139 and on every port that hosts a Web server.
plugins_timeout	This is the maximum lifetime, in seconds of a plugin. It might happen that some plugins are slow because of the way they are written or the way the remote server behaves. This option allows you to make sure your scan is never caught in an endless loop because of a nonfinishing plugin.

Continued

Table 3.3 Configuration Options

Configure Options	Corresponding Functions
safe_checks	Most of the time, nessusd attempts to reproduce an exceptional condition to determine if the remote services are vulnerable to certain flaws. This includes the reproduction of buffer over-flows or format strings, which might make the remote server crash. If you set this option to "yes," nessusd will disable the plugins that have the potential to crash the remote services, and will at the same time make several checks rely on the banner of the service tested instead of its behavior toward a certain input. This reduces false positives and makes nessusd nicer toward your network; however, this might make you miss important vulnerabilities (as a vulnerability affecting a given service might also affect another one).
auto_enable_dependencies	Nessus plugins use the result of each other to execute their job. For example, a plugin that logs into the remote SMB registry will need the results of the plugin that finds the SMB name of the remote host and the results of the plugin that attempts to log in to the remote host. If you want to only select a subset of the plugins available, tracking the dependencies can quickly become tiresome. If you set this option to "yes," nessusd will automatically enable the plugins that are depended on.
use_mac_addr	Set this option to "yes" if you are testing your local network and each local host has a dynamic IP address (affected by DHCP or BOOTP), and all the tested hosts will be referred to by their MAC address.
plugin_upload	Set this option to "yes" if you want to let nes-susd users upload their own plugins. Note that the plugins they will upload will end up in their nessusd home directory, so they won't be shared among users (except if the user who uploads the plugins is the one declared in the option "'admin_user."

Continued

Table 3.3 Configuration Options

Configure Options	Corresponding Functions
admin_users	The user listed in this option will upload his plugins into the global nessus plugins directory, and they will be shared by every other user.
rules	Path to the rules database.

Now that we have configured our server to meet the specific needs of our organization, it is time to launch nessusd into action. As root, execute the following command:

```
# nessusd -D
```

It will take a few seconds for nessusd to return a command prompt after execution. A quick **netstat** command will allow us to see if nessusd is indeed running on our system:

```
# netstat -an | grep 1241
tcp        0        0 0.0.0.0:1241              0.0.0.0:*     LISTEN
```

If the nessusd server is running on a multihomed system or there is any other reason you want to force it to listen on a specific IP address, you can accomplish this via use of the *−a* switch. Additionally, you can specify on which port **nessusd** should listen. Since **nessusd** does not display a banner after a successful connection, it is quite easy to hide a Nessus server simply by modifying the listening port. An example of this type of configuration is as follows:

```
nessusd -D -a 192.168.0.1 -p 41942
```

We've chosen port 41942 simply because attackers are less likely to scan that port unless they're doing a full 65,536 port scan. Most attackers use Nmap in its default mode, where it doesn't scan any TCP ports outside of the 1200 or so named in the accompanying Nmap-services file.

Installing a Client

The power of the distributed nessus architecture is found in accessing the nessusd servers via clients. Nessus provides clients for UNIX- and Microsoft-based platforms. In the next few sections, we take a detailed look at these clients, where to find them, and a summary on configuring them.

Using the GTK Client

There are multiple ways to connect to the nessusd server. The first and most obvious way is using the nessus GTK client installed on the nessusd server itself. To start the client, simply execute the command:

```
$ nessus
```

Enter the credentials for the user that was created previously using nessus-adduser, and then click the **Log in** button provided (see Figure 3.5). If this is the first time you're connecting to the nessusd server from this client, you will be shown the Nessus server certificate and asked if you would like to accept it. Once a complete connection has been established, the **Log in** button will be replaced with a **Log out** button. From here, you can configure the rest of your scan specifics.

Figure 3.5 Entering the Credentials for the User

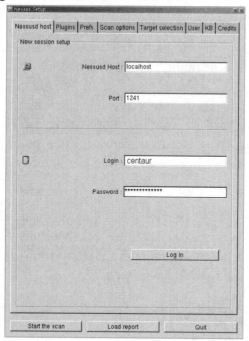

Using the Windows Client

The Windows client for Nessus is known as NessusWX (see Figure 3.6). It can be downloaded from nessuswx.nessus.org in one of three forms:

- Source
- Binary files
- Self-extracting binary files

The quickest and most comprehensive of these options is the last one. The self-extracting binary will also provide an option to extract the source during installation.

Figure 3.6 Nessus WX Setup

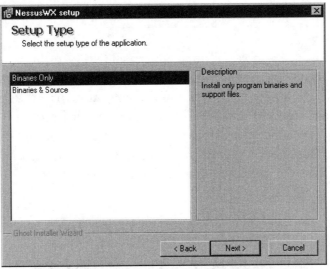

Once downloaded and installed, fire up the NessusWX client by clicking the **Nessus** icon now found on your desktop. You will then be presented with the default state of the Windows client. To set up a connection to our nessusd server, select **Communications** from the menu and then choose **Connect** (see Figure 3.7).

Figure 3.7 Selecting Communications from the Menu

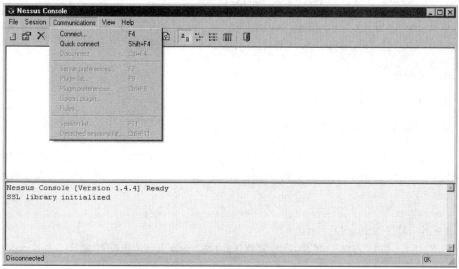

A connection dialog box will then appear, allowing you to configure the appropriate method for connecting to your Nessus server (see Figure 3.8). Enter the credentials here as we did for the GTK client, specifying the IP address of the necessarily remote nessusd server. Again, if this is the first connection, you will be prompted to accept the Nessus server certificate. After accepting this, the Nessus client will then commence the download of all plugin information from the server. This enables the client to allow for user configurability of the plugins where available.

Figure 3.8 Dialog Box Allowing You to Configure the Connection to Your Nessus Server

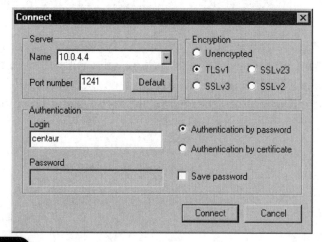

Once the plugins have been downloaded from the nessusd server, you can begin configuration for your first scan.

Command-Line Mode

The command-line version of Nessus is a much more complex piece of the Nessus puzzle. It helps greatly to be familiar with either of the GUIs and the functions they provide. For example, when you use the command-line version, you will need to specify all of the connection parameters on the command line. This includes user, password, IP address of the server, and so forth. You will also be required to have a list of target hosts in a file referenced from the command line. A quick example of executing a scan using the default settings would be to execute the following command:

```
nessus -q localhost 1241 centaur n355u5_rUl3z! ./targets.txt  \
./results.html
```

In this syntax, **targets.txt** is a simple file with an IP address per line, and **results.html** is the name of the file in which the results of the scan will be placed. If a specific configuration is required for this scan, then the *–c* switch can be used to specify this configuration file.

The command line can be used for more than just running scans without a graphical context. It is also very useful when you want to view reports from previous scans. Using the **--open-report** command-line option, you can visualize result information from previous scans.

Updating to the Latest Plugins

Running periodic and frequent scans against your networks is a good practice to get into. However, you will want to always work with the newest plugins available from the Nessus community. Failing to keep your plugins up to date can result in missing vulnerabilities for which plugins have been created only very recently. It can also result in using a less accurate version of a plugin that you do have. In any case, keeping your plugins up to date is vital to accurate vulnerability assessment.

To make plugin updating a simple process and subsequently encourage frequent updating, Nessus comes with a script named **nessus-update-plugins**, normally installed in:

```
/usr/local/sbin/nessus-update-plugins
```

Updating to the most current plugin set is as simple as executing this command. This might take a few seconds. If you are behind an HTTP proxy, this might take quite a bit longer or fail entirely unless you configure nessus-update-plugins to use your proxy settings. To configure the update script to use your HTTP proxy, create a file named .nessus-update-pluginsrc in your home directory and add the following to the file:

```
proxy_user= username
proxy_passwd= password
proxy= address_of_your_proxy:port
```

You might expect the requirement to check the authenticity of the NASL scripts with a PGP signature. However, Nessus 2.1.*x* checks this signature automatically. The plugin archive is located at www.nessus.org/nasl/all-2.0.tar.gz, and the PGP signature is located at www.nessus.org/nasl/all-2.0.sig. The signature itself is signed with the key whose public part is distributed in the 2.1.*x* plugin archive, and nessus-update-plugins does all the checking for you automatically.

In Nessus 2.0.*x*, where this signature-checking feature doesn't exist, the damage that can be done by a rogue plugin archive is pretty insignificant, due to the sandbox in which the NASL scripts are running.

Summary

Nessus is a very powerful framework and comes equipped with many powerful methods of installation. Even still, some thought is required by the security analyst who will be managing the project to deploy Nessus into the enterprise. Before enterprise deployment, you need to consider questions involving which method to use for installation, what kind of hardware to deploy on, and how frequently updates should be done. This chapter serves to start you on the path, giving you reasoning and processes to enable you to make the best decisions in both design and implementation.

Nessus is best leveraged by a sound vulnerability assessment policy and process to back it up. The studious security analyst will spend some time researching the best way to leverage the flexible framework that makes Nessus perform so well.

Configuring Nessus takes very little time—your first installation should be up and running within approximately 15 to 30 minutes. Following the steps in this chapter as highlighted in the Solutions Fast Track will make sure that no important steps are missed. Read through this chapter, and familiarize yourself with the different concepts as well as the FAQs at the end. Then, take the time to build out a Nessus server just to see how easy it is. At that point, you will be ready to pick up with Chapter 4 as you venture into your first scan.

Solutions Fast Track

Quick Start Guide

- ☑ Compiling from source is a best practice and requires negligible additional time investment.
- ☑ Nessus-installer.sh is a fully automated method of installation.
- ☑ You can install Nessus on Linux via RPM or DEB packages, emerge, or apt-get.
- ☑ There are Solaris packages available on sunfreeware.com.

Picking a Server

☑ A Nessus server should never be thought of as just another server from which arbitrary applications can be executed. Full system resources should be dedicated to the Nessus process, both for reasons of security and performance.

☑ Don't skimp on RAM or processors. When forced to decide, increase RAM.

☑ Place the Nessus server as close to the targets as possible with as few as possible network routing devices between the server and targets. Many firewalls and routers may be slowed or incapacitated due to the heavy bandwidth usage placed on them by a Nessus scan.

☑ Monitor scans closely when you first deploy Nessus, tuning Nessus to cause minimal strain on network resources.

Source or Binary

☑ Installing from source allows ultimate configurability such as passing compile options like disabling GTK.

☑ There are quicker methods such as RPMs and Solaris PKGs, but these can come with costs in security, performance, and comprehensiveness.

☑ In the end, it's a policy decision.

☑ Enterprises and best practice-oriented sites should choose source compilation.

Installation from Source

☑ Software prerequisites are GTK and OpenSSL, although these are both optional, based on compile-time options. Both are present on most modern Linux systems.

☑ Do you plan to install directly from the CVS tree, or the most recent and stable build?

☑ There are four components: nessus-libraries, libnasl, nessus-core, and nessus-plugins.

Configuring Nessus

☑ nessus–mkcert will generate a server certificate for you.

☑ nessus–adduser will allow you to configure users and their restrictions.

☑ After running nessusd –D to start the nessus listener, check to make sure it is listening on port 1241 using netstat -an. The netstat command's arguments vary with platform.

Installing a Client

☑ Use the GTK client by executing the command nessus.

☑ Use the Windows client by downloading NessuWX from http://nessuswx.nessus.org.

☑ Use the **nessus** command in batch mode to execute scans from the command line.

Updating to the Latest Plugins

☑ **nessus–update–plugins** is a script that will automatically update your plugins and restart **nessusd**.

☑ **nessus–update–plugins** fails to check authenticity or integrity of new plugins.

☑ **nessus–update–plugins** can be configured to use a proxy.

Frequently Asked Questions

The following Frequently Asked Questions, answered by the authors of this book, are designed to both measure your understanding of the concepts presented in this chapter and to assist you with real-life implementation of these concepts. To have your questions about this chapter answered by the author, browse to **www.syngress.com/solutions** and click on the **"Ask the Author"** form. You will also gain access to thousands of other FAQs at ITFAQnet.com.

Q: I want to use the cipher layer for communication between my Nessus client and server. How do I enable this?

A: You need to enable this while installing from source. After you cd into the nessus-libraries directory, run **./configure--enable-cipher** instead of the standard **./configure** command.

Q: How do I enable my Windows-based NessusWX to communicate on the cipher layer?

A: On the **nessus** server, execute **nessus-mkcert-client**. After this, locate **user-name_cert.pem** and **username_key.pem**. Concatenate these files together via cat **username_cert.pem username_key.pem >> username.pem**. Copy this resultant file to your Windows system and then select **File | Client certificates** from the menu to load this file.

Q: Are there any other clients for Nessus?

A: Yes. Tenable Security sells a commercial Windows client named NeWT.

Q: How long will it take to scan a Class C address space?

A: There is no absolute answer to this. The factors impacting the answer in your case will be proximity of the targets to the nessus server, availability of the targets, general network load, and the applications running on the targets. Your mileage may vary.

Q: I have a unique installation question that wasn't answered previously—where can I go for help?

A: Read through the rest of this book. If your question still has not been answered, then visit www.nessus.org to read their FAQ or mailing lists.

## Chapter 4

Running Your First Scan

Solutions in this Chapter:

- **Preparing for Your First Scan**
- **Starting the Nessus Client**
- **Plugins**
- **Preferences**
- **Scan Options**
- **Target Selection**
- **User Information**
- **Knowledge Base (Basics)**
- **Starting the Scan**

- ☑ **Summary**
- ☑ **Solutions Fast Track**
- ☑ **Frequently Asked Questions**

Introduction

As you are probably already aware, the realm of security problems is large, varied, and rapidly changing. Nessus' success in this realm is a result of its extensively configurable design and its large, varied, and easily augmented library of scanning modules. Nessus is the Swiss Army knife of network scanners. It can be used as a scalpel, as an axe, or as anything in between. It can provide a broad, bird's-eye view of a network, locate specific types of systems, investigate a particular service, or (if used without care) bludgeon the networked systems into complete collapse. The key to using the Nessus scanner safely and effectively is understanding the available options and how they can impact your network.

This chapter walks you through the process of planning, configuring, and running your first Nessus scan. Even if you already have experience using the Nessus scanner, this chapter might still provide insight about the different configuration choices and how you can use them to improve your scan results.

Effective use of Nessus requires careful planning beforehand. The user should have a clear goal in mind and make use of all available information to refine the scanning approach (goal and approach to be refined at each step). In this chapter, we assume that you are scanning an isolated test network or a well-known subnet of your real network. Recommended settings for your first scan are provided in the *Solutions Fast Track* section at the end of this chapter. We will discuss the issues you need to address before you start any scan, and review each section of the Nessus GUI client.

Notes from the Underground...

Variation among Nessus Versions

The Nessus client screen shots in this chapter were generated from version 2.0.9. The security environment is very fluid and so is Nessus. Future versions of the Nessus client might vary in appearance and in the organization of the different sections.

Preparing for Your First Scan

Running Nessus requires planning and practice. In guiding you through your first practice scanning session with Nessus, this chapter will also take you through your first planning session for a scan. The issues addressed here: Authorization, Risk vs. Benefit, Providing Authentication Information, and Plugin Selection, should be reviewed before *any and every* scan you perform.

Authorization

The most important thing to do before you launch a network scan is to obtain authorization, preferably in written form. Whom you should obtain this authorization from depends on the network you are testing; if you are planning to use Nessus on the internal network at your company, the CIO/CSO and senior administrative staff should be contacted. In the case of externally hosted systems, you might have to contact the hosting company or ISP and let them know of your intent to perform security scans against those systems. The tests that Nessus performs often look identical to a real attack by an unauthorized intruder, so make sure that the people monitoring system log files, intrusion detection systems (IDSs), and firewalls know when you are going to scan and from what address. There might be things you don't know about the network that could impact your scans. There might also be things about the network that could be impacted *by* your scans. If this first scan turns out to be an unannounced denial-of-service (DoS) attack, then there probably won't be a second scan.

Risk vs. Benefit

IT security can be viewed as an endless sequence of risk-benefit decisions. There is no such thing as complete security in an operational environment: some systems must be allowed to communicate with others, some services must be run, and some accounts must be allowed access. Broadly speaking, there are two kinds of risks associated with any Nessus scan: denial of service and missed information. Each type of risk must be balanced against certain benefits that might go with it (see Table 4.1).

Table 4.1 Risks vs. Benefits in a Nessus Scan

Risks	Benefits
You could create a denial of service.	You created it before someone else did.
You could miss important information by failing to scan certain targets thoroughly.	By narrowing your scan in terms of target and/or types of scan, you can run a much faster, safer scan that focuses on a specific goal.

Denial of Service

Nessus scans can be quite disruptive to certain targets. A poorly planned scan (or even a well-planned one) has the potential to shut down services, crash systems, confuse networks, and, in the case of some networked printers, generate large amounts of meaningless printout.

However, if your network contains such vulnerable targets, it is almost certainly preferable for you to discover them before someone outside the organization does. Remember that your decision to avoid activity that might disrupt your organization doesn't mean that no one else will disrupt it. This is a very sensitive issue, obviously, and needs to be discussed with all parties that depend on the network.

Missing Information

As a rule, the more detailed a network scan is, the longer it takes to complete. Nessus has many options that allow you to scan more quickly by focusing your vulnerability scan on a particular target, service, or vulnerability. It also has a tremendously useful feature, the Knowledge Base, which can be leveraged to avoid scanning the same things repeatedly. Other Nessus options help ensure that your scans are unlikely to disrupt the normal functioning of their targets.

Each of these options allows you to improve the speed or the efficiency of your scan by accepting the risk of missing something because you weren't looking for it. When you focus a vulnerability scan on certain targets, services, or types of vulnerability, you are choosing *not* to look at other targets, services, or types of vulnerability. If you use the Knowledge Base to avoid repeating a test more than once a week, you are accepting the risk that no significant problems will appear during that week. If you choose to avoid scan strategies that might impact badly on operational systems, you won't know if those systems would be so impacted until someone else tries it.

If you could be completely certain about what was happening on your network, you wouldn't need to scan it. Nessus is at its best when used as a discovery tool. Most of your scans will be streamlined one way or another by narrowing the scope of discovery, but always be aware of what you have decided *not* to look for.

Even on a small network that you understand fully, the first scan should be a careful mapping expedition to build a picture of the network and its systems. For one thing, you might be wrong. You might not really know everything about the network. (Even if you do, think how much better you will feel when Nessus agrees with you.) Beyond that consideration, though, this first scan is your first live exercise with Nessus, so it's a good idea to keep it simple.

Providing Authentication Information

Nessus can enhance its testing capabilities through the use of valid authentication credentials. Many vulnerability tests for the Microsoft Windows platform require a username and password to connect to the Registry of the target systems. Quite a few of the File Transfer Protocol (FTP) plugins also require a working username and password. When testing Cisco routers, a valid SNMP community string is required to test for problems related to outdated firmware.

When you are planning your scan, consider whether authentication could or should play a role, and have the appropriate information available.

Plugin Selection

Plugin selection is addressed in its own section, but it's important enough to be part of your initial planning. Nessus plugins are contributed by many authors (you might end up writing some, yourself) and vary considerably in the way they are written and how they operate. Think about what you want to do, select plugins that might help you do it, and check the source code of the plugin to understand how it identifies vulnerabilities. If the plugin is designed to detect a known Trojan program, for example, it might simply test for an open port that the Trojan is known to use, or it might actually send data to the suspected Trojan and compare the response with known signatures. You need to know what the plugins are doing to interpret their findings correctly.

Notes from the Underground...

Security Officers

Many people think that a security officer is a hacker who is paid by his victim to keep out other hackers. This view of security officer as outlaw-turned-lawman is very romantic and often attractive to security officers. In fact, the security officer is simply an employee of an organization. Like all other employees, the security officer is there to further the organization's goals (whatever they might be) and will be successful by working with, not against, the rest of the organization.

While the current trend is to make the IT security function distinct from network (and system) support, IT security must exist in the framework developed by network (and system) administrators. Before you install Nessus, you should sit down with the rest of the IT support staff and get as accurate a picture of the network as possible. The network and system support staff might be able to save you a lot of time and trouble. If you know where firewalls are installed, you can make sure that you have a Nessus server inside the firewall to get a fast, accurate scan. If you know that a certain subnet has only Windows desktops on it, you can restrict your scan of that subnet to Windows vulnerabilities. (Of course, you will still want to check periodically to make sure that no one has installed Linux or *BSD without telling anyone—like the saying goes: Trust, but verify!)

Starting the Nessus Client

The Nessus Client is used to configure and execute scans from the Nessus server. On a Linux (or other UNIX-like system), simply run the nessus command. On the Windows platform, click on the icon for NessusWX. To start the client, type **nessus.** You will get a display like the one in Figure 4.1.

Figure 4.1 Nessus Client Login

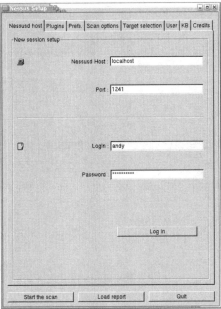

The first tab displayed is the **Nessusd host** tab. This is where you authenticate your client to the Nessus server. You will then be able to use the other tabs:

- **Plugins** Select Nessus plugins for the scan.

- **Prefs.** Specify the type of scan you want to perform.

- **Scan options** Specify the details of the scan.

- **Target selection** Specify what IP addresses will be scanned.

- **User** Create rules to constrain the scan.

- **KB** Configure the Knowledge Base (refer to Chapter 9) to allow information from previous scans to guide scans in the future.

- **Credits** Who wrote Nessus.

We address these tabs in the following sections of this chapter. Many of the configuration options involve risk vs. benefit decisions that you will have to make about your scan.

Start by typing the username in the **Login:** field and the password in the **Password:** field, and then click the **Log In** button. The display will switch to display the Plugins tab (see Figure 4.2).

Figure 4.2 Nessus Client Plugins Tab

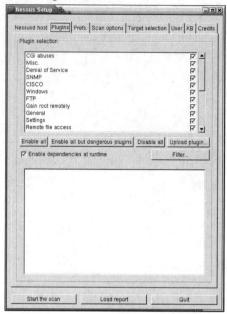

Plugins

Plugins are the meat and potatoes of Nessus. Each plugin represents one or more specific vulnerability tests that can be launched during a Nessus scan. Almost all Nessus plugins are written in Nessus Attack Scripting Language (NASL). NASL was designed specifically for developing Nessus plugins and includes a function library that makes it very convenient for performing security tests. Refer to Chapter 11 for more information about the NASL language.

For convenience, Nessus plugins are organized into functional families. The checklist of available families is at the top of the Plugins tab in Figure 4.2. Selecting a family displays all of the plugins in that family in the lower window. Checking the box next to a family activates all the plugins in that family. Once the plugins are displayed, you can select and deselect each individual plugin as you wish. Figure 4.7 shows the Plugins tab displaying the selection of the Dabber Worm Detection plugin in the Backdoors family.

If you want to be thorough, the buttons under the top window of the Plugins tab let you perform global selections and deselections of all of the plugins.

The options shown in Figure 4.2 are:

- **Enable all** turns on all plugins.

- **Enable all but dangerous plugins** turns on all plugins except those marked as dangerous.

- **Disable all** turns off all plugins.

- **Upload plugin…** brings in a new plugin (perhaps one that you have written).

If you want to use only a few plugins, clear the selections first with **Disable all** and select the plugins you want from the checklists. If you want to use all plugins except for a few, activate all plugins with **Enable all** or **Enable all but dangerous plugins** and deselect those you don't want.

Damage and Defense…

Plugins and DoS

Plugins are considered dangerous if the testing process could cause the target application or operating system to crash. The plugins in the DoS category are designed to test for issues that would allow an unauthorized intruder to crash or disable network resources. Most of the plugins in the DoS category perform the test by actually launching a DoS attack on the target system and verifying that it no longer responds. Obviously, you don't want to do this in a production environment without careful prearrangement. Note that it is left to the author to designate a plugin as dangerous. While it's unusual for an author to submit a plugin that can disable a system or a service without intending to do so, it is not uncommon for a plugin that safely checks for one vulnerability to inadvertently trigger a crash in another application or operating system.

Enable Specific Plugins

There are many plugins and plugin authors. If you are looking for a plugin for a specific task (for example, checking for a specific vulnerability), you can go to http://cgi.nessus.org/plugins and look at the plugin display options. If you are looking for something specific, select the **Plugins search** option on that page. Figures 4.3, 4.4, and 4.5 illustrate a search for plugins that test for the Windows vulnerabilities described in MS04-011.

Figure 4.3 illustrates the search for the string "MS04-011" in the report section of the plugins. Figure 4.4 shows the results of that search: three plugins specifically designed to address worms that exploit these vulnerabilities. Selecting the **Dabber Worm Detection** link displays information about that plugin as shown in Figure 4.5. The plugin information screen has an option "View the source of this plugin here" that displays the source code shown in Figure 4.6. If you have any questions about how a given plugin works or why it does or does not report a vulnerability on a given system, viewing the NASL source code can often be a useful first step.

Many plugins depend on the data obtained from other plugins to perform their specific vulnerability tests. If plugin A depends on plugin B, and you enable A, but do not enable B, plugin A will not be launched. If you check the box labeled **Enable dependencies at runtime**, as seen in Figure 4.2, Nessus will make sure that all plugins that your selection requires are enabled automatically.

Figure 4.3 Plugins search Utility at www.nessus.org

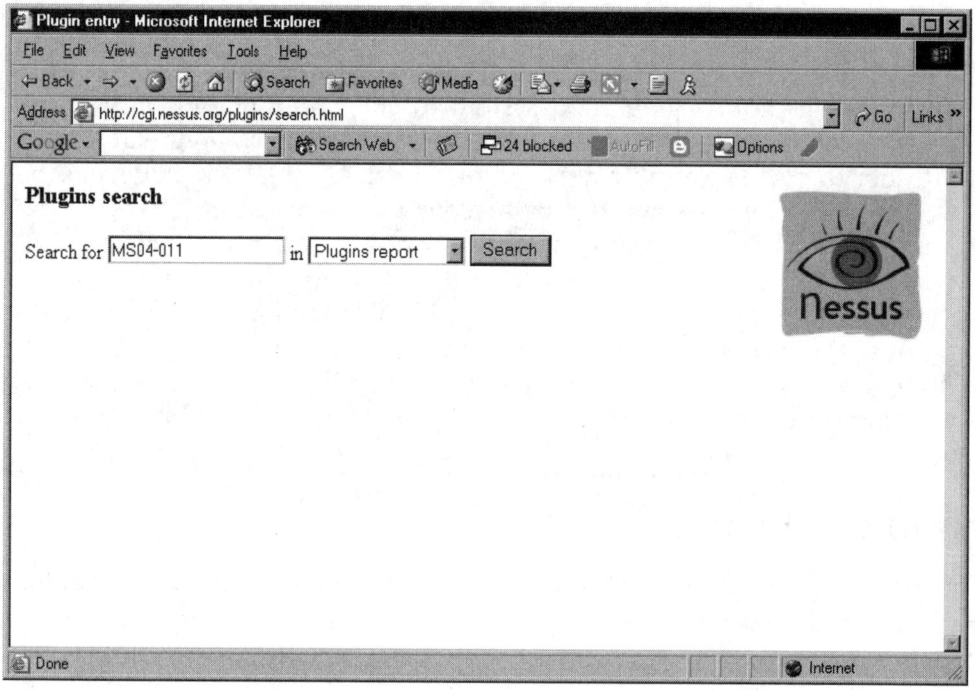

Figure 4.4 Results from Plugins search Utility at www.nessus.org

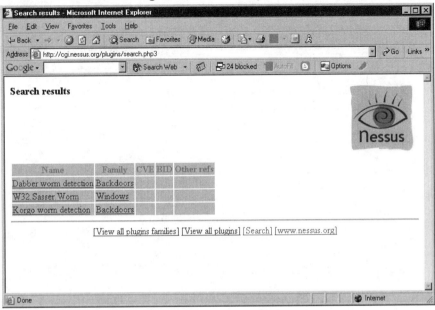

Figure 4.5 Information about Dabber worm detection Plugin at www.nessus.org

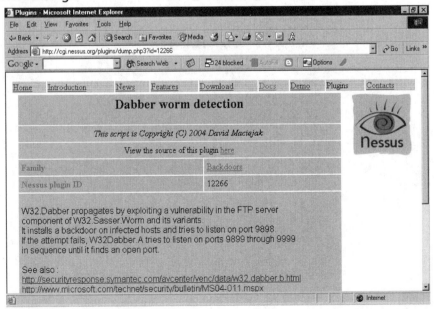

Figure 4.6 Source Code of Dabber worm detection Plugin at
www.nessus.org

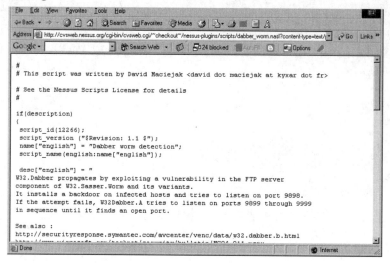

Figure 4.7 Plugins Tab Showing the Selection of the Dabber worm detection
Plugin in the Backdoors Family

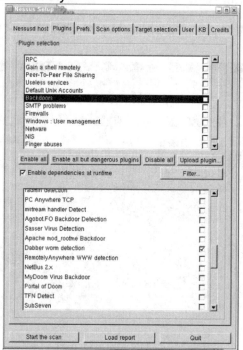

Using the Plugin Filter

An alternative to searching for plugins using the search utility at www.nessus.org is the plugin filter in the Nessus client. The filter is available through the **Filter...** button in the Plugins tab (see Figure 4.2). The filter lets you select plugins with the characteristics you want.

Figures 4.8 through 4.11 show the use of the plugin filter to select plugins that test for the Windows vulnerabilities described in MS04-011.

Figure 4.8 shows the Plugin Search window that appears when you click the Filter... button. The string "MS04-011" has been entered and the filter will be applied to the description of each plugin.

Figure 4.9 shows the results of the search. Plugins with the string "MS04-011" were found in two families: Backdoors and Windows. The Windows family is selected (but not checked), so the plugins in that family matching the search parameters are displayed.

In Figure 4.10, the Windows family has been checked, automatically enabling the plugins displayed in the lower window. Similarly, in Figure 4.11, the Backdoors family has been selected and checked, enabling the filtered plugins in that family.

Figure 4.8 Filter plugins Window

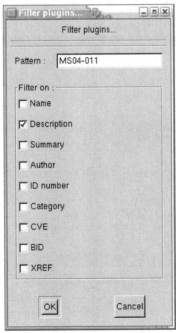

Figure 4.9 Plugin Search Results

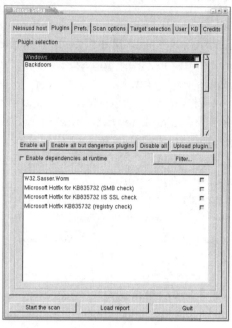

Figure 4.10 Plugin selection Window

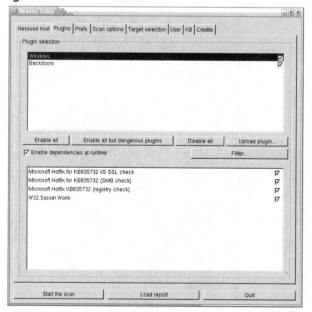

Figure 4.11 Plugin selection (continued)

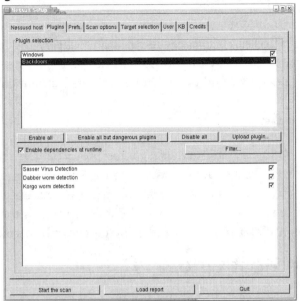

Plugin Categories

As mentioned, Nessus plugins are categorized into families based on plugin function, target, or other properties. This is very handy for quickly narrowing the field of plugins to those that interest you. For example, if you know that your target network includes Novell products, you would want to make sure that the NetWare family is enabled.

Keep in mind, however, that the classification of a plugin is a judgment call. Many plugins can arguably fit into more than one category. For example, when we performed our search for MS04-011 plugins, we found plugins for the Sasser worm in both the Windows and the Backdoors families. Since the Sasser worm attacks the Microsoft Windows operating system, the Windows family is an obvious choice. Sasser also creates a backdoor, though, so it also makes sense to assign it to the Backdoors family.

It's worth investing some time in all options to locate appropriate plugins. Use the Plugins Search utility at www.nessus.org , the Filter Plugins window feature in the Plugins tab of the Nessus client, and the list of plugins assigned to each family that might be relevant to your needs.

Plugin Information

The NASL source shown in Figure 4.6 shows an assignment of text to *desc[English]*. All plugin search features allow you to display the information stored in that variable, one way or another. It's the best way short of going through the source code to find out what the plugin is intended to do.

Preferences

Nessus offers a wide variety of different scanning protocols and approaches. The Preferences tab of the Nessus client is where you specify the options for these complex, configurable components. The arrangement of sections within this tab often changes between versions of Nessus. The order in which these sections are presented here might differ from that of the Preferences tab in your Nessus client.

Specify the Host Ping

You have probably used the UNIX *ping* utility as a simple network-diagnostic tool. It is commonly used to verify that remote systems are active and that they can be reached through the network. Success of the ping tells you that "you *can* get there from here," if not much else. Still, if you are dealing with an unresponsive web server or networked printer, it's worth checking that the remote system is reachable before worrying about why it's not responding.

Ping uses the Internet Control Message Protocol (ICMP), a member of the TCP/IP protocol suite. This protocol is meant for the exchange of information about issues of data communication. We are interested in the ECHO function of ICMP that is used by a networked system simply to confirm that another networked system is alive and reachable.

Many subnets have unused addresses. Nessus could waste a great deal of time trying to perform vulnerability scans on systems that aren't there. To avoid this situation, Nessus can do an initial scan to determine whether the hosts are there before it starts examining them in detail.

One method Nessus uses for an initial scan is ICMP ping. Unfortunately, many routers and firewalls are configured to block ICMP traffic, primarily to discourage the casual mapping of the networks they guard. Some networks won't even allow ICMP internally.

Since it's so useful to start a scan with a simple test for the presence of the target, Nessus also supports a *TCP ping*. A TCP ping sends a TCP SYN packet to a specified port on the target system. If the target port is active, it will respond with a TCP SYN-ACK packet. If the port is closed, it will respond with a TCP RST packet. If no response is received, Nessus will assume that the tested IP address is not in use and will remove it from the scan. TCP pings will work in many situations where ICMP will not. When scanning systems behind a firewall, such as in a DMZ network or on the Internet, the TCP ping type is the preferred method. To obtain the most accurate results on any network, use a list of commonly unfiltered TCP ports. Multiple ports can be specified by separating them with semicolons. The string below will cause the TCP ping plugin to test over fifteen ports that are often allowed through firewalls.

```
21;22;23;25;53;79;80;110;113;139;143;264;389;443;993;3389
```

Even with the TCP ping method, it is possible that the scan may not detect a system protected by strict firewall rules. Nessus allows you to "force scan" the entire target list, regardless of whether the system responds to any form of ping requests or not. This is usually a very time-consuming process, as each Nessus plugin is sending probes to an address that may not even be a live system. This option is only recommended in specific situations where the other techniques would not suffice.

For a thorough view of your network, you may want to use each of these three methods and compare the results.

Configuring WWW Checks

Web servers have become the workhorses of the Internet. Almost every function that was once performed by dedicated utilities in a system, authentication, file transfer, program execution, data base queries, etc., is now routinely supported as a part of web-based services. The job of scanning web servers is correspondingly complex. As a result, Nessus provides several sections of the Prefs tab that configure scans of web servers.

HTTP Login Page

Many web sites require authentication before they grant access to their pages. This section allows the Nessus user to enter the information needed to log in to a web site. The Login page, Login form, and Login form fields, respectively, specify the URL of the login page, the name of the HTTP form used for login, and the HTTP fields and values required by the form for a successful login. The actual user ID and password would then be specified in the Login configurations: section of the Prefs tab.

HTTP NIDS Evasion

Network intrusion detection systems (NIDSs) will detect and alert operators to web requests (HTTP) that match known attack signatures. Nessus allows you to configure certain HTTP plugins to automatically avoid NIDS signatures. Considering how "noisy" a full-blown Nessus scan can be, these options are usually not worth using. Basically, these options will cause certain Web assessment plugins (Nikto and Whisker) to send their requests in such a way that it will fool improperly design intrusion detection systems.

libwhisker Options

Libwhisker is a HTTP function library that is used by a variety of web assessment tools. Nessus can use these tools to detect an even wider range of Web server security flaws. The Libwhisker library can be configured to send HTTP requests in such a way that a NIDS may not be able to detect the scan. The options in this section allow you to specify an evasion technique.

Nikto

Nikto is general-purpose Web server assessment tool that utilizes the Libwhisker library. Nessus can be configured to execute this tool as part of a network scan. The options in this section allow you to configure various parameters that will be passed to Nikto when the plugin is launched:

- Force scan all possible CGI directories
- IDS evasion techniques
- Force full (generic) scan

The *Force scan all possible CGI directories* option is self-explanatory. The *IDS evasion techniques* are similar in spirit, and to some extent detail, to those in the *Libwhisker* section described. By default, Nikto will try to fit its scan to the type of server it is scanning based on that server's identification of itself. Since servers might lie about this, the *Force full (generic) scan* option overrides any identification by the server and makes Nikto try every test it has against the target server.

NIDS Evasion

Located under the Prefs tab of the user interface, the NIDS evasion options will tell Nessus to use various techniques to avoid detection. These techniques rely on the principle that many NIDS analyze each packet individually and do not take into account the cumulative effect of multiple packets. For example, imagine a bank security guard that was told to sound the alarm when he heard the phrase *stick-up*. If a bank robber enters the building and simply spelled the phrase "S-T-I-C-K-U-P", the phrase would mean nothing to the guard, but the teller would probably understand the message. The following techniques exploit a similar strategy:

- TCP evasion technique
- Send fake RST when establishing a TCP connection

The *TCP evasion technique* menu contains four options:

- none
- split
- injection
- short ttl

The default *none* option is self-explanatory. The *split* option makes Nessus send its probes one character at a time. The target will be able to reassemble the characters, but the NIDS might not. The *injection* option will make Nessus insert malformed packets with meaningless data, which the target will ignore, into the stream of probing packets. The intention is to get the NIDS to consider these packets as part of the data stream so that the meaningless data confuses the pattern of the actual probe. The *short ttl* option works on the same principle as the *injection* option; meaningless information is inserted for the NIDS to accept and the target to reject. In this option, however, it is assumed that the NIDS sensor is at least one hop from the target, and the TTL of the "garbage" packets is set to expire after reaching the NIDS but before reaching the target.

> **NOTE**
>
> The TTL, or Time-To-Live, field of a packet is intended to stop misaddressed packets from wandering the Internet forever. Each time a packet

crosses from one network to another, the value in the TTL field is decremented by one. Such a crossing is called a *hop*. When the TTL value reaches zero, the packet is no longer passed on to new networks.

Selecting the *Send fake RST when establishing a TCP connection* option makes Nessus generate a malformed RST, or Reset, packet to the target of the scan right after the *triple handshake* but before any actual scanning. The strategy is to make the packet sufficiently corrupt for the target of the scan to ignore it, but sufficiently well constructed for the NIDS to note that an RST packet has been sent and assume that the connection to the target has been terminated, thus stopping the NIDS from monitoring that connection any further.

NOTE

NIDSs are getting harder to fool with techniques like these.

Brute Force with Hydra

In theory, it should be possible to break into any system requiring a valid userid and associated password by trying every possible combination of letters, numbers, and special characters in increasingly long strings until you hit the right ones. Obviously, this is not a very efficient method and, on any given system, might not generate a good userid/password pair in your lifetime. This approach is called the *brute force* method. It's guaranteed to work eventually, but eventually might be a long time. However, if you make certain simplifying assumptions, it might be possible to restrict your search to a smaller set of possibilities that still have a good chance of getting you into the target.

For example, one such simplifying assumption could be that the userid will be a common first name among English speakers. This would reduce the candidates for userid to a few hundred. Even if you append the digits 0 through 9 to each name (mary6, john2, etc.), you are still dealing with only a few thousand possibilities. Similarly, you could assume that at least some of the passwords are English words. If so, all your password candidates might be contained in a small reference dictionary. Better still, you could look at the results gathered over decades of hacking badly chosen passwords and simply try the hundred or so most commonly chosen passwords (for example, "pass," "password," and blank).

Once you make your best guesses about userids and passwords, you could place each group of choices into respective files and try throwing them at the target until you either get access or run out of possibilities.

This is what *Hydra* does. In the *Hydra* section of the Prefs tab, you specify the maximum number of simultaneous threads you want executed at any time and provide the names of the userid and password files, respectively. Then, you check off whichever authenticated services you want to try brute forcing on your target from the list that extends to the end of the *Hydra* section.

The SMB Scope

The checkbox labeled *Request information about the domain*, if checked, instructs Nessus to retrieve information about the domain of a host Windows system, rather than from the individual host.

NOTE

Microsoft Windows systems control access through SIDs, or security identifiers. To access a system resource from an account, the account must have a SID that matches a SID associated with the resource (both the account and the resource might have more than one SID).

Configuring Login Credentials

Any plugin or package incorporated into Nessus that requires authentication to the target gets that authentication information from this section of the Prefs tab. Scans that require exchanges of authentication information take more time than port scans do, but important information can often be gleaned from "inside" a system or service using authenticated access. As always, be sure to examine your plugins to see if they depend on such access.

Notes from the Underground…

Special Credentials for Nessus Scans

It might be worthwhile to define a special userid/password authentication pair for use only by Nessus on common services on your network. Of course, the ability to establish such credentials presupposes a pretty good level of control over the systems being scanned. If you are in a large organization, you might not have such direct control over all of the systems on your network. Still, consider proposing such a credentialing system as a standard procedure for critical systems.

http | pop | ftp | nntp | imap

The fields for each of these services are self-explanatory. If you have specified a plugin that requires access to a News server, for example, you enter a valid userid/password pair in the respective fields *NNTP account:* and *NNTP password (sent in clear)*.

Of all the fields in this section, note the SMB fields in particular. Many plugins require access to the registry of a Windows system. To get that access with rights to examine the registry, you must enter a valid userid/password pair that is associated with appropriate privileges on the Windows system.

SMB configuration

While scanning and querying open ports on a Windows system can provide useful information, Windows stores a tremendous amount of system information in the Windows registry. The most reliable and relevant information about Windows is provided by plugins that require registry read access.

Read access to the registry is an administrative privilege in Windows. If you provide Nessus with the credentials for an administrative account, plugins that require registry access will operate. In addition, some other plugins that require other administrative privileges will also be effective. Administrative access provides privileges far beyond read access to a Windows system, however, and it's not a good idea to grant it too casually to any utility.

It is possible to create accounts on Windows systems that have registry read access and other specific privileges beyond those of a normal user account but without the ability to modify the Windows system configuration. If close, regular scans of Windows systems are important in your environment, consider defining a special group of local accounts or a domain account to be used for Nessus scans.

To understand the SMB configuration options in more detail, please refer to the appendices at the end of this book.

Configuring SNMP

SNMP (Simple Network Management Protocol) was developed to support a centralized, agent-based system of managing information on remote network devices. SNMP agents identify themselves with a *community* name. An agent receiving a request with the correct community name will generally honor that request (sometimes the agent will also have a list of acceptable source IP addresses for these requests).

Often, network managers will neglect to establish communities beyond the standard default community names "public" and "private." Nessus has the option of scanning for SNMP agents using a community name you specify in the field labeled *SNMP community (sent in clear)* in the *Login configurations:* section of the Prefs tab. Nessus uses a utility called *snmpwalk* to implement these scans, so your Nessus scan will inherit any problems with your installed version of this utility.

SNMP includes a command that queries an SNMP device for the "next" information record in the device's information tree. This scan uses this command to gather information from the tree. Note that some devices might loop endlessly under these scans.

Configuring Nmap

Figure 4.12 shows some of the Nmap scanning options at top of the Prefs. tab. Scrolling down this tab will reveal multiple sections, each devoted to the configuration of options native to Nessus and to options in other utilities, such as Nmap and Hydra, which have been incorporated into Nessus.

Notes from the Underground...

Default Scanner: Nmap vs. Synscan.nasl

Nmap was originally incorporated into Nessus as the default scanner. Nmap was a handy "off-the-shelf" SYN packet port scanner with a convenient, machine-parsable output. Recently, the plugin *synscan.nasl* has been added to the Nessus plugin collection and is now the default scanning option.

If you want to use the Nmap scanner, you must specify it in the Options section. If Nmap is not specified, Nessus will default to the *synscan.nasl* plugin, and the Nmap configuration options in Figure 4.12 will be ignored.

Figure 4.12 Top of Prefs. Tab

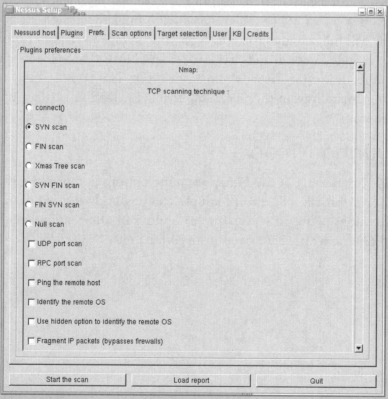

Notes from the Underground…

TCP/IP Basics

Making good decisions about port scanner options requires a basic understanding of the network protocols that underlie these scans. Communications protocols can be divided into *connection-oriented* and *connectionless* varieties. Connectionless protocols are the simpler of the two. Information is transmitted from the source without any particular measures to insure that the information is received uncorrupted (or at all) by the destination. Connection-oriented protocols, by contrast, don't send information until the source of the transmission has contacted the destination and received confirmation that the destination is prepared to accept the transmission. Once the transmission of information begins, all packets (chunks of information) transmitted are either acknowledged by the destination or retransmitted from the source.

In TCP/IP, TCP is a connection-oriented protocol and UDP is a connectionless protocol. Under the TCP protocol, the transmission source initializes communication by sending the destination a packet with the SYN flag set. The destination then responds with a packet with the ACK flag set to acknowledge that it received the source's SYN packet, and with the SYN flag set. The source then sends another packet with the ACK flag set to acknowledge that the source received the destination's packet. The entire exchange of:

- SYN source to destination
- SYN-ACK destination to source
- ACK source to destination

is called the *triple handshake*. Once this exchange is completed, a *connection* is established. Establishing a connection provides a more reliable communications channel, but it does so at the cost of extra packet exchanges and internal bookkeeping to insure that all of the information is acknowledged. A formal, although different, exchange is used at the end of the communication to *break down* the connection.

The most common methods of checking for ports on a remote system are *connect scans* and *SYN scans*. Connect scans attempt to establish a connection, as described here, from the host to possible ports on the destination host. SYN scans send the initial SYN packet of the triple

Continued

handshake to possible ports on the destination host and then receive (or don't receive) a SYN-ACK packet in response. However, instead of completing the connection with that ACK packet of the triple handshake, the scanner simply moves on to send a SYN packet to the next target port. The destination eventually times out and stops waiting for the ACK packet.

Since SYN scans involve the exchange of only two packets, and connect scans require the exchange of seven packets (three to establish the connection and four to break it down), SYN scans are faster. In addition, they are stealthier, since most operating systems are designed to recognize and log only successful connections. However, many NIDSs treat the stealthy SYN scans as hostile probes and will raise an alarm or even block the scanner from its targets. Rapid SYN scanning can also be a DoS attack, since it can crash some platforms.

The most commonly used port scan methods are *connect scans* and *SYN scans*. If there are no packet filters or firewalls between the system running the Nessus server and the target network, connect scans are the most reliable option. If you scanning systems behind a firewall or on an external network segment, using the SYN scan method will significantly reduce the amount of time it takes the port scan to complete.

Simply put, connect scans are reliable scans that will produce predictable behavior under predictable circumstances. Under more complex or unusual circumstances, they might not work at all. The behavior (and the effect) of SYN scans depends on the configuration of the network and on the nature of the scanning targets. Some operating systems will even crash under a SYN scan. However, SYN scanning is much more likely to produce reliable results than connect scanning in a network with firewalls and other specialized configurations.

Nmap also supports UDP port scanning; however, due to the nature of the protocol, the results might be inconsistent and incomplete. Still, it's worthwhile to use UDP scanning to confirm which systems are hosting common UDP services, such as DNS.

The *Port Range* section of Nmap configuration has three options:

- User specified range
- Default range (nmap-services + privileged ports)
- Fast scan (nmap-services)

The *User specified range* option makes Nmap scan the ports specified at the top of the *Scan option* tab described later in this chapter. The *Default range* is the privileged ports (those in the range 1 through 1024) and ports listed in the nmap-services file that is installed with Nmap. A *Fast scan* only probes the ports in the nmap-services file.

The Nmap *Timing policy* defines the speed at which Nmap will send scanning packets at the target, and the amount of time that it will wait for a reply. In order from the slowest to the fastest, these are:

- Paranoid
- Sneaky
- Polite
- Normal
- Aggressive
- Insane

Normal speed is fine for most of what you will want to do. *Aggressive* is quicker, but less patient about waiting for replies. It might miss some ports on some targets because it won't wait long enough to get their response. *Polite* should get every port with no problem, but can be painfully slow.

The only reason to use the *Insane* option is to see if your target can survive a DoS flood attack. *Sneaky* and *Paranoid* are both slow enough to have a chance at getting past scan detectors on the target network—which means that they are *really* slow. Use them only if you are testing scan detection on your network.

If you don't like any of these options, *Custom* will allow you to define your own timing rates. Refer to the Nmap man page and documentation for more information about custom timing options.

Scan Options

The *Scan options* tab of the Nessus Setup menu, displayed in Figure 4.13, controls the manner in which the scanning is performed. Most of the options you should be concerned with at this point are those associated with port selection.

Figure 4.13 Scan options Tab of the Nessus Setup Menu

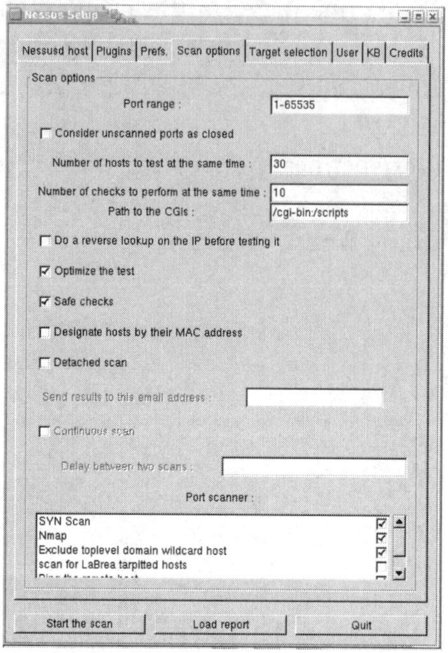

The Port Range

The *Port range:* field specifies the ports that will be scanned. The port selection applies both to the built-in Nessus scanner and to the external Nmap scanner (if the User specified option has been selected from the Port range options in the Nmap section of the Prefs. tab).

Unscanned Ports

By default, any ports not specified for scanning in the *Port range:* field are considered open and will be examined by the appropriate plugins. The *Consider unscanned ports as closed* option instructs Nessus to assume that these ports are closed and only examine the ports you have specified. It's faster, but you run the risk of missing vulnerabilities when the flawed service runs on a port outside of the TCP scan range. Don't use this option unless you have a really good reason to ignore unspecified ports.

Performance: Host and Process Count

The *Number of hosts to test at the same time:* field is the limit on the number of hosts that Nessus will look at any given time during your scanning run. The *Number of checks to perform at the same time:* field is the limit on the number of checks that Nessus will run at any given time on any given host during your scanning run. Each test on each host will be a separate process running on your Nessus server. Remember that this limits the total number of such processes to the *product* of the two values that you entered. For example, a limit of 20 hosts and 30 tests per host at the same time means that your server will be running up to 600 simultaneous processes during the scan.

Optimized Checks

By default, Nessus is not very trusting. If one plugin looks for an FTP server and fails to find it, Nessus will still run other plugins that assume the presence of the server. If the banner on an FTP server announces that it is "Joe's FTP," Nessus will still run tests appropriate to other FTP servers. The option *Optimize the test*, if checked, instructs Nessus to assume that the results of a given test actually have some bearing on whether others should be performed. This can save a lot of time, but you run the risk that some of the initial information that Nessus is getting, from either the target host or a plugin, is wrong. As with many of your configuration decisions, it comes down to how straightforward you think your network is. If you don't expect any surprises, then this is a good option to use. Before you make this decision, consider that surprises are, by definition, unexpected. Run scans without this option at least every once and a while.

Safe Checks Mode

As with optimized checks, enabling the *Safe checks* option makes Nessus less thorough in return for some other benefit. In this case, it instructs Nessus not to run tests that might crash either a service on the target host or the target host itself. As with the *Optimize the test* option, the *Safe checks* option makes Nessus draw more assumptions from the tests it does run and makes it more trusting of the self-identification of the services it scans. Unlike the *Optimize the test* option, disabling the *Safe checks* option doesn't simply run the risk of making your Nessus run take longer, but of taking out the target systems. If you run without *Safe checks*, and you should do so at least occasionally, make sure that you have warned everyone that things might get ugly, and make sure that there are up-to-date recovery procedures for every important platform.

Report by MAC Address (DHCP)

If you are scanning a network where IP addresses are dynamically assigned by DHCP, you can't expect any system to keep the same IP address beyond the next reboot. MAC addresses are much more stable. While they can be changed on some systems, they rarely are. In this case, enabling the *Designate hosts by their MAC address* option and using MAC addresses instead of IP addresses makes a lot of sense.

Notes from the Underground…

Nessus Reports and MAC Addresses

As one of your authors was reminded the hard way while trying to generate a Nessus report using MAC addresses, this option *only* works on the subnet in which the Nessus server is located. Routers do not preserve MAC addresses and Nessus knows this. If you enable this option and then try to scan through a router (scan targets outside the Nessus server's subnet), Nessus will produce the usual report using IP addresses.

Detached Scan

Nessus scans can take quite a while. Until you get used to the various options and trade-offs, they might take days on a large network. In any case, you might not want to keep your client up monitoring the scan once you've started it. If you select the *Detached scan* option, the scan runs on your Nessus server independently of the client. As with any background job, you can turn off the client and come back later after the job has finished to find out what it produced. Of course, your client won't be there to display the results when the scan finishes. If you want to take advantage of this option, you *must* either:

- Enable the *Save this session* option on the Target selection tab

or

- Enter an e-mail address to which the final report can be sent in the *Send results to this email address* field immediately below the *Detached scan* option on the *Scan options* tab.

Send Results to This E-mail Address

Specify an e-mail address for the final report (in ASCII). See *Detached scan*.

Continuous Scan

Once you have refined your scanning strategy and know what you are looking for, the *Continuous scan* option will help make your life much simpler. Enabling this option along with *Detached scan* instructs Nessus to perform scans against your target at regular intervals you specify in the field *Delay between two scans:*. You can then check back periodically to examine the results of scans that have been automatically performed and/or get e-mail reports automatically from those scans.

Configure the Port Scanner

The *Port scanner* scrolling checklist at the bottom of the Scan options tab configures important scanning options for the Nessus built-in scanner, as well as enabling or disabling Nmap scans.

Use the Built-in SYN Scanner

The SYN scan option instructs Nessus to use its built-in SYN scanner for port scans. This option is independent of the Nmap SYN scan, so if you enable both SYN scans, they will both run and you will have a completely redundant scan.

Check for LaBrea Protected Hosts

The option *scan for LaBrea tarpitted hosts* instructs Nessus to use a plugin that tests target hosts for LaBrea-type behavior to identify possible tar pits. LaBrea hosts are not common, but if you are exploring your network for the first time, you might want to consider the possibility.

Notes from the Underground...

LaBrea

Tom Liston conceived LaBrea as a way to fight back at the CodeRed worm and any other hostile scan. It works in two stages. First, it monitors traffic on its network and identifies IP addresses that haven't been assigned, so that it can respond to packets sent to those unused addresses. Second, when it receives a SYN packet on any port of any of its adopted IP addresses, it responds with a SYN-ACK packet as per the TCP/IP protocol. The source of the SYN packet then establishes the TCP connection with an ACK packet, completing the triple handshake. From that point on, LaBrea simply ignores anything that comes along that connection. Eventually, it will time out, of course, and if it's an innocently misaddressed connection, there is very little effect on the host that initiated it. If the host is scanning, however, it now has "dead" connections to as many ports it tried to scan all of the IP addresses that LaBrea is responding. If LaBrea has adopted, say, half of a class C network and the scanner is looking for privileged ports, then the scanner will have 1024*128=131072 useless connections waiting to time out.

The idea is not to stop scanning, but to slow it down to the point where it's nearly useless. Unfortunately, a LaBrea host on your network will have the same effect on Nessus.

Use the Built-in Connect Scanner

The *tcp connect()* scan option instructs Nessus to use its built-in TCP connect scanner for port scans. This option is independent of the Nmap TCP connect scan, so if you enable both TCP connect scans, they will both run and you will have a completely redundant scan.

Using Nmap to Perform Port Scans

Having configured all the Nmap options in the Prefs tab, this is where you actually enable Nmap to run as part of the Nessus scan. If this option is not checked, the configuration settings in the Prefs tab will not apply.

Whether to Ping Each Host

As discussed earlier in this chapter, you can save a lot of time by pinging a host to make sure that it's actually there and active before you start running scans on it. However, this method assumes that all active hosts will actually respond to a ping. If the ICMP or TCP ping is blocked due to a network-based or host-based firewall, the host will be ignored by the scan.

Ignore Top-Level Wildcard Host

Wildcard TLDs are like black holes in DNS name space. Any DNS domain not already assigned gets sucked inexorably into the wildcard IP address. Enabling the *Exclude top-level domain wildcard host* option instructs Nessus to avoid such hosts.

Tools & Traps....

Top-Level Domain

A *TLD*, or *top-level domain*, is a DNS domain denoted by the final suffix of a DNS name. For example, .com, .gov, and .edu are TLDs. Two-letter country codes such as .uk, .cn, and .de also denote TLDs (specifically, these are *ccTLDs* or *country-code top-level domains*).

It is possible to create a DNS *wildcard* entry for a TLD. For example, suppose a TLD denoted by .xyz were to have a wildcard assignment of 10.100.100.10. Then, *any* DNS name ending in .xyz would be guaranteed to resolve. If the name had a valid DNS record associated with it, it would be resolved according to the record. Otherwise, it would be resolved as 10.100.100.10.

As of this writing (June 24, 2004), there are several wildcard TLDs, such as the ccTLD for Christmas Island, *.cx*.

Let's try resolving syngress.cx:

```
$ dig syngress.cx +short
203.119.12.43
```

and nessusisgreat.cx:

```
$ dig nessusisgreat.cx +short
```

Continued

www.syngress.com

```
203.119.12.43
$
```

and somerandomsillyname.cx:

```
$ dig someransomsillything.cx +short
203.119.12.43
$
```

When you point your web browser at this IP address, you get the page shown in Figure 4.14. Wildcard TLDs are most often used as a way to market domain registration services. If you type **nessusisgreat.cx** into your web browser, and it doesn't already exist, you are taken to a site that offers to sell you that domain

Figure 4.14 Wildcard Web Site for .cx ccTLD

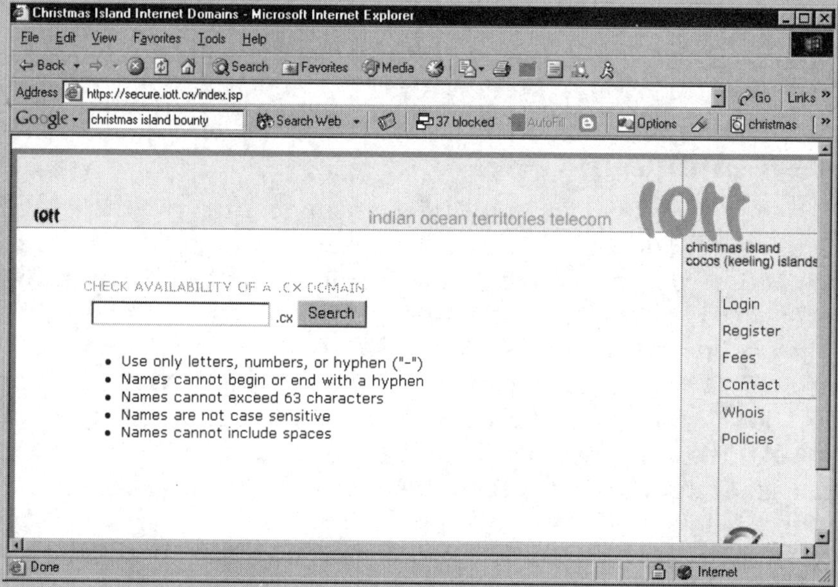

Target Selection

The *Target selection* tab is shown in Figure 4.15. At this point, you have specified just about everything about your scan except its target. For your first scan, you should probably concentrate on using the Nmap or built-in Nessus probes to get a picture of your network. Once you have a good idea, you can start selecting plugins to address specific issues of interest.

Figure 4.15 Target selection Tab

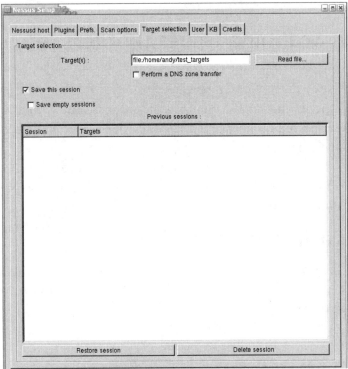

How to Select Targets

You might be tempted to enable a bunch of plugins and run Nessus against your entire network, just to see what happens. This is not a good idea. Once, one of your authors ran Nessus, trying a scan with all non-dangerous plugins enabled and ran it over about a dozen class C subnets overnight. The next morning, there was a huge pile of paper representing the combined outputs of almost every printer in two buildings. It turned out that many of the web-scanning plugins actually generated blank pages from the networked Hewlett-Packard printers. After that, Nmap was run before anything else to identify the targets that Nessus was to avoid.

Your best strategy for your first run is to select no more than five hosts as targets; preferably, targets that no one other than possibly you relies upon. The platform for the Nessus server is probably a good choice. Any desktop systems you use can be included, too. You can use your root privileges on the server and root/Administrator privileges on your desktop(s) to profile those systems from the inside and compare them to Nessus' results. You will also avoid the risk of having to explain why you chose someone else's system as a target before you got any further along the learning curve.

Common Scanning Issues (Printers, etc.)

As noted, networked HP printers might produce a small forest's worth of blank pages under a Nessus scan. System services (or systems themselves) might crash. Firewalls might be strained under the load of a packet scan. Moreover, your own scans could be impacted by host-based firewalls, NATs, or wireless VLANs where connections appear and disappear during the scan.

Scans, particularly wide-ranging network scans, need to be planned ahead of time. This makes the scans themselves run more smoothly and helps you to interpret the results more accurately.

Defining a Target Range

The *Target(s):* field on the Target selection tab accepts a single IP address, a sequence of IP addresses separated by commas, CIDR subnet notation, or any combination of these.

Tools & Traps…

Classless Inter-Domain Routing

CIDR (Classless Inter-Domain Routing) notation is a compact and flexible way to define subnets. The notation has the familiar dotted-quad form of an IP address (IPv4 for purists), followed by a forward slash (/) and a number from 0 to 32 inclusive.

For example:

```
110.212.134.56/24
```

To interpret the notation:

1. Write the dotted-quad IP address as four strings of 8 binary bits.

2. Write another four strings of binary bits in which the first 24 bits are ones and the rest zeros.

3. Logically AND the two strings.

Continued

4. Convert the result back into decimal dotted-quad notation.

```
01101110 11010100 10000110 00111000
11111111 11111111 11111111 00000000
────────────────────────────────────
01101110 11010100 10000110 00000000


110.212.134.0
```

The first 24 bits of the addresses on the subnet are fixed. The last 8 are free to vary.

The subnet addresses range from:

```
110.212.134.0 (01101110 11010100 10000110 00000000)
```

to

```
110.212.134.255. (01101110 11010100 10000110 11111111)
```

Similarly, we can read the notation 54.180.14.221/28 as:

```
00110110 10110100 00001110 11011101
11111111 11111111 11111111 11110000
────────────────────────────────────
00110110 10110100 00001110 11010000


54.180.14.208
```

Since the last 4 bits are free to vary, the subnet addresses range from:

```
54.180.14.208 (00110110 10110100 00001110 11010000)
```

to

```
54.180.14.223. (00110110 10110100 00001110 11011111)
```

Finally,

```
140.75.64.192/18


10001100 01001011 01000000 11000000
11111111 11111111 11000000 00000000
────────────────────────────────────
10001100 01001011 01000000 00000000
```

Continued

```
140.75.64.0
```

Since the last 14 bits are free, this subnet's IP addresses range from:

```
140.75.64.0 (10001100 01001011 01000000 00000000)
```

to

```
140.75.127.255 (10001100 01001011 01111111 11111111)
```

You can also type in the pathname of a file containing a list of IP addresses and ranges (one per line is the neatest way) and click the **Read file...** button. If you've already done your reconnaissance, you probably have a list of IP addresses in something like that form already.

Using Zone Transfers (Bad Idea!)

If you enter the IP address of a name server as the target and check the box **Perform a DNS zone transfer**, Nessus will attempt to download the list of IP addresses defined in that DNS server. This is problematic at best. First, many name servers these days won't let you do that. In fact, Nessus plugin 10595 tests name servers and reports zone transfers as a security problem.

More importantly, the whole point of Nessus is that *you*, the person responsible for network security, can use a powerful tool to examine what is really happening on the network. You don't need to trust any source of information other than the network itself. DNS records can be out of date or just plain wrong, and you will miss active systems.

Automatic Session Saving

While this chapter was written, it was frequently saved as it was worked on. If the laptop crashed, it could be rebooted and the chapter would be picked up where it was left off. If you enable the *Save this session* option on the Target selection tab, you are similarly protected from a Nessus crash. You will be able to restart your scanning session from the point at which it left off.

User Information

When users are defined in the Nessus server configuration, rules can be associated with each user to restrict the scans that user can perform. This is obviously a useful security feature in a situation with multiple users. Even if you are the only user of the server, such restrictions can be used to refine your scans.

The *User* tab lets you place restrictions on your scans by adding access rules. For example, if you want to specify a scan of a large network but skip a small number of systems (such as printers), you can simply specify the target network under the **Target selection** tab, and create a rule excluding the systems (specifically, their IP addresses) from your scanning range. It is also easy to apply occasional updates that add or remove systems from the exclusion list.

A wide scanning range with a few small "holes" is fairly common. However, if your scanning range is *really* fragmented, you might be better off creating a file listing only the IPs you want to scan and reading it in through the *Target selection* tab.

For more information about user rules, refer to Chapter 11.

Knowledge Base (Basics)

The Nessus Knowledge Base is discussed in detail in Chapter 9. Briefly, it augments the Continuous Scan capability described. Each test result from a scan is stored in the Knowledge Base with an assigned lifetime. Until that lifetime has expired, future automated scans will not perform that test again. If your network is pretty stable, this can be a useful option. However, you will need to do a lot of scanning before you can be sure that your network is that stable. Even then, you can't be sure that it will stay that way. As always, it's a matter of trust. Do you trust your network not to surprise you? Since you are planning to use a tool that can bypass almost any assumption about your network, we suspect that you have some doubts. Listen to them. Even if you enable this feature, run the occasional detailed scan to make sure that nothing is happening when you aren't looking.

Starting the Scan

Click the **Start the scan** button at the bottom of the Nessus Setup window. Away you go!

Notes from the Underground...

Beyond the First Scan...

Once you become comfortable with using Nessus in your initial test scans, you should plan a sequence of scans to develop an accurate map of your overall network. The details of your plan will depend on your circumstances, but the following general strategy might be useful:

- Start with a "fly-over" scan.

  - Use ICMP ping if it's not blocked, TCP ping otherwise, to see which IP addresses are in use.

  - Check for a handful of common ports on each system. At a minimum, check for 21, 22, 80, 139, and 445. If you are using TCP ping, try it on these ports.

- If you have not encountered any problems, run an OS identification scan on all the systems that you mapped in the "fly-over."

- Use the results of the OS identification scan to select targets for a complete scan of ports 1–65535.

- Using the results of all previous scans, group the active IP addresses into "target groups," each with an appropriate scanning strategy (for example, extensive use of HTTP plugins for web servers, Windows plugins for Windows systems, and so forth). Some systems might fall into more than one target group.

- Develop a scanning schedule for the target groups. In addition, continue to run "fly-over" scans on IP ranges that didn't show any active systems in case any active systems appear there.

- Repeat the entire procedure at irregular, but not infrequent, intervals.

Notes from the Underground…

Routine Scanning is Not Necessarily Regular Scanning

Once you have a routine scanning strategy, it's natural to set up a regular daily, weekly or monthly schedule and simply let it run with minor adjustments as the network grows. Bear in mind that there is an implicit assumption buried in regular schedules: that what you scan at a given time of the day, week, or month would look the same at any other time of the day, week, or month. For instance, if you have been scanning web servers every Friday evening, for six months, consider re-scheduling them for Tuesday mornings for a while.

If you keep looking in different ways, you will find different things.

Summary

Nessus is very powerful and flexible. This makes it the popular tool that it is, and, at the same time, puts *upon you* the responsibility to use it effectively. It's not a drop-in security fix. It takes practice to discover the best way to use it on any particular network.

Start small. Scan a few systems that you control and that no one else depends upon. Try different scanning options and plugins to see what they do.

Do your reconnaissance. Scan the network and map it out before you start doing widespread vulnerability checking.

When you start testing for vulnerabilities, make sure that you schedule your tests with anyone who might be affected.

Remember that your scanning strategy, like everything else security related, is a series of trade-offs. You might never want to run a potential DoS attack on your own network, but what would the cost be if someone else did it instead? Nessus runs more quickly and more safely if you tell it to trust the self-identification of systems and services, but what if they are lying?

With Nessus, you don't have to believe, you can test.

Solutions Fast Track

Preparing for Your First Scan

☑ *Do* select a small, preferably non-operational network or subnet to try out your first scans.

☑ *Do* discuss the potential risks of any scan with all relevant parties *before* you perform the scan.

☑ *Don't* forget that if there are DoS vulnerabilities on your network, someone else might find them if you don't.

☑ Always be aware of the following assumptions when you plan your scans:

- You know which IP addresses are being used on your network.

- You know what is using those IP addresses.

- You know what services are being offered at those IP addresses.

- A given service is running at the port commonly associated with it.

- A service at a given port is the service commonly associated with that port.

- You know how the firewalls and access control lists are configured on the network.

- You know what on your network is vulnerable to a DoS attack.

- Information from previous scans will be valid in the future.

- Any other assumptions that you can think of.

☑ Consider providing authentication information to Nessus if it might make the scan more effective.

☑ Check the source code of any plugins you will be using to make sure you understand how they work.

Starting the Nessus Client

☑ To start the client, type *nessus*.

☑ The "Nessusd Host" tab allows you to authenticate your client to your Nessus server, after this, you will be able to use other tabs.

Plugins

☑ Nessus plugins are organized into functional families where each plugin represents one or more specific vulnerability tests that can be launched during a Nessus scan.

☑ There are a number of plugins and plugin authors, and so thorough research must be done in order to find the plugins that suit your specific needs.

☑ Plugins can be found through using the search utility at www.nessus.org, or using the plugin filter in the Nessus client.

Preferences

- ☑ Recommendations for first scan:
    - ☑ Use ICMP host ping.
    - ☑ Use TCP SYN scan.
    - ☑ Do not use Nmap. Use the default synscan.nasl plugin.
    - ☑ Don't use WWW Checks, NIDS Evasion, Brute Force, SNMP, or login credentials.

Scan Options

- ☑ Recommendations for first scan:
    - ☑ Use port range 1–1024.
    - ☑ Enable safe checks.
    - ☑ Do not run detached scan.
    - ☑ Do not designate hosts by their MAC addresses.
    - ☑ Use the built-in SYN scanner.
    - ☑ Ping each host.

Target Selections

- ☑ Recommendations for first scan:
    - ☑ Use the address range of a test network or nonoperational subnet, preferably containing the Nessus server.
    - ☑ *Do not* scan operational systems.
- ☑ *Never* scan operational systems without notifying all potentially affected parties and obtaining appropriate prior approval.

User Information

- ☑ Recommendations for first scan:
    - ☑ Do not add rules

☑ Once you have mapped your network and located systems that you don't want to include in routine scans (like printers), add rules that deny scans to those systems.

Knowledge Base (basics)

☑ Recommendations for first scan:

☑ Do not use Knowledge Base.

☑ Once you have mapped your network and are ready to establish routine, regular scans, use the Knowledge Base to "tune" your scans to avoid scanning stable parts of your network more often than you think advisable.

Starting the Scan

☑ Click the **Start** button.

Frequently Asked Questions

The following Frequently Asked Questions, answered by the authors of this book, are designed to both measure your understanding of the concepts presented in this chapter and to assist you with real-life implementation of these concepts. To have your questions about this chapter answered by the author, browse to **www.syngress.com/solutions** and click on the **"Ask the Author"** form. You will also gain access to thousands of other FAQs at ITFAQnet.com.

Q: I've started the Nessus scan, but it doesn't seem to be doing anything. What's wrong?

A: When you start the scan, you should see a window listing the IP addresses of your first several targets and "thermometer" indicators showing you how the scans are progressing. If you don't see a list of targets at all, return to the "Target Selection" tab and make sure that you entered your targets correctly. If you see a list but no movement of the progress indicators after a couple of minutes, make sure that your Nessus server actually has access to those targets. Remember that it's traffic between the Nessus *server* and the targets that's important. If your scan depends on an initial ICMP or TCP ping, and that ping is blocked, you may need to run without it. If everything is in order, you may want to investigate the targets themselves. Some host-based firewalls may hang a Nessus scan.

Q: I've found three plugins that all seem to test for the vulnerability I'm looking for. Should I use them all?

A: Almost certainly not. The plugins may well do different things. Examine the source code of each to determine exactly what each is doing and pick the one you want. If you don't know what a plugin does, you can't interpret the results it delivers. If you can't interpret its results, there's no point in using it. *If you don't understand it, don't use it.*

Q: I've selected all the Windows plugins and I'm running them on a large network full of Windows systems. I'm completing the scans on all my targets, but there are only a handful of results from each target. Shouldn't I be getting more information?

A: Most of the Windows plugins require read-access to the target's registry, at a minimum. Make sure that you provided appropriate credentials to provide such access on these systems. Make sure that the credentials are valid. You should also make sure that your network is not blocking SMB traffic between subnets.

Q: What are some common causes of failed Nessus scans?

A: Firewalls and traffic filters that block the scans; failure to provide appropriate credentials; misunderstanding the function of plugins.

Q: My first scan is taking too long

A: One of the purposes of your initial scans is to learn how to tune Nessus for your local conditions. You can reduce the number of targets, reduce the number of plugins, or use some of the "efficiency" features discussed in this chapter. Each of these approaches involve the risk of overlooking some important feature of your targets. That's why your first scan, ideally, is on a subnet you're very familiar with so that you can compare the Nessus results to what you already know about the systems.

Q: People are complaining that my scans are breaking their systems and making their printers spew garbage.

A: If this is happening during your first scanning session, you *really* need to reconsider your target range. *Don't scan anything important until you know what you are doing.*

Chapter 5

Interpreting Results

Solutions in this Chapter:

- **The Nessus UI Basics**
- **Reading a Nessus Report**

☑ **Summary**

☑ **Solutions Fast Track**

☑ **Frequently Asked Questions**

Introduction

Nessus is a tool designed to help you evaluate risk.

"The proof of the pudding is in the eating," it's said. Ultimately the proof of a vulnerability scanner is in the reports it outputs. For the Nessus scanner to be of any use, you must be able to read, interpret, and act on the data it generates. As anyone who's worked much with the Nessus scanner will attest to, this is no simple task.

In this section, compare reading Nessus reports to learning a new language. We consider how the reports have a background, history, and context, and how one can and must understand these to fully understand what the reports are *actually* saying. We also pose some key questions that need to be asked as the reports are being read, warn of common traps and pitfalls, and describe additional sources of information that can compliment and complete the user-level reports.

We discuss two different GUI clients in this chapter, and evaluate the strengths and weaknesses of each in order to get the most out of reports.

The Nessus UI Basics

As you already know, the Nessus scanner architecture differentiates between the "server" and the "client" component. The Nessus client is responsible for generating and, in most cases, rendering the scan output. The two clients considered in this chapter are:

- The Nessus GUI Client for X
- The NessusWX Client for Windows

As far as reading the report output is concerned, both of these clients have simple and intuitive graphical interfaces. This chapter focuses more on understanding and interpreting the actual report content than the use of the point-and-click interface. Nevertheless, a brief overview of the features and functions of these two interfaces is offered for those readers who are not yet familiar with the tools at that level.

Viewing Results Using the Nessus GUI Client for X

Written primarily by Renaud Deraison and distributed from nessus.org, the Nessus GUI Client for X Windows is the definitive client for Nessus. While perhaps not always as user friendly as some would like (especially for users not accustomed to UNIX GUI environments), the UNIX client is solid, complete, and comprehensive. Any serious users of Nessus (even those more comfortable with Windows) are encouraged to familiarize themselves with the UNIX GUI client.

Using the Basic Report Viewer

By default, the Nessus Report window is divided into four different frames (as shown in Figure 5.1), showing the subnets included in the scan (or all the DNS domain suffixes, depending on how your targets were specified), the hosts included in the selected subnet (or domain), the ports found open on the selected host, and the vulnerabilities reported for the selected port, respectively. You can change the content of a frame at any time by clicking on the drop-down and making your selection—Subnet, Host, Port, or Severity—but to do so seldom makes any sense. In fact, as soon as you stray from the strict Subnet -> Host -> Port -> Severity linking, you're very likely to become confused regarding what data is actually being displayed at any given time. The actual vulnerability report is only shown when you select an item from the Severity list. Notice that this list displays all the severity *types* that were reported for the selected port.

Figure 5.1 The Nessus Client for X—Report Viewer

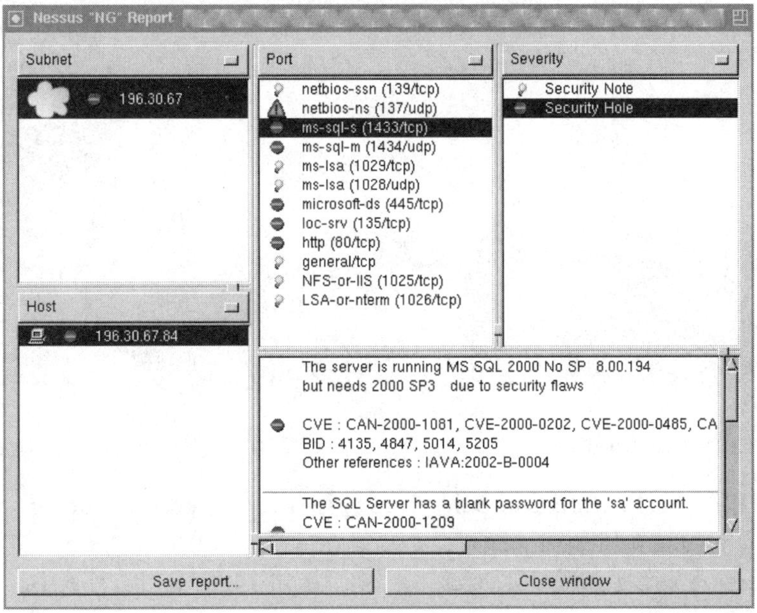

On selecting a given type, all the *vulnerabilities* of that type are displayed in the main window.

At the bottom of the window are two buttons: Save Report and Close Window. We'll expand on *saving* in the sections that follow. Notice, however, that if you close the window without saving, the scan output will be lost. This behavior differs from that of the NessusWX client, which saves the output automatically.

Saving and Exporting to Other Formats

Clicking the Save Report button allows you to save the report in a number of different portable formats, as shown in Figure 5.2.

Figure 5.2 The Nessus Client for X—Exporting Reports in Other Formats

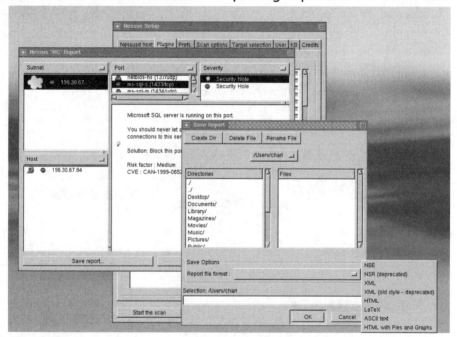

Format options include:

- **NBE** *Nessus BackEnd* reports are pipe-delimited text files in which each vulnerability is reported on a new line, making them ideal for parsing using tools like *grep*, *cut*, and *awk*. NBE is also the format used for transporting reports between two different Nessus clients. For example, later in this chapter we discuss how a report generated using the NessusWX client can be exported to the Nessus GUI Client for X so that reports with graphs can be generated. According to the Nessus documentation, an NBE report has the following format:

```
hostname|port (1)
```

or

```
hostname|port|script_id|type|data (2)
```

Format (1) indicates that a port is open. Format (2) adds a security report to the information.

Tools & Traps...

NBE File Fields

According to the Nessus documentation, the NBE file consists of the following fields (*nsr_file_format.txt,v 1.1 2000/04/13 22:35:11 renaud*):

- **Hostname** The hostname or IP address.
- **Port** The port affected. The format is port name (num/protocol); for example, www (80/tcp). It can also be general/protocol, which means that the protocol itself is affected.
- **script_id** The number of the script that generated the information. See http://cvs.nessus.org/plugins/search.html to find the name of a plugin by searching its ID.
- **type** Either INFO (security warning) or REPORT (security hole, now also WARNING).
- **data** Content of the report or warning. All the "\n" chars are replaced by ";".

The exact purpose and possible values of these fields are discussed in more detail when we cover the content of the Nessus reports later in this chapter.

- **NSR** The Nessus Report file format is no longer officially supported and has been absorbed into NBE. Essentially, the NBE file now contains all the fields in an NSR file in addition to some new ones. Later in this chapter, we describe the possible report types as being NOTE, WARNING, and HOLE, which map to the NOTE, INFO, and REPORT you'll see in the NSR output.

- **XML** According to the Nessus man pages, the Extensible Markup Language (XML) is basically a merge between a .nbe report and the .nessusrc configuration file. You won't get extra verbosity or diagnosis information in the XML report, but you'll know which plugins (and what version of these plugins) have been enabled during the scan. You can parse the XML output using software, or view it using a simple text editor. You can also view it properly formatted using a browser like Internet Explorer, provided that you also have the nessus.xsl (Extensible Stylesheet Language) file in the same directory as the XML file. The XSL file can be downloaded from the Nessus site at http://cvsweb.nessus.org/cgi-bin/cvsweb.cgi/nessus-tools/xsl/nessus.xsl and is used to describe how data received using XML is to be presented. This combination provides output almost identical to what you will see from the standard HTML report. In addition, the original XML output contains the following elements that aren't found in a regular HTML report:

  - Nessusd, libnasl, and libnessus version information

  - Enabled and disabled plugins

  - Selected global preferences

  - Selected plugin configuration settings

  - Details for the selected plugins

- **XML (old style)** This format is no longer officially supported. See the previous description of the XML format.

- **HTML** The HTML report format is a clean and browseable report of all the findings of the scan. The report is produced as a single HTML page, which is convenient for printing, e-mailing, and so forth, and lists the vulnerabilities grouped first by port number and protocol and then sorted by type. Later in this chapter, we describe the possible report types as being NOTE, WARNING, and HOLE, which maps to the Informational, Warning, and Vulnerability reports you'll see in the HTML table. Cross-references to external databases like Bugtraq, CVE, and the various vendor pages are provided as HTML links, which makes for easy browsing. More on these external links later in this chapter.

- **LaTeX** The LaTeX project web site (www.latex-project.org) states: "LaTeX is a high-quality typesetting system, with features designed for the production of technical and scientific documentation. LaTeX is the de facto standard for the communication and publication of scientific documents." Or elsewhere: "LaTeX is a simpler, faster, and better way to produce large or complex documents, and is especially appropriate for scientific community." For a Windows-based LaTeX viewer, visit http://miktex.org/ or try the UNIX X Editor "lyx," which allows you to open LaTeX .tex files and save them in .lyx format. Under UNIX, you'll also find utilities like latex2html, latex2rtf, and latex2pdf that do transforms between these formats. Unless you really know your way about the LaTeX world, however, using this format is not really recommended.

- **ASCII** This report simply generates human-readable ASCII text. The format is similar to as what you'll get from the HTML report (described in the previous section), but without the ability to browse. As the report is neither delimited nor tagged in any way, it's not particularly easy to parse, export, or even read. If you grew up with vi, you'll possibly enjoy this format.

- **HTML with Pies and Graphs** This report is also in HTML format that can be opened in any browser, but differs from the other HTML report in style and content. As this report contains graphics, it will create a directory with the name you specify and then a new subdirectory for each target host. Opening the index.html (see Figure 5.3) in the main directory will present you with some general graphs and statistics for the entire scan and an index of all the target hosts included in the report.

Figure 5.3 The Nessus GUI Client for X—The HTML Report with Graphs
Creates a Directory Structure

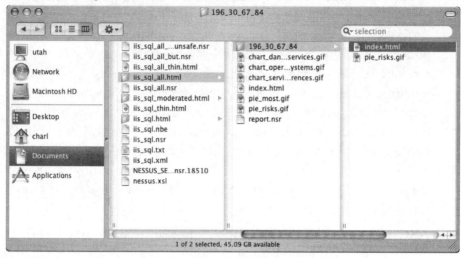

In each of the subdirectories, opening the index.html file will open the report for that host only, including a single graph that depicts the spread of Risk Factors across all the issues reported, as shown in Figure 5.4. We explore the precise meaning of Risk Factors later in this chapter.

Figure 5.4 The Nessus GUI Client for X—HTML Report Graph Showing the Impact Level Spread Over All the Issues

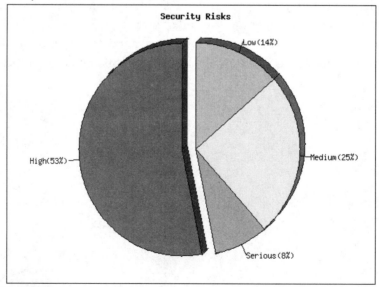

Other graphs display the most "present" and the most "dangerous" network services on the hosts scanned as well as a general most "dangerous" host. These graphs should be used for rough comparisons only and should be used very carefully as a management information tool. The percentages presented are based on a simple count of all the vulnerabilities found using the risk factor assigned by the individual NASL writer. Issues that are actually false positives are also included, and vulnerabilities that occur on multiple ports (for example, 80 and 443) will be counted twice.

NOTE

Notice that the Nessus GUI Client for X does not allow you to edit or modify the scan results before the report is exported. This means that the saved report will always contain all the scanner findings, regardless of how accurate or relevant they are. You can get around this by saving the report in NBE format and editing it there, or loading it into the NessusWX client and editing it there before loading it into the UNIX client again to be resaved in the final format of your choice. We examine this in more detail later in the chapter.

Tools & Traps...

Writing Reports to a Database

Unlike the NessusWX client, the UNIX client does not offer a "write to database" feature. However, an open-source project called "NNP"—The Nessus .nbe Log Parser found at http://personal.crybe.com/solid/projects/, parses NBE files into SQL statements, and then uses these statements to insert data to a (MySQL) database. The authors of this project (Sergei Ledovskij and Miika Turkia) describe the program as "buggy." However, it's clear that they've given the problem some thought and there's much to use for beginners and advanced users alike. The parser works as a CGI that allows users to moderate the Nessus output stored in the database before generating a simple HTML report (as seen in Figure 5.5).

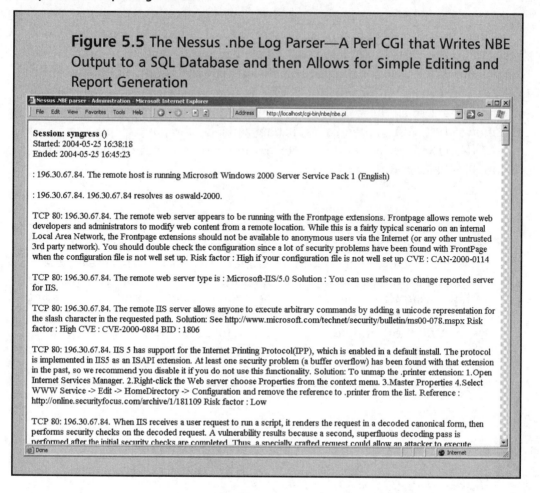

Figure 5.5 The Nessus .nbe Log Parser—A Perl CGI that Writes NBE Output to a SQL Database and then Allows for Simple Editing and Report Generation

Loading and Importing Reports

Clicking the Load Report button from the nessusd host of the UNIX X client presents you with a file browser interface with which you can select a previously saved report to load back into the interface (see Figure 5.6). You don't have to be logged in to the Nessus daemon to do this.

Figure 5.6 The Nessus GUI Client for X—Loading a Previously Saved Report for Viewing

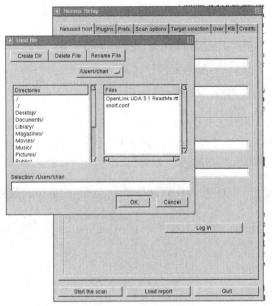

As of the time of writing (v. 2.0.10), the Nessus client will allow you to open reports that were previously saved as either NSR or NBE format, regardless of which client was originally used to save the report. This means that Nessus scan reports can be seamlessly shared between different kinds of clients, allowing you to make use of the specific client that suits your purposes at any point in your assessment.

Viewing Results Using the NessusWX Client for Windows

The NessusWX Client is a GPL product written for Windows by Victor Kirhenstein of securityprojects.org. The console will run on NT, 2000, or XP, and, while perhaps not quite as comprehensive as the UNIX client, it does have a clean, clear, and intuitive interface with features not available in the other client.

Using the Basic Report Viewer

Apart from the toolbar, the NessusWX report viewer is divided into three primary sections. As you can see in Figure 5.7, the Vulnerabilities tree on the left shows a sorted list of all the hosts included in the report output. You can expand any of the targets to see an "indexed" list of all the vulnerabilities found grouped by port number and sorted according to report type, namely:

- ⊗ SECURITY **HOLE**

- ⚠ SECURITY **WARNING**

- ❶ SECURITY **NOTE**

Figure 5.7 The NessusWX Client—Using the Report Viewer Interface

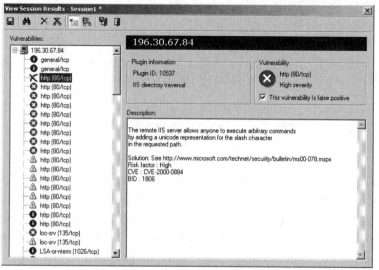

Selecting any of the vulnerabilities from the Vulnerabilities tree will cause the vulnerability information for the selected issue to be displayed in detail on the right-hand side of the window. You'll notice the target name or IP address in bold at the top, followed by two parallel panes: the left pane displays the NASL Plugin ID number and name; the right pane displays the protocol and port information, along with a check box that allows you to mark the vulnerability as a false positive. The new window below the parallel pane contains the actual vulnerability description. A detailed description of the exact implication of these different report types is given later in this chapter. At this stage, we just want to focus on how one navigates the actual interface. We'll also revisit the "false positive" check box and explore its use.

The NessusWX Results Viewer Toolbar

At the top of the NessusWX result viewer is a toolbar that gives you access to a number of simple functions:

- **Save** Saves the results of any changes you made to the report; for example, deleting or marking a vulnerability as a false positive.

- **Search** Allows you to search the report by NASL ID, port and protocol, host, and description.

- **Delete** Deletes the selected vulnerability. This is done without warning, so use it with care! Fortunately, the changes aren't permanent until you save the result. Once saved, that specific vulnerability is permanently removed from the report.

- **Delete by Plugin ID** Use this option to remove all instances of the selected NASL Plugin ID from the report, regardless of port or target. For example, if you select a vulnerability with NASL ID 10537, all vulnerabilities where this is the Plugin ID will be deleted. You can also use this option to specify another NASL ID to be deleted. This is done without warning, so use it with care! Fortunately, the changes aren't permanent until you save the result. Once saved, that specific vulnerability is permanently removed from the report.

- **Toggle False** This switch is used to set a flag marking the selected vulnerability as a false positive. False positives are endemic to network-level vulnerability scanning, and the ability to flag certain vulnerabilities as being "false" is a powerful feature of the NessusWX client. The difference between deleting a vulnerability and marking it as a false positive is that by marking a vulnerability as "false," you can still always see it in the report, but it won't be reflected in your reports, graphs, and statistics. Once deleted, the vulnerability is gone forever. Remember, the changes aren't permanent until you save the result. Chapter 7 of this book is dedicated to the question of identifying and managing false positives. A little later in this chapter, we also examine one way in which this feature of the NessusWX client can be used to improve the quality of the reports generated by the Nessus GUI Client for X.

- **Toggle False By Plugin ID** Use this option to mark all instances of the selected NASL Plugin ID as false positive, regardless of port or target. For example, if you select a vulnerability with NASL ID 10537, all vulnerabilities with Plugin ID will be marked as "false." You can also use this option to specify another NASL ID to be marked as "false." Remember, the changes aren't permanent until you save the result.

- ■ 🚪 **Exit** Exit the result viewer without saving any of the changes that were made. All changes will be lost.

- ■ 🚪 **Exit and Save** Exit the result viewer after saving all changes.

Saving and Exporting to Other Formats

As with the Nessus GUI Client for X, the NessusWX client allows you to create external reports in a number of different ways, as shown in Figure 5.8. From the Manage Session Results window there are two options—Report and Export. Both of these options create exportable reports, with the primary distinction being that "Reports" are in human-readable format, while "Export" generates out in machine-readable format. Saving output as a report also allows you the opportunity to apply filters to the report before the output is generated.

Figure 5.8 The NessusWX Client—The Session Manager Stores the Results

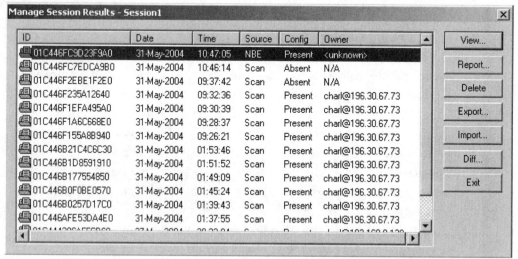

Creating Reports

The NessusWX client allows you to export your reports in three different formats: plain text, HTML, and Adobe Acrobat (see Figure 5.9).

Figure 5.9 The NessusWX Client for Windows—Saving Reports in Other Formats

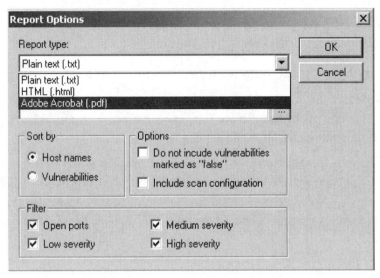

- **Plain Text** This generates the report in a nicely formatted plain-text format. It is good for reading in Notepad or copying and pasting; for example, into an e-mail or Microsoft Word document.

- **HTML** As with the UNIX client, the HTML report format is a clean and browseable report of all the findings of the scan. The report is produced as a single HTML page, which is convenient for printing, e-mailing, and so forth, and lists the vulnerabilities grouped first by port number and protocol and then sorted by type. Later in this chapter, we describe the possible report types as being NOTE, WARNING, and HOLE, which map to the High, Low, and Info reports you'll see in the HTML table. Cross-references to external databases like Bugtraq, CVE, and the various vendor pages are provided as HTML links, which makes for easy browsing. More on these external links later in this chapter. Unlike the HTML generated by the X client, this report also includes the selected plugins list and the scanner configuration settings used for the scan.

- **Adobe Acrobat** This selection will create the report as a Portable Document Format (PDF) file at the location you specify. PDF is widely recognized and very difficult to modify, and therefore is attractive as a format for report distribution. The PDF reports are almost identical to the HTML reports generated by this client, except that the format does not allow hyperlinks, for either within the report or to external sources.

For each report type, you also have the option of applying various filters to the data before the report is created, including:

- **Sort by** Sort the output in the report by hostname or vulnerability.

- **Options** Choose whether to have the issues you flagged as false positives included in the report. Choose whether to include the scanner configuration detail in the report.

- **Filters** Choose to exclude elements from the generated output. You can exclude the list of open ports or reports of type INFO (Low Severity), WARNING (Medium Severity), and NOTE (High Severity). Only items that are selected will be included in the output report.

Exporting Reports

The NessusWX client's Export function supports the several formats, as shown in Figure 5.10.

Figure 5.10 The NessusWX Client—Exporting Report Output for Further Processing

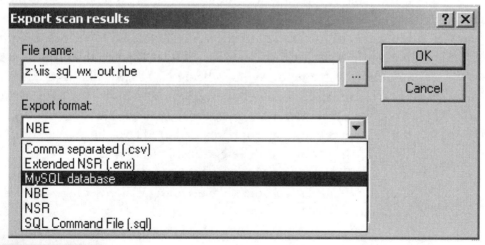

- **CSV** A Comma Separated Values (CSV) file is really an ASCII text representation of a table, where the rows are separated on to new lines and the columns are separated by commas (","). In reality, most clients that understand CSV will allow you to specify the column and sometimes even the row that has been separated. Fields are encapsulated in quotation marks so that strings can break over multiple lines. As with NBE format (described in this bulleted list), the CSV format is ideally suited for machine parsing. Both formats are also nicely suited for importing the data into productivity tools like Microsoft Access and Microsoft Excel, which can be used to perform further processing on the data and generating report and graphs. Notice that this format does not include all the information that's stored in an NBE file and is therefore not suited to exporting reports between clients. The fields in the CSV format are the same as in the NBE format and are discussed in some detail later in this chapter.

  They are:

- Target

- Port/Protocol

- Script NASL ID

- Report Type (HOLE, WARNING, or NOTE)

- Information

- **ENX** The Extended NSR file is essentially an NSR file that also contains the scan configuration data. Although this makes it the ideal format for transferring scan information between NessusWX clients, it is unfortunately not supported by the X client.

- **MySQL** This option allows you to export the scan results directly into a MySQL database. The NessusWX Settings panel allows you to specify the address, the database name, and a password for the target database. The database with all the correct permissions and the table with the correct fields and types should exist already. The interaction between Nessus and various database backends is still somewhat in its infancy. The following resource could prove useful: http://nessuswx.nessus.org/mysql.html

- **NBE** As with the Nessus GUI Client for X, Nessus BackEnd (NBE) reports are pipe-delimited text files in which each vulnerability is reported on a new line, making them ideal for parsing using tools like findstr and DOS for loops. NBE is also the format used for transporting reports between two different Nessus clients. For example, later in this chapter we discuss how a report generated using the NessusWX client can be exported to the Nessus GUI Client for X so that reports with graphs can be generated. According to the Nessus documentation, an NBE report has the following format:

```
hostname|port (1)
```

   or

```
hostname|port|script_id|type|data (2)
```

   Format (1) indicates that a port is open. Format (2) adds a security report to the information.

- **NSR** As with the Nessus GUI Client for X, the Nessus Report file format is no longer officially supported and has been absorbed into NBE. Essentially, the NBE file now contains all the fields in an NSR file in addition to some new ones. Later in this chapter, we describe the possible report types as being NOTE, WARNING, and HOLE, which map to the NOTE, INFO, and REPORT you'll see in the NSR output.

- **SQL Commands** By selecting this option, you can instruct the NessusWX client to create the entire set of SQL commands required to reproduce the selected results set into any properly formatted SQL-compliant database. Simply copy the output and use your favorite query analyzer or SQL client application to execute each command. Notice, however, that this output does not include the SQL *CREATE* commands required to build the actual tables. You need to ensure that the required tables are in place, as shown in Tables 5.1 and 5.2.

Again, the NessusWX client will allow you to select those issues you previously marked as false positives that should be included in the exported output. Select the **Do not include vulnerabilities marked as "false"** check box if you want to have false positives excluded from the exported report. Where appropriate (currently for the MySQL format only), you can also select whether you want to have the scan configuration data included in the report.

The NessusWX client can export results directly to a MySQL database that has the correct tables and formats. As of version 1.4.4, two tables are required—SESSIONS (which contains information about scanning sessions) and RESULTS (which contains the actual scan results). The tables must have the formats shown in Tables 5.1 and 5.2.

Table 5.1 Sessions

Field	Type	Description
Id	integer	Unique session identifier.
Name	varchar(255)	Session name.
Owner	varchar(255)	Scan owner (user who did the scan). NOTE: this field was added in version 1.4.0.
time_start	datetime	Date and time the scan was started.
time_finish	datetime	Date and time the scan was finished.
time_elapsed	integer	Scan duration in seconds.

Table 5.2 Results

Field	Type	Description
Session_id	integer	Identifier of a session to which this result record belongs.
Host	varchar(128)	Hostname or IP address.
Service	varchar(48)	Service name and port number.
plugin_id	integer	ID of plugin generated this record.
Type	integer	Record type: 0—open port 2—warning 3—hole
is_false	bool	1 if this record was marked as false positive.
description	blob	Security hole description.
risk_factor	varchar(32)	Risk factor extracted from original description.
cve_id	varchar(32)	Security hole's CVE ID.
Solution	blob	Solution for a problem (extracted from original description).

These tables are published by the NessusWX team at http://nessuswx.nessus.org/sql_tables.html.

Loading and Importing Reports

Selecting the Import button from the Manage Session Results window will allow you to select a previously saved report to load back into the interface. You don't have to be logged in to the Nessus daemon to do this.

As of the time of writing (v 1.4.4), the NessusWX client will allow you to open reports that were previously saved in NSR, NBE, and ENX formats, regardless of which client was originally used to save the report (see Figure 5.11). With the exception of the ENX format, which is currently not supported by the X client, this means that Nessus scan reports can be seamlessly shared between different kinds of clients, thus allowing you to make use of the specific client that suits your purposes best at any point of your assessment. As mentioned earlier, the ENX format also stores scan configuration data, which makes it ideally suited for transferring data between two NessusWX clients. Otherwise, you'll use one of the other two formats.

Figure 5.11 The NessusWX Client—Importing the Output from Previous Scans

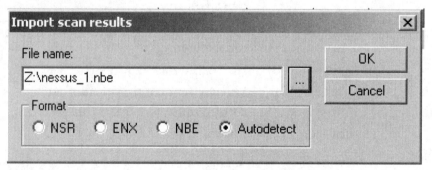

Comparing Reports

The NessusWX client offers a very convenient *Diff* feature that allows you to compare the results of two different scans. Select the first scan of the two you want to compare (A) from the Manage Session Results window and then click the **Diff** button. The NessusWX client will then offer you an interface from which you can select the second report (B) for the comparison and define the criteria against which the comparison can be done. First, you can select which elements of each report should be compared (for example: Plugin ID, Target, Port/Protocol, or description), and then choose whether you want to see all the issues that were duplicated between the reports, such as issues that were reported in both (A) and (B) or only the issues that are unique to the report that you first selected, such as issues that were reported in (A) but did not appear in (B). The client performs the comparison based on the selected criteria and creates a new report containing the resultant output that is automatically saved in the session history along with all the other reports and can then be viewed and processed in the same way.

Notes from the Underground…

Using Multiple Clients to Improve Report Quality

The question of false positives is a serious problem in network-based vulnerability scanners and is covered extensively in this chapter and elsewhere in this book. As pointed out earlier, the NessusWX client helps to address the problem by allowing you to mark selected issues as "false positives" and thus have them excluded from your final reports. Sadly, the X client doesn't yet offer such a feature. However, the X client allows you to generate an HTML report that also contains powerful management information in the form of useful graphs and statistics, a feature not present in the NessusWX client. You can get the best of both worlds by using the globally recognized NBE format to move reports to the client that best suits your purposes at any given time. For example, use the NessusWX client to run a scan and mark issues as "false positives" where appropriate. Then, export the results as an NBE file in order to use the X client to generate an HTML report with graphs and statistics. Of course, there are numerous other ways to achieve the same results, including editing the NBE files by hand, or using third-party software to generate statistical reports.

New Nessus Client

At the time of writing, a team in Germany is undertaking a project to develop a new, multilanguage GUI client for Nessus called BOSS (see Figure 5.12). BOSS, the BSI Open Source Security Suite project, is an open–source project being undertaken by Intevation GmbH and DN-Systems Enterprise Internet Solutions GmbH on behalf of the German BSI—Federal Office for Information Security.

Figure 5.12 A Preview of the New BOSS GUI

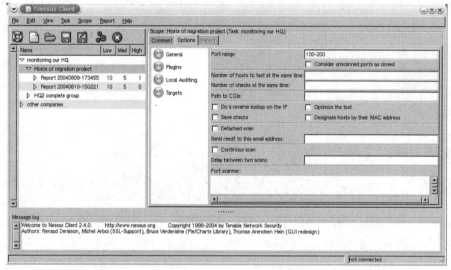

Source code, screen shots, and documentation for BOSS can be found at ftp.intevation.de/boss/.

Reading a Nessus Report

Nessus is a tool, and, like any other tool, it is only as good as the hand that wields it. The better you're able to read and interpret the scanner results, the more value you'll derive from it. Learning to read scanner output is a little like learning a new language. As you grasp the grammar and the vocabulary, the slang and the collo-quialisms, you'll find that a deep and rich pool of information becomes available to you. Of course, as with any language, there's much more to understanding Nessus reports than just knowing the vocabulary. To truly understand a language, you also need to understand something of the culture, history, customs, and tradi-tions of the people who use it. Much the same is true if you want to get the most from Nessus reports. In this section, we examine the language of Nessus reports and how to read them. To fully grasp the language of Nessus reports, we also examine the definitions of *vulnerability* and *risk* and examine the logic that a scanner applies when determining whether a given vulnerability exists.

Understanding Vulnerabilities

Nessus is a "vulnerability scanner." To understand Nessus reports, it makes sense to first understand what *vulnerability* is.

Vulnerability is understood to mean "susceptible to attack." Hence, in the context of host and network security, a vulnerability can be described as a programming, configuration, or administration error that renders the system in question somehow susceptible to attack. While Nessus always scans specific hosts for vulnerabilities, one should bear in mind that an error on one host might render another host, or the network in general, susceptible to attack. Such errors should also be considered vulnerabilities but can be much harder to spot, especially by an automated scanner. Bear this in mind as you analyze Nessus reports.

Information security theory teaches that three elements of information systems could be susceptible to attack:

- **Confidentiality** Some information is of strategic value to an organization and needs to be kept secret to maintain its value. If the confidentiality of the information is breached, the information loses its value. For example, a company's customer database is secret, and is a very valuable business asset. A telephone directory is public, and while it may still be an asset, it is considerably less valuable.

- **Integrity** Information is only valuable if it is complete and correct. Moreover, it is often only valuable if it is also *perceived* to be complete and correct. For example, a company's financial figures for previous years are valuable business planning information, but only if it is accurate. If the information is found to be incorrect, it loses its value to the company. If improperly modified, information can be rendered useless, or worse, even dangerous. Furthermore, if staff members distrust good information for some reason, they will place less reliance on the information in their decision making, and reduce the value of the information accordingly. Ironically, the same is true for the information generated by the Nessus scanner. If it's perceived to be inaccurate, it very quickly loses all its value. This is why the process of identifying and removing false positives is so important.

- **Availability** Information has no value if it cannot be accessed when and where it is required. An extreme case of this is the physical destruction of information; for example, where hardcopy records are destroyed by fire. However, more subtle examples might include an unreliable computer network. If the information is not reliably available, its value is reduced.

The Nessus reports will indicate different vulnerabilities that might allow one or more of these elements to be attacked. While the Nessus NASLs will attempt to classify the vulnerability and explain its potential impact, you as the analyst will need ask yourself which, if any, of these elements is being put at risk, and what this implies for the specific target host, the network, and the organization in general. Later in this chapter, we discuss some key questions that you should ask yourself as you view the report. The questions will help you put the scanner output into perspective and fully understand its impact on the systems you're trying to protect.

Understanding Risk

We stated earlier that vulnerability implies susceptibility to attack. Clearly, the existence of a vulnerability does not necessarily imply that the system will be attacked or that the attack will be successful. Risk is a much broader concept than vulnerability that factors in elements like the "value" of the system and the "probability" of an attack occurring. The introduction of these elements allows us to quantify risk and place it into perspective. With the risk more clearly quantified, we can compare the relative significance of the reports generated by a vulnerability scanner.

Damage & Defense…

Thinking about Attacking

Let's take a moment to look at risk and vulnerability from the perspective of an attacker. When we teach hacking courses, we tell students that an "attack" on a vulnerable system can take one of the following forms:

- **Shoot From The Hip** Remember, the attacker only needs to win once, meaning that if she can guess a password, or stumble onto a web administration backend directory, then that might be all that's needed to compromise your system.

Continued

It's much harder to secure systems than to attack them. Never underestimate how lucky an attacker can get.

- **Data Mining** An attacker will collect any snippet of information she can get, regardless of its apparent value at the time—such as usernames, directories, background information, and the like. No snippet of information is considered irrelevant, and the true impact of information leakage often only becomes apparent when all the pieces are finally put together. Countless successful compromises have been achieved simply by stringing together different snippets of seemingly innocuous information.

- **Exploit** In the classical sense, a vulnerability is "exploited" using a piece of software. Many programmatic errors, configuration errors, and so forth can be compromised in this way. Writing exploit code is both an art and a science only a very few have mastered it, leaving the rest to rely on code that is downloaded and used with very little real skill, knowledge, or control. As a result, exploit software is seldom a reliable attack vector. Have no doubt that it can and it does work, but be aware that many other attack vectors can be (and in our experience very often *are*) much more effective.

- **Brute Force** "If at first you don't succeed, force it!" Brute-force attacks are a much misunderstood attack vector. While not an "elegant" attack, the ease of automation and the anonymity offered by IP-based systems often makes brute-force attacks a viable option where other attacks fail. Try to look beyond traditional password guessing and explore other avenues for brute-force attacks: user enumeration, web directory guessing, session key highjacking, and so forth. We often demonstrate, for example, how e-commerce sites can be attacked by selecting a commonly used PIN number and cycling through all possible account numbers until one is found where that PIN has been used. In this manner, each account is only attacked once, thus bypassing security mechanisms such as account lockout.

- **Combination Attacks** In our experience, most successful compromises rely on a combination of factors, blended from this list. The system leaks a username, a vulnerable service can be exploited, but only with a valid account, and so a password must be derived using brute force. Almost all the practical

Continued

exercises in our hacking courses teach students to view attacks this way, and the thinking is consistently being affirmed by our real-life experience.

Use this thinking about attack vectors to put the risk represented by different vulnerabilities into perspective as you read through a Nessus scan report.

Understanding Scanner Logic

To understand what a scanner report is saying, we need to understand how a scanner actually thinks. Let's remind ourselves how a scanner's logic will typically work:

For each selected NASL script, the scanner will typically execute the following steps:

1. Ensure that all required NASLs are first executed, as specified by the "dependencies" list in the script.

2. Determine whether the affected service is running on the target. This is typically done by querying the Nessus Knowledge Base (KB) for the ports on which the affected service is running. If no relevant ports are found in the KB, the NASL script typically reverts to a default or might not execute at all.

3. Where possible, check whether the service banner suggests vulnerability. Mostly, this is done using simple regular expression matching.

4. If permitted by the "safe mode" setting, the NASL may attempt to verify that the vulnerability really exists. This process varies dramatically from script to script, but in essence, we're dealing with some type of prompt-and-response test. The script sends a series of values over the network and then attempts to parse the target system's response for indications that it's vulnerable. In some cases, this process might repeat a few times, with different prompts, until the script can reach a conclusion.

5. The NASL will flag a report and set the "Risk Factor" according to the findings of (3) and (4) and logic applied by the scriptwriter.

A little later in this section we discuss exactly what happens when a NASL script "flags" a report and examines all the elements of data found in a vulnerability report.

An understanding of the scanner's logic reminds us of some important truths. Some of these might seem obvious, but they bear mentioning nevertheless. Keep the following "reality checks" in mind as you read scanner reports:

- Each NASL is dependent on information it receives from other NASLs via the Knowledge Base. First, there's the obvious reliance on the NASLs listed as "dependencies." However, there's also a less obvious reliance on a set of NASLs that gather information, including things like the portscanners and find_service.nes. If any of these tests return incorrect or insufficient information for some reason, the NASL in question might fail, generating either false positives or even worse, false negatives. Take for example trojan_horses.nasl (NASL ID 11157) that attempts to detect Trojan horses by identifying open TCP sockets on ports commonly used by Trojans and on which the actual service cannot be identified. This script relies completely on previous NASLs that have listed "Unknown" services in the KB, the logic being that if something is listening on a given port and that "something" can't be identified using standard techniques, then that "something" might very well be malicious. The logic is sound in itself, but is thrown into disarray when ports are incorrectly listed as "Unknown" by *find_service.nes*. Many situations can result in this set of circumstances occurring, leading to a security report by *trojan_horses.nasl*. In this way, a perfectly secure host might be reported as already compromised by the Nessus scanner.

- Many tests are dependent on banner information. This is especially true where safe_checks is enabled, thus occasionally preventing the scanner from further prompt-and-response testing. Banners are often not updated when systems are patched, or can be masked or even modified to mislead scanners. Some systems do not update the banner information when services are patched. Some, like Microsoft's IIS, never show version changes for the duration of the product's lifetime. One also sees this frequently from Sun Solaris systems, for example, where applying a patch from Sun does not always cause the affected service banner to be updated. This type of behavior by a vendor is commonly referred to as "backporting."

- Even when NASL scripts don't just rely on banners, they're still conducted over the Internet or other networks that are often unreliable or can introduce "noise" in other ways. One example of this is transparent proxies that always respond to a TCP SYN request on web service ports, regardless of the actual target IP address. Due to this behavior, one can actually end up executing certain tests against the proxy, rather than the target server. This behavior can mislead the scanner into believing there is a web server service running on IP addresses that aren't even active.

- Even when network communications are clear and uninterrupted, the fact that we're testing over the network creates a "gap" that can make it almost impossible for a script to accurately determine the presence of a vulnerability. Imagine, for example, a script that tests for the presence of a buffer overflow vulnerability against Microsoft IIS 5. It's easy to detect the banner, but as the patch level isn't reflected in the banner, that tells us very little. The only remaining option is to actually emulate an attack and attempt to overflow the affected buffer—and that's where it gets tricky. How does the script tell if the overflow succeeded? Unless we're lucky and the service consistently fails when the exploit is run, it's extremely difficult to determine whether the exploit attack succeeded. In cases like this, NASL scriptwriters will often tend towards the side of caution and report the target as vulnerable. This is one of the chief causes for false positive reports. See *iis5_isapi_printer.nasl* (NASL ID 10661) as an example of a script that does a prompt-and-response test for a vulnerable element, but really can't determine whether the issue is present. Also see *msftp_dos.nasl* (NASL ID 10934) for an example of a script that would cause the service to fail as a test but is forced to fall back on an unreliable banner if safe_checks is enabled.

- Finally, assuming that none of the previously described conditions occurs, one still has the human element to deal with. NASL writers are only human, and one often sees NASLs generating sparse or misleading reports. Consider *bind_query.nasl* (NASL ID 105390), for example. The NASL detects DNS name servers that allow "recursive" queries, and has been classified as "Serious" by the author. The script author cautions that this may not always be the case: "If this is your internal name server, then forget this warning." However, can you imagine how often this report will be generated by a Nessus scan against an ISP's network, where large numbers of "useable" DNS servers deliberately face the Internet? The NASL writer can never understand the context in which the scans are run, so *you* have to look through the report output to the core of what's being reported and interpret that information in the light of your own environment.

Notice that the points discussed here should be seen as 'limitations' and not 'errors' and that all these issues are endemic to *all* network-level vulnerability scanners. Nessus has consistently been shown to be one of the best vulnerability scanners there is and the examples in this list should do nothing to dispute assertion. Rather, they should serve to remind us that the scanner is only a tool and will never be able to do anything a skilled human technician cannot. Indeed, the better you understand the tool with all its strengths and weaknesses, the better it will serve you.

Key Report Elements

A Nessus scan "report" consists of a number of "issues," which are in turn classified as "Holes," "Warnings," or "Infos." If you look at a Nessus issue, regardless of the client you used or the report format, there will always be certain key pieces of information for you to consider. In this section, we review each element of a Nessus issue. We list the elements in the order in which they appear in a pipe-delimited NBE format report:

- **Category** The first field of an NBE issue report is the category field, which is always either "timestamps" or "results." This value is not really a part of the report, but we mention it for completeness in case you're looking at an NBE file as you read this. In terms of reading Nessus output, you're only interested in lines with category "results."

- **Subnet** The subnet field is simply a truncation of the IP address that is performed by the Nessus client after the report has been received from the server. Nessus is not aware of the actual subnet address in which the target resides, nor is there any mapping back to the original target specification even if the target was defined as a subnet. The subnet field simply performs a logical grouping of IP addresses by Class C subnet address.

- **Hostname** The hostname field contains the IP address or DNS name for which the vulnerability is being reported. As an aside, you should note when starting your scan that DNS name and IP address are not necessarily interchangeable in terms of the behavior of the scanner, especially when scanning web servers.

- **Port** The TCP or UDP port number on which the vulnerability was discovered. The format is "port name (num/protocol)." Remember that Nessus dynamically detects what service is running on each scanned port. Thus, for example, it is not uncommon to see web server vulnerability reports on uncommon ports like 81 and 10000. However, this information is *not* shown in this field, and you should note that in the report, Nessus translates the port number shown in this field into the port name from the static /usr/local/share/nmap/nmap-service-probes file on the *nessusd* host. This field does not necessarily indicate the true function of that port or the findings of the *find_services.nes*. If no service name could be found by the server, the service name will be listed as "unknown." The keyword *general* tells us that the problem is not specific to a port but is a general TCP/UDP- or IP-level problem. For example, the script *os_fingerprint.nasl* (NASL ID 11936), which uses TCP fingerprinting techniques to determine the operating system of the target host, will report on port "general/tcp." A final point to remember is that Nessus executes scans per port. Thus, if you scan a host with multiple addresses or a service that listens on multiple ports (like HTTP and HTTPS), you'll see the same vulnerability report repeated for each port on which it was found.

- **Script ID** A unique NASL script ID number is assigned by the Nessus core team to each new NASL plugin script when it is included in the distribution. The ID is often not displayed by the GUI clients, but is included in most of the "exported" report formats (like HTML). It provides the simplest and most direct link back to the original NASL. See the Tools & Traps sidebar for how to derive the NASL script name from the ID. The ID can also be used to search for the NASL on the Nessus web site—http://cgi.nessus.org/plugins/search.html—and to query the Open Source Vulnerability Database (OSVDB—www.osvdb.org) for additional vulnerability information. Finally, the ID should be used when communicating with other Nessus users, the Nessus core team, or the NASL writer to avoid any confusion or miscommunication.

Tools & Traps…

Searching through NASLs for Specific Script IDs

Nessus NASL scripts are stored in separate files with specific names like "http_version.nasl." The files are stored in the Nessus "plugins" directory—typically (but not always) /usr/local/lib/nessus/plugins. To verify or change the location of the plugins directory, examine the following line in the nessusd.conf file:

```
# Path to the security checks folder :
plugins_folder = /usr/local/lib/nessus/plugins
```

Given a specific script ID number, a simple *grep* command is often all that's required to identify the relevant .nasl file:

```
grep 10107 /usr/local/lib/nessus/plugins/*.nasl
```

Given that the list of plugins for a current Nessus version may now exceed 4500, some distributions might have difficulties with this command—displaying an evasive "Argument list too long" error. A simple way to work around this is to use the *find* command:

```
grep 10107 `find . -name "*.nasl"`
```

Note that the *find* command has been encapsulated in back quotes (ASCII code 96), which are used in UNIX shells to evoke command execution.

Another approach that should work is:

```
ls /usr/local/lib/nessus/plugins/ | xargs grep 10107
```

This approach uses the xargs utility, which reads the filenames from the *ls* command and executes *grep* with the files as arguments.

- **Type** The report "type" is communicated by the Nessus daemon to the client via the NTP protocol as soon as a new issue is detected. Since the inception of NTP/1.1, a NASL writer who has detected a vulnerability literarily has three different function calls at her disposal: *security_note*, *security_warning*, and *security_hole*. If you use the Nessus GUI Client for X, you'll recognize the three corresponding icons in Figure 5.13.

Figure 5.13 Nessus Client Icons

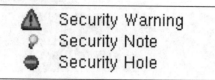

The definitions of these levels are a little sparse. However, Michel Arboi's "NASL Reference" paper offers the following guidelines:

- **NOTE** reports "miscellaneous information."

- **WARNING** reports a "mild flaw."

- **HOLE** reports a "severe flaw."

It's up to the NASL writer to select what report type to generate, and indeed many NASL scripts dynamically adjust the type based on exactly what was found and how it was found. For example, a vulnerability found with safe_checks off might be reported as a "HOLE," while the same vulnerability found with safe_checks on (using a simple banner grab) will be reported as a "WARNING." In generating the report, the NASL writer can also pass along some additional information. As of NTP/1.2, this can include the port number, protocol, and "data," which are included in the description you're shown by the client. Under the NTP protocol, the server will also pass the client the NASL ID number, which the client may choose to display. Notice that the different report file outputs use different terms in this field, which can lead to some confusion. Refer to Table 5.3 later in this chapter for a mapping between the different clients and report file formats.

- **Data** The "data" section is the actual human-readable text output of the script. Although always displayed as a single block of text, the data section logically consists of two parts. The first part (call it the "description") is the "static" part of the report—a generic description of the vulnerability that is included by the NASL writer by evoking the *script_description* function in the NASL. The second logical part of the data field (call it the "report") communicates additional information that was generated by the NASL as it executed. The NASL writer may use this facility to modify the text of the report on the fly, or to provide additional information on the vulnerability that was found. See *domino_default_db.nasl* (NASL ID 10629) for an excellent example of how this can be done. There is very little formal structure in the report data, and NASL writers are free to describe the vulnerability however they deem best. However, Nessus provides a number of sub-elements that you will often find included in vulnerability reports:

- **Name** The NASL writer can specify a "name" or a "script_name" in the script, which gives a one-line synopsis of the problem the NASL is checking for.

- **Description** The description is simply the NASL report text. It's stored inside the script or generated dynamically by the script at execution time.

- **Bugtraq ID** A SecurityFocus Bugtraq ID (BID) number. This will allow you to reference the SecurityFocus vulnerability description at securityfocus.com; for example, www.securityfocus.com/bid/**xxx** or try http://cgi.nessus.org/bid.php3?bid=**xxx**, where **xxx** represents the BID you are searching for. The Bugtraq mailing list, hosted by Symantec at SecurityFocus.com, is one of the most popular security disclosure forums on the Internet. Symantec makes a point of capturing, categorizing, and indexing newly discovered security vulnerabilities in the Bugtraq database. Each entry is assigned a unique BID number, which is referenced by the NASL.

- **CVE ID** CVE stands for "Common Vulnerabilities and Exposures" and is an initiative sponsored by the US-CERT at the U.S. Department of Homeland Security. According to the MITRE Corporation (the not-for-profit organization that manages the CVE database), the CVE is "a list of standardized names for vulnerabilities and other information security exposures—CVE aims to standardize the names for all publicly known vulnerabilities and security exposures." The ID will look like "CVE-2002-042" (a CVE entry) or "CAN-2003-666" (a CVE candidate entry), and it's a way of globally referencing vulnerabilities. The actual CVE database description of the vulnerability may seem a little sparse, that's because CVE provides more of a global key than a central repository. Using the CVE reference, you can exactly identify the specific vulnerability being tested by the NASL. CVE IDs can be cross-referenced at http://cve.mitre.org, or try http://cgi.nessus.org/cve.php3?cve=**xxx**, where **xxx** represents the CVE ID you are searching for.

- **Solution** The NASL writer may also include recommended remediation in the NASL output. Unlike commercial vulnerability scanners, Nessus does not offer an extensive database of "fixes" for the vulnerabilities it detects, nor does it offer to automatically fix the problem for you. When it comes to finding a solution for the problem being reported, you may very well be on your own. In fact, even when a solution is suggested by the NASL, it's good practice to verify the recommendation and carefully test any changes in a test environment before applying them in production. Once you've applied your changes, you'll want to verify their effectiveness by running the scan again or using a tool like *nasl* to execute the NASL again.

- **Risk Factor** In addition to classifying the report as NOTE, WARNING, or HOLE, the NASL writer may include a Risk Factor in the vulnerability description. Typically, these ratings are restricted to Low, Medium, High, or Critical, but this isn't enforced in any way, so you might also come across ratings like Serious, Medium/High, or Medium [remote] / High [local]. Serious and Critical are used almost interchangeably. There isn't any "official" index for the different risk factors, so NASL writers apply their own definitions of the ratings. The only guideline is a rule-of-thumb that suggests that the report "type" should give an indication of the impact to a system in the case of a successful attack, while the Risk Factor should provide an indication of the likelihood of an attack succeeding. William Heinbockel has built a script that categorizes NASLs and provides a script that generates statistics on how many tests of each Risk Factor can be found. His site is rather dated, but can still be found at www.rit.edu/~wjh3710/plugin_stats.html. Having said all that, we should remind ourselves of two important principles that we learned earlier in this chapter: risk is a broad and complex question and probably can't be determined objectively by someone who's not familiar with your environment, and vulnerabilities should never be seen in isolation. You need to read the scan report in its entirety and interpret it in the context of your environment to get a real understanding of the level of risk with which you're dealing. Remember what was said about NASL being like a foreign language, and apply yourself to really "reading" the report to understand the risk to you. Consider creating your own "Impact Rating," using terminology with which your organization is comfortable. One crowd that's done quite a nice job of this is the Institute for Security and Open Methodologies (ISECOM) who publish a simple definition of different Risk Types in their *Open Source Testing Mythology* manual. Again, we present this only as an example that you could use when developing your own framework.

Tools & Traps…

Report Types in Different Output Formats

In Table 5.3, we map the descriptions used for different report types to the "core" definition used in the NBE file report. Bear in mind that this is an indication of the "impact" to a system in the case of a successful attack, but it's set by the NASL author who has no real knowledge of the role and the value of the target system and therefore really isn't in a position to make this determination. You should ensure that you know exactly what's being reported and then evaluate the potential impact for yourself.

Table 5.3 Descriptions Used for Different Reports

	NOTE Reports miscellaneous information	WARNING Reports a mild flaw	HOLE Reports a severe flaw
NessusWX			
Nessus for X			
NBE	Security Note	Security Warning	Security Hole
NSR	NOTE	INFO	REPORT
HTML	Vulnerability	Warning	Informational
HTML w/Graph	Security Hole	Security Note	Information

Asking the Right Questions

Imagine that you are attending a presentation by a security vendor at a computer conference. As you listen, you're constantly asking yourself questions that help you comprehend what's being said. These questions include things like "What is this guy *actually* trying to tell me?" "What can I read between the lines?" "Is what she's saying really true?" "How does she know this?" and "What does this all mean to me?" Now imagine that the speaker's first language is not English and you have a good analogy for how you should approach reading a vulnerability scanner report.

In the previous section, we discussed what can be considered the "grammar" and the "vocabulary" of a Nessus report. However, as with any language, you need to read much deeper than that to really understand what's being said. As you read the report, regardless of how the output is being displayed, you need to constantly ask yourself certain key questions about the content. Such questions will typically include:

- **What is actually being reported?** Bearing in mind that the NASL writer is not being paid to write lengthy descriptions of the vulnerability in question, and that the NASL writer might not be a native English speaker, it's up to you to ensure you fully understand what's *actually* being reported by the scanner. In reality, a NASL doesn't report the presence of a vulnerability. What it actually reports is the result of a specific prompt-and-response test. While the NASL writer has done what she can to assist you, it's up to you to determine whether the report really implies a vulnerability, and the impact of that vulnerability. Here are some steps you can follow to help you "read between the lines" of a Nessus vulnerability report:

  - **Read the NASL itself** NASL is the true language of Nessus. If you want to understand the prompt-and-response test report, you'll have to read it in its native language. Be prepared to develop at least a rudimentary grasp of NASL syntax. (See also the Appendix at the conclusion of this book.)

  - **Read ancillary output** NASL writers will often include part of the response to their test with the output they generate. This information can be invaluable in understanding why the vulnerability was reported and its actual impact. For example,

DDI_Directory_Scanner.nasl (NASL ID 11032) is a very tidy script that (among other things) runs a brute-force test for commonly known directories on a web server. The script then goes on to list which directories were found. The presence of a cgi-bin directory, while reported by the NASL, could hardly be construed as a vulnerability. An admin directory, reported by the same NASL, could lead one to an administrative backend on the server and might represent a very serious risk. See *domino_default_db.nasl* (NASL ID 10629) for another example of this principle. In this case, the NASL differentiates between default Lotus Domino databases that exist on the server but require authentication, and those that exist and can be accessed anonymously. A huge distinction!

Figure 5.14 shows how the script *DDI_IIS_Compromised.nasl* (NASL ID 11003) reports when it believes your IIS web server has already been compromised. Under the heading "Details:" it provides evidence of why it came to that conclusion, namely that it found the files sensepost.exe, nc.exe, and upload.asp in the scripts directory of the webroot. A quick search at google.com should suffice to reveal the exact function of each of these files in an attack on an IIS web server, and hence what the impact of this report is to you.

Figure 5.14 Reading the "Ancillary" Information in a Report

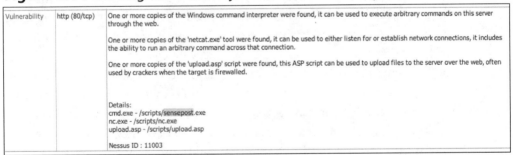

Vulnerability	http (80/tcp)	One or more copies of the Windows command interpreter were found, it can be used to execute arbitrary commands on this server through the web.
		One or more copies of the 'netcat.exe' tool were found, it can be used to either listen for or establish network connections, it includes the ability to run an arbitrary command across that connection.
		One or more copies of the 'upload.asp' script were found, this ASP script can be used to upload files to the server over the web, often used by crackers when the target is firewalled.
		Details: cmd.exe - /scripts/sensepost.exe nc.exe - /scripts/nc.exe upload.asp - /scripts/upload.asp
		Nessus ID : 11003

- **Read the report in context** You should never read a NASL report on its own. Look at the all reports for a given target to get the complete picture. A perfect example of this is the web server "false positive detector"— no404.nasl (NASL ID 10386). This script is designed to identify web servers that always respond with some form of success code to a request, regardless of whether that request can successfully be served, making accurate scanning of web servers extremely difficult. No404.nasl can often detect such behavior. The script writes a value to the Nessus KB that can be used by other scripts, but also generates a report warning you of the behavior. Now take a script like frontpage_chunked_overflow.nasl (NASL ID 11923), which checks for a buffer overflow in IIS FrontPage Server Extensions (FPSE). The current version of the script (1.10) works by making a carefully crafted HTTP POST to the affected URL and then parsing the response for an HTTP "200OK" success code. Although this NASL does check that the remote host is in fact responding with a "Server: Microsoft-IIS/5.[01] (5.0 or 5.1)," it doesn't make use of the information provided by no404.nasl and therefore wouldn't automatically detect false positives. However, when you read the report generated by no404.nsal, you'd know that the web server was behaving strangely and view the NASL report with a little more suspicion. If you look even further, you might notice that there are no other FPSE-related issues. A typical report on a machine running FPSE will include at least NASL 10077—frontpage.nasl—which reports that the "remote web server appears to be running with the FrontPage extensions." If this report is missing, it sheds a report that FPSE is vulnerable, putting it into serious doubt. In this sense, none of the informational messages produced by Nessus is irrelevant, and there are many other examples that prove this.

■ **Why was this report generated?** Once you understand what the NASL report is actually telling you, you might want to spend some time understanding why the script believes the target is vulnerable. If you've read through the script, it should be relatively easy to manually replicate the behavior of the script and trace its logic. For example, you might be able to retrieve the banner for a dated service that caused the report to be generated. Alternatively, perhaps you can observe how the web server responds with a "200 OK" result no matter what report you send it. Maybe you can use the DOS *net view* command to access the IPC$ share using a blank administrator password. Always remember, there's nothing the scanner can do that you cannot, and the scanner will always be disadvantaged because it cannot understand context, something you should be able to do very well.

■ **Is this report accurate?** Now you're in a position to decide whether the report is accurate, or whether you're dealing with a false positive. Most of the reports will be accurate, and usually this is pretty obvious. However, a number of situations can cause false positives to be reported.

By spotting these cases and weeding them out, you enhance the accuracy of the scan and ensure its credibility. This is especially important if you're going to be passing the report on to other technical people for remediation. Chapter 7 is dedicated to a discussion of how to spot false positives.

- **What are the implications of this report?** Having weeded out reports that are blatantly false, and armed with both a solid understanding of the NASL, and how it works, and a good understanding of the environment that you're scanning, you can apply your own impact rating to the issue being reported. Revisit some of the core concepts we discussed earlier in this chapter and use your knowledge of security fundamentals to put the NASL reports into perspective. Remember that there's no such thing as "zero" risk and focus your energies on mitigating the risks that are real and serious. The rating applied by the NASL writer should serve as a guide, but from our discussion of the definition of risk earlier in this chapter, it should be clear that risk is not something static. At the company we work for, we build software around the Nessus scanner that allows the analyst or the customer to adjust the risk rating as she deems appropriate for the system being scanned.

Factors that Can Affect Scanner Output

If we extend our analogy of Nessus output as a "language," then we've probably already covered many of the elements that make up a language—both the "technical" elements like grammar and vocabulary, and some "emotional" elements like culture, tradition, and the writer's personal background. One other factor that we haven't yet covered is the question of "history," which can have a huge influence on the actual meaning of the information that's being communicated. We view "history" in the context of Nessus reports as settings and variables that can impact scanner output. In this section, we explore some of the factors that can dramatically affect the contents of the report. You need to be aware of these as you read the report so that you can properly gauge the accuracy and the impact of the output.

Plugin Selection

Clearly, one of the factors that will have a big impact on the accuracy of your scan report will be the plugins you select. A detailed discussion of the plugin selection process is covered throughout this book. As with all elements of the scanner configuration, ensure that you understand the impact of the various plugin options—Enable All vs. Enable all but Dangerous, and so forth. If the plugin doesn't execute, it can't identify the vulnerability. The use of the Nessus logs (/usr/local/var/nessus/logs/nessusd.messages) to verify that the plugin executed is discussed briefly a little later in this chapter.

Tools & Traps...

Locating the nessusd.messages File

The bulk of the Nessus logs are written to the nessusd.messages file. By default, this file can be found at /usr/local/var/nessus/logs/nessusd.messages. However, this needn't necessarily be the case. The actual target for Nessus logs to be written to is specified in the nessusd.conf file at:

```
# Log file (or 'syslog') :
logfile = /sw/var/nessus/logs/nessusd.messages
```

The "logfile=..." line specifies the location of a file to which the Nessus log output should be written. Alternatively, one can enter **syslog** or **stderr**, thereby causing nessusd to log either to the standard syslog or directly to stderr. If this is the case, no nessusd.messages file will be written into.

The Role of Dependencies

By default, if a script has dependencies, that script won't be run unless the listed dependencies have been completed. This is unless you configure the scanner to "Enable dependencies at runtime," in which case the scanner will load and execute any of the NASLs that are required for the NASLs you've selected. In the end, the output is determined by which tests are run, and the plugin list is actually built at runtime. Obviously, the construction of the plugin list will dramatically affect the output of the scan.

Safe Checks

Within many NASL scripts is a decision point that reads "if (safe_checks)," where the script decides whether it should depend on a simple banner check or execute a potentially destructive attack to determine whether the target is vulnerable to a given problem. Using safe_checks is much less likely to cause disruption of service (although, as of version 2.10, only 142 NASLs consider the option), but it's also much more likely to generate false positives. As such, selecting the safe_checks flag can dramatically affect the scan output.

Notes from the Underground...

Tests that Always Return Vulnerable

With safe_checks enabled, some tests will always return vulnerable. Read this comment by Renaud Deraison in response to a question about the accuracy of certain tests against Linux Red Hat:

```
Forum:     SecurePoint - Nessus Archive

  Date:        Mar 31, 14:57

  From:          Renaud Deraison <nobody at nowhere.com>


On Wed, Mar 31, 2004 at 11:31:48AM -0500, MHewryk AT symcor DOT com
wrote:

> Hi,

> I just wonder if nessus will consider the plugins

> upgrades for Fedora or RH ES 2.0, etc?


As far as I know, RedHat backports fixes into "their" version of
OpenSSH/Apache/whatever, but do not modify the banner of the server
from the point of view of the network, and they are still "thinking
about it".
```

Continued

> If you paid for RedHat ES/AS upgrades and are tired of getting false
> positives from Nessus when scanning your systems, I recommend you
> email Mark J Cox <mjc AT redhat DOT com> and tell them that you
> want RedHat to include a tag in the banners of "fixed" programs, just
> like FreeBSD and many other distributions are doing.
>
>   -- Renaud

no404.nasl

As mentioned previously, the no404.nasl script is designed to detect web servers
that push out a generic error message using the HTTP "200OK" success code,
making them very difficult to scan for web server vulnerabilities. By storing a
"snapshot" of the error that's returned in the KB, this NASL is able to help other
scripts differentiate between truly positive HTTP responses and generic error
messages. When this process works, it can have a dramatic impact on reducing
the number of false positives from machines that exhibit this kind of behavior.
Sometimes, Nessus fails to do this (for example, because the server has a
"generic" error message that is simultaneously also random). Look for the
no404.nasl report and examine the Nessus KB for the host in question to glean
an understanding of how and how well no404.nasl is working.

Ping the Remote Host

Nessus gives you the option to first "ping" the target before scanning and then
only continue the tests if the target responds to the ping. The scanner supports
both ICMP (regular) and TCP pings, in which a number of TCP SYN packets
are sent to the host on configurable destination ports. The risk here is that with
firewalls and other network security devices, the ping packets may be filtered,
causing the host to appear dead and be dropped from the target list. This risk is
particularly real when TCP scans are used, as you need to select the ports on
which the ping packets are sent. A machine that is active on the network but not
listening on one of the selected ping ports might be missed.

Portscanner Settings

The portscan is the starting point and the basis for any vulnerability scan. The
choices you make when configuring the portscanner can have a huge impact on
the scanner output. Nessus' capability, via find_service.nes, to accurately identify
the actual service listening on an open port has largely done away with the

problem of false negatives that used to result from services listening on nonstandard ports. However, if the portscanner misses open ports, they won't be queried by find_service.nes and might never be probed for vulnerabilities, thus resulting in false negatives—serious omissions in the vulnerability scanner output. Many NASL scripts will run against default ports regardless of what the portscanner found, but others will only run against relevant ports as found by the portscanner and stored in the Nessus KB. In such cases, it's critical that the portscanner is properly configured for accurate results.

The "Consider Unscanned Ports as Closed" scanner option has a big impact on how Nessus interprets the portscanner results. By default, Nessus considers unscanned ports "open," meaning if the portscanner didn't test them, they'll be assumed "open." Selecting this option, along with the "Optimize the Test" option, inverts this behavior, instructing Nessus to assume that ports are closed, thereby speeding the test up. Of course, it might cause Nessus to miss vulnerabilities and negatively impact the quality of the scanner output.

Proxies, Firewalls, and TCP Wrappers

In modern network security architectures, a number of systems can cause a portscanner to produce misleading results. As the Nessus scanner relies so widely on the portscanner output, an incorrect portscan can have a significant impact on scanner output. Inline HTTP proxy servers, proxy firewalls, LaBrea Tarpits, and TCP Wrappers all respond to TCP SYN requests even when the port in question isn't necessarily open, and thus misleads the portscanner. Nessus keeps a record of this port as "open" in the KB and tries its best to run the appropriate tests against it. In most instances, Nessus' capability to accurately detect and identify active network services largely offsets the effect that incorrect portscanner results can have. Still, you need to be aware that if the network between the scanner and the target is acting strangely, this will affect your scanner results.

Valid Credentials

A number of NASLs will attempt to log in to services using common or default credentials. If they succeed, the NASLs will store those credentials in the KB for other scripts to use, making those scripts much more accurate and powerful. The Windows Administrator password is a good example of this. If Nessus can determine what the password is, it can perform a number of tests against the Windows registry directly and thus give you a much more accurate impression of the patch level of the machine than it would be able to do purely from the "outside." The same is true for SNMP community strings. If you know (or have an idea of) what the passwords to various services are, it might be worth configuring these in the Nessus settings. At the same time, be aware of the "snowball" effect that can occur if Nessus coincidently guesses the correct password to any of the services being scanned.

KB Reuse and Differential Scanning

Nessusd allows one to store information about scanned hosts in the Nessus KB for later use. When scanning hosts for a second scan, one can select how much work should be re-done, and how much Nessus should rely on the information gathered in the previous scan. One can even configure Nessus to report only on the differences between the information gathered in the current scan and the information stored from the previous scan. Obviously, the choices you make here will significantly impact the results that are displayed in the scan report.

And Many More...

Many more settings will impact the way the scanner behaves and can therefore impact the results. The better you understand these settings and how they're interpreted by the scanner, the better you'll be able to understand the scanner's output. Here's a brief list of some of the other settings that change the scanner's behavior in such a way that it could impact the output:

- **Optimize the test** By default, Nessus will launch all the plugins in the list, regardless of whether any of the required ports were found to be open. Selecting this option instructs Nessus only to launch a NASL script if the required ports and services were previously found and are stored in the KB. This option speeds the test up, but you might cause the scanner to miss potential weaknesses.

- **How to check if directories are writeable** This setting will determine how accurately Nessus can determine whether an FTP directory is writeable. Allowing Nessus to depend on the directory permissions can often lead to false positives. One often sees this with the FTP servers on HP printers, for example.

- **Test SSL-based services** Nessus has the capability to scan web servers that are protected using SSL. This setting tells Nessus on which ports to search for SSL-enabled services. If you leave it on "Known SSL ports," the scanner will only search for SSL on standard ports like SSL, possibly causing it to miss SSL-enabled services running on other ports. Setting this value to "All" will cause the scanner to search all ports for SSL-enabled services.

Scanning Web Servers and Web Sites

You should note when starting your scan that DNS names and IP addresses are not necessarily interchangeable as targets, especially when scanning web servers that respond differently according to the "hostname" field in the DNS request header. When scanning web servers, it's often best to scan both the host IP address and the DNS names of each of the web sites residing on the server. While this leads to large-scale duplication of reports, it might also find vulnerabilities that are web site specific and won't be detected when just scanning the IP. You should also be aware that Nessus will sometimes automatically perform a DNS lookup of the IP address specified and use the hostname returned when sending requests to a web server. This can dramatically impact results.

Web Servers and Load Balancing

One often needs to deal with cases where the target is specified as something like "www.target.com," but the target address actually refers to a load balancer and not to the web server itself. Roughly put, there are three approaches to load balancing on web servers:

- **Reverse proxy** The load balancer accepts the HTTP requests from the client, forwards them to one of the web servers, receives the reply from the web server, and then forwards that back to the client.

- **HTTP redirect** Upon receiving the first HTTP request from the client, the load balancer responds with an HTTP "redirect" of some kind. The client then makes a new request, this time for the specified target, and continues to interact with that target for the remainder of the session.

- **DNS** Various kinds of DNS voodoo can be used to specify the IP address of the server to which the client should connect. The client resolves the web server name to the IP address specified, connects, and transacts with the same web server from the start.

It's easy to see how these approaches can cause strange results from a Nessus scan. When scanning in a load-balancing environment, ensure that you understand how the load balancing is done and which element you're actually scanning.

Bugs in the Plugins

Remember that NASL scripts are just program code and are therefore susceptible to bugs, just as other code is. It's quite possible that under certain circumstances, a plugin can erroneously produce either false positives or false negatives because of simple programmer error. Make sure you update your plugin set regularly, if not every time you run a scan, and apply the principles taught earlier in this chapter to ensure that you understand each vulnerability report and why it was generated.

Tools & Traps…

Updating Nessus Plugins

It's essential to keep the Nessus plugins current, because new tests are being written all the time, and existing tests are continuously being enhanced and repaired. There are basically four different ways to update plugins:

- Download an individual NASL script from the web interface at www.nessus.org.

- Download a tarball with all the latest scripts for the current Nessus version. For Nessus 2.0.10, this can be found at www.nessus.org/nasl/all-2.0.tar.gz.

- Run the script nessus-update-plugins, which ships with the Nessus install and is typically located at /usr/local/sbin/.

- Some *nix distributions, like Debian, allow one to install a plugin set that *they* maintain via the native package manager. Be aware that these plugin lists are maintained by the OS distribution and may therefore lag a little behind the most current state.

Additional Reading

The output of the Nessus scan is always presented to you in the form of a report, in the format of your choice. To help you fully understand the report, however, there are some alternative sources of information that you can also explore. Furthering our language analogy, studying these sources can be likened to reading the history of a language or a people. It won't add to the report, but it might help you to better understand how the contents of the report were derived. There are a number of such sources you should consider, each of which is considered in its own right elsewhere in this book, so reference to them is made here for completeness only.

Configuration Files

If the report you are viewing does contain the scanner configuration that was used, you can still learn about how the scanner was configured by looking in the various configuration files.

In Figure 5.15, for example, you can very clearly see that for this scan:

- The Nmap portscanner is enabled (10336 = yes).

- The portscan was limited to a small range of ports (port_range = 80,443).

- Dependencies were loaded at startup (auto_enable_dependencies = yes).

- "Safe checks" were enabled (safe_checks = yes).

- The results generated would be a comparison against the stored results of a previous scan (diff_scan = yes).

Figure 5.15 This nessusrc File Shows What Can Be Learned by Reading the Scanner Configuration

```
 ● ● ●              Terminal — ssh — 66x50
begin(SCANNER_SET)
 Ping the remote host = no
 TCP Ping the remote host = no
 TCP SYN scan = no
 FTP bounce scan = no
 Nmap tcp connect() scan = yes
 Nmap = yes
 scan for LaBrea tarpitted hosts = no
 10796 = no
 10180 = no
 10331 = no
 10335 = no
 10336 = yes
 11840 = yes
 11219 = yes
end(SCANNER_SET)

begin(SERVER_PREFS)
 max_threads = 10
 log_whole_attack = yes
 cgi_path = /cgi-bin:/scripts
 port_range = 80,443
 optimize_test = yes
 language = english
 track_iothreads = yes
 cookie_logpipe_suptmo = 2
 checks_read_timeout = 13
 delay_between_test = 1
 plugins_timeout = 100
 disable_3001compat = no
 save_knowledge_base = yes
 kb_restore = yes
 only_test_hosts_whose_kb_we_dont_have = no
 only_test_hosts_whose_kb_we_have = no
 kb_dont_replay_scanners = yes
 kb_dont_replay_info_gathering = yes
 kb_dont_replay_attacks = no
 kb_dont_replay_denials = no
 kb_max_age = 2592000
 save_session = no
 save_empty_sessions = no
 host_expansion = none
 ping_hosts = no
 reverse_lookup = no
 detached_scan = no
 continuous_scan = no
 diff_scan = yes
 auto_enable_dependencies = yes
 safe_checks = yes
hackrack#
```

Knowing this information before reading the report will greatly assist you in understanding the output and evaluating the security posture of the target hosts.

NASL

We've stated that NASL is the true "language" of the Nessus report. The NASL script describes the set of prompt-and-response tests that are performed to reach a conclusion on the existence of a given vulnerability. Only by reading and understanding the NASL script in question can you really "get behind the scenes" of a report and evaluate its accuracy and impact. There's no need to "speak" NASL fluently; all you're aiming for is a basic grasp of the content of a script. Use this book or the NASL guide at www.nessus.org/doc/nasl.html.

The Nessus KB

The Nessus KB (Figure 5.16) is a temporary store used by Nessus to keep track of its progress and important information that'll be required later. For example, the KB will be used to store the list of open ports and the services that are believed to be listening on those ports. If "KB Saving" is enabled when the scan is run, the KB is saved to a text file that you can revisit when you read the report to help you understand what the scanner was "thinking." The KB for a given machine can usually be found at /usr/local/var/nessus/users/<your_nessus_user_name>/kbs/<target>. It's simple to read and is discussed in Chapter 9 at length. By looking in the KB, you can learn valuable information such as what plugins were run, what services Nessus associated with the different open ports, and the content of the "generic" HTTP error message.

Figure 5.16 NessusWX Client—Enable KB Saving So You Can View the KB When You Read the Report Later

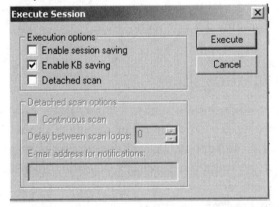

The Nessus Logs

If logging is enabled, the Nessus logfiles can also help you to better understand scanner output. The logs are covered in detail elsewhere in this book, so here are just a few specific categories of logfile entries that will often help shed light on the scanner findings:

```
user charl starts a new scan. Target(s) : 192.168.25.84, with max_hosts =
30 and max_checks = 10
```

This tells us that the scan was in fact launched against a specific target.

```
launching synscan.nes against 192.168.25.84 [24943]
```

This type of entry shows that a specific plugin was in fact launched. In this case, it's Nessus' own portscanner.

```
logins.nasl (process 24946) finished its job in 0.528 seconds
```

This type of entry tells us that the NASL completed without error. The time information can also be useful—a too-short completion time often suggests that the NASL didn't execute as expected.

```
Not launching swat_guessable_usernames.nasl against 192.168.25.84 none of
the required tcp ports are open (this is not an error)
```

This type of entry tells us that the specified NASL was never launched because the required ports were not identified.

```
Not launching apache_2_0_45.nasl against 192.168.25.84 because the key
www/apache is missing (this is not an error)
```

This type of entry tells us that the specified NASL was not launched because previously launched plugins did not identify an Apache web server on any of the scanned ports.

Forums and Mailing Lists

As an open-source product, Nessus enjoys support from a strong and vibrant user community. Renaud Deraison and the other members of the development remain actively involved in supporting and discussing the product and its use. Make use of this rich resource when using the product to learn about known bugs, quirky plugins, and advanced scanning techniques. While there are many resources on the web, the best place to start would probably be the Nessus site itself. Visit http://list.nessus.org/ or use a search engine to find what you're looking for.

Summary

Nessus is simply a tool that executes an extensive set of security tests over the network and can present you with the results in various different formats. To gain value from the scanner, you need to interpret the results of the tests yourself. To do this, you first need to understand the tests and how they are executed.

In this chapter, we liken learning to understand Nessus scanner output to learning to speak a new language. You need to understand both the "technical" (vocabulary and grammar) and the "cultural" (history and tradition) elements. In practical terms, you'll have to familiarize yourself with a number of different areas, from the theoretical definitions of "vulnerability" and "risk" to the technical details of the NASL language and the various scanner configuration settings.

We discussed that the Nessus tests are really thousands of different little programs written by separate individuals, all with different backgrounds and perspectives, and suggested some steps one could follow to really "understand" what was meant by a given report and what implication that would have with you.

Finally, we explored the impact the different scanner settings could have on the scanner results and highlighted some specific settings that could significantly impact the results of your scan.

Solutions Fast Track

The Nessus UI Basics

☑ Nessus works on a client-server model.

☑ There are currently two open-source GUI clients available: NessusWX for Windows and the Nessus UNIX client for X.

☑ A third open-source GUI client, called BOSS, is currently under development in Germany.

☑ There is also a UNIX command-line client that is not discussed in this chapter.

☑ Both GUI clients discussed allow one to view scanner output, save and export reports in various formats, and import results from previously saved reports.

☑ The two clients have different strengths and weaknesses and can be used in combination to achieve optimum results.

☑ Regardless of the client used, the Nessus scanner reports are detailed and complex and need to be carefully analyzed to be fully understood.

Reading a Nessus Report

☑ Nessus is a "vulnerability scanner." To understand Nessus reports, you need to first understand what "vulnerability" is.

☑ Risk is a much broader concept than vulnerability. With the risk more clearly quantified, we can compare the relative significance of the reports generated by a vulnerability scanner.

☑ When analyzing Nessus reports, one should temporarily put on a "black hat" and consider what vectors of attack the information being reported would present to an attacker.

☑ Use this thinking about attack vectors to put the risk represented by different vulnerabilities into perspective as you read through a Nessus scan report.

☑ To understand what a scanner report is saying, we need to understand how a scanner actually "thinks." Understanding scanner logic is key to understanding Nessus reports.

☑ A Nessus scan "report" consists of a number of "issues," which are in turn classified as "Holes," "Warnings," or "Infos." If you look at a Nessus issue, regardless of the client you used or the report format, there will always be certain key pieces of information for you to consider.

☑ A Nessus report is a little like a newspaper report and needs to be read with a critical eye. As you read the report, regardless of how the output is being displayed, you need to constantly ask yourself certain key questions about the content.

☑ Numerous settings and variables can impact scanner output and dramatically affect the contents of a Nessus report. You need to be aware of these as you read the report so that you can properly gauge the accuracy and the impact of the output. To help you fully understand a Nessus report, there are some alternative sources of information that you can explore. Studying these sources won't add to the report, but it might help you to better understand how the contents of the report were derived.

Frequently Asked Questions

The following Frequently Asked Questions, answered by the authors of this book, are designed to both measure your understanding of the concepts presented in this chapter and to assist you with real-life implementation of these concepts. To have your questions about this chapter answered by the author, browse to **www.syngress.com/solutions** and click on the **"Ask the Author"** form. You will also gain access to thousands of other FAQs at ITFAQnet.com.

Q: Of the two Nessus clients discussed in this book, which do you think is the best to use?

A: This chapter focuses on the "content" of a Nessus report and steers away from the details of the various "point-and-click" interfaces. In addition, as mentioned elsewhere in this chapter, our company has written its own interface to Nessus, which we try to use wherever we can to read and moderate reports, so it's hard to say that a particular client is "best." Nonetheless, if forced into a corner, we'd probably have to vote for the NessusWX client. The configuration is simple and far more intuitive than the X client, and the report format is much tidier than the X client is. However, the standard HTML generated by the X client is our favorite for reading reports in, and the X client does give you a higher degree of control over the configuration settings. We also use raw NBE format a lot when reading reports, as it allows us to rip through "pipes," "greps," "awks," and "cuts" very quickly.

Q: If the Nessus reports are so open to interpretation and have to be read as carefully as you suggest, aren't there other vulnerability scanners that can produce more accurate and dependable results?

A: In short: No. We really don't believe there are. This is not to say that Nessus is *better* than all other scanners, only that Nessus is not *worse*. We have two reasons for saying this. First, Nessus has consistently compared favorably with all kinds of commercial products in numerous independent reviews. While other products might have better report content or offer some features that Nessus doesn't, the Nessus scanner will always rate among the top performers in almost every important area, and most significantly so in the area of accuracy. Second, the factors that make reading Nessus reports such a skill are common to all vulnerability scanners that perform tests over the network. The same type of "prompt-and-response" logic applied by Nessus is also applied by *every* other scanner of this kind, and thus the scanners all face the same challenges. Whichever scanner you use, you'd have to learn to really "read" its reports, just as you do with Nessus. All things being equal, the dedication and approachability of Renaud and his team, along with the enthusiasm of the Nessus user community, and the "open" nature of the technology might make it easier to learn than other products, once you put your mind to it.

Q: You mentioned that you built your own software with which to moderate the scanner report and apply your own impact ratings. How exactly does this work?

A: We've built two interfaces, one in VB and one using CGIs, that allow us to quickly and easily import scanner output from the NSR format into a structured database. Once in the database, the software enables us to cross-reference our own vulnerability database, which is essentially an enhancement of the information provided in the NASL script, and also change the impact rating, add comments, and so forth. As the information is in a structured database, tasks such as searching, sorting, and mass updates become significantly easier, as does the generation of graphs, statistics, and other "management" information. Once we've finished "moderating" the reports, we can easily export them to any of the Microsoft Office products or view them using our own client interface. Please note that this software is a tool we use internally only and is not available commercially. We mention it only to demonstrate the approach and because we think that anyone who works with large Nessus reports would benefit from throwing something like this together. A few days' work in Microsoft Access with VBA should suffice to throw a rudimentary interface together.

Q: It's clear that the scanner configuration settings can dramatically impact the results of your scan. Is there then any "best" configuration to use?

A: Unfortunately, no. As you'll probably learn from this book, the scanner configuration will usually be a balance between accuracy and efficiency. The more accurate your scans, the bigger the impact, and the quicker you make the scans, the more chance you'll miss something. In terms of reading and understanding Nessus reports, the fact remains simply that you should have a grasp of the settings with which the scan was run when you read the report so that you can understand where the scanner is coming from. Without considering the scanner settings, you'll only ever have half the picture.

Chapter 6

Vulnerability Types

Solutions in this Chapter:

- **Critical Vulnerabilities**
- **Information Leaks**
- **Denial of Service**
- **Best Practices**

☑ **Summary**

☑ **Solutions Fast Track**

☑ **Frequently Asked Questions**

Introduction

When you run Nessus against your network, you might receive much more data than you bargained for. When staring at a massive report, how do you begin to know where to start fixing things, or where your real problems are? Understanding and classifying reams of vulnerability data will help you conquer the different types of vulnerabilities that have been found. Having a clear idea of what vulnerabilities are out there and in what order they need to be addressed will help you define a plan for fixing your problems most effectively.

We will begin by classifying vulnerabilities into four broad categories: critical vulnerabilities, information leaks, denial-of-service (DoS) vulnerabilities, and failure to implement best practices. Breaking down the types of vulnerabilities by type and potential impact makes it easier to realize what sorts of problems you have on your network and to provide additional information and guidance regarding the order in which the problems should be addressed.

Vulnerability classification is still an emerging field, and information security experts often have strong differences of opinion about the best way to deal with the thorny subject of classifying vulnerabilities. Some people maintain that classification should be done by the affected service, by severity, or by the operating system that is targeted. Still others take a more abstract approach, and it is this model that Nessus follows, classifying vulnerabilities by the potential impact of a successful exploit.

Critical Vulnerabilities

Critical vulnerabilities are your highest-priority problems. These represent vulnerabilities that, if exploited, could lead to code execution, privilege escalation, system compromise, or similarly dire consequences. Critical vulnerabilities should be addressed immediately due to the imminent threat to your network.

In a Nessus report, critical vulnerabilities are indicated by entries with the high- and medium-risk levels. The risk levels are set by the plugin developer and are based on a worst-case scenario of the vulnerability being successfully exploited. Several factors are weighed when considering whether a given flaw is considered critical: the ability of an attacker to exploit the flaw remotely, the privileges obtained after a successful attack, and whether the vulnerability is being actively exploited "in the wild." In general, your highest-priority vulnerabilities will be those that are remotely exploitable, do not require an existing user account on the affected system, will yield privileged access, and can be automatically and reliably exploited.

Many system administrators are already familiar with a wide range of critical vulnerabilities, mostly due to the large number of worms that take advantage of these vulnerabilities to propagate. The Sasser worm exploited a buffer overflow in the Microsoft Windows Local Security Authority Subsystem Service (LSASS); the Witty worm exploited an overflow in the ICQ protocol parser shipped with Internet Security System's IDS products; and the Slapper worm spread through a flaw in the OpenSSL library used in conjunction with the Apache Web server.

For another example of a critical vulnerability, one that wasn't turned into an automated worm or virus but is nevertheless a high-importance issue, consider the Solaris sadmind arbitrary command execution flaw. The default security settings of the sadmind RPC service allow a remote, unauthenticated attacker to execute arbitrary commands on a Solaris system as the root user. You can look at Nessus' reference page for this vulnerability at http://cgi.nessus.org/plugins/dump.php3?id=11841. Note that the risk factor is set to high, as befitting a vulnerability that would allow remote root compromise.

Notes from the Underground…

The 0-Day Market

As you might imagine, critical vulnerabilities are of the most interest to attackers, so much so that there's quite a market in the underground for new exploits, particularly those that have not been publicly disclosed or fixed by the vendor. Vulnerability scanners like Nessus will help you test your network quickly and comprehensively for known vulnerabilities, but keep in mind that new flaws are surfacing daily, many of which have been in private circulation for quite some time. This is one good reason that a vulnerability scanner is an important part of an in-depth defense, but it should never be considered the final word on whether a system is vulnerable to attack.

Critical vulnerabilities are common targets for network worms, Trojan horse programs, and automated attack tools. If your network is full of critical vulnerabilities, just one well-written worm can spell disaster and widespread compromise.

Even if your network has a solid border of tightly-configured firewalls, all it takes is one user with an infected laptop to trigger a cascade of automated attacks. The user might not even know that he's infected, but you'll certainly see the deleterious effects.

In addition to classifying critical vulnerabilities by their importance, we can also classify them by their type. Almost everyone who has worked a job that involves network security has heard of buffer overflows, but they're far from the only kind of exploitable vulnerability. Let's look at the different types of vulnerabilities that should also be considered critical:

- Buffer overflows
- Directory traversals
- Format string attacks
- Default passwords
- Misconfigurations
- Known backdoors

For this chapter's series of vulnerability explanations, let's assume that we have a well-meaning but clueless programmer/system administrator, "Bob," and a devious attacker, "Brian." This will give us a consistent framework for understanding how these vulnerabilities might be exploited and how they found their way into our systems in the first place.

Buffer Overflows

Buffer overflows are perhaps the most famous type of critical vulnerability. They are caused by a programmer's failure to limit the amount of information that can be written into a predefined buffer. When data is copied from one source (such as a network socket) into the buffer, an overflow can occur if the input data is greater than the size of the destination buffer. The programmer is responsible for checking the length value of the input prior to the copy operation.

If the length of input data is not checked, or the allocation routine for the destination buffer makes a mistake in the size of the input, the copy operation can result in memory corruption. Depending on where the destination buffer is stored in memory, this corruption can be used to hijack control of the vulnerable program. Although the exploitation details vary from platform to platform, nearly all buffer overflow flaws involving user input can result in the creation of a critical vulnerability.

For example, let's pretend that Bob has written an Internet chat system that requires users to provide their names when they connect. When developing this program, Bob uses a temporary 50-byte character buffer to store the name received from the connecting user. After all, nobody he knows has a name anywhere near that long, so 50 bytes should be more than enough room.

Now, assume that Bob's program becomes popular enough that he decides to sell it online. A copy falls into the hands of curious Brian. Brian installs the server and uses the Telnet program to connect to the service. The service asks for his name, but instead of giving it Brian, he sends a long repeated string of the letter "A." To his surprise, the chat server immediately closes his Telnet session and refuses to accept new connections. Brian then runs the chat server again, this time with the help of a debugging tool. After Brian sends the long string of "A" characters, the debugger shows that an exception occurred when trying to access the memory address 0x41414141 (the letter "A" has the hex value of 41).

Brian has seen this before. This appears to be a standard buffer overflow; the long name he provided has been copied over all other local variables in the vulnerable function and has continued on to trash program state information in the process's stack memory. This vulnerability can be exploited to run arbitrary code on the system, such as executing an interactive command shell.

Nessus uses a variety of techniques to identify network services that are vulnerable to buffer overflow attacks. When the vulnerable service runs inside a single process, it is usually not possible to actually test for the overflow without crashing the service completely. To work around this limitation, Nessus employs techniques such as version fingerprinting, banner matches, and even partial overflows to determine whether a given service is vulnerable.

Buffer overflows in real software are often somewhat more complicated than this, but usually not by much—the basic principles remain the same. In the last few years, buffer overflows have been discovered in products as diverse as gaim (OSVDB ID 3734, CAN-2004-0005), Mac OS X (OSVDB ID 3043, CAN-2003-1006), and Oracle (OSVDB ID 2449, CAN-2003-0727).

Directory Traversal

Directory traversal vulnerabilities are simply ways to access files outside a restricted directory structure. The best way to describe directory traversal attacks is by example. Let's assume our faithful but clueless Bob has installed an FTP server on his network. He has configured this server to only allow users to access the files in their home directories.

Brian has been given an account on this FTP server and is told to use it for backing up important files on his system. When Brian first connects to the FTP server, he notices that his current directory has been set to /home/brian. Being a curious-minded type, he tries to change his working directory to /home to see what other users have accounts on this system. The FTP server responds with an "Access Denied" message almost immediately; apparently, old Bob is trying to prevent people from snooping around on his server.

Like most modern operating systems, the system running the FTP server supports what are known as *parent paths*. A parent path is simply any path that references the special ".." directory name. This ".." directory always points to the directory above the current one. Brian realizes that this technique might apply against Bob's FTP server and gives it a whirl. Instead of sending a request to change to the /home directory, Brian simply asks the server to change to the ".." directory. To his glee, the FTP responds with an OK, and Brian is now able to see all of the files and directories in the /home directory.

If Brian is allowed to see the files in the /home directory, he might also be able to see system files. Consider the perils of allowing Brian to make a request like ".. /../../etc/passwd." Depending on the system configuration, access to this file could result in Brian obtaining the encrypted password hashes of all users on the system (including Bob). The encryption method used by the passwd file can be broken through an exhaustive brute-force attack, something at which any modern PC excels.

Nessus includes an impressive number of directory traversal plugins. These plugins test for traversal flaws in everything from Web applications to Trivial File Transfer Protocol (TFTP) services. The generic Web server traversal check is responsible for discovering flaws in dozens of embedded Web servers alone. Traversal flaws are one of the most common problems found with any protocol that maps user requests to local file paths.

In recent years, Apache (OSVDB ID 859, CAN-2002-0661), rsync (OSVDB ID 5731, CAN-2004-0426), and Microsoft's IIS (OSVDB ID 436, CVE-2000-0884) have all been found vulnerable to directory traversal attacks.

Format String Attacks

A format string vulnerability is another common error in the way user-supplied data is processed. In the C language, it is common to use the *printf()* functions to create and manipulate character strings. These functions take an argument known as the *format specifier*, followed by a list of values. A format specifier is simply a template, with special sequences known as *conversion specifiers* used as placeholders for the parts of the template that change.

For example, a program that prints out "Hello NAME," where NAME is something determined at runtime, will use a format specifier such as "Hello %s." The "%s" is the conversion specifier for a NULL-terminated character string. When we use this format specifier, the called function will expect a single argument after the specifier. This argument should be the memory address (pointer) of a NULL-terminated text string. The problem occurs when the format string specifier contains more conversion specifiers than there are arguments to the function. Instead of simply ignoring the extra "%" sequences, the function will use whatever happens to be in the process stack memory as the argument for the specifier.

These vulnerabilities are often found when the format specifier string is created based on data supplied by the user. If the user data contains a conversion specifier, such as "%s" or "%d," the function will try to process arguments beyond what was provided by the programmer. In most cases, this will lead to garbled output or a program crash. Talented attackers can craft their own sequence of conversion specifiers such that it results in arbitrary memory locations being written with whatever contents the attackers choose. Format string vulnerabilities are often used to overwrite a function pointer with the memory address of user-supplied data (usually shellcode). After the *printf()* function is called, any calls to the overwritten function will result in the attacker's code being executed.

Let's assume that Bob modifies his chat server to record the user's name in a log file. The following snippet of code reads the name of the new user over the network and writes it into the log file:

```
char *userdata = ReadUserName();
char *logstring = malloc(strlen(userdata)+6);
snprintf(logstring, strlen(userdata), "User: %s", userdata);
fprintf(logfd, logstring);
```

If the *userdata* character array contains a conversion specifier, the *fprintf()* call will access whatever memory happens to exist on the stack. For example, if *userdata* contains "%p" (the pointer specifier), the log file will end up with something like this:

```
User: 0xbfff601a
```

This hex value just happens to be the next value in the process's stack memory. Using conversion specifiers such as "%d" and "%n," it is possible to cause arbitrary memory locations to be overwritten, one or two bytes at a time.

Nessus checks for format string vulnerabilities in a variety of ways. Often, a version match against the service banner is sufficient to determine if the remote service is vulnerable; other times, long strings of conversion specifiers, such as "%n," are sent to force the service to crash. A few applications will actually return the resulting string to the remote client; these are tested by specifying a harmless specifier and then looking for the signature in the output.

In recent years, format string vulnerabilities have been discovered in a number of major products, including Solaris's rpc.rwalld (OSVDB ID 778, CVE-2002-0573) and Tripwire (OSVDB ID 6608, CAN-2004-0536).

Default Passwords

It is astonishing and depressing to realize how many systems are set up, configured, and deployed in the wild without anyone ever stopping to consider the peril of failing to change the password. Certainly, our bumbling Bob didn't consider that step necessary. Why, he set up his entire network without bothering to change the factory default passwords on any of the networking devices. All his Cisco routers still have logins of "cisco" and passwords of "cisco," all of his wireless access points (WAPs) are still advertising an SSID of "linksys," and he's proud of it. He considers it a measure of system administration—all those passwords are so hard to remember, after all.

Enter Brian the war-driver, stage left in a tiny VW Beetle with a huge antenna on the roof. As he passes Bob's place of employment, he detects a wireless network with a default "linksys" identifier. As an experienced war-driver, Brian has seen many different networks and is reasonably familiar with the standard usernames and passwords of most of the major pieces of networking equipment out there. Encouraged by the default SSID of the WAP, Brian pulls out his laptop, associates to the access point, and finds that a local DHCP server is more than happy to issue him an IP address. Looking at the IP and his new gateway to the Internet, Brian tries to connect to the gateway via Telnet. He sees a login prompt and tries "cisco" and "cisco" for the username and password. Just like that, he's in, and Brian now has a high degree of visibility and some degree of control over the router and Bob's connection to the Internet.

Once again, it can easily get worse. If Bob has also failed to change the enable password—the equivalent of the root account on a Cisco router—from its default setting, Brian might easily have just gained access to control the router entirely, which gives him a vast amount of power over Bob's network.

Nessus includes a massive set of plugins that test for common and default passwords. These plugins are able to identify default passwords on everything from SQL database servers to network printers. Default password vulnerabilities are extremely common on most sizable networks; many devices ship configured with a document default password. Not all system administrators are diligent about changing these default settings.

Misconfigurations

Let's take the following scenario, Bob has just been tasked with providing FTP access to the company's primary Web server, specifically to allow a Web design firm to update the content. Recalling his bad experiences with his own FTP server, Bob decides to use the tried-and-true Microsoft FTP Server that ships with Internet Information Server (IIS). While this service has had a few security problems in the past, it is already installed and would take all of five minutes to set up. Bob adds a new user account for the Web design firm, configures the FTP service to point to the Web content, and sends the account details off to his boss.

Brian is bored. He has been poking around on various FTP servers all day, looking for a place to store some illegal files for a friend of his. Bob's FTP server happens to be in the same IP range that Brian is scanning. Brian attempts to log in to the server, using the default "anonymous" credentials, and is greeted with a directory listing of the company's Web site. It appears that when Bob was configuring the new FTP service, he forgot to uncheck the "Allow anonymous access" option. The company's Web site has now been completely exposed, allowing anyone on the Internet to read and possibly modify the contents. Brian creates a hidden directory in the Web root and starts the slow process of uploading his illicit data to the server.

This particular misconfiguration is both extremely common and incredibly dangerous. One of the authors has seen an instance where the FTP service was used to backdoor the "secure login" page of a financial services organization. The intruder had simply downloaded the saved password log file once a day, for three months straight, until the backdoor was discovered. Anonymous FTP access is one of the many common misconfigurations that Nessus can detect.

Known Backdoors

The final type of critical vulnerability that we will discuss is the backdoor, or trojan horse program. These programs are designed to perform tasks such as logging keystrokes, hijacking the desktop, capturing passwords, or even relaying attacks to other systems. Given Bob's established lack of skill as a system administrator, it's quite likely that he has at least one system with a known backdoor on it. These backdoors are usually installed after an attacker has already compromised the system and wants to assure himself of having an easy and secret way to access the system later. Some backdoors, like Netbus and Portal of Doom, are quite well known. However, others are constantly being developed and discovered in the wild. Most often, a backdoor is a network service listening on an unexpected port on the compromised host, silently waiting for someone with the proper authentication credentials to log in. Many are silent upon connection until you send them the expected string, but some will actually prompt you for a login in identifiable and fingerprintable ways. Finding a known backdoor program listening on one of your systems is a critical vulnerability indicating not that you might be vulnerable to attack, but that you almost certainly have already been successfully attacked and compromised. Thanks to the global community of plugin developers, Nessus is able to detect and report a wide variety of backdoor programs. Plugins are being developed for each new backdoor as it is discovered.

Information Leaks

An information leak is a disclosure of information about your system. While it might seem at first that this isn't a big deal, in reality it can be one of the first steps in a devastating attack. Vulnerabilities classified as information leaks will allow an attacker to gather information about your system and to, in effect, conduct network reconnaissance.

Many system administrators wrongfully dismiss information leaks as a minor problem. While it's true that they don't pack the punch of a remote root compromise or other critical vulnerability, information leaks are still very real threats to your system. Let's look at some of the possible issues that can come up when information is leaked.

Notes from the Underground...

Social Engineering with Gleaned Information

One of the primary threats when dealing with information leaks is the possibility that attackers can take a little knowledge and turn it into a lot of knowledge. If they manage to discover the name of a system user or employee through a vulnerability that leaks this information, they might be able to pose as that user to the help desk and try to get their password changed. They might be able to pose as that user to the physical security department and get an official badge with their picture on it and some access rights. Moreover, they might just be able to start issuing arbitrary orders to other employees in that user's name. Depending on how well trained your employees are about social engineering, this security break might go unnoticed.

Gleaning information from a system can greatly aid or speed a technical attack. For example, consider the Lotus Notes OpenServer Information Disclosure vulnerability, viewable online at http://cgi.nessus.org/plugins/dump.php3?id=10795. In the default configuration of a Lotus Notes OpenServer, a remote client is able to browse databases on that server via HTTP, potentially learning server versions, log files, and server statistics. Let's see what a talented attacker could do with that information.

Knowing the version of a server will greatly help an attacker mount an attack. Instead of having to try exploits against all different possible versions of a server, the attacker can limit the attack to exploits that he knows will work against the version running. This will greatly speed up his attack and allow the attacker to maintain a lower profile in case network activity is being tracked by an intrusion detection system (IDS).

Being able to read the log files and server statistics will disclose even more valuable information. From the file sizes, an attacker can often determine how busy a server is, when the peak periods of activity are, and, conversely, when the server is likely to be little used. The attacker might also be able to gather usernames and authentication information—whether it's keyed or password, how many false tries are allowed before an account is locked, and so forth. This will give the attacker a better idea of how to mount an effective and undetected attack against the integrity of the server.

Now that we understand how information disclosure attacks can be a problem, let's look at some common types of information leaks, and how these can be used by a malicious attacker:

- Memory disclosure
- Network information disclosure
- Version information disclosure
- Path disclosure
- User enumeration

Memory Disclosure

One of the more common information leak vulnerabilities is memory disclosure. This problem occurs when a system forgets to clear a memory block before using it to construct a message that is sent to an untrusted party. Consider the memory block as a sheet of paper and the message itself as the graphite of a pencil. If the paper is not erased prior to a new message being written, any place on the paper that is not part of the new message could contain the contents of a previous message. The message in this case can be anything from an HTML page displayed by a Web server to an ICMP packet on the network.

Memory disclosure flaws have been discovered in everything from the Windows NetBIOS service to the network card drivers used across a wide range of operating systems. The actual impact of a memory disclosure vulnerability depends on what the affected system is doing and what the disclosed memory is used for. In some cases, this type of vulnerability can result in a remote attacker being able to capture passwords to and from the affected system.

For example, Linksys routers have a well-known vulnerability whereby they will respond to legitimate BOOTP requests with portions of the memory from their network cards in the payload (CVE-2004-0580). Given enough packets, an attacker might be able to analyze the network traffic passing through the device.

Network Information

One of the first things that any new attacker will want to do is understand your network topology. There are several ways to go about this, but most of them rely on information leaks of some sort. Once an attacker understands the topology and general configuration of your network, he can significantly lower his chances of being detected during an intrusion attempt.

Several network protocols are commonly used to obtain detailed information about the network. Simple Network Management Protocol (SNMP) is a very popular choice for configuration management, and many networks never bother to change their SNMP strings from the defaults of "public" and "private." Therefore, when Brian first attempts to scan Bob's network, a quick sweep to see which devices speak SNMP and whether they'll respond to the "public" and "private" strings is probably well worth his time. If the attempt is successful, Brian might garner all sorts of information about these devices, from their IP addresses and configuration details to their administrators' names and phone numbers. The particular details of what information is available will vary greatly between equipment vendors and their supported Management Information Bases (MIBs), but most will yield a rich harvest to an intelligent attacker.

ICMP messages are another very common method of charting a network. Depending on what devices will respond to what sorts of probes, you can learn things like the local default router, the timestamp on the devices, what ports they are and aren't listening on (which will aid in discovering what services they're running), whether they will accept source routing (most devices will not, but you never know), and other such juicy information. ICMP messages are likely to be one of the first tactics Brian employs to scan a network.

Version Information

Once hosts and basic network topology have been accounted for, the next step is to enumerate the services that are listening and to determine as much information about them as possible. Many services will advertise their vendor and exact version in the banner that is presented upon connection. Apache Web servers are fairly notorious for displaying detailed version information in the headers of every Web page they serve. For example, here are the server headers provided by a typical Apache server:

```
HTTP/1.1 200 OK
Date: Sun, 10 Aug 2004 10:17:11 GMT
Server: Apache/1.3.23 (Unix) (Red-Hat/Linux) mod_ssl/2.8.3 OpenSSL/0.9.6b
Content-Type: text/html
```

As you can see, the information returned from the Apache server includes some specific version numbers and the name of the Linux distribution on which the server is running. A talented attacker can take one look at this server string and immediately know which exploits have a high probability of working. In this specific case, Brian might choose to exploit a vulnerability in the OpenSSL library to gain remote access to this system. The most commonly used exploit for this vulnerability requires the attacker to know exactly what version and Linux distribution the server is running on to succeed in the attack. Brian can easily determine what versions of Red Hat Linux included version 1.3.23 of the Apache server and can simply choose the relevant options in the exploit code.

Many other servers are equally verbose—name servers running BIND are susceptible to disclosing their version through the *chaos txt* query; most versions of the Secure Shell server will advertise their version information during the protocol handshake, and Exchange mail servers will provide the exact release build number in the SMTP greeting message. Many Nessus plugins depend on exposed version numbers to determine whether a given service is vulnerable. This technique is used in situations in which there is simply no other way to safely check for a given flaw.

Path Disclosure

Path disclosure is one of the most commonly overlooked information disclosure vulnerabilities. A path disclosure flaw exists when a network service can be forced to return the local file or directory path for a given resource. This information can then be used to successfully exploit other flaws that depend on knowing the file path.

For example, Bob's personal Web site is hosted on a dedicated server at a large ISP. Bob has decided to start learning the PHP scripting language, which can be used to develop complex, dynamic Web sites in a short period of time. The PHP interpreter is often configured to display errors directly to the user when a problem occurs in the PHP script. This error normally contains the full path to the PHP script, the line number, and type of error that occurred. Bob has decided to create a database backend for his Web site; he makes the common mistake of placing the database username and password into a PHP script that is in the Web root. To make matters worse, this PHP script simply ends in the ".inc" extension, which means that anyone who knows the path to this file can simply download it.

Brian has developed a slight vendetta against Bob at this point; he is tired of seeing this incompetent wonk getting a fat salary. Brian has been prodding at Bob's Web site for quite some time, waiting for a chance to crack into the server and leave a nice message on the front page. As the weeks go by, Brian notices that a percentage of the Web site content appears to be pulled from a database. Brian whips up a quick script to send numerous parallel requests to one of the database-enabled pages on Bob's Web site. After Brian runs this script for a few minutes, the requests start returning a PHP error message indicating that the database server has reached the maximum number of connections. This error message happens to include the file path to the PHP script that called the database connect routine— the same PHP script that ends in ".inc" and is sitting unprotected in the Web root. Seeing this data, Brian figures out the virtual path in the Web directory and downloads this file. Five minutes later, Brian is ecstatic to discover that the password Bob uses for the database server is the same one set for the root user account on the dedicated server.

User Enumeration

The last type of information disclosure we'll discuss is user enumeration. It's certainly in Brian's interests to be able to discover legitimate account names on the system he is breaking into. A list of valid accounts will allow Brian to easily try common passwords for each account on the system, as well as increase his odds of a social engineering attack. User enumeration will allow him to map out which users might have accounts on multiple machines, thereby giving some hint as to departmental or functional organization of the network. There are multiple ways to do this, depending on the operating system and the service. Some operating systems, such as Microsoft Windows and Novell NetWare, will allow Brian to easily enumerate valid user accounts through file-sharing services.

Other services are vulnerable to a slightly different attack. Instead of simply providing a list of valid users, they allow a remote attacker to determine whether a specific account exists. A slightly obscure example is the OpenSSH Username Validity Timing Attack (OSVDB ID 2140, CAN-2003-0190), where a failed login as a legitimate user fails after a delay, and a failed login as a nonexistent user returns immediately. Using this technique, it would be possible for Brian to try usernames until he saw one with a delay. That way, even if he didn't have the password, he would know that a legitimate user account with that name existed on that machine.

As you can see, information leaks should be addressed whenever possible to prevent these types of attacks. They're not the glaring beacons of doom that critical vulnerabilities are, but they are one of the early targets of an attacker.

Denial of Service

Denial-of-service (DoS) attacks make an existing software service unavailable to the users, usually by either consuming all its resources—whether processor, memory, or network—or sending it some type of malformed signal that the service does not handle gracefully. This type of attack can be costly, in terms of both productivity and sheer finance. When a networked service is unavailable, you might lose employee hours, work, effectiveness, and business. Customers or potential customers might be turned away from an unavailable site and think less of your business because of it. The classic DoS attacks like WinNuke (a packet sent on port 139 that would cause the target machine to instantly bluescreen) and the Ping of Death (an oversized IP packet that exceeds the maximum size allowable for a packet) were just the beginning.

Currently, DoS attacks can be big business, or dirty business. Unscrupulous business folks have not hesitated to make sure that their competitors' networks were hit by a sudden and inexplicable stream of traffic that knocked them offline at just the wrong moment. This practice can be as grandiose as trying to extort payment from online sports bookies to ensure that they stay online and profitable during big betting events: "Nice server farm you've got here. Shame if something happened to it." Alternatively, it can be as petty as one person trying to knock the other offline entirely during the last few frantic minutes of bidding on a hotly contested item on eBay. In today's highly networked world, ensuring that you can access all your online resources whenever you want to is becoming ever more important.

In a more sinister approach, DoS attacks can also be used to cover a digital assault. If you know you need to do something, but that something will cause someone's IDS to light up like a Christmas tree, taking out that IDS before you launch your noisy attack is clearly to your advantage. Alternatively, you can deliberately occupy the system administrators' time and attention by flooding one machine with network requests while you launch a low-and-slow offensive on a different machine, hoping that the extremely busy and stressed system administrators will not notice.

There are several ways to launch a DoS attack. Attackers might attempt to drown your network connection in traffic, as in a distributed denial-of-service (DDoS) attack. This is the form of DoS with which most people are familiar, since the widespread DDoS attacks against major Internet sites like Yahoo.com, Microsoft.com, and sco.com have garnered a lot of press attention. However, it's not the form of DoS in which we are most interested. Nessus checks to see whether individual machines are vulnerable to DoS attacks through exploitation of the operating system or a service running on it. Through poor coding, software packages might allow excessive resource consumption, contain memory leaks, or just plain crash when they receive certain types of input. These are the DoS vulnerabilities that Nessus is concerned with and are the types of checks you'll see under this classification.

There is one important clarification to be made between different types of DoS checks. Some checks are merely banner grabs, looking for versions of software that are known to contain vulnerabilities that could lead to a DoS attack. Other checks will actually try to perform the DoS. In Chapter 8, we'll take a more in-depth look at the differences between these types of plugins.

Notes from the Underground...

Denial-of-Service Extortion Threats

An increasing and troubling trend in DoS attacks is the recent demand for payment to prevent attackers from launching a DoS attack on a system at a critical time. Silicon.com reports on the migrations of threats of this nature, from threatening online bookies right before a crucial match occurs to threatening businesses to maintain their uptime and reputation (www.silicon.com/software/security/0,39024655,39120157,00.htm). Incidents of this nature are a growing concern for ISPs, businesses, and the security community and are likely to continue to increase in frequency and severity.

Let's look at a recent example of a DoS attack, the Apache mod_ssl DoS of 2004, with Nessus-specific details available online at http://cgi.nessus.org/plugins/dump.php3?id=12100. A malformed SSL command (plain HTTP) sent to the HTTPS server running vulnerable versions of Apache with mod_ssl will trigger a memory leak, cause excessive memory consumption, and deny service to users trying to access the HTTPS server. This is a classic case of a DoS vulnerability through forced excessive use of local resources—in this case, memory utilization.

Best Practices

Best practices are a set of guidelines that define the industry-recommended way to implement a given product or solution. Although failing to adhere to best-practices might not expose a currently exploitable hole, it highlights a configuration or setup that is not in conformance with the industry's agreed-upon ideal deployment. Nessus reserves the best-practice category for vulnerabilities that are not an immediately exploitable threat but should nevertheless be changed or updated because the current setup is depreciated or suboptimal.

There are many available guides to best practices, as the following sidebar illustrates.

Tools & Traps...

Security Best-Practices Guides

A plethora of best-practices guides is availablefor network security and for administration of various types of systems. Here are a few, to give you an idea of the types of best practices being written:

- Cisco's "Network Security Policy: Best Practices White Paper" (www.cisco.com/warp/public/126/secpol.html) describes how to create a security policy, implement it, and respond to events.

- Microsoft's "Best Practices: Security Patch Management" (www.microsoft.com/business/reducecosts/efficiency/manageability/patch.mspx) describes different ways to patch your Microsoft systems optimally.

- Razvan Peteanu's "Best Practices for Secure Development" (http://members.rogers.com/razvan.peteanu/best_prac_for_sec_dev4.pdf) describes how to develop applications in a secure fashion.

Continued

- *ComputerWorld's* "Best Practices for Wireless Network Security" (www.computerworld.com/mobiletopics/ mobile/story/0,10801,86951,00.html) describes how best to securely deploy a wireless network.

Many more best-practices guides are on the market. We urge you to seek out the relevant guides for the type of network and devices you have and to read them to improve your security posture.

An example of a best-practices vulnerability is an HP printer that doesn't have a password set, as in http://cgi.nessus.org/plugins/dump.php3?id=10172. Although this does not match the classic definition of an exploitable vulnerability, the lack of authentication allows anyone to log in to the printer and change its settings, including its IP address. This is not configured ideally, and setting a password on the printer that only the rightful administrators know would greatly enhance the security of the printer. Following best-practices guidelines will make your network more secure against today's threats and against those that people in the industry see coming in the near future.

Summary

In this chapter, we looked at the different types of vulnerability classes that Nessus can analyze. Critical vulnerabilities are the most immediate and crucial threats to your network and are often the basis for worms and viruses. Critical vulnerabilities include privilege escalation, local and remote root exploits, and other major problems. Information leaks do not directly threaten the security of your machines themselves, but they divulge information that can be used to speed both technical and social attacks. Denial-of-service (DoS) vulnerabilities do not grant privileges or code execution to the attacker, but can be used to knock a functional machine offline, costing you wasted time and effort and potentially affecting your customer's view of your reliability. Best-practice vulnerabilities follow the recommended guidelines of the product manufacturer and industry experts to produce the most proactively secure configuration and setup possible.

Solutions Fast Track

Critical Vulnerabilities

- ☑ Critical vulnerabilities are immediate threats to your network and systems security.

- ☑ The exploitation of a critical vulnerability could lead to execution of arbitrary code, unauthorized privilege escalation, or some similarly crucial and high-impact consequence.

- ☑ Nessus separates critical vulnerabilities as a classification to allow the most important vulnerabilities to be addressed first.

Information Leaks

- ☑ Information leaks can disclose system or user information to an attacker.

- ☑ Data gathered from information leaks can often be used to get a foot in the door and establish credibility for a later social-engineering attack.

- ☑ Data gathered from information leaks can also be used to speed and fine-tune technical attacks, such as feeding harvested usernames to a password-cracking program.

☑ Data gathered from information leaks can also be used to target a specific vulnerability by disclosing the version of operating system or server software in use.

Denial of Service

☑ DoS vulnerabilities cause a normally available service to become unavailable. This can take the form of resource consumption, server downtime, or the crashing of operating systems.

☑ Although a DoS vulnerability is usually addressed soon after the attack traffic stops, it can still have a significant impact on business.

☑ DoS attacks can cause entire machines to crash or require a hard reset in order to restore service.

☑ DoS attacks will not lead to direct compromise in and of themselves, but they can be used to decrease the public's confidence in a business.

Best Practices

☑ Best practices are industry guidelines for implementation and maintenance agreed upon by the community.

☑ Although they are not reports of direct threats, best-practice recommendations would improve your security stance in the face of possible future threats.

☑ Savvy system administrators or security engineers will read best-practice guidelines as pertaining to their networks and attempt to make proactive improvements.

Frequently Asked Questions

The following Frequently Asked Questions, answered by the authors of this book, are designed to both measure your understanding of the concepts presented in this chapter and to assist you with real-life implementation of these concepts. To have your questions about this chapter answered by the author, browse to **www.syngress.com/solutions** and click on the **"Ask the Author"** form. You will also gain access to thousands of other FAQs at ITFAQnet.com.

Q: If a vulnerability can cause a denial of service and/or remote code execution, is it usually classified as a DoS or as a critical vulnerability?

A: In classification, the worst real possibility is usuallyconsidered the most important. Therefore, if the remote code execution is feasible, if there is proof-of-concept code, or if someone has shown how it could be done, the vulnerability is critical.

Q: Does the classification of a vulnerability in one of the four categories tell me everything I need to know about it?

A: No. In addition to the class the vulnerability belongs to, you should also consider which of your machines it's on, what defenses you have, how severe the vulnerability is, and what damage you could suffer if it were exploited. Some machines are more important than others, and some vulnerabilities will be more devastating than others.

Q: If a vulnerability is just a best practice, do I really need to care?

A: Yes, but how much will depend on your security policy and staffing. If you are very low on system administrator time, it's probably better to deal with the most important and most critical vulnerabilities first. Patch your gaping holes, and then get proactive.

Q: If a DoS vulnerability is exploited, will my machine restore itself when the attack traffic stops?

A: Some will, some won't. It depends entirely on the targeted machine and service.

Q: How do I know how much of a problem the information that I'm leaking is?

A: You might want to hire a penetration tester or security consultant to advise you, but consider whether any of that information could be used to identify avenues of further technical or social attack. How much? The damage is limited, mostly by your creativity in using the available information.

## Chapter 7

False Positives

Solutions in this Chapter:

- **What Are False Positives?**
- **Why False Positives Matter**
- **Nessus and False Positives**
- **Dealing with False Positives**
- **Dealing with a False Positive**

☑ **Summary**

☑ **Solutions Fast Track**

☑ **Frequently Asked Questions**

Introduction

Just short of missing a vulnerability, false positives (FPs) are any scanner's worst nightmare. A false positive is the inverse of a vulnerability that slipped past the scanner; the scanner reports a vulnerability when one doesn't exist. This chapter discusses what false positives are, why they are a major issue, categories of false positives, how to deal with false positives (specifically within the Nessus framework), and finally looks at some real-world examples on finding and eradicating false positives.

What Are False Positives?

Per Wikipedia—the Free Encyclopedia—"A false positive is when a test incorrectly reports that it has found what it is looking for" (http://en.wikipedia.org/wiki/False_positive). The encyclopedia correctly goes on to point out that false positives occur in all kinds of detection algorithms.

For a number of different reasons, network-based vulnerability scanners are particularly plagued by this problem. Aside from the often-vague definitions of a technical vulnerability, numerous variables and other external factors can affect the results of the test. As exploiting the actual vulnerability is seldom an option, and as a vulnerability scanner will always err on the side of caution, false positives are relatively common.

This issue is not unique to Nessus and will also affect every other scanner, whether commercial or open source. Indeed, as we will see later in this chapter, Nessus provides a number of checks and balances to ensure that false positives are kept to a minimum.

A Working Definition of False Positives

Although false positives are a known and recognized phenomenon in scientific testing, they have a very real and practical impact on the Nessus user.

For the purposes of this chapter, we're going to move a little beyond the strict, technical definition of a false positive, and also include reports that, while technically accurate, are misleading, irrelevant, or insignificant in the given context. Thus, we define two classes of "false positives":

- **Technical false positives.** These are false positives in the narrow, technical sense of the word where, for some reason, the test incorrectly returns a positive result. Specific categories of false positive found in this class include:

- **Buggy scripts.** These FPs are created when a plugin is not working correctly—because of a problem within the plugin, or within the Nessus scanner itself. Scriptwriters occasionally misunderstand the problem they're testing for, oversimplify the test, or simply make logical errors, which can cause the script to misbehave.

- **Check is technically accurate, but the service is actually patched.** A real-world example of this could be the plugin *msadcs_dll.nasl* (written by the author), which checks for the "RDS / MDAC Vulnerability." The script tests if the msadsc.dll DLL is located on the machine by sending an HTTP *GET* request for the DLL at its default location. If the DLL exists, it generates a report. However, the script has no way of knowing whether the DLL is patched, thus often resulting in a false positive. The same is true of the many scripts that rely on service banners (such as SSH, POP3, FTP, HTTP servers, and so forth). Very often, the service itself it patched, but still displays an old banner, referred to as a "backport." While Nessus does provide some mechanisms to help plugin writers counter this (see the plug-in script *backport.inc)*, many plugins still see the old banner and still report the service as vulnerable, resulting in a false positive.

- **Check is positive due to the service misbehaving.** This typically happens when a custom-made (or home-grown) application is involved. For example, some add-ons for web servers could trigger certain plugins, resulting in an FP. Another example is plugins that check for a vulnerability by determining if a service still responds after a number of checks. The script *msftp_dos.nasl* is a good example of this: it connects to a Microsoft FTP server, logs in, and sends a string that causes a buffer overflow. It then attempts to send a HELP request and waits for a response. If the FTP server fails to respond to the second request, the NASL assumes it has crashed and reports it as vulnerable. Now, if the service becomes temporarily unavailable between the first request and the second request, the NASL can mistakenly interpret this as a crash and falsely report the server as vulnerable. A number of circumstances could lead to such a temporary unavailability of the service. One simple example is load. Security technologies, like shunning firewalls, can also create this type of behavior, as can regular firewall, transparent proxies, and intrusion prevention systems (IPSs).

- **Contextual false positives.** These are results generated by NASLs that are technically correct, but might not be significant, or *as* significant as the script suggests. Such results might therefore be considered false positives, but only in the context of the specific environment in which they're being run. There are various categories of contextual false positives:

  - **Check is positive, but issue is mitigated.** These are the cases where the scanner reports a problem, the problem really exists, but the owner of the network needs to live with the problem. An example of this is when a server cannot be patched, as the patch affects the normal operation of an application. In such cases, the network administrator or security officer might have implemented a workaround or some form of mitigation.

  - **Check is positive but conditions apply.** This class of false positives also falls under the broader definition of the term. An example of this would be a script that correctly identifies a service that is vulnerable, but the attacker needs valid credentials to use the exploit. Basically, the plugin isn't smart enough to understand that the issue is there, but not exploitable. Depending on the level of security required for an environment, this might be a valid problem or could be classified a false positive. One should also take into account that some scripts do try to consider context. Take, for example, *wu_ftpd_site_exec.nasl*—a script that tests for a bounds-checking problem in some versions of wu-ftp. If script can log in to the server, it will run specific accurate tests for the vulnerability. Without credentials, the script will only parse the banner and test for vulnerable version numbers. The output of the NASL will inform you as to which of these methods was used.

  - **Check is positive but not relevant.** Here we're referring to tests that are technically accurate but, because of the *context* within which they are run, can safely be ignored. For example, the Nessus scanner does not know if the scan is launched from inside or outside a network perimeter. Issues that could be interesting from an external point of view could be irrelevant if the scan was conducted from within the perimeter. For example, the NASL script *bind_query.nasl* (also written by one of the authors) tests for DNS servers that allow recursive queries to be performed. This behavior could be considered a vulnerability on the Internet, but is probably perfectly legitimate on the internal network. This NASL generates a "Serious' report," but points out that context is important: "If this is your internal nameserver, then forget this warning." The script *traceroute.nasl* simply displays the traceroute information from the scanner to the target. This information is also very likely to be irrelevant on an internal network.

Notes from the Underground…

"Vulnerable" vs. "Exploitable"

There is always some debate in the community as to whether a scanner should detect vulnerabilities or only issues that can actually be exploited. Our feeling is that a scanner's job is to detect *vulnerabilities*, and it is the analyst's job to determine *risk*. In making this determination, the analyst will factor in questions like how difficult or easy the problem is to exploit. The scanner should always err on the side of caution—perhaps even paranoia.

For a less-experienced Nessus user, this differentiation can be hard to make. Such a user wants the scanner to say either "be worried" or "don't be worried." It is with such users in mind that we discuss the broader class of false positives referred to as *contextual false positives*.

Most false positives will fall in one of these categories, each of which has its own challenges. In the next section, we provide ways to spot an FP, and how to deal with it.

Why False Positives Matter

Why are FPs such a big deal? Surely, it would be better if the scanner detects more holes (even if they do not exist) rather than missing something crucial.

You'll sometime hear it said that the purpose of a security assessment is to help direct IT managers as to how they should invest valuable time, money, and human resources when it comes to security. The information generated by a vulnerability assessment, if accurate, can be a valuable decision-making tool. If the information is inaccurate, however, it will have exactly the opposite effect and end up wasting time, money, and human resources. Let's examine these issues individually.

False Positives Waste Your Time

The problem with false positives really becomes known when one starts looking at a large number of hosts. Imagine scanning 200 hosts; each host with 5 FPs and 25 real problems (in other words, 20 percent of the reports are false positives). If we spent three minutes on each FP determining that it is indeed false, we have wasted 200 hosts x 5 FPs x 3 minutes = 50 hours or 2 days; compared to the 10 days we'll spend on the real problems. Running Nessus regularly on these hosts becomes a nightmare—we simply don't have enough time to go through every issue. One might argue that once one finds an FP on one host, you might classify it as an FP on all the hosts—reducing the time significantly. This is a dangerous assumption, as you might miss the one host where the scanner was not wrong, and this hole could be the one used by a hacker to compromise your network.

False Positives Waste Others' Time

Of course, FPs can also waste other people's time. If security people pass bad scanner information on to the technical people actually responsible for the hosts in question, then *those* people have to waste their time attempting to understand and fix a problem that isn't there. Often, the information is "bounced" several times between the technician and the security person before it is finally agreed that the report is "false" and can safely be ignored. This will always be a frustrating experience and does little to win support for the scanner, the scanning process, or the security team. We touch on this issue a little later in this chapter.

False Positives Cost Credibility

We all know that security is a process, and often a process that's not very welcome within business. Thus, the security officer is constantly engaged in a battle of hearts, in which she tries to win IT managers, technicians, and developers over to a "secure" way of thinking. Too many false positives can cause horrible setbacks in this process. The reason for this can even be described mathematically.

If we assume that there are X number of checks within the scanner, the scanner produces FP number of false positives, P number of real problems (positives), and N number of negatives—FP+P+N=X. Let us take this equation to the extreme: a report stating that a host is vulnerable to everything the scanner checks for (for example, FP=X) is just as useless as a report stating that the host is not vulnerable to any of the checks (for example, N=X). The other extreme—when there are no FPs and the scanner only reports real vulnerabilities (P+N=X, or FP=0)—seldom occurs; it is a situation we strive toward.

This type of "bad" information will also quickly shed a bad light on the scanner, the scanner operator, and perhaps the entire security division. After a sufficient number of bad reports, the vulnerability assessment information will never again be taken seriously.

Generic Approaches to Testing

The mechanics of vulnerability testing have been debated on mailing lists and newsgroups for years. There are two methods to test for a vulnerability—call them "intrusive" and "nonintrusive." As we will see in the sections that follow, both approaches have pros and cons.

An Overview of Intrusive Scanning

The first way to test for a vulnerability is to actually exploit the vulnerability and determine if the exploit was successful. Let us look at an example. Imagine that a Microsoft IIS web server is vulnerable to the IIS WebDAV overflow (MS03-007). Exploiting this vulnerability under the correct circumstances leads to an IIS crash and full command execution with SYSTEM privileges. Renaud Deraison wrote a script that can check for this problem on a web server in an "intrusive" way: it sends the string *SEARCH /AAAA.....AAAA* (with 65535 As) to the web server within a WebDAV request. A vulnerable IIS server will crash on receiving this, and the script tests for this by checking if the HTTP server is "dead." It's an accurate way to test, but has the obvious drawback of leaving a trail of crashed IIS servers in its wake.

An Overview of Nonintrusive Scanning

There is another way to detect the WebDAV vulnerability described in the previous section—this time without actually exploiting it—and Renaud's *iis_webdav_overflow.nasl* can take this approach as well. Instead of actually sending data that will crash the IIS server, the script sends a WebDAV SEARCH request and parses the response for an HTTP 411 error code. If the error is received, the script reports a vulnerability, but with a disclaimer that "Nessus did not actually test for this flaw." In essence, this approach to testing relies on the fact that the server is IIS 5.0 and supports the WebDAV methods. It has no way of knowing whether the necessary service packs or hotfixes have been installed. Thus, this approach to testing can be significantly less accurate, but with the advantage that one doesn't have to keep rebooting IIS servers.

However, testing for vulnerabilities by actually exploiting them has other problems as well. In many cases, we cannot predict the behavior of a system when the exploit is run. In such a case, the scanner would not report the problem—although it actually exists (a false negative).

Moreover, many exploits leave the target server in an unpredictable state. An exploit that uses buffer overflow techniques can easily crash a server (or service). Nessus never uses exploit code, but rather tests for buffer overflows using random data. In a test environment, this might not be a problem, but crashing your company's production server will not win you any friends. Determining if the exploit actually worked is also not as easy as it seems. Let us assume that our exploit or method gives us the ability to execute any command on the target server, but we cannot see the output of the command (think SQL injection). How do we know if our command really executed? We could try to send Internet Control Message Protocol (ICMP) ping packets to ourselves, but what if the firewall (ours or theirs) blocks ICMP ping requests?

In addition, Nessus cannot use third-party hosts to test vulnerabilities—all the information needed to verify the existence of a vulnerability must travel between the target and the Nessus server. As such, Nessus is restricted from using some of the more advanced techniques used by exploit code in the wild.

It should be clear that intrusive tests aren't always better than nonintrusive tests. This cuts to the very heart of the issue of false positives—very often, there is simply not enough information available with which to indisputably determine whether a vulnerability exists.

Notes from the Underground…

Is Nessus a "Hacking" Tool?

It is important to note here that Nessus, unlike exploit codes, does not in any case install malicious content, malicious agents, or any other form of malware on the tested servers—an unfortunate misconception that we want to avoid in this book. To ensure all Nessus scripts are harmless, each plugin is reviewed by Renaud Deraison. This is further enforced by the fact the plugins themselves are open source, and open to scrutiny by the Nessus community.

The Nessus Approach to Testing

The Nessus scanner has the capability to use both methods of testing described in the previous section. The Nessus user can specify which approach she prefers by setting the *safe checks* configuration option. This option doesn't affect the behavior of the scanner, but should be considered by the individual NASL script when determining what approach to take. Bear in mind that the Nessus engine itself does not actually perform the checks—they are executed by third-party plugins. If the *safe checks* flag is set, the NASL may not use intrusive tests. If *safe checks* is *not* selected, the scanner will try to determine if the vulnerability exists, even if testing it could potentially crash the service. The Nessus engine only passes the setting to the plugin; the plugin decides what to do with it. Thus, many NASLs can test either "intrusively" or "nonintrusively" and select which approach to take based on the *safe checks* option. Not all NASLs have this capability, however, and the majority of scripts can only perform nonintrusive tests. At the time of this writing, there are approximately 4600 plugins, of which about 130 are "safe check" aware.

Setting plugins to use safe checks in Nessus is easy. The *safe check* option can be set as a property of an individual scan. Figure 7.1 shows the results of right-clicking on a scan, and selecting the Options tab in Windows NessusWX (version 1.4.2-HF1).

Figure 7.1 Results of the Safe Check Option

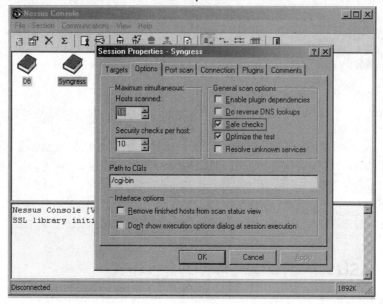

The same setting can be found on the UNIX client under Scan Options in Figure 7.2.

Figure 7.2 UNIX Client, Scan Options

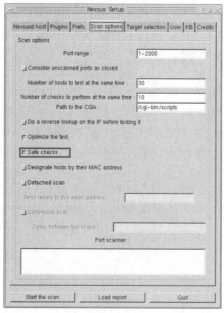

Dealing with False Positives

It should be clear by now that scan reports will sometimes contain false positives, which need to be routed out for the scan information to be useful.

Dealing with Noise

One of the biggest hindrances to spotting false positives is what we call "noise." These are reports that are technically correct but are uninteresting or irrelevant and make it hard for us to see the truly important issues. A Nessus report for hundreds of hosts, conducted from inside a perimeter, can be intimidating. One can very easily be lulled into marking real issues as FPs because the amount of data returned by the scanner is overwhelming. The first thing you want to do when trying to eliminate false positives is to move aside the "noise." The following steps can help to reduce several hundreds of possible vulnerabilities to a manageable amount of information to analyze:

1. **Identify vulnerabilities common to all hosts.** We have two different scenarios here: first, a specific plugin could misbehave in the particular environment, causing it to trigger on all hosts. A typical example is when dealing with a transparent proxy—the scanner will pick up port 80 open on all possible hosts, as the proxy picks up all the connections. The other scenario could be that all the hosts are vulnerable to a specific issue; for example, the Simple Network Management Protocol (SNMP) is enabled with a commonly used community string. In such a case, one would not want to report the issue on each host, but rather globally on all hosts.

2. **Remove issues that are not applicable.** While the traceroute to a host might be interesting from outside the perimeter, it does not carry much information when the scan is conducted on the same network segment. Other issues that fall in this category could include predictable TCP sequence numbers, ICMP timestamp replies, and so forth.

3. **Remove some of the issues only classified as informational.** This really depends on the environment in which you work in—in some cases, you should retain these issues. Issues could include SSL cipher information, port identifications (for example, "a web server is running on this port"), and OS identification.

Once one's removed some of the "noise" in this way, one can start concentrating on the "real" issues; typically, medium, high, or critical issues that do not appear to be false positives. False positives still found in the remaining reports typically fall into the category of misbehaving services or patched services.

Analyzing the Report

From this point on, the detection of false positives is difficult and essentially requires one to examine and analyze each reported issue. Issues that prove to be FPs can be marked as such or removed from the list. Here's a simple method you can apply in this process:

1. **Understand your "environment."** Earlier we discussed a broad category of false positives we labeled "contextual," and explained how these reports are technically accurate but irrelevant or less relevant because of the specifics of the context within which the tests are run. For the purposes of this chapter, such issues are also classified as false positives. With sufficient knowledge of the systems being tested, many FPs are quickly identified and eliminated because it's clear that they can't be accurate or aren't relevant.

2. **Understand the problem.** We need to understand the vulnerability— why it is a vulnerability and how it could be exploited—even if we have to do it manually. Many forums, web sites, and mailing lists deal with vulnerabilities—in fact, when you start to Google for vulnerabilities, you might find yourself flooded with information. From all these sources of information, the following four sites have proven over the years to be current, reliable, and easy to use:

   a. **www.packetstormsecurity.net** Notice the search functionality at the top of the site. Enter some keywords of the vulnerability there and you will soon be on your way to papers, exploit code, and good descriptions of the problem.

   b. **www.securityfocus.com** As the official Bugtraq mailing list archive site, it has been a favorite for ages. Click on the Vulnerabilities tab and enter the world of Bugtraq IDs (BIDs). A vulnerability can be found by searching on vendor and version, BID, CVE ID, title, or keyword. Every vulnerability has a Discussion, Exploit, Info, Solution, and Credits tab.

c. **www.osvdb.org** The Open Source Vulnerability Database, run and funded by individuals (unlike SecurityFocus, which has corporate backing) had humble beginnings, but has grown over the years to be an invaluable resource. The OSVB also uses identification numbers (OSVDBid); they are cross-linked to other IDs such as BID, CVE-ID, and ISS Xforce ID. The search functionality on the site allows searches to be performed on, among others, Nessus Script ID.

d. **www.securiteam.com** Backed by Beyond Security, SecuriTeam is known for their precise and thorough descriptions of vulnerabilities.

All of the preceding sites allow us to search for information on a specific problem, but the site's description of the problem might vary. Almost all of the Nessus plugins include a CVE ID. The CVE ID does not point to the actual issue, but rather acts as a standardized description dictionary of the issue. By searching on CVE number, we can find the standard description of the problem, and then use this description to search on the sites mentioned previously. A nice CVE ID and keyword search interface can be found at www.cve.mitre.org/cve/. Some sites like SecurityFocus and OSVDB allow us to search directly by CVE ID, Bugtraq ID, or keyword.

3. **Understand the plugin.** Once we understand the vulnerability and how the plugin works, we can begin to determine if it is indeed a false positive and into which category it would fall. To understand how a particular plugin works, you should understand the individual components and commands of the plugin. Plugins are written in a scripting language called NASL. A great source of information on this is the *Nessus Attack Scripting Language Reference Guide*, which can be found at www.nessus. org/doc/nasl.html. This document describes all the different function calls, operators, and basic syntax.

4. **Manually Verify the Results.**

a. **With the scanner.** After the environment has been changed, a patch has been applied, the scanner host (the box where Nessus is executed from) has been given elevated privileges, or scan options has been changed, we can simply run the scanner again.

b. **With other scanners.** While Nessus is one of the best scanners around, it is not the only scanner. Comparing results from different scanners is not a bad idea—in a perfect world, all scanners should have the same set of results.

c. **With NASL.** With most installations of Nessus, you will find a command-line utility called NASL (on a FreeBSD standard installation, this utility is located in /usr/local/bin/, but could vary from installation to installation). This utility allows the user to execute basic plugins directly from the command line. In some cases, using NASL directly will not give you the desired results—the NASL utility does not have the same intelligence as the actual Nessus scanner. It won't, for instance, enable SSL within the plugin if you run an HTTP-based plugin against an SSL-enabled web server. Despite this, the NASL command-line utility provides us with a quick way to test a basic plugin.

d. **By "hand."** If you've examined a NASL script and have a basic understanding of what it does, you can usually reproduce the test by hand. Here are some of the tools you'll commonly use for this:

i. **Telnet/Netcat** Some problems can be verified by simply connecting to the relevant port, sending a particular string to the service, and monitoring the output. This can easily be done using a telnet client (standard on both UNIX and Windows), or, for more advanced cases (for example, where binary data is involved), using Netcat. Source and binaries for Netcat can be found at http://netcat.sourgeforge.net.

ii. **Browser** Many HTTP(s) based problems can be reproduced by simply using a browser. Do not underestimate the power of a browser!

iii. **Using the relevant client** Of course, not all problems can be reproduced/tested using a browser or telnet. Obtaining the correct client for the service in question is always a good idea. For example, if the scanner reports VNC (remote administration software) with a blank password on a host, you might consider getting the VNC client and verifying that it is indeed the case.

iv. **Exploits** As a last resort, you can consider getting the actual exploit for the problem. Many web sites mentioned in the previous section also provide exploit code.

e. **Manual on-host inspection.** One of the best ways of verifying if a problem really exists is to manually inspect the target—by logging in locally on the target. This is not always feasible, as the target might be physically in a different location, or you might not have credentials to access the host. By checking locally on the target you can easily find out if, for example, it is indeed not running a specific service pack.

> **NOTE**
>
> Keep in mind that some exploits could crash the server or service, that many exploits are "broken" on purpose, and that some exploits are intended to cause damage to your own (attacker's) system to discourage script kiddies from using them. In many cases, a service is only potentially or theoretically exploitable. This means that a vulnerability has been found, but that the proof of concept (or exploit) has not been released. Just because an exploit is not circulating "in the wild" does not mean that the service is not vulnerable and that the issue can be marked as an FP!

False Positives, and Your Part in Their Downfall

Nessus is an open-source scanner, and plugins are written by individuals all over the world. Although the Nessus team takes great care in plugin quality control, they are human. Because hosts can be installed in many different environments and services typically have many installation options, plugins are likely to cause a false positive in a "nonstandard" environment.

If you find that a plugin does not perform as it is supposed to, you can help make it better by describing the environment, server settings, and conditions where it caused a false positive. Providing this feedback will help raise the quality of the plugin (and therefore the entire scanner), making it work better for everyone. There are a number of ways to give feedback:

- Contact the author of the plugin. Almost all plugins contains the author's e-mail address.

- Describe the problem on the Nessus mailing list and monitor the list for a response.

- If all else fails, send an e-mail to bugs@nessus.org.

Be sure to check the Nessus FAQ and the mailing list archives before asking questions or giving feedback—it is very possible that someone else already raised the question or someone has responded to the same feedback.

Dealing with a False Positive

Once we have identified an FP, we can now "treat" it in a couple of ways. The following options come to mind:

- **Leave it as an FP.** We know a particular problem is an FP and we treat it as such. This approach works nicely in a small environment, when one only looks at one or two hosts, when there are not many results (typical when looking at a properly firewalled environment), or when the results are not used by other people. As soon as we are looking at a larger number of hosts or issues, this becomes a problem—for example, "I cannot remember if problem XXX on host YYY is really an FP anymore." Reports used by more than one person are also a problem—person A might know that issue X is an FP, but person B has no idea of knowing unless she verifies it manually (again).

- **"Fix" your host or environment.** Even if you know your host is not vulnerable to a particular issue, try to understand the way the plugin tests for it and try to fix it. This could be as simple as recompiling a service or changing a banner. This way, the plugin will behave as it should and will never generate an FP on the host again.

- **Disable the plugin.** When disabling a plugin, you need to keep in mind that the plugin will be disabled for all hosts in the scan—while it might generate FPs for some hosts, it might work perfectly for others. In totally disabling the plugin, you could risk missing some real vulnerabilities on other hosts.

- **Treat or change the particular plugin yourself.** This is a very dangerous option. The plugin was written in a particular way. The fact that it generates an FP on your host does not mean it contains bugs; rather, your host or environment is misbehaving. Rather, contact the author of the plugin to explain your environment—most authors are happy to adapt the plugin.

Disabling a Nessus Plugin

Disabling a plugin for a particular scan is easy. We will show you how you can do this using both the UNIX and Microsoft clients. For our example, we will assume that the plugin with ID 12105 (LDAP information leak) is causing a false positive.

Disabling a Plugin with NessusWX

Using the NessusWX Windows client:

1. **Start the client and define a new scan.** Go to **Session -> New** and give it an appropriate name. We'll use "Syngress-12105-disabled" as in Figure 7.3.

Figure 7.3 Client Started with a New Scan Defined

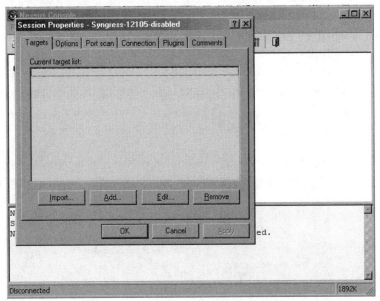

Click on **Plugins** and select **Use session-specific plugin set**. Our selection will only apply to this particular session. Now, click **Select plugins** as shown in Figure 7.4.

Figure 7.4 Selecting the Plugins

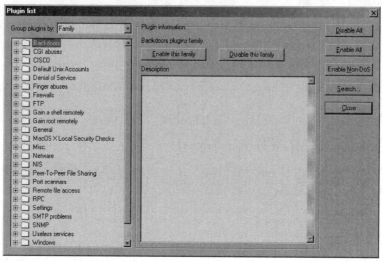

2. **Find the plugin you want to disable.** This is not always as easy as one might think, as the description of the plugin and the output of the plugin might not match. In addition, version NessusWX 1.4.2 does not give the user the ability to search per plugin ID, neither does it show it when the plugin is selected. After some searching, we find our plugin in the "remote file access" section, as shown in Figure 7.5.

Figure 7.5 Plugin within the Remote File Access Section

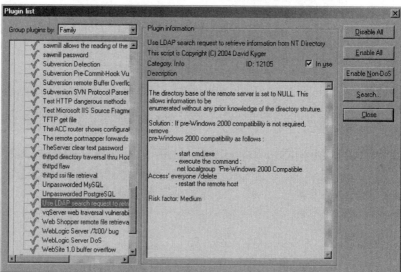

3. **Disable the plugin.** The plugin is currently "in use." To disable it, we unselect this box. After clicking **Close**, we view the plugin set again and voilà – it appears to be disabled, as shown in Figure 7.6.

Figure 7.6 Disabling the Plugin

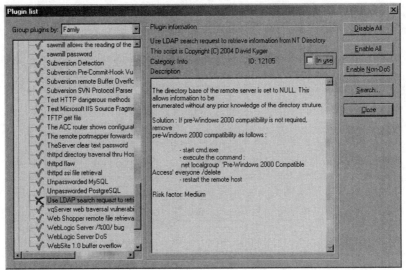

Scans run from this session will now ignore this check.

Disabling a Plugin Under UNIX

Disabling the plugin in the Nessus UNIX client is even easier:

1. **Start the client and log in.** Go to the **Plugins** tab, as shown in Figure 7.7.

Figure 7.7 Plugins Tab

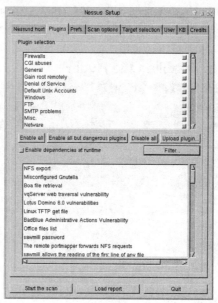

2. **Find the plugin to disable.** Here we will use the Filter functionality to assist us in finding the plugin. We click on **Filter**, select **ID number**, and enter the plugin ID (12105) in the **Pattern** field. When we click **OK**, the category and details of the plugin are displayed (see Figure 7.8).

Figure 7.8 Finding the Plugin to Disable

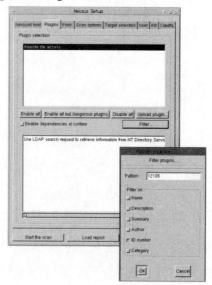

3. **Disable the plugin.** We now know that the plugin is in the *Remote file access* section. We clear the **Pattern** box, unselect **ID number** again, and click **Enable all (but dangerous)**, so we can select all the plugins. Scrolling down, we find the **Remote file access** section. We click on it, and all the plugins in this family appear. Clicking the button on the right disables the plugin (see Figure 7.9).

Figure 7.9 Disabling the Plugin

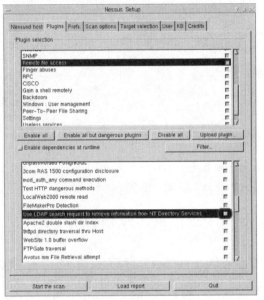

The plugin will be disabled for all scans done from the client. To enable the plugin, click on it again, and the button will appear to be going into the screen (the difference between a checked and unchecked plugin is minimal—look closely).

Marking a Result as a False Positive with NessusWX

The NessusWX client has the functionality to mark a result as an FP after a scan has completed. Once an issue has been marked as a false positive (by simply ticking the **FP** box), it is identified with a red cross next to it. Here we assume that we want to define the traceroute to an internal host as a false positive as it is not relevant to our environment. In Figure 7.10, these areas are highlighted.

Figure 7.10 Issue Marked as a False Positive

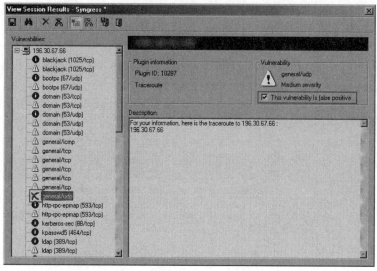

When an issue has been marked as an FP, the user has the choice to include it in HTML reporting or database export, as shown in Figure 7.11.

Figure 7.11 User Choice to Include the Issue in HTML Reporting or Database Export

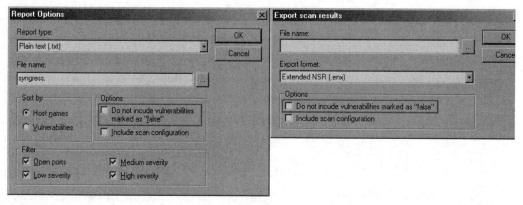

When these boxes are ticked, the issues marked as FPs are simply not included—they are not displayed in the report or database export as false.

False Positives and Web Servers—Dealing with Friendly 404s

Of all the services running on computers today (over the Internet), web servers are probably the most common. When looking externally at a network today, one finds that the majority of ports are used for HTTP or HTTPs and SMTP. The web service has become one of the most developed services—administrators and vendors are constantly looking to improve the performance and security of web servers. It then comes as no surprise that about a third of all Nessus plugins deal with web servers. Because of the complex nature of web servers, we will spend some time on FPs and web servers.

Let us look at how a web server works—a client (browser) requests a file in an HTTP request. The web server tries to find the file and return it to the client. If the file does not exist, the server reports an error (error 404 means "file not found"). If the file is protected by some means of access control list (ACL), the server responds with error 403 (forbidden). When a problem occurs when the server tries to serve the file (or execute the CGI script), it might send back error 500 (Server Error). There are many error codes, each for a different situation. If the web server can find the file, it has the permission to serve it, does not cause an internal error on the server, and returns the file with a code 200. Code 200 means that the server could respond to the request. For a complete list of status codes, refer to RFC 2616 (Hypertext Transfer Protocol—HTTP/1.1), section 10—Status Code Definitions. While the RFC describes how web server should behave, experience shows that not all vendors strictly conform to the RFC.

Let us first look at how most web server checks work. Most plugins will look for the presence of a particular script. If the server returns a 200 code, the plugin assumes that the script is present, and (if it has *safe_check* capabilities and the *safe_check* option is set) reports the issue. Other scripts might look for a 302 Redirect—the common factor is that they look at server response codes. So, what is the problem?

The following example shows what could happen. The web administration interface called Webmin listens on TCP port 10000. Webmin was written in such a way that it does conform to RFC 2616; it replies with a 200 status code every time, if the file exists or not. Figure 7.12 is a screenshot of a request for the root document.

Figure 7.12 Telnetting to a Webmin Interface

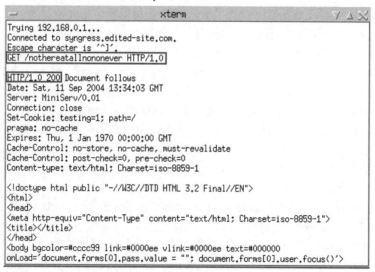

It does not matter what we request, we always get a 200 OK response. Let us request a nonexistent file and see what happens (see Figure 7.13).

Figure 7.13 Another 200 OK Response

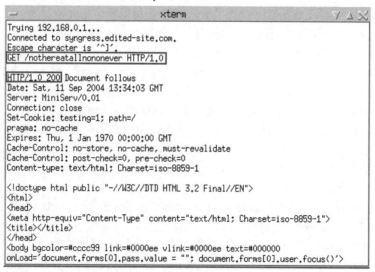

If a plugin relies on the 200 status code to generate a positive (as it does with a couple of CGI checks), this host would always show up as positive. In the same way, some web server are configured to reply with 200s (a status code that means the file is there) when a client requests a nonexistent file—it typically happens when a web server renders a "friendly" 404 message. This makes it very difficult for the plugins to determine if the file is really there, or if the web server is simply replying to all requests with a 200.

To counter this problem, Renaud and H.D. Moore wrote a plugin called *no404.nasl*. The plugin checks for a collection of files it knows will never reside on the target server (all files start with "NessusTest"). It then inspects the output of such requests; again trying to match it against known responses. When the plugin finds that the server responds with a nonstandard error message, it records the response and stores it in the Knowledge Base. Subsequent plugins can now use this—if they check for a specific offensive script or file, the dependency on the *no404* plugin will ensure that intelligence is applied. If the server responds in the same way it did when a nonexistent file was requested, the plugin assumes the file does not exist on the server rather than blindly follow the error code.

The use of *no404* dramatically improves the accuracy of the scanner when faced with nonstandard web servers.

Summary

The presence of FPs in scanner reports is probably one of the main reasons why people stop using a particular scanner. If the signal-to-noise ratio is high enough, one can lose track of the signal completely—which is as bad as having no signal at all. In this chapter, we defined different categories of false positives, looked at how Nessus deals with false positives, how to find a false positives, and what you can do to make Nessus a better scanner. The Nessus framework gives administrators and security personnel the option to investigate the inner workings of the scanner in intricate detail. This, combined with clever frontends, the option to toggle between scan modes (safe scanning), and plugins that are written to be as FP aware as possible are all moves in the right direction when dealing with FP issues. Online resources such as the OSVDB, PacketStorm, and SecurityFocus provide tons of details on how each vulnerability works and how to test for it. Armed with an open-source scanner and these resources, an analyst should be able to deal effectively with false positives.

Solutions Fast Track

☑ A false positive occurs when a scanner (such as Nessus) does a test for a vulnerability and incorrectly finds it to be vulnerable.

☑ False positives waste time (yours and anyone to whom the report is passed).

☑ False positives can be broadly categorized as technical or contextual. Technical false positive refer to problems with the scanner or plugin, while contextual false positives are more related to the environment and the perspective of the analyst running the scanner.

☑ Spot false positives by looking for results that do not make sense, like finding a Microsoft IIS problem on a UNIX server or finding problems related to patch levels when you know the patch is installed.

☑ Try to understand the problem. Refer to the original problem on mailing lists, web sites, online forums, or the web sites listed in this chapter.

☑ Determine if the false positive is generated because of your environment, or if the plugin misbehaved.

☑ Manually test if the problem really exists using other scanners, manual verification using a browser, telnet, Netcat, or an exploit.

☑ If you are sure that the plugin is not working, disable the plugin, or mark the result as a false positive in the scanner's result.

☑ Provide feedback on plugins that consistently generate false positives to the author of the plugin, or write to the Nessus mailing list.

Frequently Asked Questions

The following Frequently Asked Questions, answered by the authors of this book, are designed to both measure your understanding of the concepts presented in this chapter and to assist you with real-life implementation of these concepts. To have your questions about this chapter answered by the author, browse to **www.syngress.com/solutions** and click on the **"Ask the Author"** form. You will also gain access to thousands of other FAQs at ITFAQnet.com.

Q: What is a false positive?

A: Technically, a false positive occurs when a scanner (such as Nessus) does a test for a vulnerability and incorrectly reports its findings.

Q: How do FPs influeunce the quality of a report?

A: The more FPs in a report, the less the report reflects the actual truth; the more time is wasted on trying to correct the false findings. This wastes time and resources.

Q: Can Nessus be configured or customized to remove tests that generate known false positives?

A: Before a scan is started, each plugin within Nessus can be disabled. Entire families of tests can be disabled. After the scan is complete, the analyst can even decide to mark a finding as a false positive and exclude it in the scanner report (NessusWX client).

Q: I know a specific plugin generates a false positive. How do I report it?

A: You can report a plugin that generates a false positive to the author of the plugin or write to the Nessus mailing list.

Q: I know a specific plugin generates a false positive. How do I change it?

A: Although it is not recommended that you change plugins, you can (Nessus and all the plugins are open source). Be aware that the plugin was written in a specific way for a specific reason; don't meddle with it if you are not comfortable with NASL. In addition, remember that every new installation of Nessus will still contain the old version of the plugin.

## Chapter 8

Under the Hood

Solutions in this Chapter:

- Nessus Architecture and Design
- Host Detection
- Service Detection
- Information Gathering
- Vulnerability Fingerprinting
- Denial-of-Service Testing
- Putting It All Together

☑ Summary

☑ Solutions Fast Track

☑ Frequently Asked Questions

Introduction

To really understand Nessus, you have to know how its internal logic works and how it behaves on your network. This chapter describes how each stage of a Nessus scan is performed, with particular attention to the internal programming design of Nessus. Once you understand the logic behind the code, you will find it easier to diagnose problems relating to your scan, to create custom plugins, and to answer questions about why Nessus did or did not find a particular vulnerability. In this chapter, we look at the logical and behavioral guts of Nessus, how it works, and how it scans. We also give you a glimpse of how Nessus uses the Nessus Attack Scripting Language (NASL) to accomplish these tasks. By taking this view, you will end up with a much deeper understanding of Nessus under the hood, and be able to more easily understand where and how additional Nessus plugins should fit into the logic of the program.

Like many other vulnerability assessment tools, Nessus divides the process of detecting vulnerabilities in the network into a few major milestones, where each is dependent on the success of a previous major milestone. This process is further subdivided by the plugins themselves. Each plugin that is part of a major milestone might require additional minor milestones to be passed prior to successfully testing the vulnerability that it will later report. Behind each major milestone, you can find one or more plugins, depending on the complexity of the major milestones. A milestone doesn't necessarily indicate vulnerability. Some of the milestones used by Nessus are required for the sole purpose of allowing other plugins to detect vulnerabilities; such is the case with Microsoft HotFix enumeration (this minor milestone is officially called "Installed Windows Hotfixes"). The port-scanning milestone is usually performed by a single plugin, while the Microsoft HotFix enumeration requires about eight different plugins to succeed.

A few of the milestones are so essential that they cannot be avoided by disabling the plugins that are responsible for a specific milestone. However, you can save time by providing the milestone with the results it would otherwise generate.

Nessus will go through two preliminary, but very important to the success of the scan, major milestones before it goes on to doing vulnerability testing: host detection, the detection of whether a certain host is "alive" or "dead" (also referred to as "online" and "offline," respectively) and service detection, the detection of what ports are responsive on the remote host and the type of application or service running behind those ports. These two major milestones are essential to the success of a Nessus scan: not detecting a certain host as "alive," not detecting a certain port as open, or misidentifying its underlining service might cause us to falsely believe we are immune from vulnerabilities.

Following these two major milestones, Nessus will go into its information-gathering milestone. During this milestone, each application or service discovered during the previous service detection milestone will be examined to determine its application name and version. This allows Nessus to decide which vulnerabilities it needs to check against the application or service it discovered as early as possible. In addition, Nessus will enumerate the products, service packs, hotfixes, patches, and so forth installed on the remote host. This information can then be used by other plugins to save precious time and bandwidth, instead of each plugin needing to recreate that data. The final two major milestones are vulnerability testing and denial-of-service (DoS) testing. During these milestones, numerous plugins are launched to test the previously-discovered services. Which plugins are executed depends on the previous major milestone offering information on the type of products installed, whether a required service pack or patch was installed, and whether a prerequisite is met, as in the case of a valid username and password for authentication discovered during testing conducted by Nessus' information-gathering milestone.

As you can see, knowing what the milestones are and knowing what they do will allow you to spot problems that might prevent you from using Nessus to its fullest. Knowing these inner workings will also allow you to determine why certain vulnerabilities were not discovered, how to write new plugins to detect additional, already tested vulnerabilities, or how to improve existing plugins to better detect vulnerabilities.

Nessus Architecture and Design

Before we dive into explaining how milestones work, a brief explanation of Nessus' process forking and handling is in order. Skipping this section will not affect your understanding of the different Nessus milestones, but reading it will give you some insight into how Nessus manages the different scans and plugins, why Nessus requires a certain amount of memory and CPU to run, and why Nessus launches dozens or even hundreds of subprocesses when it scans several IP addresses in parallel.

Launching a sniffer on the network and capturing the traffic originating from the *nessusd* daemon to the tested network might lead an observer to think that Nessus initiates a scan of a network range with a ping sweep (also referred to as an ICMP sweep), followed by a full portscan of each machine, followed by a full attempt to detect services, and finally for each of the services detected by the corresponding plugins. This type of traffic might appear to have originated from a single process launched by a single nessusd daemon. In fact, the packets seen can be directly related to the enabled plugins and milestones, which we discuss in the sections that follow.

Nessus uses an individual process model: each client connection to the Nessus server will result in a new process to handle that connection. Furthermore, for each connection, the nessusd daemon spawns a new process for each host scanned. In addition, each instance of eachplugin is launched as its own process. Consequently, Nessus creates a new process for each plugin, per host, per scan.

Questions have been raised about the efficiency of this programming model: there is a common belief that calling *fork()* is slow and unwieldy, because when a process is forked, a new copy of the process and its attendant memory must be cloned and copied into memory. However, Nessus uses a copy-on-write memory model. This means that when a process is forked, the only things actually written into memory are the differences between the old process and its child; this is quite efficient.

The *nessusd* daemon and client for UNIX is written in C; however, to simplify things, plugins should be written in NASL, the Nessus scripting language. Originally, plugins were also written in C, although current development favors NASL plugins, as they are easier to debug, maintain, and write.

Without any dependence on the language in which the plugin was written, Nessus will invoke each plugin with its own built-in wrapper. The wrapper provides an environment that gives the plugin any information it might require, dependency fulfillment, and programming/networking interface. This allows the plugin writer to concentrate on writing the plugin instead of trying to make sure a dependent plugin has launched, how to transfer data between two plugins, or how to open a socket through which to send data.

Nessus launches the plugins according to three primary rules. The first rule is that no portscanning or DoS plugin will launch in parallel with other plugins; this includes all plugins that are included in the ACT_SCANNER, ACT_KILL_HOST, ACT_FLOOD, or ACT_DENIAL category. This rule was introduced to prevent Nessus from launching a port scanner while trying to crash a host, or while trying to launch two DoS plugins in parallel, making it impossible to know which actually caused the server to fail. The second rule is that if a plugin has a dependency, its dependency will need to be launched first. This allows plugins to use the results gathered by other plugins, including port numbers, service types, registry information, and authentication settings.

To illustrate how dependencies rule the success of the plugins, we will give two examples. The first is the *Buffer overrun in Windows Shell* vulnerability, whose plugin filename is smb_nt_ms04-024.nasl. Manually going over the source code of the plugin might make you believe it only depends on a single plugin; however, using the plugin_depend.pl tool you can quickly see that this isn't the case:

```
The plugin smb_nt_ms04-024.nasl depends on:
Filename: smb_hotfixes.nasl, Category ACT_GATHER_INFO, Requires Ports 139
445
Filename: netbios_name_get.nasl, Category ACT_GATHER_INFO, Requires Ports
Filename: smb_login.nasl, Category ACT_GATHER_INFO, Requires Ports 139 445
Filename: smb_registry_full_access.nasl, Category ACT_GATHER_INFO, Requires
Ports 139 445
Filename: smb_reg_service_pack.nasl, Category ACT_GATHER_INFO, Requires
Ports 139 445
Filename: smb_reg_service_pack_W2K.nasl, Category ACT_GATHER_INFO, Requires
Ports 139 445
Filename: smb_reg_service_pack_XP.nasl, Category ACT_GATHER_INFO, Requires
Ports 139 445
Filename: cifs445.nasl, Category ACT_GATHER_INFO, Requires Ports 139 445
Filename: find_service.nes, Category ACT_SCANNER, Requires Ports NONE
Filename: logins.nasl, Category ACT_SETTINGS, Requires Ports NONE
Filename: smb_registry_access.nasl, Category ACT_GATHER_INFO, Requires
Ports 139 445
```

This plugin might appear simple, as it contains only four lines of NASL code. However, it depends on other plugins, and its functionality is actually divided through those other plugins. Furthermore, the success of this plugin depends on the success of previously launched plugins.

The second example plugin is the *osTicket Attachment Code Execution* vulnerability, whose plugin filename is osticket_attachment_code_execution.nasl. Going over the dependencies of this plugin reveals an intricate tree of dependencies:

```
The plugin osticket_attachment_code_execution.nasl depends on:
Filename: global_settings.nasl, Category ACT_INIT, Requires Ports
Filename: http_version.nasl, Category ACT_GATHER_INFO, Requires Ports
"Services/www" 80
Filename: no404.nasl, Category ACT_GATHER_INFO, Requires Ports
"Services/www" 80
Filename: osticket_detect.nasl, Category ACT_GATHER_INFO, Requires Ports
"Services/www" 80
Filename: find_service.nes, Category ACT_SCANNER, Requires Ports NONE
Filename: http_login.nasl, Category ACT_GATHER_INFO, Requires Ports
"Services/www" 80
Filename: httpver.nasl, Category ACT_GATHER_INFO, Requires Ports
"Services/www" 80
Filename: www_fingerprinting_hmap.nasl, Category ACT_MIXED_ATTACK, Requires
Ports "Services/www" 80
Filename: webmirror.nasl, Category ACT_GATHER_INFO, Requires Ports
"Services/www" 80
Filename: logins.nasl, Category ACT_SETTINGS, Requires Ports NONE
Filename: DDI_Directory_Scanner.nasl, Category ACT_GATHER_INFO, Requires
Ports "Services/www" 80
```

Again, the success of this plugin is dependent on the success of other plugins that must be executed before this plugin can be launched.

The third rule is that Nessus will first launch all of the ACT_INIT plugins. Currently, there is a single plugin marked as ACT_INIT. This plugin configures the global settings that will have almost no effect on the behavior of other plugins; rather, it only affects the type of feedback will send to the user. This plugin also tells Nessus whether to launch two additional plugins (referred to as experimental_scripts)—the web server fingerprinting plugin and the anti Nessus detection plugin—and whether to run through all of the plugins, which means that the test will take longer to complete.

After Nessus finishes launching the ACT_INIT plugin, it proceeds to the ACT_SCANNER plugins. Currently, four plugins fall under this category: the *ping* plugin, which is part of the host detection milestone; the *Nmap wrapper* plugin, which is part of the service detection milestone; and two other plugins that try to determine whether scanning the remote host in question would be a waste of time. This waste of time might occur for two reasons: first, the host is a generic IP redirector, those IP addresses (also referred to as top-level domain wildcards) that when contacted will redirect all traffic to a predefined address; and second, the host being tested is part of LaBrea tarpitting, a product that takes unused IP addresses and creates virtual servers that are attractive to worms, hackers, and security scanners. More information on the product can be found at http://labrea.sourceforge.net/labrea-info.html.

After Nessus has finished with the ACT_SCANNER plugins, it now knows whether a host is "alive" and what ports and services are available on it. It next runs the ACT_SETTINGS plugins that affect the type of test Nessus will conduct. Skipping any of the ACT_SETTINGS plugins will diminish the number of vulnerabilities you detect, as these plugins allow you to define SMB username, password, and domain; to enable certain HTTP intrusion detection system (IDS) evasion techniques, and so on.

From this point, Nessus will launch the plugins according to their script ID number, lowest number first. This will not happen in most cases, as the plugin dependency rule will take precedence and certain plugins will be launched first. This usually means that all the ACT_GATHER_INFO plugins will launch prior to ACT_ATTACK, ACT_MIXED_ATTACK, and so forth, as these plugins are more sophisticated and require the results of other plugins before they can be launched successfully.

Nessus concludes the scan by launching the two ACT_END plugins. One of these two plugins will go over all the known open ports, and report which ports now appear to be closed, due to a plugin or due to the port-scanning activity. The other will go over all those ports considered unknown, meaning that the service behind them could not be detected by Nessus port scanners, plugins, or any other means. It then asks the reader of the results file what that type of port is used for. The second plugin is done mainly as a feedback method to the Nessus development team, rather than actually giving security-related information to the person using Nessus.

Host Detection

Let's look at the first milestone of a Nessus scan, the process of identifying which systems in the target range are actually "alive." As mentioned earlier, this milestone is especially important, because if a certain host appears to be "dead," Nessus will end that particular scanning thread, and report no vulnerabilities for that host.

The plugin in charge of determining whether a certain host is "alive" is ping_host.nasl. This plugin is a modular plugin, and can determine whether a remote host is "alive" by several means. The means of detection can be controlled via the Nessus client interface. Several means of detection allow you to determine whether a certain host is "alive" by methods that cannot be easily blocked by firewalls. This allows you to determine that a certain host is "alive" even if it isn't answering ICMP Echo requests (also known as ping test), or even if it has almost all its ports set on the firewall to DROP (not return any data to the user).

The plugin supports four approaches to determining whether a certain host is "alive." The first approach is to do an ICMP Echo test. During this, an ICMP Echo request is sent to the server; if it responds with any type of IP-based packet, it will be marked as "alive." To enable this option, you need to check the **Do an ICMP ping** check box under the **Prefs** menu. The second approach is to do a TCP ping. During this, a TCP SYN packet is sent to the remote server with a certain destination port and source port. The list of source ports can be predefined via the Nessus GUI by providing semicolon delimitated numbers in the edit box **TCP ping destination port(s)** under the **Prefs** menu. To enable TCP ping, check the **Do a TCP ping** check box.

The third option is to enable both, and the fourth option is to enable none. If you enable both, you are "covering all your bases," or simply leaving nothing to chance. If you enable none, you are telling Nessus that all hosts—range or single—are "alive" and require testing. Not enabling any will benefit those who cannot reliably determine whether a certain host is "alive," but will hinder those who don't want to spend time on nonexistent hosts.

For each approach, Nessus marks all the IP addresses that were not detected as "alive" with **Host/ping_failed**. However, this doesn't mean that these hosts will not be scanned during the next milestone, service detection. Only after the next milestone returns with no open ports will Nessus assume that the remote host is "truly dead."

Damage & Defense…

Firewalls

By default, most firewalls DROP packets. This means that any request sent to them on a port for which they don't have a rule will not trigger any response from the destination server. This makes it is especially hard to detect whether a certain host is "alive" if it is also not responding to ICMP Echo requests. Therefore, the success of a TCP ping relies on the ability to choose those TCP ports that are not blocked by a DROP packet rule.

Several port numbers can be used, but we suggest 21 (FTP), 22 (SSH), 23 (Telnet), 25 (SMTP), 80 (HTTP), 110 (POP3), 135 (NetBIOS), 139 (NetBIOS), 143 (IMAP), 443 (HTTPS), 445(NetBIOS), 1723 (PPTP), and 3389 (Terminal Services). This pretty much covers any Internet-based server you can find and any internal server.

Note that exaggerating the number of the TCP ports you probe will increase the time required to determine whether a certain host is "alive."

This milestone can be very time consuming when you provide Nessus with range of IP addresses, subnets, or even entire classes of IP addresses. To save time, you can limit the type of host detection to TCP ping or an ICMP ping, limit the number of ports you use for TCP ping, or prepare beforehand a comma-separated list of IP addresses to Nessus to use instead of a range.

Using Nmap, a very popular tool used for port scanning and mapping available from www.insecure.org/nmap/, you can easily accomplish the last option. Another option is to generate a list of IP addresses from your DHCP server's database; in the case of ISC's DHCP server, the list of IP addresses is stored in a text-based leases file, which can be easily converted to an comma-separated IP address list. Basically, any source of "live" IP addresses will save you time on the host detection milestone.

Service Detection

After a list of hosts is established, the next step is for Nessus to determine what services are running on these hosts. To do this, Nessus uses the ACT_SCANNER plugins. As there are different types of port-scanner technologies, different plugins can take be used. Most people will use nmap_wrapper.nes, or the newly introduced nmap.nasl. Both plugins provide a seamless interface to all of the Nmap port-scanner's configuration parameters; the difference is that nmap.nasl is written in NASL, while nmap_wrapper.nes is written in C. Other C-implemented port-scanners include SYN Scan, synscan.nes, and the TCP Connect scan nmap_tcp_connect.nes.

Damage & Defense...

Running Nmap

Running one of the Nmap wrappers, nmap_wrapper.nes or nmap.nasl, will allow you the greatest control over the port-scanning stage. Both plugins allow you configure such parameters as Host Timeout, Min/Max RTT Timeout, and Min/Max Ports Scanned in Parallel, and provide these plugins with an external file that will contain all the results for the port scan. The ability to provide this file allows you to quickly skip over the port-scanning phase and start testing for vulnerabilities.

Running any other port scanner such as synscan.nes or nmap_tcp_connect.nes will greatly reduce your success rate, as these plugins are custom made, out of date, and considered unmaintained in comparison to nmap_wrapper.nes and nmap.nasl.

Nmap and the Full-Connect Scan

Nmap, authored by Fyodor and found at www.insecure.org/nmap/, is one of the most popular scanning tools online. It boasts a wide variety of scan types that will allow you to test for listening ports in a multitude of ways. A full-connect scan is the noisiest and most obvious variety of TCP scan available. You send a TCP packet with the SYN flag set to each port, and if you receive a proper SYN/ACK response, you send a packet with the ACK flag set to complete the TCP three-way handshake and connect to the service listening on the port. While this is an obvious way to check what ports are listening on a machine, Nessus is not designed to be stealthy, just efficient.

The results from any port scanner you choose to use will be stored in the Knowledge Base as Services/known entries. Once the complete list of ports is compiled, Nessus will launch its service detection plugins to try to detect the type of service sitting behind each open port.

An Obstacle for Assessment Tools

One of the most common problems that vulnerability assessment tools face today is that as the number of products expands and unassigned port numbers are becoming increasingly scarce, products are choosing almost random port numbers for their product. This means that you might find a web server residing on port 10000, an SMTP server on port 2500, and so forth. This hinders the capability of some other scanners to detect vulnerabilities, unless they have a Nessus-like internal mechanism that is able to detect the type of service residing behind a certain port.

Nessus uses two plugins to do this job: find_service.nes and find_service2.nasl. find_service.nes is written in C, and find_service2.nasl is written in NASL. These two plugins detect the type of services for which a certain port answers. These two plugins are intelligent enough to auto detect whether a certain port is SSL protected, and to guess the type of service running behind them using fingerprinting techniques. The fingerprinting technique used by find_service.nes is to send each of the ports it knows is open a predefined string, *GET / HTTP/1.0*, after which Nessus examines the response received from the server in reply. The predefined string list Nessus uses to determine the type of service is extensive and constructed in an intricate nesting of *if else* statements, so that it will seldom incorrectly identify service behind a certain port.

Over time, the list of services that find_service.nes detects grew, and updating this plugin required the user to recompile it each time. This triggered the creation a new NASL plugin, find_service2.nasl. This plugin, like its sister plugin, tries to detect all those ports that find_service.nes was unable to detect. It does this by sending a different predefined string, *HELP*, and checking the response.

After one of these plugins detects the type of service residing behind a certain port number, it will mark it in the Knowledge Base under Known/tcp/portnumber and Services/servicetype. For example, Webmin's web interface residing on TCP port 10000 will be marked in the Knowledge Base as Known/tcp/10000 and Services/www, respectively. This information will be then used by any plugin with the port dependency of either port 10000 or Services/www under its NASL tag of script_require_ports.

Unless you specifically tell Nessus that any unscanned port should be considered closed by marking the check box under **Scan Options | Consider unscanned ports as closed**, any additional port requested by a plugin will be tried, even if it wasn't supplied in the port range. The default port range used by Nessus is 1–1024. If you supply Nessus with a port range of *1*, a single port, you will still obtain results, as the following ports will be probed for their existence:

```
2, 3, 4, 7, 9, 11, 13, 15, 19, 21, 22, 23, 25, 27, 35, 37, 53, 79, 80, 81,
90, 98, 109, 110, 113, 119, 135, 137, 139, 143, 209, 256, 257, 258, 259,
264, 360, 389, 406, 443, 444, 445, 512, 513, 514, 515, 524, 543, 548, 554,
593, 617, 625, 628, 631, 873, 900, 901, 999, 1080, 1100, 1192, 1214, 1220,
1241, 1281, 1311, 1313, 1314, 1352, 1433, 1521, 1541, 1570, 1665, 1720,
1723, 1755, 1812, 1995, 2000, 2001, 2002, 2082, 2200, 2223, 2224, 2301,
2381, 2501, 2525, 2533, 2543, 2601, 2602, 2603, 2604, 2605, 2710, 3000,
```

```
3050, 3067, 3104, 3128, 3135, 3306, 3372, 3690, 4000, 4001, 4002, 4080,
4105, 4242, 4321, 4661, 4662, 4663, 4711, 4899, 5000, 5003, 5009, 5010,
5060, 5432, 5554, 5556, 5631, 5679, 5680, 5800, 5801, 5802, 5900, 5901,
5902, 6000, 6001, 6002, 6003, 6004, 6005, 6006, 6007, 6008, 6009, 6050,
6112, 6129, 6346, 6515, 6667, 6680, 6699, 6723, 6777, 6789, 6790, 6969,
7000, 7001, 7003, 7070, 7100, 7101, 7161, 7210, 7323, 7777, 7778, 7779,
7786, 8000, 8001, 8002, 8008, 8010, 8080, 8081, 8082, 8100, 8129, 8181,
8383, 8390, 8443, 8500, 8765, 8888, 8987, 8999, 9000, 9001, 9090, 9099,
9100, 9400, 9669, 9999, 10000, 10005, 10082, 10168, 12345, 12754, 13666,
14002, 14238, 15104, 15858, 17300, 17990, 20000, 20034, 20168, 21227,
21317, 21544, 21554, 22273, 27960, 30100, 32000, 32123, 33270, 33567,
33568, 34012, 36794, 42800, 44334, 51051, 60008, 65301
```

This range doesn't mean that you will find vulnerabilities on a web server listening on port 8000, as 8000 is probed only by a limited set of plugins (28 to be exact). The rest of the web server–related plugins will look for the Services/www entry, and as this entry is only provided by the find_service.nes and find_service2.nasl plugins, most tests will not test this port for vulnerabilities.

> **NOTE**
>
> A shortcoming of not providing an inadequate, too-short or lacking port range is that any unofficially assigned port number, such as the use of port 13201 for a web server, will not be probed for vulnerabilities related to web servers. This is because the find_service.nes and find_service2.nasl plugins will not be launched against that port, which in turn will not be detected as a web server.

After Nessus identifies services, it can then go about gathering more information about what products are listening on those ports and their vulnerabilities.

Information Gathering

At this stage, Nessus uses the previous two milestones to obtain information about each host and service. The category for plugins in this milestone is ACT_GATHER_INFO. The plugins in this category are by definition constrained and verified to not cause any harm to the remote server, as they only do service queries, application fingerprinting, and general remote version analysis.

The ACT_GATHER_INFO set of plugins is by far the most numerous. Out of 4,132 available plugins (as of the time this book went to press, with Nessus version 2.1.00), 3,543 (or 85 percent) are information-gathering plugins. Even though they are called information gathering, they can determine whether a remote host is vulnerable to a certain vulnerability. The idea behind the name "information gathering" is that the plugin can be run safely without the possibility of causing harm to the service against which it is launched. This is accomplished by passively detecting the presence of vulnerabilities, either by capturing the version given by the remote host, or by testing the vulnerability in an harmless way, such as sending a cross-site scripting attack and looking for scripting code in the result.

Before any information-gathering plugin is launched, its port requirements are checked. Setting the script_required_ports NASL tag marks the port requirements for each plugin. Some types of services might reside on more than one port; in those cases, the plugin will refer to the type of port instead of the port number. One very good example for this is the use of port 80 and its corresponding service name, Service/www, in all the plugins that test web servers for vulnerabilities.

Some information-gathering plugins only gather information that will be later used by other plugins to determine whether a remote server is vulnerable. One of the more prominent plugins that belongs to this family is the NetBIOS and registry-related plugins; specifically, *Using NetBIOS to retrieve information from a Windows host* and *SMB log in*. Any plugin that requires registry access to determine whether a remote host is vulnerable to a certain vulnerability will fail unless these two plugins are launched and are successful. The first plugin will capture the NetBIOS name of the host being tested. The second plugin determines whether the guest or user-provided SMB username, password, and domain do in fact allow Nessus to connect to the remote host.

If the first plugin is successful, it will enter SMB/name in the Knowledge Base. The *SMB log in* plugin will then use this to try to log on to the remote host. Once the *SMB log in* plugin logs on to the remote host, it will mark the SMB/login, SMB/password, and SMB/domain entries in the Knowledge Base with appropriate data that will allow subsequent plugins to log on to the remote host. If both plugins are successful, a few other plugins can use the information that they provided to determine whether the remote host is missing any

Microsoft Security patches (MSXX–XXX). To save time, a new NASL was recently introduced, *Installed Windows Hotfixes* (also known as smb_hotfixes.nasl), which enumerates all existing registry keys, patches, and service packs on a remote Windows machine. The enumerated data is stored in the Knowledge Base under SMB/Registry/HKLM. Time and bandwidth are saved by storing this information in the Knowledge Base; 44+ plugins use this information when checking whether a certain service pack or patch exists.

The smb_hotfixes.nasl is dependent on five other plugins that require the success of *Using NetBIOS to retrieve information from a Windows host* and *SMB log in* and other plugins before they can assist smb_hotfixes.nasl in gathering all available service pack and patch information from a remote host.

Registry access isn't the only type of vulnerability testing that requires SMB logon to work; some tests look for files, and more specifically for their content, to determine whether a remote host is vulnerable. One such example is *Putty Modpow integer handling*, also known as putty_version_check.nasl. This plugin will try to access the content of putty.exe in several locations by way of Windows' file-sharing capabilities. Once it has accessed putty.exe, it will look for its version information, which it will then use to determine whether a remote host contains a vulnerable version of putty.exe.

Such plugin sophistication is not limited to Windows-based tests; introduced in version 2.1.0 are local tests that allow the use of an SSH client certificate to enumerate all installed packages on a remote UNIX machine. The list of local tests contains over 1,800 plugins, the majority of which are local tests for Red Hat. All local tests are preformed by a single plugin, Use *SSH to perform local security checks*, also known as ssh_get_info.nasl. This plugin will connect to a remote host, determine its flavor of RedHat, FreeBSD, Mandrake, SuSE, MacOS X, or Solaris, and then use the operating system's internal mechanism to enumerate all installed packages and their corresponding version. Once this information is stored in the Knowledge Base, any of the 1,800 plugins can simply query for the existence of a product and its version to determine whether the host is vulnerable.

It might look as though most plugins are not doing any actual testing, but this isn't completely true. Some plugins will connect to a web server, for example, and capture the version banner the server returns from which they will determine whether it is vulnerable to attack. Others will connect to every web server they see, determine whether a certain PHP script exists on it, and then query that script with a special URL to try to trigger a known response. For these plugins to be successful, the response from a vulnerable script must differ from that of an immune script, or a false positive will occur.

Damage & Defense...

Version Banners

Relying solely on version banners is likely to produce false positives. This is especially true for fixes that are backported, and whose version number remains the same while a patch to fix a certain vulnerability is introduced. If you use Nessus to scan for vulnerabilities, any test that solely relies on banners will return an extensive amount of false positives on such systems as Debian, FreeBSD, Red Hat, and so forth. To counter those cases, the Nessus Project recently introduced an include file called backport.inc that lists backported versions of products. If such a backported version is detected, no false positive will be triggered.

Most information-gathering tests that we have examined so far appear passive; they connect, send small amounts of data back and forth, and then determine whether the remote host is vulnerable by looking at the response. A more complicated information-gathering plugin is *Raptor/Novell Weak ISN*, also known as raptor_isn.nasl. This plugin checks for Raptor firewalls that have poor Initial Sequence Number (ISN) randomization, thereby making them more vulnerable to a successful TCP hijack or TCP injection attack. This script generates two successive IP packets, identical except for their randomly created IP IDs, TCP sequence numbers, and window sizes. The plugin will then send both packets to the Raptor firewall while monitoring the response it receives from the server.

If the plugin gets both packets back, it will check the ISN by comparing the TCP sequence number against the acknowledgment in both packets. If they match, the remote firewall is vulnerable to a weak ISN attack.

Vulnerability Fingerprinting

After a thread finishes gathering the information for a given host and writes its findings to the Nessus Knowledge Base, it runs through any attack plugins it's configured to use. These can include plugins in the ACT_ATTACK,

ACT_MIXED_ATTACK, and ACT_DESTRUCTIVE_ATTACK categories. These plugins will run in this order, and will highlight specific vulnerabilities present in the target(s). Because of the potentially problematic nature of some of these checks, they can be turned off while scanning. All of these represent a more aggressive attack pattern than the informational plugins described previously; they will actually execute an attack on the server, rather than just trying to determine if that version is vulnerable.

By definition, any plugin that tries to circumvent some defenses, without any adverse effect on the system availability, will be categorized as ACT_ATTACK. One such plugin example is *MS SMTP DoS*, also known as mssmtp_dos.nasl. This plugin will connect to the Simple Mail Transfer Protocol (SMTP) server, and send the proper SMTP sequence **HELO** followed by **MAIL FROM**, **RCPT TO**. Currently, this type of traffic cannot be distinguished from any other SMTP traffic. However, when the attack sequence starts, Nessus will send a **BDAT** command, which is defined as an alternative to the SMTP's command DATA, followed by a **b00mAUTH LOGIN**, which allows us to determine whether a remote server is vulnerable by examining the response we receive. An immune server should respond with **503 5.5.2 BDAT Expected**; however, a vulnerable server will not respond in this way, allowing us to determine that this server is vulnerable to attack.

> **NOTE**
>
> This vulnerability was discovered in 2002 in Microsoft's SMTP server. The flaw involves how the service handles a particular type of SMTP command used to transfer the data that constitutes an incoming mail. By sending a malformed version of this command, an attacker could cause the SMTP service to fail. This would disrupt mail services on the affected system, but would not cause the operating system itself to fail. For additional information regarding this vulnerability, see www.securiteam. com/windowsntfocus/5XP0L2A6AS.html or www.securiteam.com/ exploits/5AP0O1P6MK.html.

Not all ACT_ATTACK plugins try to trigger a problem in the remote server; some just try to determine if some type of attack is feasible. To determine the feasibility of an attack, most ACT_ATTACK plugins rely on the results of previously launched NASLs. One such plugin is *DB4Web directory traversal*, also known as db4web_dir_trav.nasl. This plugin directly relies on the success of the no404.nasl, httpver.nasl, http_version.nasl, and webmirror.nasl plugins. These plugins in turn rely on the DDI_Directory_Scanner.nasl, http_login.nasl, www_fingerprinting_hmap.nasl, and logins.nasl plugins. This dependency tree allows the db4web_dir_trav.nasl plugin to accurately detect the presence of the vulnerability without "falling prey" to servers that act in a similar way to DB4Web.

The no404 plugin is a very important part of the effort Nessus makes to reduce the number of false positives it generates. The purpose of no404 is to try to determine what information can be used in the response of a web server to determine that it doesn't contain a certain file. The httpver.nasl plugin's purpose is to determine whether the remote web server supports the extended HyperText Transfer Protocol (HTTP) protocol. The http_version.nasl plugin's purpose is to determine the vendor of the web server running on the remote host, so that Apache tests will not be launched against Microsoft's IIS web server. Finally, the webmirror.nasl plugin's purpose is to determine which Common Gateway Interfaces (CGIs), also known as user-driven pages, are available on the remote server.

By taking into account all the data provided by the plugins on which the webmirror.nasl plugin is dependent, the script can accurately determine whether a remote host is vulnerable. The plugin, for example, can know which type of operating system the DB4Web is running under, whether the remote host supports HTTP/1.1's keep-alive connection so it can speed up the test, and whether it responds with the error code 404 for files you request that do not exist, again allowing you to speed up the test and increase its accuracy.

Damage & Defense...

Nessus Speed

Nessus has greatly improved the speed at which it can test web servers by improving its internal mechanisms responsible for querying a remote web server for the existence of certain files. The internal mechanisms support HTTP/1.1's keep-alive, allowing Nessus to use a single open socket for all its web queries, instead of constantly opening new sockets and closing them after a test has finished.

Continued

However, this might adversely affect servers that do not properly support HTTP/1.1's keep-alive standard; one such example is Novell. Novell has sent an advisory regarding this problem to its customers in TID2966181. However, such an incident is rare; this issue was reported in June 2003.

If that's an ACT_ATTACK, what's an ACT_MIXED_ATTACK? ACT_ATTACK plugins are safe to use even when safe checks are enabled—they are unlikely to take down your server. An ACT_MIXED_ATTACK is a script that can be used with the safe checks off in a potentially destructive fashion, or with the safe checks on as a potentially safe attack—although with less certainty of assuring you that your server is vulnerable or not. Let's look at an example of this type of check: the *ntpd overflow* plugin, also known as ntp_overflow.nasl.

In this plugin, the test starts by determining whether the Network Time Protocol (NTP) is enabled on the remote host. If safe_checks() has been enabled, it will initiate a subsection of code that will try use NTP's internal provided information to determine the version of NTP server running. If this version falls under the version range that is known to be vulnerable, the script will mark the vulnerability as present. As mentioned previously, this can be problematic when servers are backported to include fixes for vulnerabilities. The problem of backported security fixes is avoided if safe_checks() are disabled: in that case, an actual buffer overflow attack will be mounted against the NTP server. Using the plugin with safe-checks() disabled makes the test much more accurate, and allows you to discover vulnerabilities in products that weren't considered vulnerable prior to this plugins fun.

The third category of vulnerability assessment plugins that the Nessus daemon will run is the ACT_DESTRUCTIVE_ATTACK plugins. These will not be tried unless safe checks are turned off, as they always have the potential to do something destructive to the target system, such as lock out accounts, crash services, or exploit a running service.

One example of such a plugin is the SMB log in with W32/Deloder passwords, also known as smb_login_deloder.nasl. This plugin will try to determine whether a remote host has been compromised by the W32/Deloder worm. The worm will try to modify an existing account, usually administrator, with a predefined set of passwords. Trying a list of passwords on a certain username can cause that account to become locked out, which is why this plugin is marked as destructive.

For each of these classes of attacks (ACT_ATTACK, ACT_MIXED _ATTACK, and ACT_DESTRUCTIVE_ATTACK), Nessus will run through all the available and appropriate attacks as noted in the Knowledge Base, and then move on to the next class. When all the vulnerability fingerprinting is done, Nessus will look at one last class of vulnerabilities before generating a report.

Denial-of-Service Testing

Nessus also has the capability to test a server or a network against known DoS vulnerabilities. It is usually inadvisable to do this against a production network during business hours, as you might cause excessive delays if your DoS scans show your network to be vulnerable (by downing it). Plugins labeled ACT_DENIAL, ACT_FLOOD (in Nessus 2.1.*x* only, although it might be incorporated into an upcoming mainline release), and ACT_KILL_HOST can simulate a real DoS attack.

The DoS checks are the last milestone in the scan of hosts just in case they are successful: it would be poor design to knock your Web server offline at the start thereby making it impossible to scan with all the other plugins and tools available to find vulnerabilities. Moreover, even within the class of DoS testing, the host-killing checks are last, so as not to deprive other checks of their host's uptime for as long as possible. Let's look at the options for these types of tests:

Here's a simple case, the *Microsoft's SQL TCP/IP denial of service* also known as mssqlserver_dos.nasl. This particular vulnerability from 1999 caused the Microsoft SQL server to crash, this occurred when it received a packet whose payload contained more than two null characters.

The plugin relies on the results of *Microsoft SQL TCP/IP listener is running,* also known as mssqlserver_detect.nasl. The plugin starts by checking whether TCP port 1433 is open. If it is, the plugin establishes a TCP connection to that port and sends a packet with six NULL bytes. To check whether the attack was successful, the plugin will try to reconnect to TCP port 1433; if it is unable to connect, it will report that the vulnerability has been confirmed to exist.

In Nessus version 2.1.00, a new category was introduced—ACT_FLOOD. Plugins in this category require the capability of Nessus to send a constant stream of data to a remote host in order for the DoS to occur. Because such attacks can use large amounts of bandwidth, they have been marked for easy exclusion as category ACT_FLOOD.

For an example of a flooding DoS attack, let's look at the *MacOS X Directory Service DoS* plugin, also known as macos_x_directory_svc_dos.nasl. This plugin attempts to cause the MacOS X's directory services to no longer respond to any connection by flooding it with more than 250 connections. The attack itself is no more bandwidth consuming that opening and closing a socket; however, 250 connection attempts are unusual for a "normal" plugin. The final category of DoS plugins is ACT_KILL_HOST. This includes all plugins that try to kill the operating system itself. An example is the *Linksys Gozila CGI denial of service*, also known as linksys_gozila_cgi_DoS.nasl, which attacks the CGI on a Linksys device.

The attack consists of single connection to the web server available on the Linksys device and requesting the Gozila.cgi with no parameters. Unlike the previous example, you can see that we are not wasting bandwidth; we can trigger the issue with a single request. The difference between ACT_KILL_HOST and ACT_FLOOD is that we will use the function *end_denial* at the end of the plugin, which will try to confirm whether the remote host is still alive. Nessus determines whether a remote host is still alive by trying to connect to one of the remote host's TCP ports, and seeing if such a connection is possible.

Putting It All Together

Throughout this chapter, some data in the Knowledge Base was used for the benefit and improvement of every plugin. This is by no means accidental. The Knowledge Base has become one of the most important features that Nessus has in its arsenal that make it usable, extendable, and accurate. One plugin can concentrate on grabbing data from the registry, while others concentrate on taking that data and deducing from it whether you are vulnerable. However, the Knowledge Base is not a flawless implementation.

The Knowledge Base is unfortunately a one-way communication; a plugin will be unable to use it for two-way communication with other plugins running simultaneously. Nessus writes to the Knowledge Base from the plugin process to the host-specific process over a socket pair. Processes always get their own copy of the Knowledge Base once they are spawned from the main process, and any updates to the Knowledge Base will not affect their copy. This implementation has pros and cons. One of the obvious pros is that no shared data is used, and as such, no locking and unlocking mechanism is required, which will speed up the entire process of scanning hosts. In addition, any process that will, even by mistake, not unlock one of the entries in the Knowledge Base will have no effect on any of the other processes. One obvious con is that two plugins running simultaneously will not be able to use the Knowledge Base as a means of talking to each other, and in theory make the testing procedure work better. Another con is that multiple copies of the Knowledge Base are kept, thereby requiring more memory than storing a single copy of the Knowledge Base that every plugin will use.

As you can see from the way the Knowledge Base is implemented, Nessus' process model ensures that a problem in a specific plugin will not cause the entire scan (or even the scan of a particular host) to fail or stale. This includes those instances where a plugin might segfault, causing a segmentation fault to the process running it, or any other problem, such as when a plugin takes too long to complete.

The Knowledge Base is stored under the configuration directory of Nessus, under the path hierarchy of /[installation path of nessus]/users/[user used to logon to Nessus]/kbs/[IP or hostname]. For example, in our installation, the Knowledge Base information for host 192.168.1.62 is stored under /usr/local/ var/nessus/users/beyondsecurity/kbs/192.168.1.62. Knowing where the Knowledge Base is stored, and knowing how to parse the content found, will allow you to debug any problems that might arise. Nessus by default will not store any Knowledge Base information after the scan is completed. To keep a copy of the Knowledge Base after the scan is completed, check the **KB | Enable KB saving** check box.

Once you have such a Knowledge Base entry, parsing it is not a big problem. The data format used in the Knowledge Base files is in text, and can be easily parsed by a Perl script. For each entry written in the Knowledge Base, Nessus stores the time, in milliseconds since 1970.

This is followed by the type of Knowledge Base entry. There are five types available: ARG_STRING defined as 1, ARG_PTR defined as 2, ARG_INT defined as 3, ARG_ARGLIST defined as 4, and ARG_STRUCT defined as 5. The most common types are strings and integers; in both cases, the data is stored in strings, so the number "1" will be stored as "1" and not as its binary counter-part 0x01.

The next thing is the name of the Knowledge Base entry, which is delimited from with an equal sign (=). The value's end is marked with a new line. This means that each line will be the entire Knowledge Base entry; if new lines exist within it, they will be replaced with the string \n, to avoid confusion.

Some lines in the Knowledge Base are informational, some are scan settings, and others contain vulnerability values. The first step when trying to determine why a certain scan has not completed successfully would be to verify that the plugin was in fact launched. For example, assume we are trying to see if our *SMB log in* plugin was launched against our host. The first step is to find out that the *SMB log in* plugin's number is 10394. Once we know this, we can look for the entry *Launched/10394* in the Knowledge Base; if it exists, the plugin was successfully launched. Next, we can determine whether the plugin was successful by determining whether it called one of the security_hole, security_note, security_warning, and so forth functions. This is determined by looking for the *Success/10394* entry. You can see what type of vulnerabilities were discovered by looking for entries that start with *SentData/[plugin id]*; each of these entries is a single result like you can find in other types of results files Nessus can generate. Any data that is shared between plugins will be saved with its corresponding Knowledge Base name and value.

During the scan, Nessus will generate a temporary report file in the NBE format. This temporary file is created under the /tmp directory. This file contains temporary results discovered by the scan; once the scan is completed, this file will be converted to whichever format you desire. The file-naming convention is random enough to hinder the possibility of a symbolic link attack—an attack that can be used in those cases where temporary filenames can be guessed beforehand and symbolically linked to another file, but have the constant convention of "nessus-" followed by six random bytes.

Notes from the Underground...

(plugin_depend.pl)#!/usr/bin/perl

```perl
# This Perl script receives a filename as its first parameter.
# This filename is considered to be a NASL, for each of the dependencies
# listed in it it will open them, and find any additional dependencies,
# once it is done with all the dependencies it will print them as a list.
```

Continued

```
#
# Coded by Noam Rathaus of Beyond Security Ltd.
# It is released under the GNU Public Licence (GPLv2)
#
use strict;

my @OpennedList;
my @Dependent;
my $debug = 0;
my $Filename = shift;
plugin_open($Filename);


print "------------\n";
print "The plugin $Filename depends on:\n";
foreach my $Depend (@Dependent)
{
 plugin_show($Depend);
}
print "------\n";

sub plugin_show
{
 my $Filename = shift;
 my $Category;
 my $RawPorts;
 my @Ports;
 if ($debug)
 {
  print "Filename: $Filename\n";
 }

 my $Buffer;
 if (open(BASE_PLUGIN, $Filename))
 {
```

Continued

```perl
 while (<BASE_PLUGIN>)
 {
  $Buffer .= $_;
 }
 close(BASE_PLUGIN);

 if ($Buffer =~ /script_category\(([^\)]+)\)/gs)
 {
  $Category = $1;
 }

 if ($Buffer =~ /script_require_ports\(([^\)]+)\)/gs)
 {
  $RawPorts = $1;
  while ($RawPorts =~ /([^\,]+)\,?/gs)
  {
   push @Ports, $1;
  }
 }
}

 print "Filename: $Filename, Category $Category, Requires Ports
@Ports     \n";
}

sub plugin_open
{
 my $Filename = shift;
 if ($debug)
 {
  print "Filename: $Filename\n";
 }

 my $Found = 0;
```

Continued

```
foreach my $Openned (@OpennedList)
{
 if ($Openned eq $Filename)
 {
  if ($debug)
  {
   print "Already opened\n";
  }
  return;
 }
}


push @OpennedList, $Filename;

my $Buffer;
if (open(BASE_PLUGIN, $Filename))
{
 while (<BASE_PLUGIN>)
 {
  $Buffer .= $_;
 }
 close(BASE_PLUGIN);

 if ($Buffer =~ /script_dependencies?\((([^\)]+)\);/gs)
 {
  my $Dependencies = $1;
  while ($Dependencies =~ /"([^"]+)"/gs)
  {
   my $TempDepend = $1;
   my $Found = 0;
   foreach my $Depend (@Dependent)
   {
    if ($Depend eq $TempDepend)
    {
```

Continued

```
        $Found = 1;
        last;
       }
     }


    if (!$Found)
    {
      push @Dependent, $1;
    }
   }
  }


if ($debug)
{
  print "Depends:\n";
  foreach my $Depend (@Dependent)
  {
    print "$Depend\n";
  }
  print "------\n";
 }
}


foreach my $Depend (@Dependent)
{
  plugin_open($Depend);
 }
}
```

Summary

In this chapter, we saw how the internal logic of the Nessus server works when scanning. We discovered that each machine is assessed and scanned independently in a host-based model. We looked at the many different types of plugins that are available for the Nessus server, and the order in which they are checked and run for each host. We discovered the many configurable options that will allow us to optimize our scans for our network and our scheduling.

Solutions Fast Track

Nessus Architecture and Design

☑ Nessus uses an individual process model—each client connection to the Nessus server will result in a new process to handle that connection; in addition, within each connection, the scan launched is host based.

☑ Generally speaking, Nessus will launch the plugins in numerical order according to the plugin ID. This order does not occur in practice, as Nessus' internal plugin scheduler performs optimizations, dependencies, and reordering of plugins according to a few rules.

☑ The nessusud daemon and client for UNIX is written in C; however, to simplify things, plugins should be written in NASL, the Nessus scripting language.

Host Detection

☑ Each host is assessed independently, up to the maximum number of hosts that might be concurrently scanned.

☑ You can use TCP pings, ICMP pings, or both for host detection.

☑ TCP pings are the default choice for host detection.

Service Detection

☑ By default, a full-connect TCP portscan is used to determine what ports are listening on any given machine.

☑ Once the open ports have been established, the nessusd daemon will use the find_service.nes binary and the find_service2.nasl script to identify what service is running on each port.

☑ Find_service.nes depends on direct output of the service, whereas find_service2.nasl uses the HELP command to retrieve useful data.

Information Gathering

☑ Plugins used for information gathering run right after services have been identified for each machine.

☑ Information-gathering plugins can probe the machine, grab banners, send crafted packets, and so forth, but they will not perform any active attack.

☑ There are far more of these plugins than any other type.

Vulnerability Fingerprinting

☑ Plugins capable of performing actual attacks will be used for vulnerability fingerprinting.

☑ There are three types of vulnerability fingerprinting plugins: attacks that are unlikely to cause actual harm, attacks that can be potentially destructive, and attacks that can be configured either way.

☑ The use or nonuse of destructive attacks in a scan is regulated by the use of safe checks.

Denial-of-Service Testing

☑ Denial-of-service (DoS) testing is performed last in any given thread. This is to ensure that if the host is knocked offline or the service does go down, all other indentifiable vulnerabilities have been found.

☑ Flooding attacks are present in Nessus 2.1, but not yet present in the mainline Nessus code train.

☑ The last attacks to be performed are those that might knock the entire host offline, thereby preventing any further testing.

Putting It All Together

☑ When all threads have completed scanning, Nessus will check the contents of the temporary NBE it created during the scan and generate a report from the data collected there.

☑ Data from each machine, by default, is grouped individually in the report, so you will see a full assessment of the vulnerabilities of each machine, one at a time.

☑ The Knowledge Base information can be stored on the machine in a form of a file, allowing easy debugging of possible false positives.

Frequently Asked Questions

The following Frequently Asked Questions, answered by the authors of this book, are designed to both measure your understanding of the concepts presented in this chapter and to assist you with real-life implementation of these concepts. To have your questions about this chapter answered by the author, browse to **www.syngress.com/solutions** and click on the **"Ask the Author"** form. You will also gain access to thousands of other FAQs at ITFAQnet.com.

Q: Why is it important to understand what all these plugins do?

A: Nessus is modular by design. If you want to write your own plugins for extended scanning, it's a good idea to have an understanding of the architecture of Nessus so you know what type they are and where to add them. You wouldn't want to accidentally put a destructive or DoS plugin before all the informational checks; you could lose valuable data that way.

Q: What is the Knowledge Base?

A: The Knowledge Base is where Nessus stores the information it gathers as it goes through a scan. At any point, the Knowledge Base will contain information about what on the network Nessus has discovered so far.

Q: What if I do things in the wrong order?

A: Unless you are writing your own plugins, Nessus will automatically select the correct order for plugins to run based on the class of plugins to which they belong. If you write your own, make sure that you assign them to the appropriate class.

Q: Will the Nessus server behave the same way when scanning if I use a local client or a remote one?

A: The scanning behavior will be the same. All scans are performed by the server; the client just selects options for the server and the scan, then lets the server to do its job.

Q: Where can I find out more about NASL and its syntax?

A: You can read the appendix in this book, or look online at www.nessus.org/doc/nasl2_reference.pdf.

Q: Why are things scanned in a particular order?

A: Maximum gain of information for minimal disruption. The hosts are identified and fingerprinted and the servers are identified first for efficiency reasons. Then the information-gathering phase, attack phase, and DoS phase are ordered that way to ensure that the best data is gotten out of a scan before the machine or service is knocked offline, if you have configured options that allow it.

## Chapter 9

The Nessus Knowledge Base

Solutions in this Chapter:

- **Knowledge Base Basics**
- **Information Exchange**
- **Limitations**

☑ **Summary**

☑ **Solutions Fast Track**

☑ **Frequently Asked Questions**

Introduction

In 2000, Nessus introduced the then "experimental" Knowledge Base saving feature. The original Nessus Knowledge Base was an in-memory list of data gathered during a vulnerability assessment. With the release of Nessus 1.0.5, however, Nessus servers gained the capability to save the Knowledge Base to disk for use in future scans.

The merits of the Nessus Knowledge Base, or KB, are obvious. As use of the Knowledge Base increases, one almost has to wonder how any scanner could operate without it. The Knowledge Base allows Nessus to use information gleaned from a past scan of a system to enhance and speed the scan being performed. Even more important, though, is that one plugin can use data gathered by a previously running plugin, decreasing the number of interactions with each host and making plugin development easier. A perfect example of this is the current implementation of Microsoft HotFix checks. In the original implementation, each check made a connection to the remote registry to examine its relevant key/value pairs. The "Installed Windows Hotfixes" check released in 2004 instead makes a single remote registry connection and proceeds to populate the Knowledge Base. Subsequent Nessus Attack Scripting Language (NASL) scripts need only query the local Knowledge Base to glean this information.

The aim of this chapter is to get the reader familiar with the workings of the Nessus Knowledge Base. The chapter highlights how the Knowledge Base works and how you can use it to maximum benefit.

It should also be noted that at the current way the Nessus Project is going, the Knowledge Base is becoming an increasingly vital part of the plugins.

Knowledge Base Basics

This section (as its title implies) is aimed at covering the basics of the Nessus Knowledge Base. We will discuss briefly how the Knowledge Base is implemented and how it can be used and configured by the user.

What Is the Knowledge Base?

The Nessus Knowledge Base is quite simply the list of information gathered about a host being tested. It allows plugins, or tests, to share information about the target system allowing for both more intelligent testing and more conservative use of bandwidth and processing power. Please keep in mind, as we discuss *plugins*, *tests*, and *scripts*, that these terms are interchangeable in the world of Nessus. The Knowledge Base feature allows Nessus to restrict tests to only those that are pertinent to the host being tested. For example, Nessus currently contains about 650 distinct tests for CGI abuses. (The Common Gateway Interface, or CGI, is a standard for external gateway programs to interface with information servers such as HTTP servers). These tests would be pointless against a server that does not have a running HTTP daemon. To conserve bandwidth (and to distinguish itself from many of the regular scanners available today), Nessus will first determine if a web server is running on the server (on port 80 or any others within its configured scan range) and will set a key within the Knowledge Base for "Services/www" with its value being the corresponding discovered httpd port; for example, "Services/www=8181". Tests that require a web server to be present will first make a call to the Knowledge Base to determine the value for "Services/www" before continuing.

As stated, Knowledge Base saving has been compiled in by default since version 1.1.0. You can confirm this by running *nessusd* with the "dump configuration" flag (-d). This flag causes the server to dump its compile time options.

```
[haroon@nessus-server]$ /usr/local/sbin/nessusd -d
This is Nessus 2.0.10 for Linux 2.4.22-1.2174.nptl
compiled with gcc version 3.3.2 20031022 (Red Hat Linux 3.3.2-1)


Current setup :
        Experimental session-saving      : enabled
        Experimental KB saving           : enabled
        Thread manager                   : fork
        nasl                             : 2.0.10
        libnessus                        : 2.0.10
        SSL support                      : enabled
        SSL is used for client / server  communication
        Running as euid                  : 500
```

The Knowledge Base is considered "fresh" for a user-configurable period of time. During the specified time, the Knowledge Base will be consulted for information about the host. This will affect the actions performed by the scanner on subsequent scans within the specified time window. In short, Nessus can be configured to only conduct vulnerability tests against ports reported to be open by the Knowledge Base. This reduces the traffic generated by the scanner (effectively

preventing the scanner from first doing a portscan of the target host), but introduces the possibility that the scanner could "miss" a port that has opened
between the time the Knowledge Base has been created and the current scan.
These options are covered in more detail later in this chapter.

Where the Knowledge Base Is Stored

The Knowledge Base is stored on the Nessus server and is created by default in
the `/usr/local/var/nessus/users/<username>/kbs` directory, where `<username>`
refers to the Nessus user who initiated the test. These directory locations can be
configured by passing compilation options to the configure scripts during the
install process. Each host tested results in the creation of its own Knowledge Base
file, which is named for either the IP address or the fully qualified domain name
(FQDN) of the tested host.

```
[root@nessus-server]# ls /usr/local/var/nessus/users/mh/kbs/
127.0.0.1         192.168.0.1      192.168.0.123   womwom.sensepost.com
172.16.110.128    192.168.0.100    192.168.0.50    www.sensepost.com
```

Using the Knowledge Base

Options pertaining to the Knowledge Base can be found under the KB tab of
the GUI Nessus client.

Figure 9.1 gives the user a series of configuration options that might seem
daunting at first but are actually quite intuitive. We will discuss them one at a time.

Figure 9.1 Configuration Options

The check box highlighted in Figure 9.1 is the option that enables Knowledge Base saving on the Nessus server. This setting is not selected by default, preventing the user from making changes to the Knowledge Base-specific configuration options that follow. Checking the box brings us to the screen in Figure 9.2.

Figure 9.2 Knowledge Base Saving Enabled

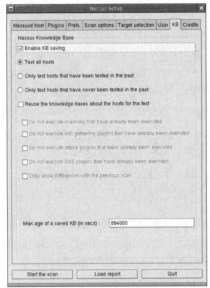

Even with the Knowledge Base saving option activated, the Nessus client defaults to a "neutral" configuration. As you can see in Figure 9.2, the default settings cause the Knowledge Base to be saved, but do not allow it to affect subsequent scans. Therefore, the Nessus server will write the Knowledge Base to disk, but will never consult it for subsequent scans on the same hosts.

The following options, selected via option buttons, allow the user the option to scan all hosts, scan only hosts without a valid Knowledge Base, or only hosts that have a valid existing Knowledge Base. These options can be used in different situations to great effect. For example:

- An administrator performs a scan on an entire subnet to determine her key critical hosts. The Knowledge Bases of noncritical hosts are removed from the /kbs directory. With the option to "Only test hosts that have been tested in the past," the scanner will not try to discover new hosts in the subnet on subsequent scan runs and thus will only test the hosts the administrator has chosen as key hosts.

- An administrator performs a scan on an entire subnet and generates his results. A few days later, he discovers that new hosts have been added to the subnet. Running the scanner with the "Only test hosts that have never been tested in the past" option instructs the scanner to run tests only on the new hosts that it finds, serving to both enumerate new hosts and to list vulnerabilities found in those new hosts. This option is powerful in a number of scenarios. For instance, consider that a company can only afford high network utilization once per week. And so, once per week, the administrators run a scan over all hosts. They then scan each day for any hosts that were missed due to being powered off, taken home, or newly introduced into the environment since the last scan.

- It is important to highlight the pitfalls of network topologies such as those using DHCP when using the previous Knowledge Base saving settings, and possibly overcoming this pitfall by using the MAC address setting option.

Note that until this point, the last five check boxes in Figure 9.2 are grayed out, precluding the user from selecting them. Selecting the "Reuse the Knowledge Bases about hosts for the test" check box allows the user to select these five check boxes (see Figure 9.3).

Figure 9.3 Knowledge Base Reuse

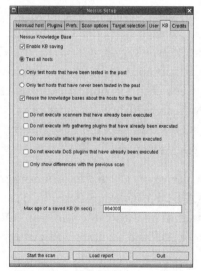

The first four check boxes correspond directly to the following Nessus plugin categories:

- ACT_SCANNER

- ACT_GATHER_INFO

- ACT_MIXED_ATTACK, ACT_DESTRUCTIVE_ATTACK, and ACT_ATTACK

- ACT_DENIAL, ACT_KILL_HOST, and ACT_FLOOD

Users familiar with NASL will notice that there are two other categories at the time of this book's publication: ACT_INIT and ACT_SETTINGS. Both of these serve to set global variables used by other plugins, but not to actually interact with systems, and thus cannot be deactivated by use of the Knowledge Base.

The remaining text info box in Figure 9.4 allows the user to enter the maximum age in seconds for a Knowledge Base. After this number of seconds, the information in the Knowledge Base is considered stale and must be rediscovered. Again, this setting is important to decrease the odds that the Knowledge Base does not decrease the accuracy of a scan by using data that has become inaccurate as the target systems' configuration changes over time.

Figure 9.4 Knowledge Base Age

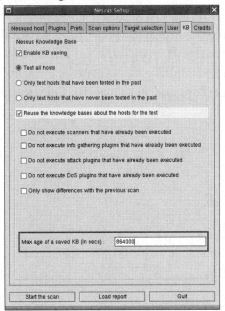

As can be seen in Figure 9.4, the default maximum age for a saved Knowledge Base is 864,000 seconds, or 10 days. If no value is specified here, a more conservative default of 3,600 seconds, or one hour, is used. The maximum age of the Knowledge Base is the maximum lifetime, in seconds, of a Knowledge Base. After this lifetime passes, the entire Knowledge Base is considered obsolete and is disregarded by the scanner and thus regenerated on the next scan.

Selecting the first option "Do not execute scanners that have already been executed" will result in the scanner running without portscanning or ping scanning the target host. This lowers the resultant noise on the network by consulting the Knowledge Base for a list of hosts and open ports on those hosts. All data normally generated by the ACT_SCANNER plugins will be pulled from the Knowledge Base instead. The three check boxes that follow limit the execution of information gathering, attack, and DoS (Denial of Service) plugins respectively. An administrator who has just added new plugins either manually or through the nessus-update-plugins script might choose to select all of the check boxes to ensure that only the new plugins are executed. This is only advisable, of course, if you have performed a scan using the older plugins recently enough for the data to be trusted. Don't just look for new vulnerabilities or you'll miss hosts that have very old vulnerabilities on the network!

The remaining option highlighted in Figure 9.5 "Only show differences with the previous scan" is selected to generate "differential scans." Using differential scanning, an analyst or administrator is able to repeatedly scan her subnet/network for the duration of the Knowledge Base lifetime while keeping the returned information/reports minimal, preventing an administrator to constantly read about vulnerabilities that the organization has decided to leave active or mitigate later. This option will have the Nessus scanner return only differences between the Knowledge Base and new scan findings to the user.

Figure 9.5 Differential Scanning

Knowledge Base Saving: Caveats

A few caveats must be kept in mind when reusing saved Knowledge Bases. One can easily picture a host that starts a vulnerable web server after it has been scanned. If the saved Knowledge Base is used to avoid rescanning the host, then it is a certainty that the new service will not be discovered and probed for vulnerabilities. The saved Knowledge Base function should therefore be used with caution and is best used against relatively tightly controlled subnets when testing for a few select vulnerabilities. It is also important to use a relatively short maximum lifespan.

A second caveat and a very real danger that should be considered is that of sensitive information disclosure through access to the Knowledge Base files. With the increasing use of the Nessus Knowledge Base, we are quickly reaching the point where access to the Knowledge Base files is worth as much as access to an actual Nessus report. By default, the /usr/local/var/nessus/users directory (which stores the Knowledge Base

Continued

> files) restricts access to the Knowledge Base files to the root user. Relaxing the permissions on this directory could result in inadvertently sharing sensitive data with other users on the same machine or attackers who can gain even low levels of illicit privilege on the system.

Information Exchange

As mentioned earlier, the primary aim of the Nessus Knowledge Base is to facilitate the sharing of information between tests (plugins) to remove redundancy during testing. We will now quickly examine exactly how the Knowledge Base can be used within NASL scripts. After reading this section, the reader should be able to use calls to write to and read from the Nessus Knowledge Base to improve her scripts.

How Plugins Use the Knowledge Base to Share Data

This section uses examples to illustrate how entries can be written to and read from the Knowledge Base using the various Knowledge Base related calls. This topic is probably best explained by example. For an illustration, let's say we run a "clean" scan (in other words, no existing Knowledge Base) against the target womwom.sensepost.com. The scan completes, finding a host of vulnerabilities present on womwom.sensepost.com's web server. Examining the Nessus Knowledge Base created for this host (/usr/local/var/nessus/users/mh/kbs/womwom.sensepost.com) reveals about 1,800 lines of text. One must bear in mind that about 1,725 lines of the Knowledge Base can be attributed to the Nessus server committing to the Knowledge Base its list of successfully launched tests against the target. These entries are then used in subsequent tests to ensure that plugins are not rerun if Knowledge Base saving is enabled and the appropriate check boxes have been selected. There would be more lines in the Knowledge Base file if the test had not excluded potentially destructive plugins.

A quick *grep* for the word *Port* in the newly created womwom.sensepost.com Knowledge Base file will give us an example of data stored in the Knowledge Base.

```
[root@nessus-server]# grep "Port" womwom.sensepost.com
1086039322 1 Ports/tcp/25=1
1086039322 1 Ports/tcp/22=1
1086039322 1 Ports/tcp/111=1
```

```
1086039322 1 Ports/tcp/443=1
1086039322 1 Ports/tcp/631=1
1086039322 1 Ports/tcp/1241=1
1086039322 1 Ports/tcp/1234=1
```

An Nmap scan against the same host confirms our Nessus results.

```
[root@blowfish]# nmap -sT womwom.sensepost.com

Starting nmap 3.48 ( http://www.insecure.org/nmap/ ) at 2004-05-31 23:43
SAST
Interesting ports on womwom.sensepost.com (XXX.XXX.XXX.XXX):
(The 1650 ports scanned but not shown below are in state: closed)
PORT      STATE SERVICE
22/tcp    open  ssh
25/tcp    open  smtp
111/tcp   open  rpcbind
443/tcp   open  https
631/tcp   open  ipp
1234/tcp  open  hotline
1241/tcp  open  nessus

Nmap run completed -- 1 IP address (1 host up) scanned in 0.385 seconds
```

The results match, as they should, considering that nessusd has merely run a wrapped *nmap* command to gather the same information. Nessus goes on, however, and a host of plugins like find_service.nes and find_service2.nasl then attempt to determine the service running behind these open ports. Once a plugin has determined the running service, it makes a call to the Knowledge Base by using NASL's register_service(port, proto) call. This call defines two items in the Knowledge Base:

- Known/tcp/port   = proto
- Services/proto   = port

For illustration, we make a simple alteration to the nasl that confirms the existence of a Nessus daemon running on a host (nessus_detect.nasl). All we need to do here is add the following lines:

```
-snip-
# nasl modified for simple test
register_service(port: port, proto: "FooBar");
-snip-
```

Running the scan again against the host womwom.sensepost.com returns the exact same portscan result as before. A *grep* (or *egrep* in this case) for Services or Known (identified services) in the new Knowledge Base file returns the following:

```
[root@nessus-server]# egrep "Known|Services" womwom.sensepost.com
1086039325 1 Known/tcp/111=portmapper
1086039325 1 Services/portmapper=111
1086043077 1 Services/www=443
1086043077 1 Known/tcp/443=www
1086043079 1 Services/unknown=111
1086043082 1 Services/www=631
1086043082 1 Known/tcp/631=www
1086043083 1 Services/smtp=25
1086043083 1 Known/tcp/25=smtp
1086043083 1 Services/ssh=22
1086043083 1 Known/tcp/22=ssh
1086043083 1 Services/unknown=1241
1086043083 1 Services/www=1234
1086043083 1 Known/tcp/1234=www
1086043093 1 Services/nessus=1241
1086043093 1 Services/FooBar=1241
1086043103 1 Known/tcp/1241=nessus
1086043103 1 Known/tcp/1241=FooBar
```

Also worth noting here is that the Nessus scanner has managed to correctly identify and register the web server running on port 1234:

```
1086043083 1 Services/www=1234
```

NASL also provides the set_kb_item(string: name, string: value) and get_kb_item(string: name) functions to set and retrieve single key-value pairs from the Knowledge Base. The function get_kb_list(string: name) is almost the same as the get_kb_item function, except, as its name suggests, it returns a list to the calling script. To demonstrate how a NASL would make use of these functions, we create two simple dummy plugins (sense.nasl and post.nasl).

sense.nasl:

```
# This script written to demonstrate kb writing <haroon@sensepost.com>
if(description)
{
 script_id(123123);
 script_version ("$Revision: 1.2 $");
 name["english"] = "sense";
 script_name(english:name["english"]);


desc["english"] = "
Pointless test in order to set a kb item.
We will set a key of Weird/non_existent/key
with a value of Moo
Risk factor : Info";

 script_description(english:desc["english"]);
 summary["english"] = "Sets pointless KB item";
 script_summary(english:summary["english"]);
 script_category(ACT_GATHER_INFO);


 script_copyright(english:"This script is not worth Copyrighting (nwC) 2004
haroon meer");
 family["english"] = "Misc.";
 script_family(english:family["english"]);
 script_dependencie("find_service.nes");
 exit(0);
}


 set_kb_item(name: "Weird/non_existent/key", value:string("Moo"));
```

Once this plugin has been run, we can peek ahead to check for a successful Knowledge Base write by manually *grep'ing* the resultant Knowledge Base file:

```
[root@nessus-server]# grep Weird womwom.sensepost.com
1086049000 1 Weird/non_existent/key=Moo
```

So far, so good! Now we write another simple (and pointless) NASL to read the value from the Knowledge Base and display the results.

post.nasl:

```
# This script written to demonstrate kb reading <haroon@sensepost.com>
if(description)
{
 script_id(223123);
 script_version ("$Revision: 1.2 $");
 name["english"] = "post";
 script_name(english:name["english"]);


desc["english"] = "
Pointless test in order to read a kb item.
We will retrieve the value for the key
Weird/non_existent/key


Risk factor : Info";


 script_description(english:desc["english"]);
 summary["english"] = "reads pointless KB item";
 script_summary(english:summary["english"]);
 script_category(ACT_ATTACK);


 script_copyright(english:"This script is not worth Copyrighting (nwC) 2004
haroon meer");
 family["english"] = "Misc.";
 script_family(english:family["english"]);
 script_dependencie("sense.nasl");
 exit(0);
}


 val = get_kb_item("Weird/non_existent/key");
 security_note(data:"We extracted the following key from the KB for this
host" + val, port:0);
```

The post script simply creates a value called "val," which is populated by the value returned from the Knowledge Base using the get_kb_item("Weird/non_existent/key") call. The last line simply returns the string through the report viewer. Note also the script_dependencie("sense.nasl") line that needs to be included in our post.nasl script. This ensures that the sense.nasl will be run prior to the running of post.nasl should the configuration be set to include dependencies at run time. We can see this dependency by using the GUI client and selecting the NASL in question.

Clicking the button in Figure 9.6 spawns the Dependencies window in Figure 9.7. It would be worth noting the outcome when other plugins' (not as simple as this) dependences are not met, and they use that dependence to share data.

Figure 9.6 NASL Script Details

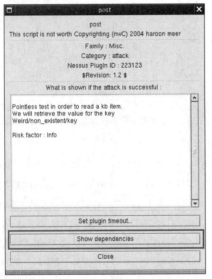

Figure 9.7 Dependency Check

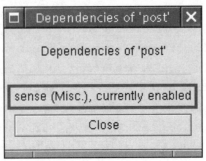

The result of the scan is shown in Figure 9.8 for the sake of completeness, but illustrates that post.nasl successfully read the key/value pair written to the Knowledge Base by sense.nasl.

Figure 9.8 Nessus Report Viewer (Single Knowledge Base Key/Value)

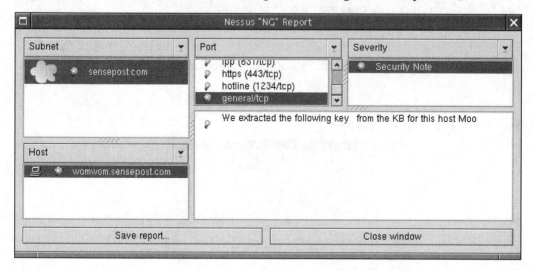

The get_kb_list(string: name) function has the additional benefit of accepting a literal Knowledge Base entry name or a wildcard (for example, "Services/www" or "Services/w★"). Since the Knowledge Base might hold multiple lines with the same key, the function get_kb_list() returns a hash. The requesting NASL then needs to either wrap the request in a call to make_array(), or make use of a *foreach* loop to iterate through all items in the hash.

A simple change to sense.nasl allows us to set multiple values for our key:

```
set_kb_item(name: "Weird/non_existent/key", value:string("Moo"));
set_kb_item(name: "Weird/non_existent/key", value:string("Doe"));
set_kb_item(name: "Weird/non_existent/key", value:string("Ray"));
set_kb_item(name: "Weird/non_existent/key", value:string("Me"));
set_kb_item(name: "Weird/non_existent/key", value:string("Far"));
set_kb_item(name: "Weird/non_existent/key", value:string("So"));
set_kb_item(name: "Weird/non_existent/key", value:string("La"));
set_kb_item(name: "Weird/non_existent/key", value:string("Ti"));
set_kb_item(name: "Weird/non_existent/key", value:string("Doe"));
```

While this example is highly contrived, there are many cases where multiple plugins add a key-value pair to the Knowledge Base resulting in this type of situation. The corresponding change that needs to be made to our post.nasl is made incredibly easy thanks to NASL's make_list() function.

-post.nasl-

```
val = make_list(get_kb_list("Weird/non_existent/key"));
 foreach item (val)
 {
   answer = answer + ", " + item;
 }


 security_note(data:"We extracted the following keys from the KB for this
host" + answer, port:0);
```

-post.nasl-

The *foreach* loop used here iterates through the array and merely appends the new array element to the answer variable. This answer variable is then reported to the user (see Figure 9.9).

Figure 9.9 Nessus Report Viewer (Multiple Returned Values)

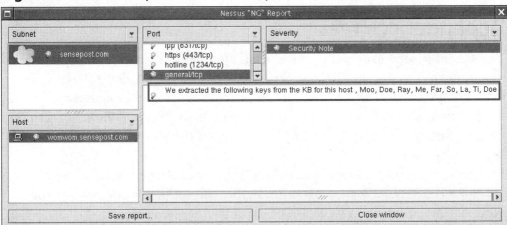

The Type of Data that Is Stored

Theoretically, the Nessus Knowledge Base can be used to store just about any type of data that one comes across during an assessment. Most plugins restrict themselves to writing data to the Knowledge Base that is worth sharing with other plugins. For example:

- **Information about the scan** ("What tests did I run?")
- **Information about a test** ("Did the test succeed?")
- **Information about the target** ("Open Ports/Service Banners/Service Descriptions")
- **Information about the results** ("3 Info messages and 1 Critical during this scan!")

The value of a key begins immediately following the equal sign and is terminated by the newline character.

```
1086051533 1 ftp/banner/21=BLEH_BLEH_ BLEH_BLEH_ BLEH_BLEH_ BLEH_BLEH_
BLEH_BLEH_ BLEH_BLEH_ BLEH_BLEH_ BLEH_BLEH_ BLEH_BLEH_ BLEH_BLEH_
BLEH_BLEH_ BLEH_BLEH_ BLEH_BLEH_ BLEH_BLEH_BLEH
1086051588 1…
```

Dependency Trees

The simplistic sense.nasl and post.nasl examples used earlier in this chapter served to introduce the concept of script dependencies in the Knowledge Base. With more complex tests that are built on top of more layers of protocols, keeping track of these dependencies becomes a little more challenging. We now examine the smb_lanman_browse_list.nasl script to explain the concept of NASL script dependency trees.

The smb_lanman_browse_list.nasl script has the relatively modest goal of obtaining the remote host's browse list. Before this script can successfully run, however, it requires the completion of the following two scripts: netbios_name_get.nasl and smb_login.nasl. With the option to "enable script dependencies at run-time" set, the scanner will attempt to launch those plugins if they have not already run. netbios_name_get.nasl in turn requires cifs445.nasl, while smb_login.nasl requires netbios_name_get.nasl, cifs445.nasl, logins.nasl, and find_service.nes. cifs445.nasl is in turn dependent once more on find_service.nes. This might seem convoluted, but it's actually a reasonable dependency tree that shows that the plugin authors are abstracting the process appropriately, working to both avoid duplicating code between plugins and to create a framework for building other SMB/NetBIOS-related plugins.

Limitations

While the Knowledge Base is an invaluable addition to Nessus' architecture, it does have some shortcomings inherent in its current design. This short section is aimed at ensuring that the user is aware of the possible complications that could arise when making use of the Nessus Knowledge Base.

Using get_kb_item and fork

We explained earlier the use of get_kb_list() when dealing with multiple key/value pairs. When the singular get_kb_item() is used to retrieve a list, the plugin forks for every additional returned value. This technique has both pros and cons, allowing us to write really small tests when dealing with multiple keys, but at the same time adding a level of complexity that we need to be careful of. Returning to our post.nasl after having created multiple entries in the kb using sense.nasl, we have:

```
-post.nasl-
# This script written to demonstrate kb reading <haroon@sensepost.com>

if(description)
{
  script_id(223123);
  script_version ("$Revision: 1.2 $");
  name["english"] = "post";
  script_name(english:name["english"]);

desc["english"] = "
Pointless test in order to read a kb item.
We will retrieve the value for the key
Weird/non_existent/key


Risk factor : Info";
```

```
script_description(english:desc["english"]);
summary["english"] = "reads pointless KB item";
script_summary(english:summary["english"]);
script_category(ACT_ATTACK);

script_copyright(english:"This script is not worth Copyrighting (nwC) 2004
haroon meer");
family["english"] = "Misc.";
script_family(english:family["english"]);
script_dependencie("sense.nasl");
exit(0);
}
```

security_note(data:"We extracted the following keys from the KB for this host" + get_kb_item("Weird/non_existent/key"), port:0);

```
-post.nasl-
```

Note that this time, we call security_note() just once. The call to get_kb_item(), however, will return a list, causing the plugin to fork for every unique key/value pair returned. This results in the report shown in Figure 9.10.

Figure 9.10 Nessus Report Viewer (Multiple Key/Value Pairs)

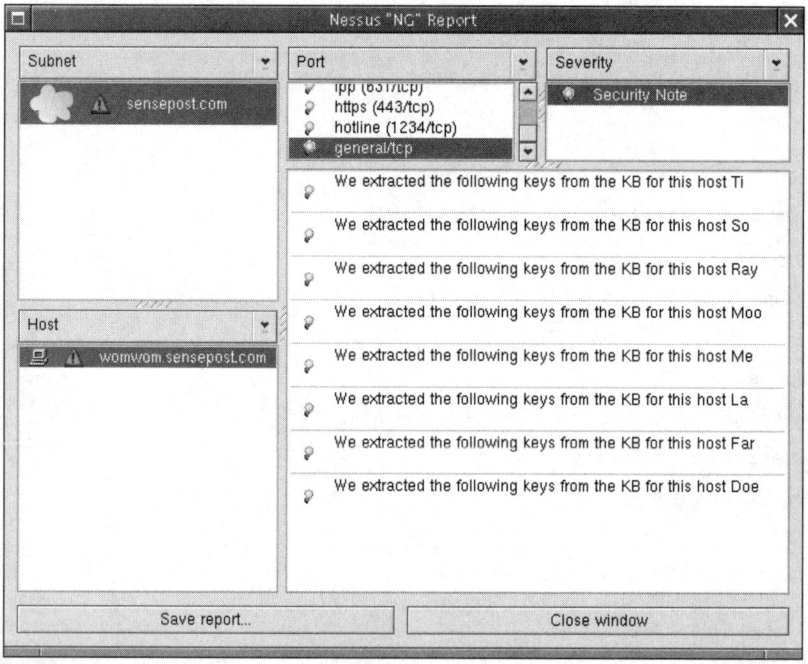

This forking needs to be kept in mind when dealing with sockets. A call to open a socket made prior to the fork will potentially result in multiple children trying to write to the same socket at the same time.

Tools and Traps...

Knowledge Base Saving in a DHCP Environment

Astute readers will have spotted the inherent danger of saving Knowledge Base files based on IP addresses or DNS names on a network running the Dynamic Host Configuration Protocol (DHCP). In such cases, it is possible for hosts on the network to be out of sync with the data contained in the Knowledge Base. For example, hosts A, B, and C are scanned and their respective Knowledge Bases are stored. During the lifetime of these Knowledge Bases, however, the hosts' DHCP leases expire and are redistributed to other hosts. This then leads to the new hosts inheriting the Knowledge Bases of the hosts that previously had their IP addresses! This is almost certainly the worst kind of inaccuracy possible when using the Knowledge Base, but also the easiest to guard against.

In a DHCP environment, the user/analyst should turn on the **Designate hosts by their MAC address** option under the **Scan options** tab. Selecting this check box will cause Nessus to save entries into the Knowledge Base using the host's Ethernet MAC address instead of its IP address. Since MAC addresses are unique physical numbers tied to the hosts' network cards by the hardware manufacturers, they serve as excellent unique identifiers when IP addresses aren't reliable. Remember, though, that MAC addresses are at Layer 2, the data link layer, and are thus only useful on a LAN. You can't communicate with a host through a router and still discover the host's MAC address. As we discussed in Chapter 3, you'll need to place a nessusd server on each network for which you want to identify hosts by their MAC addresses.

Summary

The Nessus Knowledge Base gives power to both the analyst writing tests, and the administrator running the scanner. The analyst benefits from being able to write more efficient, less bandwidth-hungry tests, while the administrator benefits from decreased network traffic while maintaining his security posture at acceptable levels. The decision to use Knowledge Base saving and to limit future scans based on data stored within the Knowledge Base is a tricky one, however, and should be carefully examined before execution.

The bulk of the settings governing the use of the Knowledge Base during a scan can be found under the KB tab of the Nessus Setup GUI on the client. Theses settings can be used to enable or disable Knowledge Base saving, and to guide what the scanner can do with the stored Knowledge Base data and for what period of time. A Nessus user might choose to scan or ignore hosts with existing Knowledge Bases and might choose to run different permutations of the NASL script families based on the information stored in the target host's Knowledge Base.

Making use of the Knowledge Base to store data that should persist (at least for the duration of the scan) makes good sense and is a technique that has been used to increasing effect as time goes on. Simply making use of the correct calls to retrieve these stored values and being aware of the Knowledge Base's possible limitations is important when writing NASL scripts.

Solutions Fast Track

Knowledge Base Basics

☑ The Knowledge Base is the list of information gathered on a single tested host.

☑ This information is referenced during the running scan and can be configured to serve as a data store for subsequent scans on the host for a configurable period of time.

☑ Selecting the Enable KB Saving option under the KB tab will by default save Knowledge Bases per host but will still redo all subsequent scans from scratch unless other options are set.

☑ The scanner can be configured to ensure that only "New Hosts" (hosts that are discovered by the scanner that do not have a corresponding Knowledge Base) or "Old Hosts" (hosts that do have Knowledge Bases) are tested.

☑ One can choose to ignore scan categories on hosts with valid Knowledge Bases.

☑ Differential Scanning can be enabled under the KB tab to limit scanner output to results that have no history in the relevant host's Knowledge Base.

Information Exchange

☑ Entries are stored and retrieved from the Knowledge Base in the form of key/value pairs.

☑ The scanner can be configured to dynamically "Enable dependencies at run-time" to ensure that plugins are ordered well, such that key values are set in one plugin before they are required by another.

☑ Values can be written and read by making use of set_kb_item() and get_kb_item()/get_kb_list() calls, respectively.

Limitations

☑ Using get_kb_item() to retrieve a set of values in a single call causes the NASL to fork for every returned value. This could cause complications if multiple children attempt to communicate with the same socket opened prior to the *fork()*.

☑ One should consider the fact that scanned hosts could change within the window period of a Knowledge Base's lifetime, potentially causing a scanner to overlook issues until the Knowledge Base expires. It is thus important to set short-enough lifetimes for the Knowledge Bases via the GUI **KB** tab.

☑ DHCP'd environments are prone to complications with reusable Knowledge Bases, but this can be mitigated somewhat by making use of Ethernet MAC addresses instead of IP addresses as Knowledge Base filenames. When using this replacement mechanism, remember that every host you want to scan must have a nessusd server running on its local network (LAN).

Frequently Asked Questions

The following Frequently Asked Questions, answered by the authors of this book, are designed to both measure your understanding of the concepts presented in this chapter and to assist you with real-life implementation of these concepts. To have your questions about this chapter answered by the author, browse to **www.syngress.com/solutions** and click on the **"Ask the Author"** form. You will also gain access to thousands of other FAQs at ITFAQnet.com.

Q: Is there a difference between using get_kb_item() and get_kb_list()?

A: Yes. get_kb_item() will fork for every new key/value pair returned (when dealing with multiple returned entries), while get_kb_list() will not.

Q: Is it dangerous to always keep my Knowledge Base valid for the default 10 days?

A: *Dangerous* is a relative term. The risk that one must live with (if limiting the actions of certain tests) is that the target host might have changed within that time window in its configuration, vulnerability set, or even IP address!

Q: If I disable KB saving, does Nessus stop using the KB?

A: Saving the KB doesn't affect the behavior of Nessus, rather it only affects whether Nessus keeps a record of the KB it generated during the scan.

Chapter 10

Enterprise Scanning

Solutions in this Chapter:

- **Planning a Deployment**
- **Configuring Scanners**
- **Data Correlation**
- **Common Problems**

☑ **Summary**

☑ **Solutions Fast Track**

☑ **Frequently Asked Questions**

Introduction

Enterprise vulnerability scanning is quite complicated, and as such requires a certain amount of planning, preparation, and adjustment. The key factors for effectively scanning the enterprise for security vulnerabilities are easy administration, periodic scanning, and accurate results.

There is no trivial way to take a scanner such as Nessus and use it to scan the entire enterprise network. Simply pointing it toward the network and scanning will not be enough. This chapter shows some of the caveats that make this process difficult. You'll learn, for example, why simply scanning the entire network from a single point is often not viable. This involves exploring distributed scanning, differential reporting, report correlation, and automated updating.

At this point in the book, we expect that you are most likely already using Nessus for regular security testing, and are looking to take it up a notch—from maintaining a list of hosts you regularly scan, to scanning your entire enterprise and using the results to improve your enterprise's security status.

Planning a Deployment

In the following section we will help you outline your plan for deployment.

Define Your Needs

Before scanning your enterprise network for security holes, you must remember that simply scanning anything that has an IP address will not bring you the expected benefits unless you can handle the huge number of vulnerabilities that are likely to appear in the report.

Our experience shows that on a typical vulnerability scan in a medium-to-large enterprise, each host scanned returns an average of 3 high-risk, 5 medium, and about 10 low-risk vulnerabilities. Quick math will show that scanning a small subnet of 100 hosts will return around 300 high-risk vulnerabilities and about 1,800 vulnerabilities in total. This computation doesn't take into account that some vulnerabilities might be the same on different computers, or that the same vulnerability might exist on different ports on the same machine. According to an old Chinese proverb, "if *what we know* is the contour of a circle, and *what we do not know* is the inside of that circle, the *more we know* the less *we know that we do not know.*" We therefore must prepare beforehand so we're not overwhelmed by the amount of information we will receive once we start scanning the network. We will divide the preparation into three parts: planning, preparation, and segmentation.

Planning

Some companies consider their customer database their most critical asset. Others consider the CEO's laptop most sensitive. Others still will mark their file server as the important one. Just as this is different for each company, each company's security needs are different, and so is the understanding of what "enterprise scanning" requires.

The easiest way to identify your most critical assets is to answer the following question: How much money and time will you lose if "something bad" happens to that asset? The definition of "something bad" is your worst-case scenario; this might be the deletion of a critical file or perhaps your database falling into the hands of your competition. Once you answer that question, you will see that scanning anything and everything doesn't necessarily solve the problem of scanning your most critical assets, as too much information is just as bad as too little. If you fail to notice vulnerabilities in your most critical assets because the report overflows with data about your least important hosts, you've simply missed important vulnerabilities for a pitiful reason.

When customers say they are uncertain of what is critical and what is not, it is good practice to revert to this list of items, ordered with more critical resources first:

1. Centralized servers (DNS, mail, file, database)
2. Financial servers and workstations
3. Management servers and workstations
4. Servers and workstations containing marketing data and plans
5. Sales servers and workstations
6. All remaining hosts

This list is a good starting point in identifying what the company management should worry most about an attacker compromising.

Scanning the right assets in the right way (most important first, or, alternatively, the most critical more frequently) will help you understand what is required to protect your critical machines.

This will prevent you from being overwhelmed by information and subsequently giving up the idea of scanning your enterprise. We have seen many cases of companies that reached the unfortunate conclusion that vulnerability scanning is "impractical," just because they were scanning the wrong parts of the network or just too much of it. This made it impossible for them to realize the obvious benefits if the vulnerability scanner was used properly. They threw away a tool that would be perfectly useful if it was simply tuned to only examine the most critical systems.

New security holes surface daily, and in order to be effective, you should plan to run your scans on a regular basis. It would be impractical to try to handle dozens and sometimes hundreds of reports illustrating the security vulnerabilities of the enterprise network without first prioritizing which reports are most important.

By the end of this section, you will be able to develop a list of critical assets (identified by hostnames, IP addresses, or even IP ranges) ordered by how important they are to your organization. Next to each asset, list what their acceptable "bill of health" is. You might decide that some servers must be completely free of vulnerabilities, while others might have medium- and low-risk vulnerabilities only. At the very least, do not accept any "high-risk" vulnerabilities on any of the critical assets. In addition, write down a point of contact for each asset, as this will be required once you start generating reports and need someone to address the issues found, and the frequency with which you will scan the asset. Table 10.1 shows one way of organizing the list of assets.

Table 10.1 Asset List

Asset Name	IP Ranges/ Hostnames	Expected Results	Manager Name and E-Mail	Frequency of Scans
HR database	192.168.1. 50–250	No open ports No vulnerabilities	Joe Smith joes@ acmecorp.net	Daily
R&D file servers	192.168. 1.3–10	No open ports except file sharing and HTTP No high or medium vulnerabilities	John Williams johnw@ acmecorp.net	Every other week

When it comes to the frequency of scans, we prefer *more* versus *less*. By *more*, we mean that running the scan once a day is preferable to running it once a month. Although this might sound extreme (we can imagine you're now thinking, "Do I really need to scan my network on a daily basis?"), you need to remember the recent Sasser worm. The Sasser worm hit the Internet just three weeks after the vulnerability was discovered. This means that a monthly vulnerability scan could have missed this vulnerability altogether, and as a result you would have missed the need to install this critical patch. This vulnerability discovery to worm creation window has actually been steadily shrinking. We cannot stress enough how important the frequency of your scans is to their success in preventing worm outbreaks at your site.

NOTE

Here are some vulnerability statistics from ICAT, available at http://icat.nist.gov/icat.cfm?function=statistics. In the first five months of 2004, 313 new vulnerabilities were discovered. In the year 2003, the total count was 1,007, and in the year 2002, the total number of vulnerabilities discovered was 1,308. Year 2001 holds the record for the last four years with 1,506.

The CERT reports, available at www.cert.org/stats/, show even higher figures. The number of vulnerabilities reported to CERT in the year 2003 was 3,784; in 2002, the number was 4,129; and in 2001, the count was 2,437.

According to SecuriTeam.com, an online vulnerabilities database, an average of about five new vulnerabilities are discovered each day. The total number of new vulnerabilities reported on the web site during the first five months of the year 2004 was over 750.

Most network administrators and security managers are extremely busy people who will find it difficult to handle a dozen or more scanning results a day, especially when they need to give these results the required attention. We will therefore show you in later sections ways to reduce the amount of reports generated to just one or two. Each of these reports will only show the changes since the last scan (if any) by using differential report generation.

Preparation

In many organizations, different managers are in charge of different assets. Each of these managers needs to be prepared for the vulnerability scans on his or her assets. In fact, in most cases, the scans will find vulnerabilities in the assets for which the managers are responsible, so it's a good idea to prepare them for the potentially bad news. Furthermore, vulnerability scans are very "noisy"—the relevant network and system administrators need to be prepared to see abnormal log entries, higher CPU and memory consumption, and an increase in network traffic during the scanning phase.

Notes from the Underground....

The Importance of Prior Notification

One of the authors was once present during a vulnerability scan that was done without prior notification to some of the system and database administrators. During the scans, some of the Solaris systems and the Oracle databases exhibited strange and abnormal log entries, all caused by the fact that the vulnerability scanner was sending unusual requests as part of the vulnerability assessment. Not knowing that a scan was in progress, the administrators immediately assumed the database was failing and started to run corrective measures.

You might be able to guess what happened next. The corrective actions, which were trying to fix a nonexisting problem, corrupted the database and destroyed the information stored on that machine. Hours of labor could have been saved if the administrators had been notified in advance of the pending scan and that unusual events would potentially occur during that time.

A good way to make sure everyone is aware that you are implementing enterprise-scaled vulnerability assessment is to invite the different managers to a meeting where you present the following:

- An overview of Nessus' capabilities.

- Different aspects of Nessus' effects.

- Live scans of a test environment, preferably a machine or subnet of low importance. This will better illustrate how the scan affects the machines and demonstrate the scanning process.

This last point, the demonstration of a live scan, should probably involve a look at the log messages generated on the target machines and might include a look at the network traffic through a sniffer like tcpdump or Ethereal.

By the end of this section, all of your asset managers should be aware of your intention to regularly scan them. They should understand that these scans will result in vulnerabilities being highlighted, which will then need to be addressed.

Finally, remember the politics of the situation. If you want a manager to be most responsive to vulnerability data, or any data presented by the security team, it's important to work hard to avoid an adversarial relationship. Approach the manager with a helpful tone and do what you can to make the process easier. Otherwise, you might find that either vulnerability scanning gets shut down or the results ignored. You can often help managers most by giving them a preliminary report, allowing them the chance to fix vulnerabilities and get a second scan in one to three day's time. This helps managers show that they are responsive and that vulnerabilities get a short lifespan on their watch.

Segmentation

As discussed earlier, your network contains different kinds of assets, each of which might have a different type of confidential material on it. The scan results, and scanning in general, might reveal sensitive information, such as usernames, weak passwords, hidden directories, and, of course, security vulnerabilities in those assets. To minimize information leakage, you should consider segmenting your scans, breaking them up so no one report contains information about the entire enterprise.

Segmentation allows you to test each of your assets while not providing confidential information about one set of assets to a manager of another set. In computer security, we're always thinking about risk avoidance and risk mitigation. In this situation, we're trying to decrease both the probability that sensitive information leaks and how much information a single leak can carry. Giving information about one asset's vulnerability to eight people instead of two roughly quadruples the risk. Remember, that person might turn against the organization, potentially criminally. He might drop the report on the ground inadvertently; he might get mugged. It's far easier to deal with these events if the report that's used maliciously contains less information.

There's more than just vulnerability information at stake, though. Nessus can be configured with or discover sensitive information, including logon information for Windows, brute-forcing results, SNMP community names, and so forth, and as this type of information can show up in the vulnerability reports, you should segment the results in such a way that only the people who need access to each piece of information actually receive it. Another benefit of segmentation is that it allows you to use load-balancing techniques to optimize the scan based on your network topology and host concentrations.

Network Topology

Your organization's network topology largely affects the quality of the results you receive. For example, results from scanning the internal network (or MZ network) from your DMZ network will differ from a scan done from your internal network. Each of these scans is equally important, and the different results provide insight into your network's security situation. The difference is mainly caused by the effect that firewalls and other network devices have on the scan, as they allow or block connections, route or reroute traffic, according to a predefined rule set.

Therefore, a critical question to answer during the planning phase is, "what do you want to find?" Are you trying to see what a normal employee would be able to do to your file server, or what a night cleaning crewmember could do without having a valid username and password combination? Are you trying to find out what an Internet attacker would be able to do to your web server, or what a hacker could do if he successfully compromises the DMZ?

Each of these questions is equally important and requires a different type of deployment.

NOTE

At first glance, it might seem logical to install a scanning server on each of your different networks (DMZ, MZ, privileged network, etc.) and run VA scans from each to the rest of the organization. However, that would probably be a waste of time, as high-risk vulnerability on a sensitive host, no matter who has access to that network, should always be considered critical. Hiding a vulnerability doesn't fix it—it will eventually resurface. Network segmentation is an added protection, but should not be an alternative to fixing vulnerabilities.

The actual benefit of scanning the network from different points of view is in providing you with a feel of what needs to be addressed immediately and what can wait. For example, a high-risk vulnerability on your web server connected to the Internet needs greater attention than a high-risk file-sharing related vulnerability on the same web server does, as no outsider should have access to the related file-sharing port.

When segmentation is involved, we always recommend separating your network topology into two parts— internal and external—before dividing it further. "Internal" refers to the networks that are accessible only to employees, while "external" consists of all the hosts that are accessible from the Internet.

Your external topology should be scanned from an external server, imitating as much as possible an external attacker. The internal topology should be scanned from an internal server with full network access, imitating to the greatest extent possible an internal attacker

NOTE

You should remember that when you receive the results for the external scans, every vulnerability should be accounted for, as it has been proven in the past that something considered a medium-risk vulnerability can quickly develop into a high-risk problem. In addition, low-risk vulnerabilities sometimes indicate that something is wrong: unnecessary services are installed on a hardened server, or incorrect rules are configured on the firewall. For example, your scan might find an unnecessary portmap or rpcbind process on a UNIX box and rank that as a low priority. A week later, when researchers release a remote-root vulnerability in Sun's rpcbind, the risk due to that unnecessary service is much higher. It's better to address even low-priority issues early, before the vulnerability escalates or a new one is discovered.

Bandwidth Requirements

One of the more important aspects of enterprise scanning is that unlike a one-time penetration test, typically done quarterly or even annually, enterprise scanning is done on a daily, weekly, or monthly basis. As such, network effects of the scan, such as bandwidth utilization or intrusiveness of the scans, are especially important.

Unfortunately, no network can provide us with unlimited bandwidth, and no two points on the network can use the complete bandwidth allowed by the network hardware without affecting other points on the network. Therefore, you must take into consideration that scanning your network will affect your network's overall performance. To complicate things even further, interoffice communications infrastructure tends to be even more restricted, and instead of 10/100/1000Mb per second, we can expect those communication lines to be 1Mb per second or less. In any case, this bandwidth needs to be shared with our coworkers—saturating the connection with our vulnerability scan will result in inaccurate scan reports due to packet loss, and lost of connectivity and functionality to our coworkers. Although Nessus does not consume much bandwidth if properly configured, scanning across a low-bandwidth and high-latency connection is not recommended unless there are no other alternatives.

How can we handle the problem of scanning multiple physical locations? One easy solution is to place a server in each location to make sure the available bandwidth between the scanning server and the network being scanned is at least 10Mb.

However, a better solution would be to first understand how much bandwidth Nessus requires, and enumerate any locations that do not meet these requirements. Before we lay out the bandwidth requirements, let's look at what affects bandwidth consumption. One simple rule of thumb is that a host with no open services requires far less bandwidth to scan than a server hosting multiple web servers, each running on a different port. The fewer services a host has, the fewer plugins Nessus will need to launch against it; thus, the lower bandwidth the Nessus scans will consume.

We have used freely available open-source tools to verify the bandwidth requirements needed for an average host. The tools are very easy to obtain, and require no knowledge of programming and very little technical skills. First, we need to use the ever-popular packet-capturing tool tcpdump (available from www.tcpdump.org). You can use simple capturing filters to capture only those packets originating from the scanning computer to the scanned host. We also use further filtering of the captured packets to prevent the capture file from becoming too large and difficult to handle.

For example, testing a port-80 scan using the filter host 192.168.1.243 and port 80 allows the capture of all traffic originating from and destined for port 80. After capturing the entire Nessus session, you can generate statistics on the captured traffic. To do so, open the capture file using Ethereal (available from www.ethereal.org) and choose **Statistics | Summary** (see Figure 10.1). Alternatively, if you want to create more in-depth graphs and statistics, you can use the tool tcpstat (available at www.frenchfries.net/paul/tcpstat/) with gnuplot (www.gnuplot.info). Tcpstat is able to take raw tcpdump files and generate numerical data from them. This numerical data combined with gnuplot allows you to take any numbers and crunch them into a graph.

We used the following steps to capture packets, take the capture file and convert it to numerical data, and generate from it an easy-to-analyze graph. We start with our packet-capturing command:

```
tcpdump -w iis.dump "host 192.168.1.243 and port 80"
```

Once a substantial amount of data is captured, we convert it to statistical information using:

```
tcpstat -r iis.dump -o "%R\t%B\n" 1 > iis.total.data \
tcpstat -r iis.dump -f "dstport 80" -o "%R\t%B\n" 1 > iis.up.data \
tcpstat -r iis.dump -f "srcport 80" -o "%R\t%B\n" 1 > iis.down.data
```

We then generate the corresponding graph by opening gnuplot and typing the following at the prompt:

```
set term png small
set data style lines
set grid
set yrange [ -10 :  ]
set title "IIS Bandwidth"
set xlabel "seconds"
set ylabel "KBytes/s"
plot "iis.total.data" using 1:($2/1024) smooth csplines title "Total"\
    , "iis.up.data" using 1:($2/1024) smooth csplines title "Up"\
    , "iis.down.data" using 1:($2/1024) smooth csplines title "Down"
```

The result of gnuplot will appear on the screen, and can be redirected to a file. For example, writing these lines to a file called gnuplot.script and running **gnuplot gnuplot.script > picture.png** will generate a file called picture.png containing the desired graph.

Now that we know how to generate the information, let's understand the different phases of Nessus scans and how much bandwidth they generate using the method just illustrated.

Portscanning Phase

During the portscanning phase, Nessus can use Nmap or a similar portscanner to determine what ports are open on a particular host. The Nmap "connect scan," which uses a single TCP 72-byte packet with its SYN flag set, is Nessus' default method to detect open ports. This packet is sent to each of the ports you configure Nessus to scan. Nessus by default will scan all ports between 1 and 15,000.

The number of packets sent depends on the latency of the scanning host, the network, and the host being scanned. On a very low latency and high-bandwidth network, this portscan can take roughly 1.5 seconds.

Doing some quick math brings us to:

15,000 x 72 = 1,080,000 bytes

The response packets require roughly the same amount of bandwidth. Dividing that by 15 seconds brings us to 720,000 bytes per second, or 720KBps. Although this isn't very high, multiplying this by a few dozen hosts will generate enough traffic to temporarily bring a 100Mbit (roughly 12.5Mbytes per second) network to its knees. In addition, this large amount of packets will strain the firewalls and network devices responsible for connecting your scanning host with the host being scanned.

Moreover, not all traffic is created equal. We see in Figures 10.2 and 10.3 that the portscan phase generates average traffic—this average is controlled by how long we wait for a response from the host being portscanned. We will use this waiting time to reduce the bandwidth requirements, by setting the value to 1 millisecond (with the value of *Maximum wait between probes (ms)*). In addition, notice that there is a minimal difference between the bandwidth consumption of a TCP Connect() scan and a SYN scan.

Figure 10.1 Ethereal Summary

Figure 10.2 Portscan (1–15000)

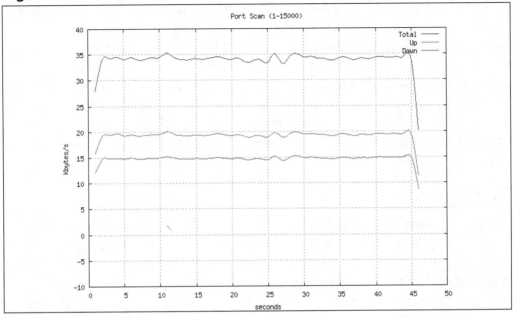

Figure 10.3 Portscan—SYN (1–15000)

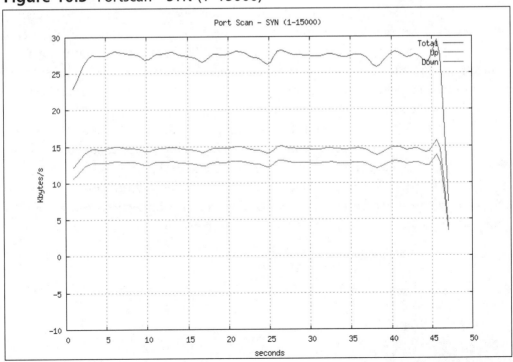

We can easily control how fast the portscan proceeds and the average bandwidth being consumed by choosing settings other than the defaults Nessus uses for Nmap. Of course, these changes will affect the time it takes to portscan the host, but at the moment, we are more concerned about bandwidth utilization than scanning speed. Note that our goal in enterprise scanning is an optimal configuration where no interaction with the scanning server is required after our early tuning, and thus we can just sit back and receive reports, while Nessus scans at its own speed consuming predetermined bandwidth. The process is automatic, and we don't really care how long it takes, just that the results are accurate and as unobtrusive as possible.

Testing Phase

During this phase, Nessus takes each port reported open by Nmap and runs a service detection process on it to determine the service type of that port (for example, HTTP, SMTP, POP3, etc.). For each service detected, Nessus will then run its arsenal of plugins. The more ports and applications you have on your machine, the more bandwidth consumed. However, since you can control the number of plugins that are run simultaneously, you can easily control the utilized bandwidth during this phase.

By launching Nessus against a default IIS web server and analyzing the traffic generated, we can see that the upstream bandwidth required averages 30KB per second, while the downstream is an average of 239KB per second. Running a similar scan against a default Apache web server will return different results: for the upstream an average of 13KB per second, and for the downstream an average of 73KB per second.

An average is one thing but as the two graphs in Figures 10.4 and 10.5 show, a more elusive bandwidth requirement issue hides behind it, as there are impressive bandwidth peaks going well over the 500KBps for Apache and over the 1,000KBps for IIS. However, in both cases, they are the downstreams—the responses from the server. This means that asymmetric connections can be used while it might appear that this was not the case before.

Figure 10.4 Apache Scan (port 80/www)

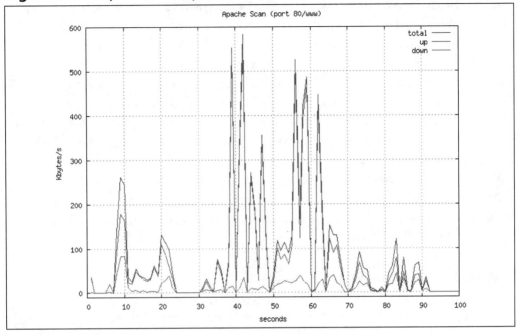

Figure 10.5 IIS Scan (port 80/www)

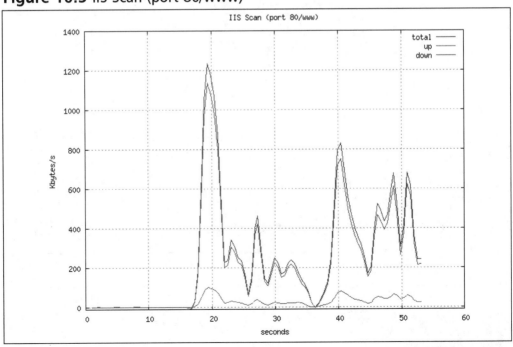

There is one obvious difference between **Apache Scan (port 80/www)** and **IIS Scan (port 80/www)**. The **IIS Scan (port 80/www)** is a slow starter, while the *Apache Scan* appears to consume an average bandwidth throughout the scan.

This difference in bandwidth consumption is due to the type of plugin "sophistication" Nessus uses—when the web server is detected to be Apache, Nessus will run certain tests, whereas if IIS is detected, those tests will not be run.

You should note that HTTP is not a special case—most protocols are just as bandwidth intensive as HTTP, if not more. For the sake of comparison, NetBIOS (the protocol used when scanning for vulnerabilities affecting ports 135, 137, 139, and 445) will yield a higher bandwidth usage on an unpatched Windows 2000 system when it is provided with a username and password combination in comparison to when it is only allowed to use NULL (anonymous) sessions, as shown in Figures 10.6 and 10.7.

Figure 10.6 SMB Traffic (NULL Session Only)

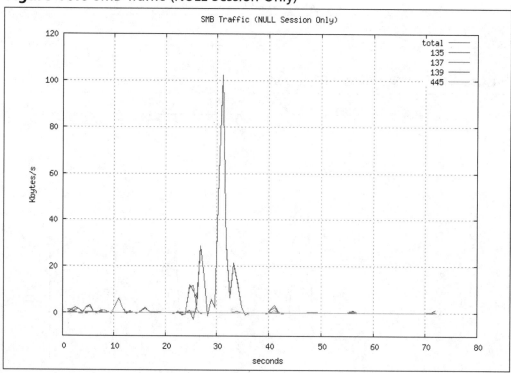

Figure 10.7 SMB Traffic (Authenticated Session)

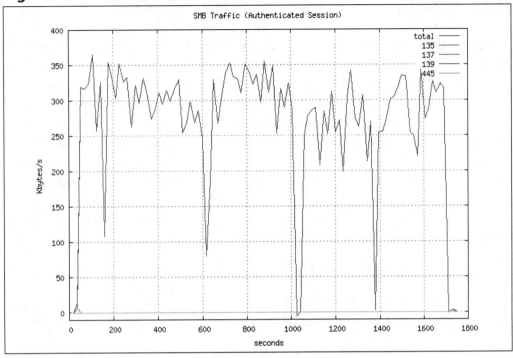

The provided username and password allow Nessus to use two important functionalities—registry access and remote share access—which in turn result in more plugins becoming relevant. These two functionalities are time consuming (making the scan take longer to complete) and consume a great deal of bandwidth. However, given valid credentials, they provide very important information; for example, notification of backdoors, worm infections, and policy breaches, including expired passwords, locked accounts, administrative group members, and so forth.

So, what does this all mean? It means that Nessus' bandwidth requirements aren't negligible, and that in most cases they cannot be dismissed as unobtrusive. Furthermore, the different types of operating systems (OSs) and applications being checked affect how much bandwidth is consumed.

There are now two big questions: How can we minimize the average bandwidth being consumed, and where can we place the scanning server without affecting the network's bandwidth utilization?

The first question is easy to answer. You can minimize the average bandwidth consumed by configuring Nessus to run fewer tests in parallel by tweaking the value *Number of checks to perform at the same time* via the graphical user interface GUI or by setting the value of *max_threads* found in nessusd.conf.

The best time to employ this tweaking, changing the value of *max_threads*, is whenever there are more than several hosts we want to scan, preferably with the same network mask, or at least on the same physical network (provided they are not separated by network devices or firewalls). Doing so accomplishes two important things. First, it minimizes the strain a scan will have on the network, and second, it minimizes the load on the scanning server itself. At the moment we are more interested in the first goal. The subsequent question will be better explained in the section *Configuring Scanners*, where we explain how to spread the scan over several physical servers, while not necessarily increasing the maintenance workload. We will do this by managing the servers from a centralized location, automating them so they update themselves send the generated reports back to that central location.

Automating the Procedure

Before installing Nessus daemons on several computers, we must first create a test plan that will answer the following questions:

- How do we verify that the scanners do not cause harm to our network?

- How do we monitor the bandwidth usage that might be incurred by our scanning?

- How do we verify that the scanners are working properly and are in fact finding vulnerabilities?

Similar to the Hippocratic Oath taken by physicians, the most important part of the enterprise scanning is to make sure the network does not suffer from being scanned. The network can suffer due to unresponsive applications, high CPU, memory usage, or by traffic congestion. Our scanning servers can cause any of these problems.

These effects will need to be prevented. To avoid problems in applications or bandwidth congestion, you need to prepare some sort of test lab where several nonproduction servers will go through the same scanning as you are planning to use.

The test lab will allow you to verify the effects on your network of setting the port range, plugins to run, network scan speed, and so forth. This test lab will create a scanned environment that is as real as possible, allowing you to detect issues that might arise in the actual scans and solve them before they can cause problems in your real environment.

The test lab will also ensure that you are not running scans with incorrect settings. For example, running Nessus with a port range of 1–1024 and telling it to regard all other ports as closed will have an adverse effects on the results of your scan. Any service above port 1024 will be considered closed—numerous applications use ports higher than 1024: Oracle, MySQL, MSSQL, IRC, and Proxies, to name a few. Those applications will not be tested for vulnerabilities, and you might never notice.

To avoid such incorrect settings from affecting the results of your scans, you will need to create self-made "honeypots" that you know are vulnerable to a certain extent. These honeypots will be used to verify that Nessus is in fact running correctly. We do not need to actually use commercial honeypots—all we require is to understand our network structure enough and expect certain vulnerabilities to appear. For example, if we know a certain Windows machine wasn't patched with the latest MSXX-XXX patch, we can use one of Nessus' tests as a marker that our scans are working correctly and that we are able to access the registry to detect that missing patch.

We assume from now that you created your test lab, ran some Nessus scans, verified that they are not affecting your test lab's network, and you are running them as correctly as possible finding all the vulnerabilities that appear in the test lab servers. Does this mean that we are finally ready to scan the enterprise? Again, we must reiterate that you are still missing a crucial part of making Nessus work correctly—this important part is what makes the difference between recurring vulnerability assessment and one-time vulnerability assessment.

One of Nessus' most important features is its capability to update tests amazingly frequently. Nessus is installed with an easy-to-use script that will update the plugin library used by the scanner. The script, trivially called nessus-update-plugins, downloads a file from the www.nessus.org web site, extracts its content to the plugin folder, and restarts the Nessus daemon, making the update process as smooth and automated as possible.

However, the script's behavior leaves more to be desired. How can you verify that the update process was successful for every Nessus daemon you have on the network? How can you make sure all Nessus daemons are in fact up to date? How can you roll out any custom-made plugins you create? How can you avoid the Nessus daemons downloading a big file from the Internet, possibly slowing the Internet connection? And, how can you avoid giving direct access to the Internet to each of these Nessus daemons?

All of these questions can be answered using a more centralized approach to updating the Nessus engine. The required materials for centralizing the plugin-updating mechanism are a web server and some scripting skills. The update mechanism is composed of five stages:

1. Download the update.

2. Unpack the update.

3. Install the update.

4. Restart the Nessus daemon.

5. Report success.

Each stage will be done as much as possible in a single operation, making the update mechanism as redundant and safe as possible. In addition, it will guarantee that if a stage fails, the centralized server is informed. To implement the download stage, we suggest you either use the wget utility (which features the ability to Proxy, HTTP Authenticate, Resume, Retry, and many other nifty features) or implement a file downloading script via some external libraries, like Perl's amazingly popular LWP module.

We suggest you modify the downloading process so it does not download the same file each time it updates, as nessus-update-plugins does, but rather have some type of versioning mechanism where you can keep track of what version the Nessus daemon last attempted to update.

The version does not have to be more than a simple counter increasing by one each time you decide to roll out an update to your Nessus daemons, or perhaps a timestamp. After the download is complete, the updating mechanism will inform the web server that it was successful in downloading the update.

Our next stage is extraction and installation of the update. You do not have to separate the two stages, although it is recommended that you verify that the extraction was successful before trying to overwrite files—some extraction programs will partially overwrite the files if the archived file was corrupted, making your installation unstable or even unusable.

The installation of new plugins (unlike overwriting existing plugins) has no effect until the Nessus daemon is restarted; therefore, we must restart the Nessus daemon before continuing.

Restarting Nessus via a HUP signal (as is done by nessus-update-plugins) has no effect on the scan that is currently in progress—the scan will continue scanning as if nothing had happened.

This is both and bad. It's good because it doesn't stop our current scan, but it is bad because it doesn't reload any new scripts, making the current scan only partial (without all the new or updated plugins). We cannot avoid this, but we can modify our update mechanism to recognize such an event and alert us that a scan was in progress while the update was running, so that we can make a decision on whether we want to rerun that scan.

You can easily verify whether a scan is currently in progress by obtaining the list of running processes on the Nessus daemon and looking for the string *testing* (followed by the IP being tested). If this string appears, a scan is currently in progress. If not, you can safely signal a HUP at the end of the update mechanism or even restart the Nessus daemon service.

Once the Nessus daemon restart process has completed by either a HUP signal or a full-fledged stop and start, the script should again report to the web server that it has successfully restarted Nessus. The cautious administrator might also want to verify that Nessus has successfully HUPed/restarted by checking the */var/log/messages* (or any other file configured by the nessusd.conf file) for the string *nessusd x.x.xx started* (if Nessus was started/restarted) or for the string *Caught HUP signal - reconfiguring nessusd* (if Nessus was HUP'ed).

Unfortunately, we can't cover the aspects of automatically updating each Nessus daemon, including its libraries, and binaries using a mechanism similar to the one discussed previously, as it is too complex to be covered here. However, we can suggest using other means of updating that are equally good and relatively safe. By using Debian's apt-get, you can constantly check whether the Nessus you are using is up to date. Debian's unstable distribution is updated with the latest version of Nessus. At the time of writing, Nessus 2.0.10 is available by Debian. By simply running the command **apt-get -t unstable update**, followed by **apt-get install -t unstable nessusd nessus**, whenever a new version is available it will be installed on the machine.

Nessus' client provides two different ways of determining configuration and version information on a remote Nessus daemon. One is the **-p** parameter that allows you to obtain a list of the server and plugin preferences. The parameter can also work from a remote location where the only requirements are a username and password or client-side certificate (depending on the authentication mechanism used by the Nessus daemon). The other is the **-P** (uppercase) parameter that allows you to obtain a list of plugins installed on the server. This parameter, as the previous one, can be used from a remote location.

Instead of using the **-p** and **-P** parameters on your own and parsing the results returned, we recommend using the update-nessusrc script (available at www.tifaware.com/perl/update-nessusrc/). This easy-to-use Perl script takes an existing configuration file and is able to display the differences between your configuration file and the remote Nessus daemon. The differences include version changes, different plugin settings, and new, removed, or changed plugins. Unfortunately, the update-nessusrc script does not support command-line parameters that control the host to which it connects or change the username and password combinations it uses. However, by modifying the updated-nessusrc script and adding support for such a parameter, you can make the script incredibly handy.

The Nessus daemon keeps track of its actions through the log files. These log files can therefore be used to maintain a good record of what was scanned, when it was scanned, and how long it took. As going over the Nessus daemon log file manually is no easy task, we suggest using nessustail.pl (available from Nessus' nessus-tools package). The tool is a very easy-to-use Perl script that will comb through the message log created by the Nessus daemon and highlight potential problems such as segfaults, interruptions, HUP signals, and plugins that were too slow to finish.

Configuring Scanners

We'll now look at specific ways to deploy distributed scanning in terms of scanning topologies, examining the advantages and disadvantages of each.

Assigning the Tasks

Once we have decided what we want to scan, we need to start dividing the scans between the different hosts. When we divide the scans, we need to make sure we do not breach the confidentiality of the different departments by placing a single server scanning administratively separate networks, we do not cause too much traffic across the network by placing the server in a single place and scanning the whole network from it, and that we can still control the servers placed around the network even if they are in the different parts of the network.

There are three possible distributed scanning topologies you can use: *Star*, *Flat*, and *Islands*. Each topology has its advantages and disadvantages. We will start with the islands topology, as it is the easiest to explain. The islands' goal is to install Nessus daemons that are completely isolated from each other, thus maintaining the highest form of separation between the different departments. In the islands topology, there is no single point of control to the servers, and each network has its own Nessus client connecting to the server.

Advantages of the islands topology include:

- Information cannot leak between departments.

- Any problems with one server's scans does not affect the others.

- Each server can have an independent administrator. This administrator doesn't gain any additional access to other servers or other scanning servers.

- No additional firewall or networking devices rules need to be placed between the departments or between the Nessus client and the server.

- The different servers can provide different points of view of the same hosts (for example, DMZ vs. MZ).

Disadvantages of the islands topology include:

- Maintenance overhead because there is no centralized management.

- Higher hardware costs, as more servers are required.

- No centralized updates server can be created.

- Data cannot be correlated between different servers, or brought in to a centralized database for report consolidation.

The next topology we will discuss is the flat topology, which provides real increases in scalability over the islands topology, although it raises bandwidth requirements. In the flat topology, the Nessus daemons are installed all over the network. The network itself is fairly open between the departments and allows traffic to flow unobstructed. In this type of topology, the Nessus client can be used to manage the servers practically from any location. As the network is wide open, a single Nessus daemon can scan several departments.

Advantages of the flat topology include:

- A single server can scan the entire network.

- Management can be done virtually from any point of access on the network.

- A centralized update server can be used to update all the different Nessus daemons.

- Reports can be consolidated between the different servers.

- No additional firewall or networking devices rules need to be placed between the departments or between the Nessus client and the server.

Disadvantages of the flat topology include:

- Information may leak between two reports, as servers can house more than a single network vulnerability report.

- As a single server can be used to scan the entire network, it becomes a single point of failure with regard to the enterprise's vulnerability scanning.

- A single server cannot provide different views of the network's vulnerabilities (for example, DMZ vs. MZ).

- A single server causes higher bandwidth consumption across the organization compared to distributed servers.

The last topology we will discuss is the star topology. In this topology, the Nessus daemons are servers spread cross the organization that are all connected (in addition to their normal network access) to a management network. In this topology, we can manage all the servers from the management network, and can use this network to transfer data between the servers and to update these servers. However, the servers themselves cannot interconnect, as the management network allows only access to the centralized network.

Advantages of the star topology include:

- Information cannot leak between departments.

- Bandwidth consumption is divided between the servers.

- It provides different views of the network's vulnerabilities (for example, DMZ vs. MZ).

- A centralized update server can be used to update all the different Nessus daemons.

- Reports can be consolidated using a centralized server housing all the data.

Disadvantages of the star topology include:

- Management can only be done from a single point.

- Higher hardware costs are incurred, as more servers are required.

- Reports cannot be consolidated by interconnecting two servers.

- Additional firewall and network devices rules need to be placed between the departments and the management network.

- A single administrator would have control over the entire set of Nessus daemons, with the ability to inadvertently breach the different departments' confidentiality.

System Requirements

The Nessus daemon by itself isn't a large memory or CPU consumer. An idle Nessus daemon, with no clients attached, will consume virtually no CPU time, and around 1MB of memory. A disconnected Nessus client memory consumption is around 1.5MB. Once a connection is made, the daemon's memory consumption will jump to around 2.5MB, and the client's memory consumption will jump to around 5.5MB. Any additional Nessus client connecting to the daemon will consume an additional 1.5MB of memory.

Using these figures, we can safely assume that the Nessus daemon can hold a few dozen open connections with Nessus clients. However, the numbers given do not provide an accurate picture, as they do not include the memory consumption requirements needed once a scan starts. The memory consumption will vary greatly during the portscan phase and the plugin running phase, as different plugins are loaded, executed, and unloaded.

The Nmap process requires around 3.5MB of memory for each host it portscans with TCP connect() scan and OS fingerprinting. By default, Nessus issues scans for up to 255 hosts in parallel, which means that a heavily used network can easily consume all available memory during the portscanning phase.

This calculation doesn't take into account the fact that the Nessus daemon will spawn an additional process for each host it scans, consuming roughly an additional 1.5MB of memory per host scanned. This process is responsible for launching the different plugins (the NASL and NES files).

Running the Nessus client with a Nessus daemon, where we configured the Nessus daemon to run one plugin at a time, will cause the Nessus daemon to consume roughly 10MB of memory in total. Using the same configuration, but configuring it to run two plugins at a time, will make the memory consumption jump at times to 12MB, but the average memory consumption will remain around the 10MB mark as Nessus waits for the two plugins it has launched to finish prior to launching two new ones. This is true even if the first plugin finishes several minutes before the second plugin .

Table 10.2 illustrates the memory consumption of the Nessus daemon vs. the number of simultaneous plugins being used (when scanning a single host).

Table 10.2 Memory Consumption of the Nessus Daemon

Number of Plugins	Peak Memory Consumption	Average Memory
1	10MB	10MB
2	12MB	10MB
3	17MB	12MB
4	21MB	16MB
8	35MB	28MB
16	38MB	32MB
32	77MB	50MB
64	92MB	60MB

NOTE

You will need to modify the value of **max_checks** in the nessusd.conf file to go over the 10 plugins mark. To go over the 64 marker, you will further need to modify the nessus-core/nessusd/pluginlaunch.c file and change the value of MAX_PROCESSES from its default value of 32 to whatever you desire and then recompile.

The calculation for more than one host is a bit more difficult, and requires a long trial and error process to get the memory consumption requirements. As a rule, the **nessusd** process requires an average of about two times as much memory for any additional host for the peak memory requirement, and about one and a half times the memory needed for the average memory. We do recommend, however, as memory is a relatively inexpensive component, to equip the scanning servers with at least 1GB of RAM to answer most of your memory needs for scanning. You need to remember that you do not want to scan too many hosts in parallel, or use too many plugins in parallel, as both of these are bandwidth consumers. The Nessus daemon consumes plenty of CPU but it is not a CPU hog, as the utilization of CPU consumption depends on two main factors: the number of hosts being tested and the number of plugins being launched. As more hosts are tested and more plugins are launched in parallel, the CPU time for processing of the network data increases, and with it, the CPU loads. As in many other tasks, increasing memory has a greater effect on Nessus' speed than using a faster processor.

> **NOTE**
>
> The Nessus daemon does not support Symmetric Multi Processing (SMP) in its native code, and will not benefit from it more than any other non-native-SMP program running on the computer. We therefore recommend running the Nessus daemon on a dedicated machine, instead of installing it on a multipurpose server.

Scanning for a Specific Threat

Every once in a while, a new threat arises in the form of a critical advisory. The new vulnerability may affect more than one host on your network, but you are not certain which ones. It would appear that your viable solution would be to scan your entire network for all vulnerabilities and filter out that new vulnerability in which you are interested. However, scanning the entire network is neither simple nor quick.

We suggest this alternative. Scan your network with a limited set of plugins, which allows you to scan your entire network in a very short timeframe while trimming down the amount of vulnerabilities found to just those about which you are concerned. The only shortcoming of this type of scan is that you will need to make sure that all the plugin dependencies are met—open ports, dependent plugins, and so forth.

The dependencies requirement can easily be met by setting the parameter **auto_enable_dependencies** to **yes** in your configuration file and choosing the plugin numbers you are interested in enabling. As an alternative to changing your configuration file, you can use the tool update-nessusrc mentioned in the previous section. One of the tool's parameters is **--includes** followed by ID numbers. These ID numbers are the plugin IDs. Plugin IDs are unique identifiers for the specific test you are interested in using. For example, if we want to test for Microsoft's MS04-011 (incidentally, this patch addresses the vulnerability that the Sasser worm exploits), we need to first locate the appropriate plugin filename. In our case, there are several related plugins—we choose to use the registry-based smb_nt_ms04-011.nasl. Inspecting the file smb_nt_ms04-011.nasl, and looking for the entry **script_id** will reveal that the script's ID is 12205. We will use this number to run **update-nessusrc -c "" -f "" -r "" -i "12205" basic**, where **basic** is the default Nessus configuration file, **12205** is the relevant script ID, **-c** sets the name of the categories you want to enable, and **-f** sets the name of the families you want to enable.

NOTE

Remember that before you start scanning using this configuration file, you need to set the **auto_enable_dependencies** to **yes**. Failing to do so will return scan results that are misleading, as some of the tests plugin 12205 depends on will not execute.

In some cases it is better to meet (or avoid meeting) the plugin dependencies on your own, as the dependencies directly affect the behavior of certain plugins and the "path" (or method) that is used to discover a certain vulnerability. However, this is only recommended to those who are fully aware of the consequences of not meeting a given dependency—the most problematic outcome is that you might completely miss the presence of the vulnerability you were looking for.

Notes from the Underground...

Testing New Plugins

When you want to test your newly acquired or created plugin that depends on other plugins for such things as registry access, the NASL command-line interpreter will be insufficient, as it does not support Knowledge Base access or meeting of dependencies. The only viable solution in this case would be to run that test using a configuration file that specifically requests this newly formed plugin as the only plugin to execute, and that you mark the **auto_enable_dependencies** to **yes**.

We can easily illustrate the difference between meeting the dependencies and failing to do with an example of plugins that have the **script_exclude_keys** entry in them. Each plugin that has the **script_exclude_keys** entry in it will not be executed if a plugin has previously set the key this entry lists to exclude, such as in the case of **tcp_chorusing.nasl**.

NOTE

The **tcp_chorusing.nasl** plugin checks whether a remote Windows 95/98/Me machine answers to the same packet more than once—this will happen if it has more than one TCP/IP stack bound on that adapter.

The **tcp_chorusing.nasl**'s plugin logic is as follows: If the key SMB/WindowsVersion (which **tcp_chorusing.nasl** excludes) is set, the remote host is a Windows XP/2000/2003, and as such is certainly not vulnerable to this attack. However, if the key is not set, it will go about testing the vulnerability against the remote machine, using a real attack packet. Therefore, plugins partially answering to the dependency required by the test (plugins that set a value to SMB/WindowsVersion) will cause the plugin to test each host it finds on the network for the vulnerability.

In addition to the exclude behavior, certain plugins read Nessus' internal information Knowledge Base and act according to the information given there. Therefore, if we want to control the plugin's behavior, we will need to prevent the Knowledge Base information from being written. One way of doing this is to stop certain plugins from running by not meeting or only partially meeting their dependencies.

Notes from the Underground…

The Nessus Community and Plugins

Unlike other commercial vulnerability assessment tools, Nessus enjoys a large community of plugin developers and plugin maintainers. However, as there is no paid quality assurance team making sure the plugins are accurate, false positive free, and informative, the Nessus community requires your assistance. The most helpful feedback you can provide the Nessus community is its ability and inability to detect vulnerabilities, and, if possible, new plugins that detect those vulnerabilities. It is important to note that if you do find a problem with any of the Nessus plugins, you should report as much information regarding the host being tested and e-mail all the information to the bugs@nessus.org.

Best Practices

In the following section we will outline the best practices you should keep in mind.

Divide and Conquer

It is important to avoid sensitive information unintentionally appearing in reports that are available to less-classified personnel. Both the Nessus configuration file and the reports generated might contain sensitive information such as usernames, passwords, domain names, and so forth. As different divisions of your company are exposed to different types of sensitive information, you should run a separate scan for each division to keep reporting tools separate.

Segregate and Limit

In some companies, a different person from the one who installed the Nessus daemon might control the Nessus client. In such cases where it is not possible to further separate the Nessus daemons between the different networks, it is important to create daemon-based rules to prevent users from scanning networks and hosts that they don't need to.

The Nessus daemon's internal configuration file allows creation of rules that allow this segregation and limitation to be done easily. A rule is basically composed of an action: *reject*, *accept*, and *default* followed by an IP and associated network mask. The rules can be serverwide, user based, or client based. As we do not have control over the client-based rules, you should mainly concentrate on server-wide and user-based rules.

> **NOTE**
>
> Client-based rules are set by the Nessus client and offer no protection from someone using your Nessus daemon to scan a host it shouldn't.

Serverwide rules block a certain range of IPs from being scanned by the server. They are relevant to all users who connect to the Nessus daemon, and cannot be overridden by choosing a different user. User-based rules block a certain range of IPs, as before, from being scanned by the server, but they are dependent on the user who logged on to the system. A certain user might be able to scan host A, and another might not—it all depends on the username used to log on to the Nessus daemon.

We recommend placing a limited range of IPs that hosts can scan on each of the Nessus daemons you install, and extending that range as required. These rules will prevent the scanning host from accidentally being used to scan the entire network or even a single host you didn't intend to scan, such as sensitive servers, production networks, and so forth.

Certificates for the Forgetful

The Nessus daemon supports two authentication methods: password-based and certificate-based. We will not discuss why one is better than the other, but from our experience, certificates are easier to move and handle, and are more secure against snooping and capturing, while passwords can be captured, guessed, forgotten, and so forth. As such, we recommend that you install your entire Nessus daemon installation base with certificate authentication instead of password-based authentication. Both have no implications on anything but the logon phase where the Nessus client connects to the Nessus daemon.

Speed Is Not Your Enemy

Having a faster connection with lower latency between your scanning server and the host being scanned improves the speed at which you can scan the host and the reliability of your results. A host scanned over a low-bandwidth WAN connection with a high percentage of packets lost will produce a greater percentage of both false positives, usually from denial-of-service (DoS) tests, and false negatives, which generally come with web-based tests.

It is therefore important to make sure that you conduct your scans through an optimal network connection, and that this connection offers as much bandwidth as you require and introduces as little latency as possible.

Keep a Watchful Eye

It is easy to lose track of the last time you received the results from a particular scan. Sometimes, a scan will only return partial results. This is especially true when you are working with large-scale networks where a momentary reset of a router, firewall, or other network device might cause hosts to disappear, artificially thinning your reports.

It is critical to always be aware of what vulnerabilities have been fixed and what new vulnerabilities are present as a result. Tracking these vulnerabilities and including them in the reports you receive can help you make certain that everything is working properly.

Data Correlation

In this next section, we'll focus on data correlation, especially in regards to the reports that are developed.

Combining Reports

Obviously, the most important part of Nessus isn't the scan itself, but rather the scan's results. While reading dozen of Nessus reports using the Nessus GUI can prove difficult, you can easily solve this problem by building your own vulnerability database. A comprehensive database often contains reports about all of the servers that were found to be vulnerable, along with the vulnerability identification numbers, descriptions, and risk factors. Once you've entered the data into a database, it's easy to query it and reveal which parts of the network are the most vulnerable, which vulnerabilities affect most of your servers, which servers contain a particular worm's affected vulnerabilities, and so forth.

Preparing Your Database

Before we can begin, we will need to prepare the database. For this section, our examples will use MySQL as our database server, because it is freely available for both the Linux and Windows operating systems, and is easy to use. However, any other database server can be used, instead. No matter which database server you choose, it will need to hold at least one database and one table where your information can be stored. You can easily parse Nessus' NBE (Nessus BackEnd) file format with any program that can interpret content that is delimitated by the pipe sign (|).

The fields the Nessus' NBE returns are IP address, affected port, script ID, vulnerability type, and description. To begin, we will first need to create a table that contains these fields. We will start by using the following SQL query:

```
CREATE TABLE ScanResults (
                    ID INT AUTO_INCREMENT,
                    IP TEXT,
                    Port TEXT,
                    PluginID INT,
                    Type TEXT,
                    Description TEXT,
                    PRIMARY KEY ID (ID)
);
```

You might need to modify the script depending on your database configuration.

The aforementioned table will be used to hold our scan results, which we will parse using the following Perl script:

```
#!/usr/bin/perl
# nbeparser.pl - Nessus NBE parser
# Thanks to A.M.I for helping with the Voodoo
use strict;
use DBI;

my $db = "nessusdb";
```

```perl
my $dsn =
"DBI:mysql:database=$db;host=localhost;port=3306;mysql_read_default_file=/etc
/mysql/my.cnf";
my $user = "nessusdb";
my $pass = "nessusdb";


my $dbh = DBI->connect($dsn, $user, $pass, {'RaiseError' => 1});


my $filename = shift;
open(NBE, "$filename") || die "File not found\nYou need to provide this
program with a valid filename to parse.\n";


while (<NBE>)
{
 my @values = split(/\|/, $_);


 my $SQL = "INSERT INTO ScanResults SET IP='".$values[0]."',
Port='".$values[1]."', PluginID='".$values[2]."', Type='".$values[3]."',
Description=".$dbh->quote($values[4])."";


 print "$SQL\n";


 my $sth = $dbh->prepare($SQL) or die "Cannot prepare statement:
$DBI::errstr\n";
 $sth->execute() or die "Cannot execute statement: $DBI::errstr\n";


 $sth->finish();
}


$dbh->disconnect();
close(NBE);
```

You can run this script on a system that has a Perl interpreter installed by typing the following at a command line. Root or administrator privilege will not be necessary, so make sure to run this command as an ordinary user:

```
nessus-user $ ./nbeparser your_real_report_name.nbe
```

If the script has successfully completed, you should now have your own Scan Results table that contains the outcome data of the Nessus report file whose name you specified on the command line; in this case, **your_real_report_name.nbe**. From here on, you should be able to query your database and find the information that you need from this report.

This script is not a perfect solution, however. It is, in fact, a very simplistic piece of code and is therefore unable to handle tasks that are more complex. For more complex (especially enterprise-scalable) applications, you'll need to write your own. We'll outline the limitations here to help you realize when you've outgrown the script. First, this script can't verify whether the results you seek are already there. Moreover, it can't tell you the date that your results were generated. Additionally, the resulting database table does not differentiate between different reports' filenames. Therefore, a unique line is generated for any entry found in the results file. Thus, if you accidentally run the script on the same results file, duplicate entries will appear in your database. What this comes down to is that the table is too simplistic to support any form of differentiation of data. This means that it is difficult to discern which vulnerabilities are old problems and which ones have recently appeared.

Outside of differentiation, this script will not work in a model where you scan the same targets from multiple points. For example, it isn't possible to show the same target's vulnerability results from the DMZ and the privileged network. In short, it's just a basic structure to get you started.

Adding additional columns can solve some of these problems, but before we do that, let's look at some queries we can execute to find useful information from the database. Let's start by finding which vulnerability affects the most computers on our network. We first need to find out what script IDs we have affecting our network, so we will execute:

```
select DISTINCT PluginID from ScanResults;
+----------+
| PluginID |
+----------+
|    12205 |
|    10394 |
|    10400 |
|    10150 |
|    11011 |
+----------+
```

We then need to take each PluginID and count the number of entries it has in the database. We will use the following SQL statement:

```
select COUNT(*) from ScanResults WHERE PluginID='11011';
+----------+
| COUNT(*) |
+----------+
|        8 |
+----------+
```

After going through all the different PluginIDs, we can conclude that PluginID 11011 is the one that affects the most machines in our network.

If we look up this plugin's description, we learn that this test detects whether the remote servers support NetBIOS, and that we forgot to eliminate the same host being affected more than once by this vulnerability. We will recount using this SQL statement:

```
select COUNT(DISTINCT IP) from ScanResults WHERE PluginID='11011';
+--------------------+
| COUNT(DISTINCT IP) |
+--------------------+
|                  4 |
+--------------------+
```

It seems almost all of our vulnerabilities appear in all four hosts we scanned, and that we don't have a single vulnerability that we need to give special attention to before the others. This is in fact false—if we take into account the severity of the vulnerabilities, one vulnerability will be more important to highlight than the others.

Let's start by finding how many High/Medium/Low risk vulnerabilities we have in the database. For the sake of simplification, we will consider a *Serious* risk factor as equal to *High*. We can count the number of vulnerabilities according to their risk factor by executing the following SQL statement:

```
select COUNT(*) from ScanResults WHERE Description LIKE '%Risk factor :
High%' OR Description LIKE '%Risk factor : Serious%';
+----------+
| COUNT(*) |
+----------+
|        1 |
```

```
+----------+
select COUNT(*) from ScanResults WHERE Description LIKE '%Risk factor :
Medium%';
+----------+
| COUNT(*) |
+----------+
|        4 |
+----------+
select COUNT(*) from ScanResults WHERE Description LIKE '%Risk factor :
Low%';
+----------+
| COUNT(*) |
+----------+
|        1 |
+----------+
```

We can easily see that we have a High/Serious risk factor vulnerability. We can cross-reference this by counting the vulnerabilities that occur more than once on our network by using the SQL **UNION** statement. We will come back to this in the next section, which covers differential scanning.

Now that we know we have a High/Serious risk factor vulnerability, we can pull its PluginID and search for an explanation about this vulnerability either from the description that comes with that entry in the database or by going to http://cgi.nessus.org/plugins/dump.php3?id=XXXXX and replacing XXXXX with the PluginID.

```
select PluginID from ScanResults WHERE Description LIKE '%Risk factor :
High%' OR Description LIKE '%Risk factor : Serious%';
+----------+
| PluginID |
+----------+
|    12205 |
+----------+
```

Going to http://cgi.nessus.org/plugins/dump.php3?id=12205 shows that the plugin that reports this vulnerability is named *Microsoft Hotfix KB835732 (registry check)*, and that this problem is solved by installing the patch available from www.microsoft.com/technet/security/bulletin/ms04-011.mspx.

One of the greatest benefits of using a database is that you can easily compare two different results that were generated from two different network locations; for example, DMZ vs. privileged network. We first need to modify our database table to include an *Exposure* column, and insert the results gathered from the different sections of the network.

We start by adding a new column named *Exposure*:

```
ALTER TABLE ScanResults ADD Exposure TEXT;
```

We will mark all existing records with the word *Privileged*, using the following statement:

```
UPDATE ScanResults SET Exposure='Privileged';
```

Now we should restart the scan, and insert the results using this script. However, before we rerun the scan, we will add to the SQL statement the string:

```
Exposure='DMZ'
```

Resulting in:

```
my $SQL = "INSERT INTO ScanResults SET IP='".$values[0]."',
Port='".$values[1]."', PluginID='".$values[2]."', Type='".$values[3]."',
Description=".$dbh->quote($values[4]).", Exposure='DMZ'";
```

We will now have the same table as before, but with new entries that illustrate the state of vulnerability from an internal network (privileged) and from an external network (DMZ). The first neat thing we can do is compare the results we received from the privileged network with that of the DMZ and see which vulnerabilities we solved by segmentation alone.

The following SQL statement can be used to find out which vulnerabilities "disappeared" due to scanning from the two different locations:

```
SELECT CurrentScan.IP, CurrentScan.Port, CurrentScan.PluginID FROM
ScanResults AS CurrentScan LEFT JOIN ScanResults ON (CurrentScan.PluginID =
ScanResults.PluginID AND CurrentScan.Port = ScanResults.Port AND
CurrentScan.IP = ScanResults.IP AND CurrentScan.Exposure !=
ScanResults.Exposure AND ScanResults.Exposure = 'DMZ') WHERE
CurrentScan.Exposure = 'Privileged' AND ScanResults.Exposure IS NULL;

+---------------+----------------------------+----------+
| IP            | Port                       | PluginID |
+---------------+----------------------------+----------+
| 192.168.1.4   | netbios-ssn (139/tcp)      |  11011   |
| 192.168.1.13  | netbios-ssn (139/tcp)      |  11011   |
```

```
| 192.168.1.138 | netbios-ssn (139/tcp) |    11011 |
| 192.168.1.243 | netbios-ssn (139/tcp) |    11011 |
+---------------+-----------------------+----------+
```

The following SQL statement will reveal which new vulnerabilities have "appeared" due to scanning from the two different locations:

```
SELECT ScanResults.IP, ScanResults.Port, ScanResults.PluginID FROM
ScanResults AS CurrentScan LEFT JOIN ScanResults ON (CurrentScan.PluginID =
ScanResults.PluginID AND CurrentScan.Port = ScanResults.Port AND
CurrentScan.IP = ScanResults.IP AND CurrentScan.Exposure !=
ScanResults.Exposure AND ScanResults.Exposure = 'Privileged') WHERE
CurrentScan.Exposure = 'DMZ' AND ScanResults.Exposure IS NULL;
Empty set (0.00 sec)
```

The following SQL statement will reveal which vulnerabilities "persist" between the two different locations:

```
SELECT ScanResults.IP, ScanResults.Port, ScanResults.PluginID FROM
ScanResults AS CurrentScan LEFT JOIN ScanResults ON (CurrentScan.PluginID =
ScanResults.PluginID AND CurrentScan.Port = ScanResults.Port AND
CurrentScan.IP = ScanResults.IP AND CurrentScan.Exposure !=
ScanResults.Exposure AND ScanResults.Exposure = 'DMZ') WHERE
ScanResults.Exposure = 'DMZ' AND CurrentScan.Exposure = 'Privileged';
```

```
+---------------+-----------------------+----------+
| IP            | Port                  | PluginID |
+---------------+-----------------------+----------+
| 192.168.1.243 | microsoft-ds (445/tcp) |    12205 |
| 192.168.1.13  | microsoft-ds (445/tcp) |    10394 |
| 192.168.1.243 | microsoft-ds (445/tcp) |    10400 |
| 192.168.1.4   | microsoft-ds (445/tcp) |    10394 |
| 192.168.1.4   | netbios-ns (137/udp)  |    10150 |
| 192.168.1.243 | microsoft-ds (445/tcp) |    10394 |
| 192.168.1.138 | microsoft-ds (445/tcp) |    10394 |
| 192.168.1.13  | netbios-ns (137/udp)  |    10150 |
| 192.168.1.243 | netbios-ns (137/udp)  |    10150 |
| 192.168.1.4   | microsoft-ds (445/tcp) |    11011 |
| 192.168.1.13  | microsoft-ds (445/tcp) |    11011 |
| 192.168.1.138 | netbios-ns (137/udp)  |    10150 |
| 192.168.1.138 | microsoft-ds (445/tcp) |    11011 |
| 192.168.1.243 | microsoft-ds (445/tcp) |    11011 |
+---------------+-----------------------+----------+
```

Even though the example is simplistic, you can see the benefit you receive from using the database as your information-generating tool. Scanning the hosts from the DMZ revealed that all our firewall was doing was blocking port 139, which as you can see is insufficient in blocking most vulnerabilities.

There are other means of inserting data into a database; specifically, NessusWX (available from http://nessuswx.nessus.org), Nessus' Windows-based client. NessusWX can generate SQL statements that you can paste into your SQL server, or directly insert entries into a MySQL-based database. We find NessusWX's capability to use a SQL server better than storing the results in a file, but as the data cannot be manipulated before it is entered, we prefer using our own scripts to insert data into the database.

Differential Reporting

Differential reporting and the trend analysis information you can generate from it allows you to easily spot changes on your network. Differential reporting allows you to compare one scan against another, and receive only the changes caused when a new vulnerability has been discovered, a new host is added to the network, or a new service is operating. This allows you to reduce the size of the report you receive, and the overload generated due to it, while still allowing you to be successfully alerted to new security problems on your network.

You can generate differential reports using either of two methods: scan normally and use a database to generate differential data, or use Nessus' built-in differential reporting features through the configuration. Choosing the latter only requires marking the scan as differential, by either editing the configuration file used by Nessus or setting the **save_knowledge_base, kb_restore**, and **diff_scan** entries to **yes**. Alternatively, you can change these values via the GUI by activating the **KB | Enable KB saving, Reuse the knowledge bases about the host for the test**, and **Only show differences with the previous scan** options.

Once the scan has completed, the results you receive are only those new vulnerabilities, ports, or hosts that weren't present in the previous scan. The shortcoming from this type of scan is that you cannot generate any additional information from the results; for example, what was fixed, what vulnerabilities are still present although found a certain timeframe ago, and so forth. Another disadvantage of this type of differential data is that it is hard to determine what has changed. Some plugins return dynamic data, such as the plugin that retrieves the SMTP banner. Since the banner might contain the current time, it will be different between every two scans you conduct and will constantly appear in the differential results, even though nothing actually changed with regard to that vulnerability.

You can partially minimize this effect by excluding the information-gathering plugins from being launched again against the hosts by choosing **KB | Do not execute info gathering plugins that have already been executed**, or by setting the **kb_dont_replay_info_gathering** entry in the configuration file to **yes**. However, this would defeat the purpose of scanning the computer for all possible vulnerabilities, including any information-gathering plugins (consider, for example, a situation where an information-gathering plugin was enhanced—you will never get to see these enhancements since the new version will never run). Furthermore, it risks keeping outdated information in the Knowledge Base.

NOTE

By default, Nessus keeps records in the Knowledge Base for a period of 10 days. If you are interested in waiting more than that between differential scans, change the value of **Max age of saved KB (in secs)** found under **KB** tab, or modify the value of **kb_max_age** from 864000, which equals 10 days, to any other value.

Now that you know how to use Nessus' built-in feature for differential scanning, we'll look at how to use your database to generate similar and better differential information from the same scans. In the previous section, we implemented the table structure. In this section, we'll take things a step further by modifying the table to include an additional column to accommodate our differential scan data. This column, that we'll label ScanDate, will enable us to set the date at which the report is generated. We'll do this by implementing the following SQL statement:

```
ALTER TABLE ScanResults ADD ScanDate DATE;
```

In addition, we will need to modify the nbeparser.pl script, from the previous section, so that it includes the ScanDate column. The value to which we will set the ScanDate will be the reserved word **NOW()**. MySQL will, in turn, convert this to the date and time at which an entry was inserted. This change to the script will result in:

```
my $SQL = "INSERT INTO ScanResults SET IP='".$values[0]."',
Port='".$values[1]."', PluginID='".$values[2]."', Type='".$values[3]."',
Description=".$dbh->quote($values[4])."', ScanDate=NOW()";
```

Now, we'll generate two separate scans. The first scan will be conducted today, without making any changes. Next, we will alter our network so that it appears that one of our hosts is no longer responding. Additionally, we will turn off a few of our services on another one of our hosts. This will enable us to create a second scan that will now appear as if it is being completed one day after our first scan. Once we've imported results from both scans into our database, we can start to derive meaning from the resulting data. From here on, we will assume your database contains results for scans that were completed for the same range of IP addresses.

Let's begin by pulling any scan dates with which we can work. This can be easily accomplished by using the following SQL statement:

```
select DISTINCT(ScanDate) from ScanResults;

+------------+
| ScanDate   |
+------------+
| 2004-06-15 |
| 2004-06-16 |
+------------+
```

Now, we can provide a list of hosts that were discovered during the scan and a list of hosts that were absent using the following SQL statement:

```
SELECT DISTINCT(CurrentScan.IP) FROM ScanResults AS CurrentScan LEFT JOIN
ScanResults ON (CurrentScan.IP = ScanResults.IP AND CurrentScan.ScanDate !=
ScanResults.ScanDate AND ScanResults.ScanDate = '2004-06-15') WHERE
CurrentScan.ScanDate = '2004-06-16' AND ScanResults.IP IS NULL;
Empty set (0.00 sec)


SELECT DISTINCT(CurrentScan.IP) FROM ScanResults AS CurrentScan LEFT JOIN
ScanResults ON (CurrentScan.IP = ScanResults.IP AND CurrentScan.ScanDate !=
ScanResults.ScanDate AND ScanResults.ScanDate = '2004-06-16') WHERE
CurrentScan.ScanDate = '2004-06-15' AND ScanResults.IP IS NULL;

+--------------+
| IP           |
+--------------+
| 192.168.1.52 |
+--------------+
```

The first statement returns a list of the new hosts that appeared on the network, and the second statement returns a list of IPs that have dropped off the network. As you can see, host 192.168.1.52 is absent from the second scan's results.

We can now create similar lists for both ports and vulnerabilities. Let's start by using the SQL statement that will retrieve the new ports that differed between our two scans:

```
SELECT DISTINCT(CurrentScan.Port), CurrentScan.IP FROM ScanResults AS
CurrentScan LEFT JOIN ScanResults ON (CurrentScan.Port = ScanResults.Port
AND CurrentScan.ScanDate != ScanResults.ScanDate AND ScanResults.ScanDate =
'2004-06-15') WHERE CurrentScan.ScanDate = '2004-06-16' AND
ScanResults.Port IS NULL;

Empty set (0.05 sec)


SELECT DISTINCT(CurrentScan.Port), CurrentScan.IP FROM ScanResults AS
CurrentScan LEFT JOIN ScanResults ON (CurrentScan.Port = ScanResults.Port
AND CurrentScan.ScanDate != ScanResults.ScanDate AND ScanResults.ScanDate =
'2004-06-16') WHERE CurrentScan.ScanDate = '2004-06-15' AND
ScanResults.Port IS NULL;
```

Port	IP
mysql (3306/tcp)	192.168.1.243
x11 (6000/tcp)	192.168.1.52
loc-srv (135/udp)	192.168.1.243
ssh (22/tcp)	192.168.1.52
unknown (1029/udp)	192.168.1.243
ftp (21/tcp)	192.168.1.243

Here it's easy to spot that host 192.168.1.243, which is present in both scans, had some ports from the first scan close before our second scan was run. Additionally, we can see that host 192.168.1.52 had a port open in the time period between the scans. Moreover, this host is absent from our second scan. However, these two facts are not equal in importance. Simply put, if host 192.168.1.52 is no longer there, its open and closed ports are meaningless to us. Once we recognize this, we can easily filter out host 192.168.1.52 from our results by creating a more complex SQL statement:

```
SELECT DISTINCT(CurrentScan.Port), CurrentScan.IP FROM ScanResults AS
CurrentScan LEFT JOIN ScanResults ON (CurrentScan.Port = ScanResults.Port
AND CurrentScan.ScanDate != ScanResults.ScanDate AND ScanResults.ScanDate =
'2004-06-16') WHERE CurrentScan.ScanDate = '2004-06-15' AND CurrentScan.IP
NOT IN ('192.168.1.52') AND ScanResults.IP IS NULL;

+--------------------+---------------+
| Port               | IP            |
+--------------------+---------------+
| mysql (3306/tcp)   | 192.168.1.243 |
| loc-srv (135/udp)  | 192.168.1.243 |
| unknown (1029/udp) | 192.168.1.243 |
| ftp (21/tcp)       | 192.168.1.243 |
+--------------------+---------------+
```

In the **NOT IN** clause, we place any IPs that previously appeared as being absent from the previous scan, thus filtering them out from the information in which we are interested. A very similar SQL query can show the vulnerabilities that have been addressed:

```
SELECT DISTINCT(CurrentScan.PluginID), CurrentScan.IP, CurrentScan.Port
FROM ScanResults AS CurrentScan LEFT JOIN ScanResults ON
(CurrentScan.PluginID = ScanResults.PluginID AND CurrentScan.ScanDate !=
ScanResults.ScanDate AND ScanResults.ScanDate = '2004-06-15') WHERE
CurrentScan.ScanDate = '2004-06-16' AND CurrentScan.IP NOT IN
('192.168.1.52') AND ScanResults.PluginID IS NULL;

+----------+---------------+-------------+
| PluginID | IP            | Port        |
+----------+---------------+-------------+
|    11580 | 192.168.1.254 | general/udp |
+----------+---------------+-------------+


SELECT DISTINCT(CurrentScan.PluginID), CurrentScan.IP, CurrentScan.Port
FROM ScanResults AS CurrentScan LEFT JOIN ScanResults ON
(CurrentScan.PluginID = ScanResults.PluginID AND CurrentScan.ScanDate !=
ScanResults.ScanDate AND ScanResults.ScanDate = '2004-06-16') WHERE
CurrentScan.ScanDate = '2004-06-15' AND CurrentScan.IP NOT IN
('192.168.1.52') AND ScanResults.PluginID IS NULL;

+----------+---------------+------------------------+
| PluginID | IP            | Port                   |
+----------+---------------+------------------------+
```

```
|     10916 | 192.168.1.243 | microsoft-ds (445/tcp)   |
|     12054 | 192.168.1.243 | microsoft-ds (445/tcp)   |
|     10915 | 192.168.1.243 | microsoft-ds (445/tcp)   |
|     12209 | 192.168.1.243 | microsoft-ds (445/tcp)   |
|     10481 | 192.168.1.243 | mysql (3306/tcp)         |
|     10914 | 192.168.1.243 | microsoft-ds (445/tcp)   |
|     11890 | 192.168.1.243 | loc-srv (135/udp)        |
|     10913 | 192.168.1.243 | microsoft-ds (445/tcp)   |
|     10092 | 192.168.1.243 | ftp (21/tcp)             |
+-----------+---------------+--------------------------+
```

With these two statements, you can spot which new vulnerabilities appeared (in this case, a vulnerability whose script ID is 11580) and which vulnerabilities appear to have been addressed (in this case, vulnerabilities with script IDs 10916, 12054, 10915, 12209, 10481, 10914, 11890, 10913 and 10092).

This wealth of information can be very useful for an administrator when handling a large network, as some vulnerabilities might take longer to fix, in which case seeing them appear and reappear in every report you receive might degrade your ability to understand this as well as your ability to follow the reports as a whole. In contrast, showing you only the changes between the two scans, while giving you the ability to generate a complete report at will, gives you the best of both worlds, seeing the data both in full and differential formats.

Another feature that we can incorporate using simple SQL queries is the ability to see vulnerability trends, or how long a certain vulnerability has been around on the server in question, as data can be easily fetched by its scan date. To better illustrate this, we added some data into the database, after starting new services on the machine 192.168.1.243.

We start by requesting a list of all the unique PluginIDs we can find in the table:

```
SELECT DISTINCT(PluginID) FROM ScanResults
+-----------+
| PluginID  |
+-----------+
|     11834 |
|     12264 |
|     10287 |
|     10916 |
```

```
|    10342   |
|    12054   |
|    11835   |
|............|
|    11580   |
|    10719   |
+------------+
```

Then we use an SQL statement that will show for a particular PluginID and an IP, how long that vulnerability has been present:

```
SELECT IP, Port, ScanDate FROM ScanResults WHERE PluginID='10481' ORDER BY
IP, Port;
```

```
+---------------+-------------------+------------+
| IP            | Port              | ScanDate   |
+---------------+-------------------+------------+
| 192.168.1.243 | mysql (3306/tcp)  | 2004-06-15 |
| 192.168.1.243 | mysql (3306/tcp)  | 2004-06-17 |
+---------------+-------------------+------------+
```

We specifically chose a vulnerability that was there, disappeared, and reappeared. As you can see, this vulnerability appeared to have been fixed, but resurfaced later—a very valuable piece of information. Why has this vulnerability resurfaced? Was some kind of firewall rule changed? Was this vulnerability only partially addressed? This information would be hard to come by if you didn't use this type of differential information gathering.

NOTE

You can use, as we did in this query, the **ORDER BY** directive of SQL to prevent the same vulnerability from appearing on the same IP, but on different ports, from confusing the trend the SQL statement returns.

We now want to generate some graphs from the data we collected. We'll do this by using MySQL's capability to generate on-the-fly comma-separated value (CSV) files and the SQL statement's power to return the number of entries it has for a specific row. The following SQL statements will return for each risk factor the number of entries divided by the different scan dates. We also added the raw data returned by each of the SQL statements:

```
SELECT ScanDate, COUNT(ScanDate) FROM ScanResults GROUP BY ScanDate INTO
OUTFILE 'vuln.total.data';
+------------+-----------------+
| ScanDate   | COUNT(ScanDate) |
+------------+-----------------+
| 2004-06-15 |              77 |
| 2004-06-16 |              55 |
| 2004-06-17 |              54 |
+------------+-----------------+
```

```
SELECT ScanDate, COUNT(ScanDate) FROM ScanResults WHERE Description LIKE
'%Risk Factor : High%' OR Description LIKE '%Risk Factor : Serious%' GROUP
BY ScanDate INTO OUTFILE 'vuln.high.data';
+------------+-----------------+
| ScanDate   | COUNT(ScanDate) |
+------------+-----------------+
| 2004-06-15 |              10 |
| 2004-06-16 |               6 |
| 2004-06-17 |               6 |
+------------+-----------------+
```

```
SELECT ScanDate, COUNT(ScanDate) FROM ScanResults WHERE Description LIKE
'%Risk Factor : Medium%' GROUP BY ScanDate INTO OUTFILE 'vuln.medium.data';
+------------+-----------------+
| ScanDate   | COUNT(ScanDate) |
+------------+-----------------+
| 2004-06-15 |              10 |
| 2004-06-16 |               7 |
| 2004-06-17 |               7 |
+------------+-----------------+
```

```
SELECT ScanDate, COUNT(ScanDate) FROM ScanResults WHERE Description LIKE
'%Risk Factor : Low%' GROUP BY ScanDate INTO OUTFILE 'vuln.low.data';
+------------+-----------------+
| ScanDate   | COUNT(ScanDate) |
```

```
+-----------+-----------------+
| 2004-06-15 |              25 |
| 2004-06-16 |              21 |
| 2004-06-17 |              18 |
+-----------+-----------------+
```

All you need to do now to generate a nice graph from this data is to use the following gnuplot script:

```
set term png small
set data style lines
set grid
set yrange [ -10 :  ]
set title "Vulnerability Trends for IP 192.168.1.243"
set xlabel "Date"
set ylabel "Number of Vulnerabilities"
set xdata time
set timefmt "%Y-%m-%d"
set xrange ["2004-06-15":"2004-06-17"]
set format x "%d-%m"
set yrange [0:]
plot "vuln.total.data" using 1:($2) title "Total"\
     ,"vuln.high.data" using 1:($2) title "High"\
     , "vuln.medium.data" using 1:($2) title "Medium"\
     , "vuln.low.data" using 1:($2) title "Low"
```

The utility will generate a graph similar to what is shown in Figure 10.8.

Figure 10.8 Trend for 192.168.1.243

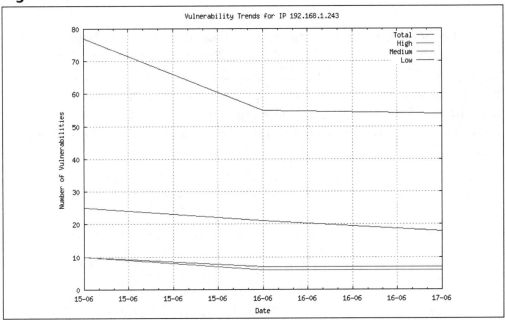

The more extensive data you have, the more interesting and useful this graph becomes. Taken over time, this graph illustrates how vulnerabilities are progressing for this particular host. Continuing our data mining, we would now like to count the number of vulnerabilities divided by dates and IPs by issuing the following SQL statement:

```
SELECT ScanDate, IP, COUNT(IP) FROM ScanResults GROUP BY IP, ScanDate;

+------------+---------------+-----------+
| ScanDate   | IP            | COUNT(IP) |
+------------+---------------+-----------+
| 2004-06-15 | 192.168.1.243 |        31 |
| 2004-06-16 | 192.168.1.243 |        15 |
| 2004-06-17 | 192.168.1.243 |        17 |
| 2004-06-15 | 192.168.1.254 |        18 |
| 2004-06-16 | 192.168.1.254 |        19 |
| 2004-06-17 | 192.168.1.254 |        17 |
| 2004-06-15 | 192.168.1.4   |        21 |
| 2004-06-16 | 192.168.1.4   |        21 |
| 2004-06-17 | 192.168.1.4   |        20 |
```

```
| 2004-06-15 | 192.168.1.52 |          7 |
+------------+---------------+----------+
```

The only piece of information we are lacking is those vulnerabilities that are persistent. A vulnerability can be declared persistent if it persists for a long time and is present in every scan. Thinking graphically, we mean that the vulnerability's line starts on one end of our graph and proceeds to the other without segmentation. By performing the following query, we can get a perspective for each plugin we tested for, when it was first detected, and how many hosts were affected:

```
SELECT ScanDate, COUNT(ScanDate), PluginID, Port FROM ScanResults GROUP BY
ScanDate, PluginID, Port ORDER BY PluginID, ScanDate;
```

```
+------------+------------------+----------+------------------------+
| ScanDate   | COUNT(ScanDate)  | PluginID | Port                   |
+------------+------------------+----------+------------------------+
| 2004-06-15 |               1 |    10028 | domain (53/tcp)        |
| 2004-06-16 |               1 |    10028 | domain (53/tcp)        |
| 2004-06-17 |               1 |    10028 | domain (53/tcp)        |
| 2004-06-15 |               1 |    10092 | ftp (21/tcp)           |
| 2004-06-17 |               1 |    10092 | ftp (21/tcp)           |
|..................................................................|
| 2004-06-16 |               2 |    12053 | general/tcp            |
| 2004-06-17 |               2 |    12053 | general/tcp            |
| 2004-06-15 |               1 |    12054 | microsoft-ds (445/tcp)|
| 2004-06-15 |               1 |    12209 | microsoft-ds (445/tcp)|
| 2004-06-15 |               3 |    12264 | general/icmp           |
| 2004-06-16 |               3 |    12264 | general/icmp           |
| 2004-06-17 |               3 |    12264 | general/icmp           |
+------------+------------------+----------+------------------------+
```

You can easily spot in this query output what vulnerabilities appear more than others, and what vulnerabilities are particular to certain hosts.

To summarize, as the data is in a relational database, you can generate a multitude of SQL statements to go through this data and analyze it. The data can be further extended to contain such columns as *assignee*, the person in charge of fixing a particular vulnerability, *ignore* allowing you to ignore certain results from future reports, and so forth. We explain the *ignore* column in better detail in the next section.

Filtering Reports

The previous section focused on the benefits of differential reporting and how to generate differential reports. In this section, we look at how to filter out wrong or misleading content from your reports. This will enable you to filter out enterprisewide false positives and irrelevant vulnerabilities, generate reports containing less information than the original database, and divide the reports based on the type of operating system. In other words, you will be able to locate the relevant data that you seek.

As before, we'll be using a MySQL database containing the single table with its differential data that we created in the previous section, and the Perl script that we used to insert the data into the table. We will start by generating a table of IPs vs. operating systems with a simple SQL statement:

```
SELECT IP, MID(Description, LENGTH('The remote host is running ')+1,
LOCATE(';', Description)-LENGTH('The remote host is running ')-1) AS OS
FROM ScanResults WHERE PluginID='11936' GROUP BY IP, OS;

+---------------+-------------------------------+
| IP            | OS                            |
+---------------+-------------------------------+
| 192.168.1.243 | Microsoft Windows 2000 Server |
| 192.168.1.4   | Microsoft Windows XP          |
+---------------+-------------------------------+
```

This SQL statement looks through the database for all the records of the Nessus plugin *OS Identification*. When such entries are found, they are grouped together. The result from the *Description* column is made a bit more readable by using MySQL's string handling functions.

NOTE

OS detection algorithms, whether they are ICMP based or use Nmap's fingerprinting technique, are rarely accurate or consistent. Therefore, if you want to better generate reports divided by OS types, we suggest that you build an additional table where you can enter and maintain IP vs. OS information manually.

You can also limit your data to a certain IP or IP range. As our table contains numerous records, we will need to eliminate all extraneous data, fix the most critical issues, and then handle those issues that remain. We can use simple queries to filter out IPs, by using *IP='192.168.1.254'* as our query string. Alternatively, we can use a range of IPs by using *IP IN ('192.168.1.52','192.168.1.254')*. Furthermore, we can create a subset of the network by using an *IP LIKE '192.168.1.%'*.

At times, you might need to scan a large part of the network, but not the entire network. In such an instance you can use Nmap's capability to parse the value of an IP/netmask pair into a list of IPs: *nmap –sL 192.168.1.1/29*. This will create a list of IPs that fall under that range. The same can be done for 192.168.1-2.1-2, which will return the list 192.168.1.1, 192.168.1.2, 192.168.2.1, 192.168.2.2. This list can then be taken to the SQL queries *WHERE* section, and provided as is.

To save time, use the table from Table 10.1 and insert it into the MySQL table. Be sure to select the relevant IPs by asset instead of only by the IP. Now, be sure to use the following table structure for your records:

```
CREATE TABLE AssetList (

                ID INT AUTO_INCREMENT,

                AssetName TEXT,

                IPs TEXT,

                ExpectedResult TEXT,

                Contact TEXT,
                Frequency TEXT,

                PRIMARY KEY ID (ID)

);
```

After entering the details into the table, use the IP addresses found in the *IPs* column to filter out the data in the ScanResults table.

Most enterprise networks are bound to have a few irrelevant vulnerabilities. Nessus was built to report everything, and then let someone else sort through the results. That way, it's possible for you to define what is important and what is not. This makes it possible for you to be sure that you do not miss any vulnerabilities, because Nessus will not ignore any. However, when you are dealing with a large-scale network, this can result in a few hundred irrelevant vulnerabilities. For example, items like administrative privilege vulnerabilities will appear when

Nessus is provided with the administrative credentials required to remotely access the workstations' registry.

As all our data is in the database, we can quickly weed out these records by explicitly deleting the records from our database where a certain PluginID is equal to a certain number, or by adding a new column to the ScanResults table that marks the record as irrelevant. The second option enables you to reactivate those entries in the future as changes occur in the corporate policy regarding that vulnerability.

Additionally, some vulnerabilities are simply false positives, caused by a variety of issues. Unfortunately, fixing these false positives requires time and effort. The quickest fix requires a familiarity with Nessus' scripting language and the ability to find and repair the underlying problem. Therefore, we must adopt an approach similar to the solution we used with the irrelevant vulnerabilities described in the previous two paragraphs. To do this, we must mark those vulnerabilities that are false positive as irrelevant. We will also need to locate and fix the root cause of the false positive, by e-mailing bugs@nessus.org, reporting it online at http:// bugs.nessus.org/, or e-mailing the Nessus mailing list (available at http://list. nessus.org). Alternatively, you can fix the offending NASL on your own, or contact the NASL's author—a contact e-mail address is usually available at the top of each Nessus Plugin.

Third-Party Tools

In this section, we highlight some third-party tools you can use to assist your deployment, maintenance, and usage of Nessus.

Extracting Information from a Saved Session Using sd2nbe

The Nessus daemon has the capability to store information about scanning sessions in a file for resuming interrupted scans. This option is normally used to recover sessions; however, it is not limited to that. You can take the information saved in the session and convert it to an NBE data file using the sd2nbe tool available from www.tifaware.com/perl/sd2nbe/. Once the session information is in NBE format, we can open it using the Nessus client or convert it to HTML or XML.

Nessus Integration with
Perl and Net::Nessus::ScanLite

You might have thought of building a wrapper to the Nessus command-line client to automate your deployment and to automatically schedule scans. To make this easier, you can use Net::Nessus::ScanLite, a Perl module that allows you to implement your very own Nessus client. The Perl module is almost a complete command-line Nessus client, supporting all of the Nessus client features and offering an API to easily use the results of a scan.

Using simple scripts, you can connect to the Nessus daemon, grab the results, and dump them directly into the database without generating a single file. You can also extend this to create a complete Perl-based web interface where you choose what IP to scan. That same Perl-based web page can call the script that runs Nessus, and return the results. This tool is available from http://search.cpan.org/~jpb/Net-Nessus-ScanLite-0.01/.

Users who have trouble installing the necessary dependencies can use the automated CPAN installation, which takes care of all the dependencies required.

NOTE

As this is a book written by security professionals who are paid to be paranoid, we'll always suggest using the nonautomated installation mechanism that allows you to check PGP signatures instead. The following automated process does not check PGP signatures, and its documentation admits to weak security:

"There's no strong security layer in CPAN.pm. CPAN.pm helps you to install foreign, unmasked, unsigned code on your machine. We compare to a checksum that comes from the Net just as the distribution file itself. If somebody has managed to tamper with the distribution file, they may have as well tampered with the CHECKSUMS file. Future development will go towards strong authentication."

(Source: http://search.cpan.org/~jhi/perl-5.8.0/lib/CPAN.pm# SECURITY)

As this documentation reminds you, an attacker who compromises the CPAN servers can replace the Perl module that you're installing while also replacing the checksum on the same server. The only way to avoid having a vital piece of your security infrastructure compromised by an attacker's hostile code is to check that code's PGP signature before installing it. Avoid using easy methods that ignore this risk, especially on your organization's security infrastructure. Exercise best practices to avoid this infrastructure compromise or you might find yourself losing control of the system, and your job!

Executing the following commands will install the module:

```
# perl –MCPAN -e shell
cpan> install Net::Nessus::ScanLite
```

A very easy way to manage multiple Nessus daemon installation is by using a web interface. Several such web interfaces have been written as open-source projects. One such project is the Vulnerability Scanning Cluster (VSC). The VSC interface was written in PHP and uses the MySQL database as its backend for storing information. VSC allows users to manage hosts by hierarchical order, to select different scanning policies, to schedule future and recurring scans, and to view scan results. The tool is available from www.sourceforge.net/projects/vscweb/.

Nessus NBE Report Parsing Using Parse::Nessus::NBE

If you already have several Nessus reports in NBE data format and want to process them without much hassle, you can use the Parse::Nessus::NBE module. This module handles the regular expressions work for you, leaving you to simply request different types of information within the reports. Parse::Nessus::NBE can locate banners, open ports, plugins, numbers of vulnerabilities, web directories discovered, NFS-related issues, OS types, SNMP related issues, OS type statistics, service statistics, and vulnerability statistics.

This tool is available from http://search.cpan.org/~dkyger/Parse-Nessus-NBE-1.1/. Again, new users can use the following automated CPAN installation to handle the required dependencies, but should remember the resulting risk to their organization's security infrastructure. Those choosing this method can execute the following commands to install:

```
# perl –MCPAN -e shell
cpan> install Parse::Nessus::NBE
```

Common Problems

Several problems might arise while you are using the Nessus daemon to scan your network. These problems are not necessarily related to bandwidth or a vulnerability, but rather to a product vendor's improper handling of abnormal and unexpected traffic being directed at their product.

In this section, we divide the problems that might surface when scanning your network with Nessus into the following categories: aggressive scanning, volatile applications, and printer carnage. Toward the end of this section, we also describe another shortcoming that might show up when running Nessus against your enterprise's workstations. These workstations might be turned off during some part of the scan or change their IPs due to a restart, and the results pertaining to these workstations need to be addressed differently.

Aggressive Scanning

The type of portscan performed on your network has an effect on the stability of numerous types of hardware and software. We need to remember that while the main goal of the portscan phase is to detect open ports, it needs to do so while making sure that the software and hardware being scanned will "survive" the portscan, so that we can detect vulnerabilities in that software/hardware and do not needlessly reduce their uptime.

The Nessus daemon uses Nmap for its portscanning back engine, and as such, it supports all of Nmap's portscanning techniques, including TCP connect(), SYN, FIN, Xmas Tree, SYN FIN, FIN SYN, and NULL. Each scan type has a different effect on the software and hardware being scanned. As we are not testing the vendor's product endurance to portscanning but rather searching for vulnerabilities, we will want to use the closest thing to a normal user's connection: TCP connect(). Other scan types can cause inadvertent DoS conditions.

NOTE

Even though TCP connect() is considered the slowest scan type, it emulates in closest resemblance what a normal user would go through to connect to a remote host's ports.

You can also configure through Nessus the speed at which Nmap tries to connect to the remote server. The speed settings range from *Paranoid*, the slowest, to *Insane*, the fastest. Faster scans will often result in inaccurate results, as Nmap fails to get a response from the target on one port before giving up to start a new test on another port. Nessus' default settings are set to *Normal* speed, which tries to run as quickly as possible without overloading the network and without missing hosts/ports. We recommend against changing Nmap's scanning speed from the Normal settings, as the benefit of scanning faster is minimal in comparison to the potential problem of not detecting a certain port as open.

The Nmap settings that have a more visible effect on the portscanning speed, while not compromising the accuracy, are *Min RTT Timeout*, *Max RTT Timeout*, and *Initial RTT Timeout*. These three settings tell Nmap how long to wait for a response. The *Initial RTT Timeout* sets how long Nmap will wait for the first packets to return— there is no need to set this value any higher than the network's current maximum latency (the time it takes an ICMP packet to return from that host). The *Min/Max RTT Timeout* tells Nmap the range of the roundtrip time it can expect from the network. Limiting the range too much will cause Nmap to lose or discard packets, while setting it to a wide range will cause Nmap to scan more slowly.

We recommend setting the *Initial RTT Timeout* to 1000 (milliseconds) for LAN networks and to 3000 (milliseconds) for WAN networks, and setting the *Min* and *Max RTT Timeout* to .5 the *Initial* for the *Min* and 1.5 times for the *Max*.

One last Nmap setting that has an effect on the speed of the scan is *Host Timeout*. By setting this parameter, you are telling Nmap when to "give up" on a certain host and consider the current open-port list final. Nmap will consider any packet that was dropped as a lost packet and not as a closed port, and as such, when a firewall or firewalled host is scanned, it will take longer to return open port results. Nmap has no default timeout setting, and will continue to scan the firewall several times before giving up. The *Host Timeout* setting allows you to define this timeout interval, and prevent Nmap from spending several hours on the same host for just the portscanning phase.

We recommend setting the Host Timeout to 21,600,000 (milliseconds); that is, roughly 6 hours. However, if your network is fast, and you have no need to scan firewalls or hosts behind a firewall, you can lower this setting to achieve a faster scan. Remember, don't lower it too much, as portscanning takes time.

Volatile Applications

Not all of the possible problems stem from portscanning alone. Many applications are easily affected by Nessus' interaction on the ports on which they listen. Application developers expect the program connecting to it to behave in a certain way, according to the predefined protocol. A web server developer may assume that the client is always a web browser; an FTP server developer is likely to consider an FTP client to make incoming connections. This means that the QA process of the program is likely to run a client that behaves in a normal way, and doesn't send unexpected content.

The Nessus plugins are far from perfect in this respect. They were built to detect vulnerabilities. A vulnerability stems from the combination of a misbehavior on the part of the client and the server's poor reaction to that misbehavior. As such, Nessus plugins are likely to misbehave from the server's point of view. In addition, many of the Nessus plugins do not just assume a vulnerability exists because of the remote server type and version, but rather actually try to probe more deeply, usually attempting to exploit the problem.

By attempting to exploit vulnerabilities, Nessus tends to create fewer false positives, as a system that isn't vulnerable won't be successfully exploited. This is more accurate simply because it simulates the attacker's interaction with a vulnerability. Checking for vulnerabilities by attempting their exploitation also leads to detecting vulnerabilities in products not previously known to be vulnerable. One such example is the infamous AUX/LPT/COM1 DoS vulnerability. This vulnerability stems from the fact that when you request one of these reserved names as a filename from a remote web server, the server's attempt to access that filename will cause it to hang and subsequently disrupt the web server's service to clients. As this vulnerability affects more than a single server, the same plugin that detects it on Vendor X's product can detect it on Vendor Y's product as well, as the attack works for both products in a similar manner.

This behavior, however, affects a wider range of products than that which the Nessus plugin was built to detect, causing problems when you scan products that are relatively obscure, went untested by security analysts, weren't properly upgraded to prevent such problems, and so forth. These machines might crash when scanned or their applications might stop responding, requiring a restart of the affected applications or even the entire server.

Another issue that can arise from badly written products is the effect a certain plugin might have on the tested machine when not conforming to the vendor's specified protocol. From the point of view of the person who developed an application, anyone connecting to his or her port is trying to access the developer's service and thus knows what product is listening on that port, and as such will use the proper syntax. This isn't necessarily the case when a vulnerability scan is communicating with that port, especially in those cases where the scanner doesn't even know what application is listening. Before you disregard this, think about how many different web servers exist, from mainstream servers to small server programs on network printers that don't even respond to every HTTP command.

A badly written protocol implementation might be waiting for a *QUIT* command, and if such a command does not arrive, it might fail to close the connection (such as is the case with some SMTP servers). Due to this, Nessus' plugins launched against that port that fail to send the *QUIT* command will create a new connection that the product will never close. Over the course of multiple plugins that interact with the product's port, the scan will cause the product to create multiple sockets, consuming valuable resources and overloading the machine it is run on, and also possibly causing the failure of the server altogether.

This issue can also manifest itself during the portscan, as no data is sent to those ports. A badly written application might try to read a set size of bytes from the socket, and as no data is sent, the product will freeze waiting for more bytes or otherwise fail.

In most of the cases we mention here, where the product fails, the behavior is in fact a problem in the product and not in the Nessus scanner, and the product's failure to handle unexpected input without failure should itself be addressed as a vulnerability. For example, older Cisco routers might still hang when receiving Nmap's UDP scan packet on their syslog port, UDP 514. However, such unexpected behavior may end up causing the program to fail without your knowledge of the cause. Therefore, it is important to make sure that the majority of your critical products are properly tested for robustness to portscanning and testing during the testing lab phase discussed earlier. One of this book's authors used Nmap to scan a Cisco router and caused it to hang so badly that it lost its configuration, requiring a router administrator to enter the configuration line by line at the router's console. All this from a single UDP 514 packet! This type of failure could have been prevented with a router firmware patch deployed proactively and served as a DoS vulnerability, but it disconnected a network for 30 minutes. This problem should probably be found in a lab, instead of on the production network.

Another issue that might occur due to Nessus launching plugins against a specific product is that the product might not be designed to receive numerous simultaneous connections. You need to remember that Nessus makes scans run faster by launching more than a single plugin against each host. Badly written products may not support such multiple connections, and may as a result fail to address new connections or even crash. This type of behavior is difficult to predict and might occur even if you have done previous tests in a test lab, as the problem may require particular circumstances only likely in production use, such as high CPU load or network utilization.

Printer Problems

One of the most common problems occurs when scanning network appliances, especially printers. Scanning a printer can waste money in a form that isn't easily replaceable or recoverable. Some printers using old firmware versions handle portscans amazingly badly—they begin to print huge amounts of garbage, wasting large amounts of paper and ink or toner. This is because the printer wastefully thinks that the scan is someone trying to print something.

Printers aren't the only piece of network appliance affected by such scans. Voice over IP (VoIP) products, billing devices, automated teller machines (ATMs), time clock machines, parking systems, and basically any other product that answers to IP traffic but wasn't coded to handle unexpected input well or tested for security vulnerabilities by the manufacturer may display erratic behavior during the scan. The effects a scan would have on such devices aren't always wasteful as in the case of a printer, but going through your corporate building and restarting all the time clock machines is something you will want to avoid.

NOTE

Think of the situation in which your scan brings down all the time clock machines in your organization during the night, and you are violently awakened at 6:00 A.M., after the shift changed and find out that no one can clock in. Not only will this cause havoc in the corporation, it will also get you out of bed earlier than expected.

At least in the case of printers, the Nessus daemon now incorporates a test to specifically detect whether the IP being scanned is a printer, and, if this is the case, prevent the scan from testing that IP's printing-related ports. Still, we suggest that you avoid testing network devices whenever possible, unless you can verify that scanning these devices doesn't cause them to misbehave.

Scanning Workstations

Scanning workstations is very tricky. Workstations are restarted frequently, and might not be available during scanning hours, especially when scans occur in the middle of the night. In addition, scanning workstations might affect their reaction speed; the workstation might change its IP address due to Dynamic Host Configuration Protocol (DHCP) usage, and its vulnerabilities should usually be rated differently from servers' vulnerabilities.

We still believe that scanning workstations is an essential part of your organization's way of addressing the security issues on your network. Despite the inherent challenges, we recommend that you put forth the extra effort and scan workstations as part of your regular network security scanning.

If the corporate servers are secure, but you have over 10,000 workstations wide open to attack, your network cannot be considered secure. A single worm entering the internal network can affect these workstations and thus the rest of the network, by disturbing them due to the worm exploiting the vulnerability and as an effect bringing the network down due to the resultant excessive worm traffic. This is no imaginary scenario: MSBlaster and Sasser are just recent examples of worms that affected both corporate servers and workstations. Networks that made sure their servers were secure were still affected by the worm attacking their workstations.

The issue isn't just limited to these worms that affect only Windows-based machines. UNIX machines have been attacked by a small number of worms as well. Additionally, worms that attack IIS, Apache, OpenSSL, Microsoft SQL Server, and others will affect development networks as well. A worm attacking your development network still affects your corporate servers, where the loss of revenue occurs immediately when a developer is unable to update a production server application because his workstation has to be taken offline for worm removal.

NOTE

Another reason why development machines are so important to scan is that they often run experimental versions of operating systems or applications, typically without recent service packs, as those machines get reinstalled frequently. You should make sure those machines are protected from the rest of the network if they cannot be secured.

One of the problems mentioned previously is that workstations might not be available for scanning. This is especially true for employees who work in shifts, or turn off their workstations once they leave the office. For these workstations, scanning during off-peak hours is futile, as the machines cannot be scanned when they're off. However, these workstations are no less critical than those computers that are kept constantly on.

NOTE

You have to remember that the weakest link in your network's security is the computer that an attacker can compromise most easily. The CEO's secretary's computer is sometimes as valuable as the CEO's computer in terms of intellectual property. Additionally, most firewall policies grant much more privilege to an arbitrary internal computer than they do to outside computers. Attackers who compromise a single internal machine and use it to attack others are in much better shape than when they had no internal access.

Another problem is that workstations tend to have a weaker CPU and less memory compared to servers. As such, they will be more affected by Nessus' scans. The Nessus scan on those hosts will cause them to consume more resources than usual. As this cannot be avoided, we suggest considering running the workstations scans at off-peak hours, while keeping in mind that you need to instruct the employees to avoid turning off their computers when they leave.

Another problem that rises from large-scale corporate networks is the frequent use of DHCP. The protocol is used in most corporations to avoid the need to statically assign IP addresses to each workstation on the network. This in turn causes a problem for someone trying to understand what host was vulnerable at the time of the scan, as the IP it was allocated might be now, at the time of reading the vulnerability report, assigned to a different computer. This problem can be easily avoided by instructing the Nessus daemon to report vulnerabilities by the MAC address, or Ethernet card hardware address, of the vulnerable computer instead of by its IP address. This feature can be activated via the configuration file's **use_mac_addr** entry.

The last point to consider about workstation scanning is that not all vulnerabilities can be measured in the same way as when you're scanning a corporate server. A workstation wide open for file sharing might not be as critical as a corporate server having the same vulnerability. This is because a workstation's stored information is usually less valuable than that of the corporate server, and this is true in most cases where a centralized server stores all the information (documents, spreadsheets, and so forth). The problem is much harder to solve, and requires better planning of what tests you want to perform on the workstation and what data you want to filter out from the reports prior to going over them.

Summary

Once a security an officer concludes that enterprise scanning is needed, he or she is usually baffled by the big questions: "How do I do it? And how much effort must I put into that?" These two questions are answered in detail in this Enterprise Scanning chapter. We all know that planning your deployment is important, and this is the case with Nessus.

Nessus requires preparation of your network for the bandwidth requirements of the scanner. Measuring these requirements is not always easy, but with a few tricks and the right third-party tools, you can measure these requirements, and understand the effect they will have on the network.

Bandwidth utilization is greatly affected by the different types of topologies you use to deploy the scanning servers. The different topologies also affect the hardware requirements and the necessary preparations for the day when you will need to scan a specific vulnerability instead of using the complete arsenal of vulnerability tests at your disposal.

As simply scanning your network is not enough, you need to place these results in some centralized location and start sorting out the relevant data. Once the data is placed in a database, we can use it to correlate the different results provided by the differential exposure to vulnerabilities from multiple locations throughout an organization. We can also use the database to see how the vulnerabilities have progressed over time. Most importantly, once the data has been placed in a single location, we can filter out any false positives and irrelevant vulnerabilities.

You are not obliged to do everything from scratch—several third-party tools exist that you can use to ease your usage of Nessus in the organization. These tools are free to use and you can extend them to further suit your needs. As with everything in life, there are several common problems with running Nessus in your organization. Some problems can be easily avoided, while others can be detected beforehand in the test lab so that their impact can be minimized.

Solutions Fast Track

Planning a Deployment

☑ Make a list of your network's assets, who is responsible for them, and to whom the results should be mailed.

☑ Invite all the network's assets owners and managers to an overview of Nessus' capabilities, and the effects they have. Give a live demonstration.

☑ Use a test lab to determine the network bandwidth requirements your organization can afford.

☑ Automate the server's process of scanning and updating.

Configuring Scanners

☑ Choose a topology that suits your needs.

☑ Buy any additional hardware you require.

☑ Practice scanning for a specific threat, as in the case of a critical Microsoft advisory.

Data Correlation

☑ Use a database instead of files to store all the results.

☑ Correlate the results you receive from scans to help you concentrate on the most serious vulnerabilities.

☑ Generate differential results from the data stored in the database.

☑ Generate complex results using sophisticated SQL statements.

☑ Filter out from the database irrelevant vulnerabilities and false positives.

☑ Use third-party tools to ease the use vulnerability assessment in your organization.

Common Problems

☑ Avoid problems caused by scanning too aggressively.

☑ Test relatively unknown software and hardware in a test lab to avoid unexpected problems.

☑ Try to avoid scanning printers to save paper resources.

☑ Scan your workstations during working hours to avoid illusive hosts, or instruct your employees to leave their workstations turned on for the night.

Frequently Asked Questions

The following Frequently Asked Questions, answered by the authors of this book, are designed to both measure your understanding of the concepts presented in this chapter and to assist you with real-life implementation of these concepts. To have your questions about this chapter answered by the author, browse to **www.syngress.com/solutions** and click on the **"Ask the Author"** form. You will also gain access to thousands of other FAQs at ITFAQnet.com.

Q: Is it feasible to scan my entire enterprise network periodically?

A: The question is not whether you should scan your entire network, it is whether you can afford *not* to scan it. Not knowing what vulnerabilities you have in your network is certainly not going to help you secure the organization. This chapter should give you some ideas on how to manage this obviously challenging task.

Q: How often should those scans run? You discuss daily/weekly scans, but we can hardly cope with our current rate of quarterly network audits!

A: As noted earlier, the Sasser worm started spreading in just over three weeks after the vulnerability was discovered. This "window of exposure" is getting smaller and smaller all the time, and demonstrates the need to perform vulnerability scans on a weekly basis. The real question is how to handle the wealth of information you will start receiving once the scans are configured to run automatically and frequently. The answer is technological: differential reporting, data mining through databased results, and eliminating false positives, using the techniques outlined in this chapter.

Q: When dealing with other departments, I have difficulties explaining why a certain vulnerability needs to be addressed. This is especially true when dealing with knowledgeable technical people such as system administrators and programmers. How can I convince them that the problem is indeed serious and should be dealt with promptly?

A: As a person in charge of security in your company, you probably have a good understanding of why security is a concern. We found that this is not always the case with other technical people who do not deal with security issues daily. However, this approach can be reversed. Security is an interesting subject for most technical people, and in many cases system administrators or programmers will be extremely happy to participate in a security workshop that explains the concepts and demonstrates the risks. By exposing potentially resistant staff to the subject and raising their awareness to the risks, you will increase the level of cooperation and will find it easier to communicate any security concerns. People tend to cooperate better once they have a better understanding of what the challenges are—this can usually be done without training them to be security experts... Focus on cooperating with them, educating them, and framing your discussions within both the risks and the business needs. Finally, as much as possible, understand the technology and risks yourself, so you can explain them to others realisticly and convincingly.

Q: How scalable are the solutions presented in this chapter? Will they work in my complicated network?

A: This chapter is based on our own experience overseeing implementations of enterprisewide vulnerability scanning solutions. If you break the huge task of scanning your entire enterprise into smaller tasks (like we did in this chapter) and then further distribute the tasks as appropriate among the different networks you have, you will see that although not trivial to set up, once the setup is working, the benefits are tremendous. Applying techniques such as distributed scanning and report correlation make it possible to use the Nessus scanning tool across the enterprise.

Chapter 11

NASL

Contributed by Renaud Deraison

Solutions in this Chapter:

- **Why NASL?**
- **Structure of a NASL Script**
- **An Introduction to the NASL Language**
- **The Nessus Knowledge Base**

☑ **Summary**

☑ **Solutions Fast Track**

☑ **Frequently Asked Questions**

Introduction

When I initially announced the use of the Nessus Attack Scripting Language (NASL) within Nessus, many users disapproved, since it was not a "known" language such as Perl or Python. Over time, the use of a dedicated language turned out to be a good design decision, since it gives us, as developers, full control of the virtual machine used by the individual plugins. The use of NASL dramatically simplifies the maintenance of the plugins; bug fixes and enhancements can be applied to the NASL interpreter itself, avoiding the need to modify each and every plugin. For example, each of the network-related functions—such as connecting to a system or receiving data from it—are defined at the scripting engine level, not the plugin level. If we want to improve the way in which network connections are made, we only need to modify the NASL interpreter, and not the thousands of plugins that use these functions.

In this chapter, I explain why the NASL language was written, how it works, and why it is best suited for vulnerability detection. Then I explain how to write a NASL script for use within Nessus, how the Knowledge Base (KB) can be used, and how the contribution process works if you want to submit your own plugins to the community.

Why NASL?

In 1998, the first version of Nessus was released with around 50 security checks, otherwise known as "plugins." These plugins were implemented as shared libraries, written in the C programming language, and renamed to have a .nes file extension. The goal of this approach was to separate the scanning engine (nessusd) from the security checks it performs. This separation provided Nessus with a modular and easily extensible architecture. At the time, using shared libraries to write plugins made a lot of sense; it allowed us to quickly create new plugins based on existing C programs.

A few months after the initial release of Nessus, I had written nearly 200 plugins this way. Compiling these plugins would take up to 30 minutes on my 200MHz Pentium PC (which was a beefy computer at the time). During that same time, I was investigating ways to help people upgrade the plugin set without having to recompile the entire Nessus package. In short, the C plugins were showing their limits, as they were slow to install and complicated to upgrade.

I wrote a small script called "plugins-factory" (which is still included in the Nessus distribution but fortunately is not used) that would take a C plugin and compile it into a shared library (.nes). The idea behind this was to write a plugin update script that would download the latest C plugins from the web, compile them, and then install them. Due to the obvious security implications, the idea never went anywhere.

After looking into the currently available scripting languages, Perl stood out as the best language to use for Nessus plugins. However, Perl had several pitfalls at the time:

- Large memory footprint
- Sending and receiving raw packets was not well supported
- No reliable way to control the underlying virtual machine

This last point was, by far, the most important. From a high-level view, every security check in a scanner basically does the same thing; it connects to some port on the remote host, "does some stuff," and then deduces if the remote host is vulnerable to a given flaw. The best way to tune every security check is not to edit them individually, but to tune to the virtual machine that executes them. For example, when we added SSL support to Nessus, we did not have to modify any of the existing plugins; we only modified the way the socket functions work underneath. Another concern with using Perl as the plugin language was that almost all advanced functionality was only available through external modules. These modules each have their own set of required packages and system libraries. I was afraid that users would contribute really nice plugins, but the external package requirements would complicate the installation process. By having a dedicated language, I decided to make life a bit more difficult for contributors, but much simpler for end users. This is how the Nessus Attack Scripting Language was born.

I started to write a language, tentatively called "NASL," whose goals were the following:

- Each script must be self-contained (in one file)
- Easy to install for the end user
- Easy to learn for the contributors
- Small memory footprint
- Designed for network security checks

- Strong security

- Easy to modify and extend

- Support multiple languages

The result was a library now referred to as "nasl1," which had some pitfalls (for example, it was really slow and would be too lax regarding syntax errors), but overall, it did its job properly. Over 1,000 security checks were written in this first version of NASL. Initially, speed was not much of a concern; it will always take more time to establish a TCP session than the NASL interpreter would spend parsing the plugin code.

However, as the number of plugins increased over time, and as people started using Nessus to scan more and more hosts, nasl1 was eventually considered too slow for the task. The original code was difficult to extend, and the decision was made to simply rewrite it.

In 2001, the libnasl library was rewritten by Michel Arboi to extend the language and fix the pitfalls that existed in nasl1. This rewritten library was dubbed "nasl2," and became the biggest new feature in Nessus 2.0. We are very happy with nasl2, as it reaches all our goals for our embedded language:

- **Self-contained scripts** Each NASL script contains both the code that checks for the flaw and a description of the plugin itself. Initially, I had considered using an external file for the description, but dismissed this idea due to the complexity it would introduce.

- **Easy to install for the end user** NASL is a self-contained package that can be configured to use the OpenSSL library. Any user with a copy of the GNU C Compiler (gcc) and GNI Bison (bison) could easily build and install the NASL language interpreter.

- **Easy to learn for the contributors** NASL looks very much like C, with some Perl-isms. If you have ever programmed or scripted in the past, the learning curve is small. The big difference between C and NASL is the lack of pointers and memory management.

- **Small memory footprint** A typical Nessus check will only require a few hundred kilobytes of memory, which means that more plugins can be launched at the same time.

- **Designed for network security checks** NASL is designed to establish connections, send data, and parse the results. It comes with a number of function libraries that implement high-level protocols. Example protocols include SMB, NFS, RPC, SMTP, HTTP, and many more. All these libraries are written in NASL.

- **Strong security** NASL checks cannot access the local file system, execute system commands, or connect to third-party hosts (they can only establish connections with the remote host currently being tested). Additionally, the lack of pointers and memory management results in a language that is not vulnerable to buffer overflows. This makes NASL a very strong language for developing security checks and reduces the time it takes to publish new plugins. We do not have to worry about the security of the scanner itself when writing a new plugin.

- **Easy to modify and extend** The current implementation of the NASL interpreter is very clean from a code perspective. This makes the addition of new operators or built-in functions very easy, while maintaining backward compatibility with older implementations of the library.

- **Support for multiple languages** NASL was initially designed to support a great number of languages, but the limitations of ASCII encoding were not taken into account. At this time, only the French language implementation has made much progress. Many languages, such as Japanese, cannot be represented in the extended ASCII character set. The number of new plugins being written every day, as well as the frequent modifications to old plugins, would place large demands on any translation effort. We have investigated ways to have better support for non-English languages, but at this time, this goal has been delayed.

Why Do You Want to Write (and Publish) Your Own NASL Scripts?

The Nessus engine (nessusd) is not a vulnerability scanner; it's a network engine that launches a set of plugins against every host on the network. The Nessus engine is responsible for launching plugins in the right order, facilitating communication between the plugins, and managing the resources they require.

What this really means is that as a user, you have the ability to write plugins that perform network security checks, and almost any other type of networkwide test (such as policy compliance). For example, if your corporate policy is to use

Apache 1.3 instead of Apache 2.0, you can easily write a plugin that verifies that every system with an active web server is indeed running the correct version of Apache. If your company requires the use of SSH.com's SSH server instead of OpenSSH, writing a compliance check is also very simple. Finally, if you deal with Windows hosts and your corporate policy is to deploy patches using Microsoft's Software Update Services (SUS), you can easily write a plugin that will warn you whenever a Windows host is not configured to use your company SUS server.

You might also want to write your own security checks because Nessus.org has not published a check for a vulnerability with which you are dealing. Although the Nessus project does its best to provide plugins for as many vulnerabilities as possible, many situations would result in a plugin not being written. When a flaw is reported in a product with a very small user base, the Nessus plugin developers might choose to spend their time working on a plugin that applies to a larger group of people instead. Unsupported shareware products and software that provides a specific function to a niche industry are both candidates for exclusion. This is not to say that if someone submitted a plugin that it would be rejected, just that these are a lower priority than the dozens of critical flaws discovered in mainstream products every week.

If you write your own security check, we encourage you to submit it to the Nessus community. The best way to submit your plugin is to post it to the *plugin-writers* mailing list (please refer to Chapter 12). Your plugin will be reviewed and potentially included with the Nessus distribution. Once your plugin has been accepted, the Nessus development team will automatically maintain it. This means that if the NASL API changes (and it is constantly being improved), your plugin will be updated and will continue to work with newer versions of Nessus. Publishing your plugin allows you to write it once and let a team of dedicated people maintain it in the future.

Structure of a NASL Script

A NASL script is divided in two sections. The first section is called the "script description" and contains NASL code that is used by the Nessus engine. This code contains information such as the unique plugin identifier, a short name for the plugin, its dependencies, and other attributes that are used to control how and when this plugin is launched. This section defines what the users will see in the client interface as well as what ends up in the final report. The description and name fields in this section are just as important as the test code itself; if end users are not able to determine what this plugin does or understand the significance when they review the report, they might inadvertently ignore a serious vulnerability on their network.

The second section is called the "script body." This code is the actual meat of the plugin; it is responsible for testing the actual vulnerability and reporting any relevant data. How this section is written depends on quite a few factors. Some plugins will gather data and report it, others will query saved data and trigger alerts based on the contents, and a handful will just configure other parameters of the scan and exit.

Internally, this means that the Nessus engine actually executes every script in two different ways. When the Nessus engine first starts, it will set the "description" variable to TRUE and then execute every plugin once. This allows the engine to build a dependency tree and provide a list of available plugins to the Nessus client software. During the actual scan, each plugin is launched once for each target on the network, with the "description" set to FALSE. If for some reason the description section does not contain an **exit ()** call at the end, the engine will continue processing the plugin. To prevent any problems during the initialization phase, the engine will disable all network-related functions, reducing the impact of buggy plugins.

The Description Section

This section must call the following functions:

- **script_id(<number>)** The unique ID number of this plugin. Each plugin is attributed a unique ID that that will not change over time. Traditionally, Nessus scripts use the 1xxxxx space (10000, 10001, and so on...). If you intend to develop private scripts that you do not intend to distribute, it is recommended you use the 9xxxxx ID space.

- **script_name(english:"<name>")** The short name of the script, it should be relevant to the tested vulnerability.

- **script_description(english:"<description>")** A concise description of the flaw tested for by the plugin, how it can be resolved, and the potential risk. If the plugin generates dynamic output (for example, it reports the version number of a remote service), this description should explain what the script does. Plugins that generate dynamic output specify argument to the "data" parameter of the **security_hole()**, **secu-**

rity_note(), and **security_warning()** functions in the script body. A good description is around 10 to 20 lines long, contains a solution, and a risk factor. Although the description is "free form," we highly recommend that it include the solution and risk factor, as it helps user prioritize the report. The following example is from Nessus plugin #11591:

```
desc = "The remote host is running 12Planet Chat Server - a web based chat
server written in Java.

The connection to this server is done over clear text, which means that
an attacker who can sniff the data going to this host could obtain the
administrator password of the web site, and use it to gain unauthorized
access to this chat server.

Solution : None at this time
Risk factor : Low";
```

- **script_summary(english:"<name>")** A one-line description of what the plugin actually does.

- **script_category(<category>)** The script category is used by the Nessus engine to determine when the plugin should be launched. The following categories exist:

  - **ACT_INIT** The plugin fills the Knowledge Base and must be launched before anything else.

  - **ACT_SCANNER** The plugin is a port scanner or a "pinger" that determines if the remote host is alive.

  - **ACT_SETTINGS** The plugin processes user-specified preferences that might affect the rest of the plugins (some preferences are stored in the Knowledge Base).

  - **ACT_GATHER_INFO** The script will gather information about the remote services (for example, it grabs the banner, determines what service is running on which port, and so on…). Most of the scripts in this category fill the Knowledge Base with data that is used by other scripts.

  - **ACT_ATTACK** The script nonintrusively tests for a flaw and is likely leave "noisy" logs on the tested system.

- **ACT_MIXED_ATTACK** The script will perform an intrusive check if "safe checks" are disabled (for example, attempt to reproduce a buffer overflow condition), and will perform a nonintrusive check if "safe checks" are disabled. The nonintrusive check might have a higher chance of false positives.

- **ACT_DESTRUCTIVE_ATTACK** The script might disable the remote service while performing the test. Scripts in this category will be disabled if the "safe checks" option is set.

- **ACT_DENIAL** The goal of the script is to disable the remote service. Scripts in this category will be disabled if the "safe checks" option is set.

- **ACT_KILL_HOST** The goal of the script is to crash the tested system. Scripts in this category will be disabled if the "safe checks" option is set.

- **ACT_FLOOD** The script might crash the tested system and potentially affect the network itself. Scripts in this category will be disabled if the "safe checks" option is set.

- **ACT_END** The script must run after every other script has finished.

- **script_copyright(english:"<copyright>")** A one-line sentence that states who holds the copyright on this script.

- **script_family(english:"<family>")** The family to which the script belongs. A plugin might fall into more than one family. For example, if a buffer overflow was found in Microsoft's IIS web server, it could logically be placed into both the "Gain a shell remotely" and "Windows" families. When these situations come up, the rule of thumb is to associate the plugin with the family to which the vulnerability is closest. For example, a flaw in IIS is would be placed into the "Windows" family, since it is an integral part of the Windows operating system. By the same logic, a buffer overflow in a Novell product would be placed into the "NetWare" family. Selecting the proper family is often a difficult task, since one flaw might affect various operating systems and services. This becomes particularly complicated when dealing with a flaw in an application library that is used by a wide variety of products. We have been investigating other categorization techniques, but have not developed a better method at this time.

If you intend to share your script with the community, avoid creating your own family name and use one of the following standard names instead:

- **Backdoors** The plugin tries to detect backdoor services and Trojan horse programs. This family also applies to vendor-installed maintenance accounts and other "official" backdoors.

- **CGI abuses** The plugin looks for flaws in a web application (PHP, CGI, and so forth).

- **CISCO** The plugin looks for flaws in a product made by Cisco.

- **Denial of Service** The plugin looks for flaws that would result in a denial of service (DoS) if exploited.

- **FTP** The plugin looks for flaws in a File Transfer Protocol (FTP) service.

- **Finger abuses** The plugin looks for flaws in the venerable "finger" service.

- **Firewalls** The plugin looks for flaws specific to firewalls and proxy servers.

- **Gain a shell remotely** The plugin looks for flaws that would result in arbitrary code execution, such as buffer overflows and format string attacks.

- **Gain root remotely** The same as "Gain a shell remotely," but affecting services running as the root user (the most powerful account on UNIX systems).

- **General** The plugin performs a task that is not directly related to vulnerability detection, such as service discovery.

- **Misc.** The plugin does something that does not fit into one of the other families.

- **NIS** The plugin looks for flaws in Sun's Network Information Service (formerly called "yellow pages").

- **NetWare** The plugin looks for flaws affecting Novell NetWare products.

- **Peer-to-Peer file sharing** The plugin detects various peer-to-peer (P2P) file sharing services.

- **Port scanners** The plugin is either a portscanner or "pinger."

- **RPC** The plugin looks for flaws in a Sun RPC service.

- **Remote file access** The plugin looks for flaws that can be exploited to obtain remote file system access.

- **SMTP Problems** The plugin looks for flaws in Simple Mail Transfer Protocol (SMTP) services.

- **SNMP** The plugin looks for flaws in Simple Network Management Protocol (SNMP) services.

- **Untested** The plugin has not been well tested and might provide inaccurate results.

- **Useless services** The plugin looks for services that are not required and might represent a security risk (they might have been relevant in 1972, but should no longer be allowed on the network).

- **Windows** The plugin looks for flaws related to the Microsoft Windows operating system.

- **Windows User Management** The plugin looks for flaws related to user accounts on Microsoft Windows systems.

The following functions are not strictly required, but should be used as needed:

- **script_bugtraq_id(ID1, ID2, ...)** Associates the plugin with one or more Bugtraq ID values. Bugtraq identifiers are managed by SecurityFocus (www.securityfocus.com/bid). This information is incorporated in the final report.

- **script_cve_id("CVE-XXXX-YYYY", "CVE-XXX2-YYY2", ...)** Associates the plugin with one or more CVE identifiers. CVE is a vulnerability dictionary that is managed by the Common Vulnerabilities and Exposures project (http://cve.mitre.org). This information is incorporated in the final report.

- **script_xref(name:<name>, value:<value>)** Associates a plugin with an arbitrary reference type and value. Currently, this function is used to link Nessus plugins with IAVA (U.S. Government) and OSVDB (www.osvdb.org) identifiers, as well as standard HTTP URLs. This information is incorporated in the final report.

- **script_timeout(timeout)** Specifies the number of seconds that the plugin is allowed to run before it is killed. This prevents a buggy plugin or slow service from causing a scan to hang indefinitely. If this function is not called, the default of three minutes will be used. If your particular plugin will take longer than this, make sure that this function is called. Calling this function with the parameter of zero (0) will allow the script to run indefinitely.

- **script_dependencies("name1.nasl", "name2.nasl", ...)** Defines a list of other plugins that must run before this one. This is particularly useful if your plugin requires information from the Knowledge Base that is placed there by another plugin. Be careful when adding dependencies, because it is possible to create a circular dependency tree that will result in *bad things* happening inside the Nessus engine (a recursive function will consume all available stack space). You may notice that some plugins also call script_dependencie(); this is the older syntax for this function and behaves exactly the same way.

- **script_require_ports(port1, port2, ...)** Instructs the Nessus engine to not launch this plugin if *all* of the listed ports are closed.

- **script_require_keys(key1, key2, ...)** Instructs the Nessus engine to only launch this plugin if *all* of the listed Knowledge Base keys are defined.

- **script_exclude_keys(key1, key2, ...)** Instructs the Nessus engine to only launch this plugin if *all* of the listed Knowledge Base keys are *not* defined.

An Introduction to the NASL Language

If you are familiar with C, Perl, or PHP, you should have no problem picking up the NASL language. Since NASL was designed to perform network checks, the language is focused on string manipulation and networking. Everything else was designed to be out of your way; you do not need to worry about memory management, pointers, or operating system peculiarities. NASL was designed to run from within the Nessus engine and does not have the capability to read data from the console or otherwise interact with the host system (with a few exceptions in the case of "trusted" scripts). In a way, you can view a NASL script as an elaborate configuration file that tells the Nessus engine what to do. You can launch scripts in a stand-alone mode, using the command-line NASL interpreter, but some functions are dependent on the environment provided by the Nessus engine. For example, scripts run from the command line are not able to automatically negotiate SSL-wrapped services or manipulate the Knowledge Base. The **display()** function is available for debugging purposes; it is one of the few functions designed for use outside of the Nessus engine.

Writing Your First Script

When writing NASL scripts, it is common practice to test them with the *nasl* command-line interpreter before launching them as part of a Nessus scan. The *nasl* utility is part of the Nessus installation and takes the following arguments:

```
nasl [-t <target>] [-T tracefile] script1.nasl [script2.nasl …]
```

where:

- **-t <target>** is the IP address or hostname against which you would like to test your script. The NASL networking functions do not allow you to specify the destination address when establishing connections or sending raw packets. This limitation is as much for safety as for convenience and has worked very well so far. If this option is not specified, all connections will be made to the loopback address, 127.0.0.1 (localhost).

- **-T <tracefile>** forces the interpreter to write debugging information to the specified file. This option is invaluable when diagnosing problems in complex scripts. An argument of "-" will result in the output being written to the console.

This utility has a few other options covered later in this chapter. For a complete listing of available options, execute this program with the *-h* argument.

For our first NASL script, we will write a simple tool that connects to an FTP server (on TCP port 21), reads the banner, and then displays it on screen. The following NASL code demonstrates how easy it is to accomplish this task:

```
soc = open_sock_tcp(21);
if ( ! soc ) exit(0);
banner = recv_line(socket:soc, length:4096);
display(banner);
```

Let's walk through this small example:

```
soc = open_sock_tcp(21);
```

This function opens a TCP socket on port 21 of the current target (as specified with *nasl –t*). This function returns NULL on failure (the remote port is closed or not responding) and a nonzero file descriptor on success.

```
banner = recv_line(socket:soc, length:4096);
```

This function reads data from the socket until the number of bytes specified by the "length" parameter has been received, or until the character "\n" is received—whichever comes first.

As you can see, the function **open_sock_tcp()** takes a single, non-named argument, while the function **recv_line()** takes two arguments that are prefixed by their name. These are referred to as "anonymous" and "named" functions. Named functions allow the plugin writer to specify only the parameters that he needs, instead of having to supply values for each parameter supported by the function. Additionally, the writer does not need to remember the exact order of the parameters, preventing simple errors when calling a function that supports many options. For example, the following two lines produce identical results:

```
banner = recv_line(socket:soc, length:4096);
banner = recv_line(length:4096, socket:soc);
```

Save this script as "test.nasl" and execute it on the command line:

```
$ /usr/local/bin/nasl -t ftp.nessus.org test.nasl
** WARNING : packet forgery will not work
** as NASL is not running as root
220 ftp.nessus.org Ready
```

If you run *nasl* as a nonroot user, you will notice that it displays a warning message about "packet forgery." NASL scripts are capable of creating, sending, and receiving raw IP packets, but they require root privileges to do so. In this example, we are not using raw sockets and can safely ignore this message.

Now, let's modify our script to display the FTP banner in a Nessus report. To do so, we need to use one of the three special-purpose reporting functions: **security_hole()**, **security_warning()**, and **security_note()**. These functions tell the Nessus engine that a plugin is successful (a vulnerability was found), and each denotes a different severity level. A call to the **security_note()** function will result in a low-risk vulnerability being added to the report, a call to

security_warn() will result in a medium-risk vulnerability, and **security_hole()** is used to report a high-risk vulnerability. These functions can be invoked in two ways:

```
security_note(<port>)
```

    or

```
security_note(port:<port>, data:<report>, proto:<protocol>)
```

In the first case, the plugin simply tells the Nessus engine that it was successful. The Nessus engine will copy the plugin description (as registered with **script_description()**) and will place it into the report. This is sufficient for most plugins; either a vulnerability is there and we provide a generic description, or it is not and we do not report anything. In some cases, you might want to include dynamic text in the report. This dynamic text could be the version number of the remote web server, the FTP banner, the list of exported shares, or even the contents of a captured password file.

In this particular example, we want to report the FTP banner that we received from the target system, and we will use the long form of the **security_note()** function to do this:

```
soc = open_sock_tcp(21);
if ( ! soc ) exit(0);
banner = recv_line(socket:soc, length:4096);
security_note(port:21, data:"The remote FTP banner is : " + banner,
proto:"tcp");
```

If you execute this script from the command line, you will notice that the "data" parameter is written to the console. If no "data" parameter was specified, it will default to the string "Successful." When this plugin is launched by the Nessus engine, this data will be used as the vulnerability description in the final report.

Now that our plugin code has been modified to report the FTP banner, we need to create the description section. This section will allow the plugin to be loaded by the Nessus engine:

```
if ( description )
{
        script_id( 90001);
        script_name(english:"Simple FTP banner grabber");
        script_description(english:"
```

This script establishes a connection to the remote host on port 21 and
extracts the FTP banner of the remote host");

```
        script_summary(english:"retrieves the remote FTP banner");
        script_category(ACT_GATHER_INFO);
        script_family(english:"Nessus Book");
        script_copyright(english:"(C) 2004 Renaud Deraison");
        exit(0);
}


soc = open_sock_tcp(21);
if ( ! soc ) exit(0);
banner = recv_line(socket:soc, length:4096);
security_note(port:21, data:"The remote FTP banner is : " + banner,
proto:"tcp");
```

After you have saved this plugin to disk, you can verify the syntax of the
code using the *nasl* interpreter. The *-p* option will tell *nasl* to only parse the
plugin, it will not actually execute the NASL script. If the command **nasl –p
yourscript.nasl** results in no output, then the syntax of the plugin is correct. To
add your plugin to the Nessus installation, copy it to the Nessus plugins directory
and send the main "nessusd" process a "HUP" signal. The location of the plugin
directory will depend on your system; it can usually be found in
/usr/local/lib/nessus/plugins or /usr/lib/nessus/plugins. You will need root privileges to add your plugin to this directory and restart the server:

```
# cp test_script.nasl /usr/local/lib/nessus/plugins/
# killall -HUP nessusd
```

After restarting the server (with the "HUP" signal), open the Nessus client
and connect to the server. After authenticating, verify that your new plugin
shows up in the family "Nessus Book" shown in Figure 11.1.

Figure 11.1 Nessus Book

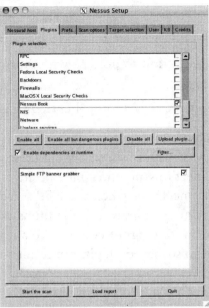

Now, disable every plugin except this one, and run a test scan against the FTP server of your choice. You should obtain the report shown in Figure 11.2.

Figure 11.2 Nessus "NG" Report

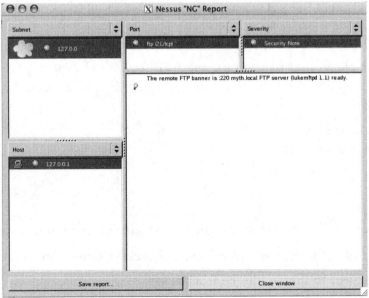

If the results look like Figure 11.2, it worked! However, this plugin is still not 100-percent Nessus compliant:

- It assumes that FTP servers are bound to listen on port 21.

- It establishes a connection to port 21 without first making sure that the port is actually open.

- It does not respect the FTP protocol entirely.

These issues might seem minor, but can cause serious problems in the overall performance and accuracy of a Nessus scan. Fixing these issues will prevent unnecessary network connections, potential false positives when other services are using port 21, and false negatives when the FTP server is running on a non-standard port. Recent versions of Nessus include thousands of unique plugins; small problems across the entire plugin tree can have a noticeable impact on the scan results. Even a single misbehaved plugin can result a measurable drop in scan performance and cause havoc across the target network.

So, let's fix each issue to make this plugin more "Nessus friendly."

Assuming that the FTP Server Is Listening on Port 21

During the scan, Nessus builds what we call a Knowledge Base (KB). Basically, every script can write down facts about the remote host—the ports that are open, the banner of various services, the version of installed software and patches, and so on. By using the KB efficiently, you can speed up your test and make it "smarter"—the trick is to know which plugins provide the KB data your plugin needs.

For example, instead of assuming the FTP server is always on port 21, you can ask the KB to tell you the port number of any FTP discovered by the service detection plugin.

```
port = get_kb_item("Services/ftp");
if ( ! port ) port = 21;
soc = open_sock_tcp(port);
```

This code means:

- I want to know the port of an FTP service on the tested system.

- If no FTP service was identified, fall back to using port 21.

- Connect to the remote FTP service.

Every identified service is located under the "Service/xxx" hierarchy in the KB, where "xxx" is the name of the detected service. If the remote host happens to run two FTP servers—one on port 21 and another on port 2121—Nessus will detect this condition and will execute your script twice; once with a port value of 21, and once with a value of 2121. Internally, this actually results in the plugin spawning off a cloned copy of itself for each value stored in that KB key. If the service has not been recognized, we fall back to port 21—useful in situations where the service detection plugin encounters a problem. When running this plugin from the command line, the KB does not exist, so providing a default value is the only way we could test this script from outside the Nessus engine.

Establishing a Connection to the Port Directly

Since the Nessus engine usually performs a portscan, there's no need to connect to a port that has already been detected as closed. It wastes bandwidth and time—especially if the target system is behind a firewall. The NASL function **get_port_state(<port>)** will tell you if a port is closed. It returns 0 if the port is known to be closed, and 1 if the state is unknown (not in the portscan range) or open. We will modify our plugin to check the state of the port before trying to establish a connection to it:

```
port = get_kb_item("Services/ftp");
If ( ! port ) port = 21;
If ( ! get_port_state(port) ) exit(0);
soc = open_sock_tcp(port);
```

Respecting the FTP Protocol

One last assumption has been made so far: the FTP banner is sent as one line. In reality, FTP banners might split up across multiple lines. This is common practice with many large FTP servers (such as ftp.lip5.fr), which provide the terms of use in the banner itself. Our plugin would fail because it only reads the first line.

The FTP protocol defines that all lines starting with the string "220-" are followed by another line, while lines starting with the string "220-" signify the last line of the banner. Our plugin will need to be modified to take this into account:

```
port = get_kb_item("Services/ftp");
if ( ! port ) port = 21;
if ( ! get_port_state(port) ) exit(0);
```

```
soc = open_sock_tcp(port);
banner = line = recv_line(socket:soc, length:4096);
while ( line =~ "^220-" )
{
        line = recv_line(socket:soc, length:4096);
        banner += line;
}


security_note(port:port, data:"The remote FTP banner is : "  + banner,
proto:"tcp");
```

This modification will cause the script to read the first line of the banner from the server and then continue to read data as long as the new line starts with "220-." As each new line is received, the data is added to the variable "banner."

In this particular case, this functionality has already been implemented as the **get_ftp_banner()** function in the "ftp_funcs.inc" script library. We will now modify our plugin to use this library:

```
include("ftp_func.inc");
        port = get_kb_item("Services/ftp");
        if ( ! port ) port = 21;
        banner = get_ftp_banner(port:port);
        security_note(port:port, data:"The remote FTP banner is : " + banner,
        proto:"tcp");
```

There are many advantages to using library functions, such as **get_ftp_banner()**, instead of writing the code ourselves. If a new type of FTP server becomes popular, one that provides the banner in a slightly different way, only a single library function would need to be modified to support it. Additionally, many of the library functions will use smart caching techniques to reduce the number of connections made to the server. The first time the **get_ftp_banner()** function is called, it will store the FTP banner in the KB. Each successive call to this function will first check the KB for the banner and return it if one is found, removing the need for each plugin to connect to the FTP server on its own. Considering that in any given scan, there might be dozens of plugins that all need to analyze the FTP banner, this is a huge improvement in terms of efficiency and bandwidth usage.

Wrapping It Up

Now that our plugin is "smarter," we need to modify the description section to indicate that this script must be run after the find_service.nes service detection plugin. The find_service.nes plugin is responsible for determining what type of application is running on each port found during the portscan phase. Almost every plugin in the Nessus distribution depends on this plugin or its slightly more advanced sibling, find_service2.nasl. We use the **script_dependencie()** function to tell the Nessus engine that our plugin must always be launched after find_service.nes.

```
if ( description )
{
        [...]
        script_copyright(english:"(C) 2004 Renaud Deraison");
        script_dependencie("find_service.nes");
        exit(0);
}
```

Once this is done, we copy the plugin over our old one in the Nessus plugins directory, restart the Nessus engine, and launch a test scan. Since the new plugin is able to identify FTP servers on any port, you will need to enable one of the portscan plugins to find FTP services on ports other than 21.

More Advanced Scripting

You now know the basics of writing a NASL plugin, how to access the Knowledge Base, and how to report a vulnerability. Let's explore some of the interesting built-in functions and libraries of the NASL language.

String Manipulation

NASL is quite flexible when it comes to working with strings. String operations include addition, subtraction, search, replace, and support for regular expressions. NASL also allows you to use escape characters ("\n", and so forth) using the **string()** function.

How Strings Are Defined in NASL

Strings can be defined using single quotes or double quotes. When using double quotes, a string is taken "as is"—no interpretation is made on its content—while strings defined with single quotes interpret escape characters. For example:

```
A = "foo\n";
B = 'foo\n';
```

In this example, the variable "A" is five characters long and is equal to "foo\n", while variable "B" is four characters long and equal to "foo", followed by a carriage return. This is the opposite of how strings are handled in languages such as C and Perl, and can be confusing to new plugin developers.

We call an interpreted string (defined with single quotes) a "pure" string. It is possible to convert a regular string to a pure string using the **string()** function. In the following example, the variable "B" is now four characters long and is equal to "foo", followed by a carriage return.

```
A = "foo\n";
B = string(A);
```

If you are familiar with C, you might be used to the fact that the zero byte (or NULL byte) marks the end of a string. There's no such concept in NASL— the interpreter keep tracks of the length of each string internally and does not care about the content. Therefore, the string "\0\0\0" is equivalent to three NULL byte characters, and is considered to be three bytes long by the **strlen()** function.

You may build strings containing binary data using the **raw_string()** function. This function will accept an unlimited number of arguments, where each argument is the ASCII code of the character you want to use. In the following example, the variable "A" is equal to the string "XXX" (ASCII code 88 and 0x58 in hexadecimal).

```
A = raw_string(88, 0x58, 88);
```

String Addition and Subtraction

NASL supports string manipulation through the addition (+) and subtraction (−) operators. This is an interesting feature of the NASL language that can save quite a bit of time during plugin development.

The addition operator will concatenate any two strings. The following example sets the variable "A" to the value "foobar", and then variable "B" to the value "foobarfoobarfoobar".

```
A = "foo" + "bar";
B = A + A + A;
```

The subtraction operator allows you to remove one string from another. In many cases, this is preferable to a search-and-replace or search-and-extract operation. The following example will result in the variable "A" being set to the value "1, 2, 3".

```
A = "test1, test2, test3";
A = A - "test";  # A is now equal to "1, test2, test3"
A = A - "test";  # A is now equal to "1, 2, test3"
A = A - "test";  # A is now equal to "1, 2, 3"
```

String Search and Replace

NASL allows you to easily search for one string and replace it with another, without having to resort to regular expressions. The following example will result in the variable "A" being set to the value "foo1, foo2, foo2".

```
A = "test1, test2, test3";
A = str_replace(find:"test", replace:"foo", string:A);
```

Regular Expressions in NASL

NASL supports **egrep(1)**-style operations through the **ereg()**, **egrep()**, **ereg_replace()** functions. These functions use POSIX Extended regular expression syntax. If you are familiar with Perl's regular expression support, please keep in mind that there are significant differences between how NASL and Perl will handle the same regular expression. The *Wikipedia* (http://en.wikipedia.org/wiki/Regular_expression) has a great description of regular expressions in general and the differences between each type.

The **ereg()** function returns TRUE if a string matches a given pattern. The string must be a one-line string (in other words, it should not contain any carriage return character). In the following example, the string "Matched!" will be printed to the console.

```
if (ereg(string:"My dog is brown", pattern:"dog"))
{
        display("Matched\n");
}
```

The **egrep()** function works like **ereg()**, except that it accepts multiline strings. This function will return the actual string that matched the pattern or FALSE if no match was found. In the following example, the variable "text" contains the content of a UNIX "passwd" file. We will use **egrep()** to only return the lines that correspond to users whose ID value (the third field) is lower than 50.

```
text = "
root:*:0:0:System Administrator:/var/root:/bin/tcsh
daemon:*:1:1:System Services:/var/root:/dev/null
unknown:*:99:99:Unknown User:/dev/null:/dev/null
smmsp:*:25:25:Sendmail User:/private/etc/mail:/dev/null
www:*:70:70:World Wide Web Server:/Library/WebServer:/dev/null
mysql:*:74:74:MySQL Server:/dev/null:/dev/null
sshd:*:75:75:sshd Privilege separation:/var/empty:/dev/null
renaud:*:501:20:Renaud Deraison,,,:/Users/renaud:/bin/bash";

lower_than_50 = egrep(pattern:"[^:]*:[^:]:([0-9]|[0-5][0-9]):.*",
string:text);
display(lower_than_50);
```

Running this script in command-line mode results in the following output:

```
$ nasl egrep.nasl
root:*:0:0:System Administrator:/var/root:/bin/tcsh
daemon:*:1:1:System Services:/var/root:/dev/null
smmsp:*:25:25:Sendmail User:/private/etc/mail:/dev/null
$
```

```
ereg_replace(pattern:<pattern>, replace:<replace>, string:<string>);
```

The **ereg_replace()** function can be used to replace a pattern in a string with another string. This function supports regular expression back references, which can replace the original string with parts of the matched pattern. The following example uses this function to extract the Server: banner from an HTTP server response.

```
include("http_func.inc");
include("http_keepalive.inc");
reply = http_keepalive_send_recv(data:http_get(item:"/", port:80), port:80);
if ( ! reply ) exit(0);

# Isolate the Server: string from the HTTP reply
server = egrep(pattern:"^Server:", string:reply);
if ( ! server ) exit(0);
server = ereg_replace(pattern:"^Server: (.*)$",
       replace:"The remote server is \1",
       string:server);
display(server, "\n");
```

Running this script in command-line mode results in the following output:

```
$ nasl -t 127.0.0.1 ereg_replace.nasl
The remote server is Apache/1.3.29 (Darwin)
$
```

The NASL Protocol APIs

The Nessus installation includes quite a few function libraries written in the
NASL language. These libraries are located in the plugin directory and use the
".inc" filename suffix. Almost every plugin in the Nessus distribution uses these
libraries in one form of another. They provide you with high-level access to protocols that would be both time consuming and error prone to implement on a
per-plugin basis. Once your plugin starts using the NASL function libraries, any
improvements to those libraries will be passed to your plugin as well. This section
presents some of the most widely used protocol libraries and the functions they
provide.

HTTP

To use the HTTP APIs, your script should **include()** the http_func.inc and
http_keepalive.inc libraries. These libraries work together to provide simple, efficient access to the HTTP protocol. If you write a script that uses this API, you
should set "http_version.nasl" as a dependency of your plugin. The http_ver-
sion.nasl plugin in turn depends on a large number of fingerprinting and web

server analysis scripts. These scripts are responsible for initializing various sections of the Knowledge Base that are used by the HTTP function libraries.

These two libraries contain the following functions:

- **get_http_port(default:<port>)** Returns the port number on which a web server is listening. If no web server has been identified on this system, the specified port parameter will be returned. This function uses a call to **get_kb_item()**; one instance of this plugin will for spawned for each active web server. Additionally, this function will verify that the web server is actually active and responsive before returning it to the calling plugin. This last step is required to work around a few broken web server implementations, which can slow the scan.

- **get_http_banner(port:<port>)** Returns the banner of the remote web server listening on the specified port. This banner will be stored in the KB and subsequent calls to this function will result in the cached banner being returned.

- **http_get(item:<file>, port:port)** Returns a HTTP GET request that is automatically configured to use the correct version of the HTTP protocol for that host and port.

- **http_keepalive_send_recv(port:<port>, data:<req>)** Sends an HTTP request to the remote host and returns the results. If the remote host supports persistent HTTP connections, then the connection state is maintained for the lifetime of the plugin. Any subsequent calls to this function will reuse this connection, reducing the latency and overhead associated with creating a new connection.

- **cgi_dirs()** Returns an array containing all the directories that contain CGI executables or dynamic pages (by default, this function returns "/cgi-bin", "/scripts", and "/"). The webmirror.nasl and DDI_Directory_Scanner.nasl plugins will populate this list through web crawling and directory guessing techniques, respectively.

- **can_host_php(port:<port>)** Returns FALSE if the remote web server is known to not be able to host PHP dynamic pages; it returns TRUE otherwise. Many plugins that test for flaws in PHP web applications will use this function to save bandwidth and reduce scan time.

- **can_host_asp(port:<port>)** Returns FALSE if the remote web server is known to not be able to host ASP dynamic pages. Many plugins that test for flaws in ASP web applications will use this function to save bandwidth and reduce scan time.

In the following example, let's imagine that the PHP page "foo.php" is vulnerable to a directory traversal attack—requesting foo.php?file=/etc/passwd will return the content of file "/etc/passwd". To check for this flaw, we will use **cgi_dirs()** to get a list of directories that might contain dynamic pages. For the sake of brevity, we have not included the description section of this plugin, but make sure that any HTTP plugins you write have a call to the **script_dependencie()** function for "http_version.nasl".

```
# Determine on which port the remote web server is listening
port = get_http_port(default:80);
# If there is no port or if the port is known to be closed, quit
if ( ! port || ! get_port_state(port) ) exit(0);

# Loop through all the CGI directories and request foo.php?file=/etc/passwd
foreach dir ( cgi_dirs() )
{
 # Make an HTTP GET request
 req = http_get(item: dir + "/foo.php?file=/etc/passwd", port:port);
 res = http_keepalive_send_recv(port:port, data:req);

 # If there is no reply, it means the remote server is dead - quit
 if ( res == NULL ) exit(0);

 # Alert if we see the contents of /etc/passwd in the reply
 if ( egrep(pattern:"root:.*:.*:0:[01]:.*", string:res ) )
 {
  security_hole(port);
  exit(0);
 }
}
```

FTP

To use the FTP APIs, your script should **include()** the ftp_func.inc library. You do not need to set any dependencies to use this API.

This library contains the following functions:

- **get_ftp_banner(port:<port>)** Returns the banner of the FTP service that is listening on the specified port. Just like the **get_http_banner()** function call, it will store the banner in the KB and return a cached copy if possible.

- **ftp_log_in(socket:<socket>, user:<user>, pass:<password>)** Authenticates to the remote FTP server using the supplied username and password, returning a nonzero value if the server accepts the login request. The socket parameter must have been initialized with **open_sock_tcp()** prior to this function being called.

- **ftp_recv_line(socket:<socket>)** Reads a reply from the remote FTP server. If the reply is a multiline message (such as a long banner), it will return all associated lines.

- **ftp_get_pasv_port(socket:<socket>)** Sends a *PASV* command to the remote host, parses the response, and returns the decoded port number to use for data transfers. The socket parameter should be associated with an active TCP connection that is already authenticated to the FTP service.

- **ftp_recv_data(socket:<socket>, line:<line>)** Reads the data sent by the FTP service after a RETR (download) request. The socket parameter should be associated with an active TCP connection to the port number returned by the **ftp_get_pasv_port()** function. The line parameter should be the reply from a previous *RETR* command (see the plugin ftp_rhosts.nasl for an example).

- **ftp_recv_listing(socket:<socket>)** Reads the data sent by the FTP server after an NLST or LIST (directory listing) request. The socket parameter should be associated with an active TCP connection that is already authenticated to the FTP service.

NFS

To use the Network File System (NFS) APIs, your script should **include()** the misc_func.inc and nfs_func.inc libraries.

Nessus contains a nearly complete NFS client API. It allows you to mount and unmount NFS partitions, and read the content of a directory or a file. Of course, these functions are dependent on the target system being configured to allow access to the NFS exports in the first place.

Since all the NFS functions are written in NASL, they are independent from the underlying operating system. This means that even if your system does not support the NFS protocol, Nessus will still be able to interact with remote NFS services.

When dealing with the NFS protocol, you will to need to use two privileged (port 1024 or less) UDP sockets; one to communicate with the actual nfsd daemon (RPC 100003) and another to access the mountd daemon (RPC 100005). The following example obtains the port numbers for the nfsd and mountd RPC services, and then associates a privileged UDP with each.

```
nfsd_port = get_rpc_port(program:100003, proto:IPPROTO_UDP);
if ( ! nfsd_port ) exit(0);
nfsd_socket = open_priv_sock_udp(dport:nfsd_port);


mountd_port = get_rpc_port(program:100005, proto:IPPROTO_UDP);
if ( ! mountd_port ) exit(0);
mountd_socket = open_priv_sock_udp(dport:mountd_port);
```

After using this example code to configure the sockets, the following NFS functions are available:

- **mount(socket:<mountd_socket>, share:<sharename>)** Attempts to mount the specified remote share. It returns NULL on failure, or a file handle (fid) on success.

- **readdir(socket:<nfsd_socket>, fid:<fid>)** Returns the contents of a directory pointed to by the specified file handle. It returns NULL on failure, or a list of entries on success.

- **cwd(socket:<nfsd_socket>, fid:<fid>, dir:<dir>)** Changes the current working directory to one specified in the "dir" parameter. The "fid" parameter must point to the current working directory. This function returns NULL on failure, and a file handle pointing to the new directory on success.

- **open(socket:<nfsd_socket>, fid:<fid>, file:<filename>)** Opens the specified filename inside the directory associated with the "fid" parameter. It returns a file handle pointing to the opened file on success, and NULL on failure.

- **read(socket:<nfsd_socket>, fid:<fid>, length:<length>, off:<off>)** Reads data from the specified file handle (created by **open()** function), limited to the number of bytes specified by the "length" parameter, and starting at the offset specified by the "offset" parameter.

The following example attempts to mount the root file system ("/") of the remote server, over the NFS protocol, and then read the first 4096 bytes of the "passwd" file.

```
include("misc_func.inc");
include("nfs_func.inc");
nfsd_port = get_rpc_port(program:100003, proto:IPPROTO_UDP);
if ( ! nfsd_port ) exit(0);
nfsd_socket = open_priv_sock_udp(dport:nfsd_port);

mountd_port = get_rpc_port(program:100005, proto:IPPROTO_UDP);
if ( ! mountd_port ) exit(0);
mountd_socket = open_priv_sock_udp(dport:mountd_port);

root = fid = mount ( socket:mountd_socket, share:"/");
if ( ! fid ) exit(0); # Could not mount / - exit

# Go to /etc
fid = cwd(socket:nfsd_socket, fid:fid, dir:"etc");
if ( ! fid ) exit(0);

# Open the file "passwd" in /etc
fid = open(socket:nfsd_socket, fid:fid, file:"passwd");
if ( ! fid ) exit(0);
```

```
# Read the first 4096 bytes of the file, starting at offset 0
content = read(socket:nfsd_socket, fid:fid, length:4096, off:0);
if ( ! content ) exit(0);


umount(fid:root, socket:mountd_socket);
close( nfsd_socket );
close ( mountd_socket );
display("The remote password file contains :\n", content);
```

The Nessus Knowledge Base

As mentioned earlier in this chapter, plugins have the capability to store and retrieve data that can be accessed by other scripts. This system is called the Knowledge Base, or simply KB, and is covered extensively in Chapter 9. The Knowledge Base stores one or more values for a given name. This name is a simple descriptive identifier for the data that it references. During the course of a Nessus scan, each target system is provided with its own individual KB. As each plugin obtains more information about the system, it will slowly populate the KB with data. Other plugins can access this data to information about a service, retrieve a password successfully guessed by another plugin, or set a flag stating that a certain patch has been applied.

The NASL API provides three functions for manipulating the Knowledge Base:

- **set_kb_item(name:<name>, value:<value>)** Creates the Knowledge Base entry specified by the "name" parameter, with the data specified in the "value" parameter. The value can be an integer, a string, or simple Boolean flag such as TRUE or FALSE. If a KB entry already exists for the specified name, both the old and new values are kept. Any given KB entry can have an indefinite number of values associated with it.

- **get_kb_item(<name>)** Retrieves the value of the KB entry specified by the "name" parameter. If the specified entry does not exist, this function will return NULL. If the specified entry has multiple values, the calling script will be executed multiple times, each time with a different return value for **get_kb_item()**.

- **get_kb_list(<name>)** Similar to **get_kb_item()**, except that instead of retuning a single value, it will return a list of matching values. Unlike **get_kb_item()**, this function will never result in the calling script being executed multiple times. The **get_kb_list()** function supports wildcards when specifying the entry name. For example, calling **get_kb_list("Services/*")** will return all the ports for which a service has been identified.

Summary

In this chapter, we discussed the beginnings of the NASL language, the original design requirements, and how the language has evolved to meet the challenges of modern vulnerability assessments. We then analyzed the structure of a NASL script and walked through the process of creating a new Nessus plugin from scratch. After reviewing many of the advanced features of the NASL language, we introduced the protocol libraries and how they can be used to develop robust Nessus plugins. Finally, we concluded the chapter with a brief review of the Knowledge Base and the NASL functions that are used to access it.

Solutions Fast Track

Why NASL?

☑ No existing scripting language met the requirements for Nessus plugins.

☑ Plugins written in C or Perl were unwieldy and could be a security risk.

☑ The NASL language was designed specifically for security testing.

☑ NASL scripts are self-contained and easy to update.

☑ The NASL interpreter code is clean and easy to extend.

Structure of a NASL Script

☑ NASL scripts are composed of two sections: the script description and the script body.

☑ The script description contains information about the script itself.

☑ The script body contains the NASL code that performs the vulnerability test.

☑ The Nessus engine uses the script description to manage the plugin set.

An Introduction to the NASL Language

☑ If you already know C, Perl, or PHP, learning NASL is straightforward.

☑ Complex network tests can be accomplished in only a few lines of code.

☑ NASL provides a wide range of string-matching and manipulation techniques.

☑ The NASL libraries encompass a wide range of complex network protocols.

The Nessus Knowledge Base

☑ Plugins communicate with each other by setting variables in the Knowledge Base.

☑ The Knowledge Base is only available when a script is launched by the Nessus engine.

☑ During a Nessus scan, each system has its own Knowledge Base.

Frequently Asked Questions

The following Frequently Asked Questions, answered by the authors of this book, are designed to both measure your understanding of the concepts presented in this chapter and to assist you with real-life implementation of these concepts. To have your questions about this chapter answered by the author, browse to **www.syngress.com/solutions** and click on the **"Ask the Author"** form. You will also gain access to thousands of other FAQs at ITFAQnet.com.

Q: What were the main reasons behind the development of the NASL language?

A: When the need for NASL was first realized, none of the current scripting languages met the requirements for virtual machine security, resource usage, and cross-platform support.

Q: You mention that the Nessus engine is not technically a vulnerability scanner; has anyone developed another use for the Nessus engine and NASL language?

A: Not at this time, but don't let this stop you if you want to be the first. Recent versions of Nessus now include the capability to access remote machines over the SSH protocol. This feature could be easily extended to allow remote patch deployment, network monitoring, and almost any other administration task, simply by creating a custom set of plugins. The NASL protocol libraries already have full access to the SMB protocol, allowing remote administration of Windows systems as well.

Q: At one point, the concept of "trusted" scripts was introduced. What are "trusted" NASL scripts?

A: In an effort to completely remove the old "C" plugins from Nessus, the development team has created a system that allows specific scripts to perform "dangerous" functions, such as system command execution. These scripts have a cryptographic signature placed at the very top of the file; if this signature is not verified against the official Nessus certificate, the plugin will not be allowed to access these dangerous functions. Trusted scripts will become much more common starting with Nessus 2.2.

Q: The NASL protocol API section does not seem to be complete. Where can I obtain more information about the functions in the NASL libraries?

A: Please refer to the NASL reference in Appendix A of this book. The latest version of the NASL reference can be online, linked from the www.nesssus.org web site.

## Chapter 12

The Nessus User Community

Solutions in this Chapter:

- **The Nessus Mailing Lists**

- **The Online Plugin Database**

- **Reporting Bugs via Bugzilla**

- **Submitting Patches and Plugins**

- **Where to Get More Information and Help**

☑ **Summary**

☑ **Solutions Fast Track**

☑ **Frequently Asked Questions**

Introduction

Nessus enjoys widespread support in the field of computer security today in no small part due to the work of its principal authors. However, design and coding excellence will take a product only so far. What sets Nessus apart from other network vulnerability assessment tools is its openness and its user community.

Thanks to its openness, anyone can browse the source for Nessus and its plugins to learn how they work. Moreover, with the knowledge gained, anyone can contribute to the Nessus Project by adding features to and fixing problems in the existing software base, deriving new plugins from existing ones, and developing third-party tools and resources.

Thanks to its user community, such contributions are indeed being made. In terms of software, you can currently find a Nessus client for Windows, several Web-based interfaces for configuring and managing scans, various tools for displaying and managing results, programming interfaces such as the Net::Nessus::ScanLite and Parse::Nessus::NBE Perl modules, and a continuous stream of plugins, all authored by dozens of individuals and businesses not explicitly part of the Nessus Project. In terms of resources, Hugo van der Kooij's Nessus FAQ and Edgeos' Nessus Knowledge Base have recently emerged to help the community better understand Nessus. The user community even contributes by simply submitting signatures for previously unidentified services in response to instructions in reports from the various fingerprinting plugins. This form of contribution alone has proven extremely valuable, for it has enabled Nessus to leapfrog its competition in the area of service fingerprinting.

In his paper entitled "Shoulders of Giants" (available at www.cyber.com.au/users/conz/shoulders.html), Con Zymaris argues that open-source software will dominate competing paradigms. Essentially, open source allows a project to get a head start by avoiding the need to reinvent the wheel and to gather momentum more quickly through the free exchange of ideas. Further, as a project grows to dominate its field, whatever paradigm it might follow, it tends to draw interest away from its competitors in a snowball effect. Only time will tell if Nessus follows this path, but the future looks bright.

The Nessus Mailing Lists

The Nessus mailing lists are the primary means by which the user community interacts. There are five lists currently, as shown in Table 12.1. The signal-to-noise ratio for the three discussion lists is generally quite high. Their tone is professional and academic, not as collegial as, say, *Snort-users* with its drinking game, but not full of flame wars either.

Table 12.1 Description of the Nessus Mailing Lists

List	Description	Average Weekly Volume
nessus	Discussions about all things Nessus.	61
nessus-announce	Announcements of new releases. Moderated.	under 1
nessus-cvs	CVS commits to the Nessus source tree. Read-only.	58
nessus-devel	Discussions about software enhancements and fixes.	6
plugins-writers	Discussions about writing plugins and the NASL language.	7

Of the discussion lists, *nessus* is the most active, broadest in scope, and probably most useful to the average reader. Much of the traffic consists of questions and answers rather than actual discussions, and topics include Nessus and NessusWX, the plugins, vulnerabilities themselves, third-party add-ons, and so forth. *Nessus-devel* tends to be much more discussion oriented, with the focus on revisions to Nessus and the NASL language. For example, past threads have focused on overhauling plugin families and adding 64-bit support to Nessus. *Plugins-writers* leans more toward questions and answers, generally how to accomplish something in NASL or whether plugins are properly testing for vulnerabilities. None of these lists has an actual charter, though, and in practice there's a fair amount of overlap among them, so don't worry too much about which list is the most appropriate. If you're still hesitant, browse the archives to get a better feel for each list's suitability.

All of the lists are operated using Mailman, a powerful and popular open-source mailing list management package. If you subscribe to other mailing lists on the Internet, chances are that you're already familiar with Mailman; if not, don't worry, since Mailman is tightly integrated with the Web. That is, you can subscribe to any of the mailing lists or access their archives by visiting http://list.nessus.org/ (see Figure 12.1).

Figure 12.1 Web Interface to the Nessus Mailing Lists

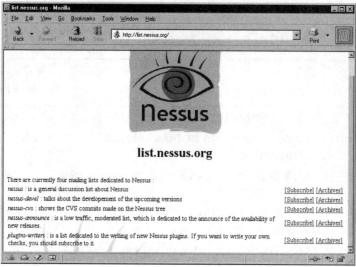

Subscribing to a Mailing List

Mailman gives you the option of subscribing to one of the Nessus mailing lists either through a Web-based interface or via e-mail. Regardless of which method you choose, subscribing is a two-step process: First, you submit a request to subscribe, and then you confirm that request. After that, you should be added to a list automatically and receive a welcome message with general instructions for using the list and a list password that you will need to configure your list settings.

If you want to join the *nessus* mailing list, here's what you have to do:

> **NOTE**
>
> In the following examples, replace the final instance of *nessus* in URLs and the leading instance in e-mail addresses with the name of the desired mailing list. Note that all of the Nessus mailing lists use lowercase names.

- If using the Web-based interface, point your Web browser to http://mail.nessus.org/mailman/listinfo/nessus. In the middle of the page is a form for subscribing. Enter your e-mail address, fill in the other fields as desired, and click **Subscribe**.

- If using e-mail, send a message to nessus-request@list.nessus.org, with the command *subscribe* as either the subject or the only line in the message body.

- In a short time you should receive an e-mail from Mailman asking you to confirm your request. Visit the link included in the e-mail or reply to it to do so.

Notes from the Underground...

Identifying Messages from the Nessus Mailing Lists

When delivering messages sent to any of the Nessus mailing lists, Mailman uses a special value for the SMTP envelope sender to facilitate bounce processing. Specifically, it appends the string *–bounces* to the address of the mailing list; for example, for *nessus* it's *nessus-bounces@list.nessus.org*. Further, mail transfer agents such as sendmail and postfix place the envelope sender in the Return-Path message header and use it in the UNIX From line.

You can take advantage of these two facts to whitelist messages sent to the Nessus mailing lists, have them bypass spam filters, or automatically filter them into separate folders. For example, the following procmail recipe will automatically file messages from any of the Nessus mailing lists into a folder named Nessus:

```
:0:
* ^Return-Path: .*-bounces\@list\.nessus\.org
Nessus
```

If you're using Outlook 2000/2002, you can achieve the same functionality by adding rules to filter on this header for each mailing list to which you've subscribed:

If the folder Nessus doesn't yet exist, select **File | New | Folder** to create it under your mailbox and click **OK** when finished.

1. Select **Tools | Rules Wizard**.

2. Click **New**.

3. If using Outlook 2002, make sure **Start from a blank rule** is selected.

Continued

4. Select **Check messages when they arrive** if it isn't already selected, and then click **Next**.

5. Check **with specific words in the message headers** (you might have to scroll down to see this option) and click on **specific words** under **Rule description** at the bottom.

6. Enter **Return-Path: nessus-bounces@list.nessus.org** in the textbox and click **OK**.

7. Click **Next**.

8. Check **move it to the specified folder** if necessary and click on **specified** in **Rule description** at the bottom.

9. Select the folder **Nessus**, and click **OK**.

10. Click **Finish**.

11. Click **OK**.

Mailman supports a number of options for message delivery. For example, you can choose to receive messages bundled as a single digest once a day, not receive your own postings, or disable delivery in the event you're away on vacation or are just too busy. Go to the Member Options page at http://mail.nessus.org/mailman/options/nessus, enter your list password, and click **Log in** to review or change these options. If you don't know your list password, click the **Remind** button to have Mailman send you your password. You can also use that link to unsubscribe from the mailing list. As before, you will need to confirm your request.

NOTE

Exercise care if you decide to change your list password: Mailman sends passwords out in the clear both in response to clicking the **Remind** button on the Member Options page and as part of a monthly reminder.

Sending a Message to a Mailing List

To send a message to one of the discussion lists, simply address it to the list name at list.nessus.org; for example, nessus@list.nessus.org. Shortly after Mailman receives it, the message will be redistributed to the list's subscribers based on their user settings. Currently, you do not need to subscribe in order to post a message to one of the Nessus mailing lists; however, messages from nonsubscribers are held for review, which can result in significant delays.

Before you actually send your first message, review these general guidelines:

- If you're asking a question, check the Nessus FAQ (http://hvdkooij. xs4all.nl/NessusFAQ/) and search the list archives first. You might find the answer without having to wait for an answer or even subscribe to a list!

- Give your message an appropriate subject header. For example, a message with the subject "Compilation Problems with SuSE 9.0" has a better chance of attracting attention than a message entitled simply "Help."

- Start a new thread rather than posting a new question to an existing thread. People might have decided not to follow a particular thread, and this ensures that they don't miss your message.

- Use Bugzilla rather than the mailing lists to report bugs. It's okay, though, to post a message to a list to point people to your bug report to alert them to the problem if you think the problem is serious.

- Trim quoted text when replying to a message.

- Consider directing replies to the mailing list unless otherwise requested so that everyone has the option to participate in the thread and so that they'll appear in the archives. In addition, unless otherwise requested, do not CC posters too, since the lion's share on the Nessus mailing lists are themselves subscribers.

- If you are trying to manage your subscriptions using e-mail, append **–request** to the list's name and send your messages to the corresponding address (for example, for *nessus* it's nessus-request@list.nessus.org).

- Don't send test messages to the list. If you need to send a message, just do so. Otherwise, if you haven't received messages for a while and are curious, check the list's archives. If people are indeed sending messages and you're not receiving them, visit the list's Member Options page (for example, http://mail.nessus.org/mailman/options/nessus) and log in with your e-mail address and list password. You will see a notice at the top of the page that follows if Mailman has suspended your subscription for excessive bounces. If it has, follow the instructions Mailman provides to re-enable mail delivery after you've corrected any problems. Regardless, sending test messages will only aggravate other subscribers.

NOTE

By default, Mailman archives messages sent to the Nessus mailing lists, munging e-mail addresses of senders somewhat in an effort to foil spammers. Including a special header line in your messages—either **X-Archive: no** or **X- No-Archive: yes**—instructs Mailman to not archive your messages. Realize, though, that doing so reduces the value of the list's archives.

Accessing a List's Archives

Archives of every Nessus mailing list are currently available on the Web through mail.nessus.org. Access to the archives is open, even to various search engine robots and Web crawlers.

For example, to browse, the archives for *nessus*, point your Web browser to http://mail.nessus.org/pipermail/nessus/. For each month for which archives are available, you can view messages by date, subject, author, or thread, or retrieve the entire collection as a UNIX mbox file (see Figure 12.2).

Figure 12.2 Web Interface to the Nessus Mailing List Archives

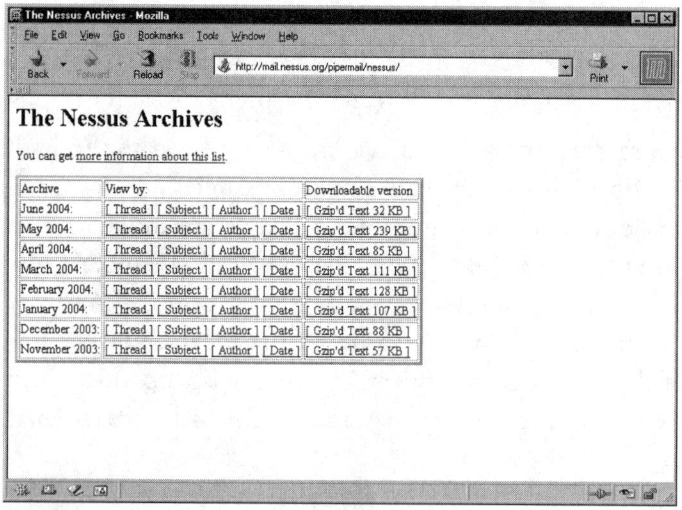

The mailing list archives on mail.nessus.org currently lack a built-in search capability (although we do hope to have one in place by the time you read this). This can be mitigated somewhat by searching Google with the *inurl* query modifier. For example, you could locate the announcement of version 2.0.10's release with the following query: `inurl:mail.nessus.org inurl:nessus-announce 2.0.10`. This tells Google to search for the string *2.0.10* and restrict results to documents with both *mail.nessus.org* and *nessus-announce* in the URL.

Notes from the Underground…

Alternative Archives

Several other sites also archive one or more of the Nessus mailing lists; you can find them using a straightforward Web search. Two such sites deserve special recognition. Refer to them if the archives on nessus.org are temporarily unavailable or don't meet your needs.

- 10 East's Mailing list ARChives (MARC) service maintains archives of *nessus*, *nessus-announce*, and *nessus-devel* extending back nearly to the birth of Nessus and provides a view by thread within date as well as a search capability. Visit http://marc.theaimsgroup.com/?l=nessus (replace *nessus* with another list name if desired) to see the archives for the mailing list *nessus*.

- Gmane gateways several of the mailing lists both from and to Usenet newsgroups and offers access to them via NNTP and the Web. If you prefer to keep your mailbox uncluttered, refer to *nntp://news.gmane.org/*: gmane.comp.security.nessus.general is for *nessus*, gmane.comp.security.nessus.announce is for *nessus-announce*, and gmane.comp.security.nessus.devel is for *nessus-devel*.

The Online Plugin Database

One of Nessus' strengths is its extensive and continually updated collection of plugins, over 2,150 as of June 2004. This sheer number, though, can lead to problems. For example, sometimes Nessus determines that a vulnerability exists, and you need to better understand how it arrived at that determination, perhaps because the sysadmin of a supposedly vulnerable system contends that it's a false positive. In addition, sometimes you need to learn which plugin tests for a particular vulnerability, perhaps to help management assess the risks of the latest worm *du jour*.

The Online Plugin Database, available at http://cgi.nessus.org/plugins/, can help resolve such problems. It supports several means of access: view by plugin family, view by popularity (determined by accesses to the Online Plugin Database and covering only plugins with a CVE ID, Bugtraq ID, or some other type of cross-reference), list recent additions, and search plugins by keyword.

Clicking on a plugin's name or ID from any of these pages leads to an overview of that plugin, including its family and description, cross-references if available, and even notes contributed by users. It also contains links to the plugin's source (only if written in NASL), a list of plugins in the same family, and cross-references. See Figure 12.3 for an example.

Figure 12.3 Overview of a Plugin

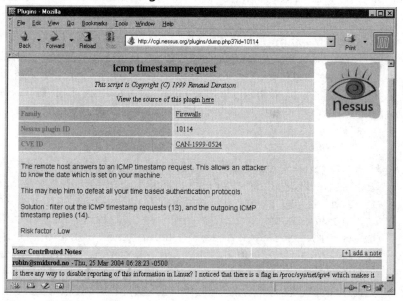

User-contributed notes are a relatively new feature, introduced in 2003. They are particularly interesting, as they can help users understand precisely how a plugin operates, the vulnerabilities for which it tests, or steps to address those vulnerabilities. If you have a question or want to alert others about a particular plugin, feel free to add a note.

Staying Abreast of New Plugins

The Online Plugin Database offers two ways to learn about new Nessus plugins: a Web page at www.nessus.org/scripts.php, and, for those who use a news aggregator, an RSS feed at www.nessus.org/rss.php. The first lets you select the most recent 10, 20, 40, or 80 additions, and the second shows only the most recent 20 plugins. In either case, you'll get a list of plugins and their descriptions.

> **NOTE**
>
> These resources list only new plugins; they don't say anything about changes in existing plugins. Thus, if you need to maintain a consistent set of plugins for your scans, don't blindly trust the output of either resource before running *nessus-update-plugins*.

Reporting Bugs via Bugzilla

The Nessus Project's Bug Tracker, located at http://bugs.nessus.org/, uses the popular Bugzilla software to track bugs (and enhancement requests) in Nessus, its associated plugins, the Nessus installer, NessusWX, and Web sites in the nessus.org domain. It offers several advantages compared to posting a message to one of the mailing lists or e-mailing someone directly:

- It ensures that your bug report will not be overlooked.

- It keeps you abreast of efforts to fix the problem through a series of e-mail alerts.

- It helps project developers coordinate and prioritize their efforts to address bugs.

- It reduces duplication of effort by serving as a reference for the user community.

So, if you think you've uncovered a bug in Nessus or a related product, first check with Bugzilla to see whether it's a known issue and, if not, report it using Bugzilla.

Querying Existing Bug Reports

Bugzilla provides two methods for searching bug reports: a simple *QuickSearch* and a general query. You can access both from the project's Bug Tracker homepage.

In a QuickSearch, Bugzilla treats search terms as case-insensitive substrings; for example, *nasl* matches reports containing the strings *NASL* and *libnasl*, as well as *nasl* itself. By default, a QuickSearch covers only unresolved bugs, although you can extend the search to all bugs by prefixing the query with the word *ALL* (must be uppercase). Finally, if you enter a bug number as the only search term, Bugzilla will return the corresponding bug report in its entirety. To perform a QuickSearch, enter a search term or two in the form at the lower left of the page, and then click **Show**. For example, Figure 12.4 illustrates how you might perform a QuickSearch for unresolved bug reports of Nessus on AMD's 64-bit processors.

Figure 12.4 A QuickSearch

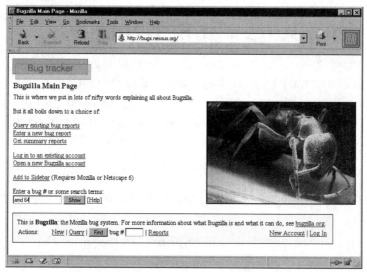

In a general query, you have a large degree of control over the search: you can select from a wide variety of search methods (for example, substrings, whole words, regular expressions, case-sensitive, and so forth), limit the fields in which the terms occur, and even restrict results by date. To perform a general query, click the link labeled **Query existing bug reports** and fill out the form that follows as desired. For example, Figure 12.5 illustrates how you might fill out the form to perform a general query similar to the earlier QuickSearch but limited to only those bugs affecting the UNIX-based nessus client. If you find this form daunting, you can generally obtain good results by just entering your search terms in the **Summary** field and clicking **Search**.

Figure 12.5 A General Query

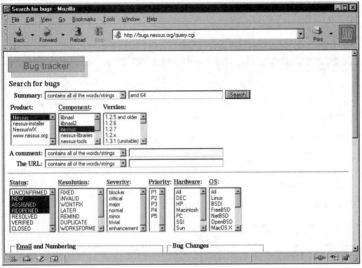

If any entries match your query, you will see a list, as in Figure 12.6. Click on the bug **ID** to view the report in detail.

Figure 12.6 Query Results

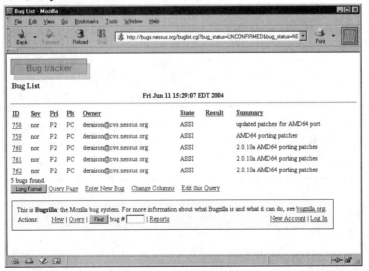

Creating and Logging In to a Bugzilla Account

While you can query Bugzilla anonymously, you must log in to a Bugzilla account to report a new bug or update an existing one. To create an account, visit http://bugs.nessus.org/createaccount.cgi and enter your e-mail address along with, if you want, your name (see Figure 12.7).

Figure 12.7 Bugzilla Account Creation

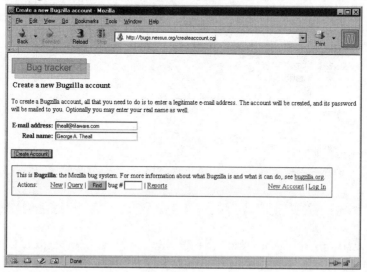

Bugzilla will create the account and send you an e-mail with your login name (typically your e-mail address) and a randomly generated password. After this, you can change your account password or preferences using the form at http://bugs.nessus.org/userprefs.cgi.

> **NOTE**
>
> As currently configured, bugs.nessus.org does not accept Web traffic encrypted with SSL. Exercise care if you decide to change your Bugzilla account password.

To log in to your Bugzilla account, visit:
http://bugs.nessus.org/query.cgi?GoAheadAndLogIn=1
or click on the **Log In** action at the bottom of any of Bug Tracker's pages. Bugzilla uses cookies for authentication, so make sure your browser is configured

to accept them, at least from bugs.nessus.org. Enter your e-mail address (or account name, if different) and password, and then click **Login**. (If you have forgotten your password, you can fill out a form in the middle of the page to submit a Change Password Request.) Once you've authenticated, Bugzilla will display the general query page.

Tools & Traps…

Cookies

By default, the cookies that Bugzilla uses for authentication last, for all practical purposes, indefinitely; even across machine reboots. This can be a problem when accessing Bugzilla from a shared machine. To have a browser forget those cookies, visit http://bugs.nessus.org/relogin.cgi or click on the **Log out** action at the base of any of Bug Tracker's pages. This link appears only if you're actually logged in.

Submitting a Bug Report

Let's suppose you uncover a bug and search Bugzilla only to determine that you're the first to come across the issue. You understand that the best approach is to report the bug through Bugzilla—but how do you do it?

Before you submit a bug report, first verify that the bug is reproducible and then try to narrow it down. For example, if *nessusd* appears to hang during a scan, examine the process list to see if there is a common set of plugins running and look at the *nessusd* message log to see which targets are in the process of being scanned. Now, rerun the scan. If it completes successfully, take note of the problem but don't submit a bug report; just chalk up the earlier hang to sunspots, user error, or the like. If it hangs a second time, check again which plugins and targets are active. If they are the same, examine the plugins or targets themselves for issues you might not have been aware of earlier. Perhaps you had selected a UDP scan with a large port list (such scans can take up to 24 hours per host). Perhaps the targets aren't real, but merely part of a LaBrea tarpit (enable plugin #10796, *scan for LaBrea tarpitted hosts*, to detect such hosts and flag them as dead). Even if you are unable to solve the problem yourself, your efforts will mean a higher quality bug report.

Now you're ready to use Bugzilla:

1. Log in to your Bugzilla account as just described.

2. Click **New action** at the base of the Query page or go to **http://bugs.nessus.org/enter_bug.cgi**.

3. Select which product the bug affects. The choices are:

   - **Nessus nessusd** the UNIX-based nessus client, plugins, and the like.

   - **nessus-installer** The stand-alone installation script for Nessus.

   - **NessusWX** A Nessus client for Windows.

   - **www.nessus.org** Web sites in the nessus.org domain.

4. Enter information about the bug in the form that follows; see Figures 12.8.a and 12.8.b. Choose the appropriate values from the list boxes, especially the Component field, and enter a helpful summary and description. (Note that Bugzilla automatically fills in the Platform and OS fields based on your browser. You might have to change them; for example, if you're using a desktop PC running Windows to report a problem with nessusd.)

5. Click the **Commit** button at the bottom of the form to file the bug report. If everything goes okay, Bugzilla will show you a copy of your bug report.

6. Add an attachment (for example, process trace, log segments, patches, and so forth) while viewing the bug report, if appropriate.

If you also want to announce your discovery (for example, if it involves unexpected and dangerous behavior), send a message to one of the mailing lists and be sure to point people to your bug report.

Figure 12.8.a A New Bug Report

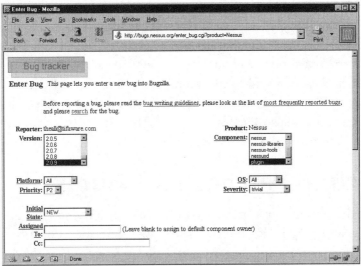

Figure 12.8.b A New Bug Report (continued)

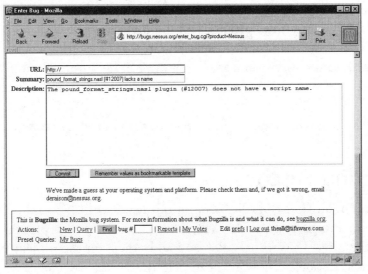

It's important that you include as many details in your report as you think are appropriate and be as specific as possible. It's also important that you limit your report to relevant details. Put yourself in the shoes of the person who will be addressing your report. What exactly does he or she need in order to replicate the problem? Is there anything special about your installation? If you need help, refer to the general Bug Writing Guidelines, available at http://bugs.nessus.org/bugwritinghelp.html.

Bugzilla will notify you by e-mail once it has filed your initial bug report and every time the report is changed, until it is eventually closed. Occasionally, the person handling your report will add a comment to your report requesting additional information, which will result in another e-mail from Bugzilla. To respond, log in to your Bugzilla account and add comments or attach files while viewing the bug report. You can also do this if you simply learn something new about a bug, or even if you weren't the one to file it.

Submitting Patches and Plugins

Throughout the project's history, many individuals and companies have written enhancements and plugins for their own purposes and then contributed them to the project. Renaud Deraison, the project leader, estimates that third parties have been responsible for around 30 percent of the plugins written during the past two years.

You don't have to be a programming whiz to contribute in this fashion, though; even simple editorial patches will improve the quality of Nessus. For example, if you notice while browsing a plugin that one of the CVE IDs is wrong, you could submit a patch that corrects it. In addition, if you feel the documentation is lacking in some fashion, you could rewrite it and submit that as an enhancement request.

Contributing is what matters, however your skill level, interests, and time allow.

Submitting Patches

You can, and should, use Bugzilla to point out issues with Nessus; for example, bugs or shortcomings in the code itself, the documentation, any of the plugins, or even in the project's Web sites. Renaud and others on the project team will address them as resources allow. You can help the process by including patches to the existing code in your bug report or enhancement request whenever possible. Be sure to use unified diff format (`diff -u ...`) against the most current release.

Submitting Plugins

With the large number of vulnerabilities uncovered on a daily basis, it should come as no surprise that plugins do not exist for every vulnerability. If you need a certain plugin but one doesn't exist, we encourage you to write your own (see Chapter 11) and contribute it to the user community.

When writing your plugin, you might find it convenient to use an existing plugin as a template. This is indeed a common practice—Renaud estimates that 90 percent of plugins currently are derived in some fashion from others. Post a message to *plugins-writers* if you need help or want to see if someone else is working on a similar plugin.

Once you've written and tested your plugin, e-mail it directly to Renaud at deraison@nessus.org. Use a value such as **99999** for the script ID to avoid confusion. Renaud will review your contribution and add it to the plugin database, at which point, others will get it when they next run *nessus-update-plugins*.

Where to Get More Information and Help

The Nessus Web site is a good starting point for more information on Nessus. Two sections are of particular interest: Documentation (www.nessus.org/documentation.html) and Related Tools (www.nessus.org/related/index.html). Be sure visit the mailing list archives, under Documentation as they contain a wealth of knowledge. And the section entitled Related Tools offers links to nearly all of the resources discussed in this chapter.

The Nessus FAQ, available at http://hvdkooij.xs4all.nl/NessusFAQ/, is another excellent source of information. Thanks to a facelift in spring 2004, the Nessus FAQ offers a collection of questions and answers and a form to comment on existing answers

If you're interested in information about configuration settings in the Nessus client or server components, visit The Nessus Knowledge Base at www.edgeos.com/nessuskb/. There you will find information about every option and configuration variable in both the Nessus client and server.

In some cases, the user-contributed notes in the Online Plugin Database (http://cgi.nessus.org/plugins/) offer valuable insight into plugins and their corresponding vulnerabilities.

Finally, if all else fails, post a question to the *nessus* mailing list. Many bright and helpful people on the list would be happy to help you.

Summary

The user community forms an active and important part of the Nessus Project. By submitting bug reports, enhancement requests, and new plugins, and developing third-party tools, the user community improves the quality of the project. In addition, through resources such as the mailing lists, user-contributed comments in the Online Plugin Database, and the Nessus FAQ, the user community serves as an educator, enriching and expanding the user community. We hope that through this chapter, and indeed this entire book, we have provided you with the knowledge you need so that you too can join the community if you're not already a part of it and help make Nessus even better than it is today.

Solutions Fast Track

The Nessus Mailing Lists

☑ Five mailing lists: *nessus* (general discussion about Nessus), *nessus-announce* (announcements of new releases), *nessus-cvs* (CVS comments to the Nessus tree), *nessus-devel* (discussions about upcoming versions of Nessus), and *plugins-writers* (discussions about writing plugins).

☑ Subscribe or view archives at http://list.nessus.org/.

☑ Include **X-Archive: No** header to prevent message archival.

The Online Plugin Database

☑ Access the database at http://cgi.nessus.org/plugins/.

☑ There are several methods for viewing plugins: by family, recent releases, or popularity. You can also search for strings in names, descriptions, summaries, references, and the like.

☑ The RSS feed at www.nessus.org/rss.php lets you track plugin additions.

☑ Follow links in the plugin overview to read references to associated CVE entries, Bugtraq IDs, and the like.

☑ User-contributed notes might accompany plugin overviews to improve understanding of a plugin or the vulnerabilities for which it tests.

Reporting Bugs via Bugzilla

☑ Bugzilla is available via the Web at http://bugs.nessus.org/.

☑ Bugzilla handles both bug reports and enhancement requests.

☑ Entries cover Nessus and its plugins, the Nessus installer, NessusWX, and nessus.org.

☑ Search terms in a QuickSearch are case-insensitive substrings.

☑ You must create an account to enter a new bug report or to update existing ones.

☑ E-mail messages track activity.

Submitting Patches and Plugins

☑ Contribute in whatever way you can; code and editorial changes are both of value.

☑ Submit patches as part of a Bugzilla bug report or enhancement request.

☑ Use existing plugins as templates when writing new ones.

☑ E-mail plugins directly to Renaud Deraison: deraison@nessus.org.

Where to Get More Information and Help

☑ For guidance on configuring and running scans, see the Documentation section of the Nessus Web site at www.nessus.org/documentation.html.

☑ For information about products and tools that work with Nessus, see the Related Tools section of the Nessus Web site at www.nessus.org/related/index.html.

☑ For general queries, consult the *nessus* mailing list and its archives along with the Nessus FAQ at http://hvdkooij.xs4all.nl/NessusFAQ/.

☑ For configurable settings in the Nessus client and server, browse The Nessus Knowledge Base at www.edgeos.com/nessuskb/.

☑ For insight into plugins and their corresponding vulnerabilities, view the user-contributed notes in the Online Plugin Database at http://cgi.nessus.org/plugins/.

Frequently Asked Questions

The following Frequently Asked Questions, answered by the authors of this book, are designed to both measure your understanding of the concepts presented in this chapter and to assist you with real-life implementation of these concepts. To have your questions about this chapter answered by the author, browse to **www.syngress.com/solutions** and click on the **"Ask the Author"** form. You will also gain access to thousands of other FAQs at ITFAQnet.com.

Q: Where can I find a list of tools that work with Nessus?

A: Unfortunately, there is no definitive list of such tools. If you don't find what you're looking for on the Related Tools page at nessus.org (www.nessus.org/related/index.html), examine the Nessus FAQ (http://hvd-kooij.xs4all.nl/NessusFAQ/), post a query to one of the mailing lists, or use your favorite Web search engine.

Q: I posted a question to one of the Nessus mailing lists, but no one responded. Should I resend it?

A: First, visit the list's archives to verify whether the message actually made it to the mailing list. Understand that mail is a batch process, and delays up to several days are possible. In addition, realize that mail from nonsubscribers is moderated, a process that might take several days. If your message has yet to appear, wait a week before resending. If it is available in the archives, give readers plenty of time to respond. History shows that few questions on the mailing lists go unanswered completely, but some responses come after a week or more. Posting your question repeatedly in a short period of time does little to convince readers of your message's importance—and much to aggravate them.

Q: I stopped receiving messages from one of the Nessus mailing lists. What happened?

A: Use your e-mail address and list password to log in to the list's Member Options page (for example, http://mail.nessus.org/mailman/options/nessus).

If your subscription is disabled, you will see a notice at the top of the page along with an explanation as to why. One likely cause is that Mailman received a number of consecutive bounces after sending messages to you; once a preset limit (typically seven) is reached, Mailman disables your subscription and sends you a note. These bounces generally indicate a problem with your mail server (you might have exceeded your mail quota, for example), so investigate the problem on that end first.

Q: How can I learn more about composing queries in Bug Tracker?

A: Visit www.mozilla.org/bugs/text-searching.html.

Q: I tried searching Bugzilla for a bug that I know exists, but I can't find it. Why?

A: Searches by default cover only unresolved bugs. If you can't find an entry you know exists, make sure you're searching all bugs. If doing a QuickSearch, prefix your query with the word *ALL*; in a general query, you must select all the values in the Status field.

Q: Why hasn't a bug I reported two weeks ago been fixed?

A: Before you complain too loudly, first make sure that the problem is not on your end. Check the bug report in Bugzilla to make sure someone has not requested additional information. While Bugzilla would have sent you an e-mail of such a request, understand that mail is sometimes lost, and that ultimately the responsibility to respond lies with you. If there aren't any requests and the bug is serious, you might send the person to whom it was assigned a gentle reminder by e-mail; otherwise, be patient, and use your time to pinpoint the problem and develop a fix for it.

The NASL2 Reference Manual
Contributed by Michael Arboi

Michel Arboi <mikhail@nessus.org>

2004-08-25

Abstract

This is the NASL2 reference manual ($Revision: 1.48 $). It describes the language syntax and the internal functions. If you want tips on how to write a security test in NASL, read *The Nessus Attack Scripting Language Reference Guide* by Renaud Deraison <deraison@nessus.org>.

1 Introduction

1.1 History

Please read *The Nessus Attack Scripting Language Reference Guide*.
Here is what the man page says:

> NASL comes from a private project called "pkt_forge", which was written in late 1998 by Renaud Deraison and which was an interactive shell to forge and send raw IP packets (this pre-dates Perl's Net::RawIP by a couple of weeks). It was then extended to do a wide range of net– work-related operations and integrated into Nessus as "NASL".

> The parser was completely hand-written and a pain to work with. In Mid-2002, Michel Arboi wrote a bison parser for NASL, and he and Renaud Deraison re-wrote NASL from scratch. Although the "new" NASL was nearly working as early as August 2002, Michel's laziness made us wait for early 2003 to have it working completely.

1.2 Differences between NASL1 and NASL2

- NASL2 uses a real Bison parser. It is stricter and can handle complex expressions.

- NASL2 has more built–in functions (although most of them could be back ported to NASL1).

- NASL2 has more built–in operators.

- NASL2 is much quicker (about sixteen times).

- Most NASL2 scripts cannot run under NASL1.

- And a few NASL1 scripts cannot run under NASL2 (but fixing them is easy).

- NASL2 user-defined functions can handle arrays.

1.3 Copyright

This document is (C) Michel Arboi. Permission is granted to reproduce this document as long as you do not modify it (and leave this copyright in place, of course).

1.4 Comments

Please send comments to Michel Arboi mikhail@nessus.org.

I checked the spelling of this document with an American dictionary, however the grammar may be incorrect.

2 The NASL2 grammar

2.1 Preliminary remarks

- A comment starts with a **#** and finishes at the end of the current line. It is ignored by the lexical analyzer.

- You may insert "blanks" anywhere between two lexical tokens.

- A blank may be a sequence of white space, horizontal or vertical tabulation, line feed, form feed or carriage return characters; or a comment.

- Token are parsed by a lexical analyzer and returned to the parser.

  - As the lexical analyzer returns the longer token it finds, expressions like a+++++b without any white space are erroneous because they will be interpreted as a++ ++ + b i.e. (a++ ++) + b just like in ANSI C[1]. You have to insert spaces: a++ + ++b

  - You cannot insert spaces in the middle of multiple character tokens. e.g. x = a + +; will not parse. Write x = a ++;

2.2 Syntax

```
decl_list      instr_decl

               instr_decl instr_decl_list

instr_decl     instr

               func_decl;
```

```
func_decl      function identifier ( arg_decl ) block
arg_decl        /*nothing*/
               arg_decl_1
arg_decl_1     identifier
               identifier , arg_decl_1
block          { instr_list }
               { }
instr_list     instr
               instr instr_list
instr          s_instr  ;
               block
               if_block
               loop
s_instr        aff
               post_pre_incr
               rep
               func_call
               ret
               inc
               loc
               glob
               break
               continue
               /*nothing*/
ret            return expr
               return
if_block       if ( expr ) instr
               if ( expr ) instr else instr
loop           for_loop
               while_loop
               repeat_loop
               foreach_loop
for_loop       for ( aff_func ; expr ; aff_func ) instr
while_loop     while ( expr ) instr
repeat_loop    repeat instr until expr ;
foreach_loop   foreach identifier ( array )  instr
```

array	expr
aff_func	aff
	post_pre_incr
	func_call
	/*nothing */
rep	func_call **x** expr
string	STRING1
	STRING2
inc	**include** (string)
func_call	identifier (arg_list)
arg_list	arg_list_1
	/*nothing*/
arg_list_1	arg
	arg , arg_list_1
arg	expr
	identifier : expr
aff	lvalue **=** expr
	lvalue **+=** expr
	lvalue **-=** expr
	lvalue ***=** expr
	lvalue **/=** expr
	lvalue **%=** expr
	lvalue **> >=** expr
	lvalue **> > >=** expr
	lvalue **< <=** expr
lvalue	identifier
	array_elem
identifier	IDENTIFIER
	x
array_elem	identifier **[** array_index **]**
array_index	expr
post_pre_incr	**++** lvalue
	- lvalue
	lvalue **++**
	lvalue **-**
expr	(expr)

```
                        logic_expr

                        arith_expr

                        bit_expr

                        post_pre_incr

                        compar

                        INTEGER

                        STRING2

                        STRING1

                        var

                        ff

                        cst_array

                        ipaddr

        logic_expr      expr and expr

                        !  expr

                        expr or expr

        arith_expr      expr + expr

                        expr - expr

                        - expr

                        expr * expr

                        expr / expr

                        expr % expr

                        expr ** expr

        bit_expr        ~ expr

                        expr & expr

                        expr ^ expr

                        expr -- expr

                        expr >> expr

                        expr >>> expr

                        expr <<expr

        compare         expr >< expr

                        expr >! < expr

                        expr =~ string

                        expr ! ~ string

                        expr < expr

                        expr > expr

                        expr == expr
```

	`expr ! = expr`
	`expr >= expr`
	`expr <= expr`
`var`	`identifier`
	`num_arg`
	`array_elem`
	`func_call`
`ipaddr`	`NTEGER . INTEGER . INTEGER . INTEGER`
`num_arg`	`$INTEGER`
	`$*`
`cst_array`	`[ l_array ]`
`l_array`	`array_data`
	`array_data , l_array`
`array_data`	`atom`
	`string => atom`
`atom`	`integer`
	`string`
`loc`	**`local_var`** `arg_decl`
`glob`	**`global_var`** `arg_decl`

`INTEGER`	is any sequence of decimal digit (preceded by an optional minus sign), or **0** followed by a sequence of octal digits, or **0x** followed by a sequence of hexadecimal digits.
`IDENTIFIER`	is any sequence of letters (uppercase or lowercase) or digits, starting with a letter. The underscore sign is treated as a letter. Note that "**x**" is not exactly an identifier because it is the "repeat" operator, but can be used for function or variables names.
`STRING1`	is a string between simple quotes.
`STRING2`	is a string between double quotes.

2.3 Types

NASL2 handles the following data types:

1. **integers** Any sequence of digits with an optional minus sign is an integer. NASL2 uses the C syntax: octal numbers can be enter by starting with **0** and hexadecimal with **0x** (i.e. 0x10 = 020 = 16)

2. **strings**, which can exist in two flavors: "pure" and "impure"[2].

    (a) "Impure" strings are entered between double quotes and are not converted: backslashes remain backslashes. "Impure" strings are transformed into "pure" string by the internal **string** function.

    (b) "Pure" strings are returned by **string** or are entered between simple quotes. In this case, a few escape sequences are transformed[3].

3. **arrays**, which can be indexed with integers[4] or strings[5].

4. And the **NULL** value, which is what you get if you read an initialized variable, or what internal functions returns in case of severe error. Read the warning below!

5. **Booleans** are not a standalone type. The comparison operators return **0** for FALSE and **1** for TRUE. Any other value is converted :

    ■ The undefined or null value is FALSE.

    ■ Integers are TRUE if not null; **0** is FALSE.

    ■ Strings are TRUE if not empty. So "**0**" is TRUE (it is false in Perl or in NASL1).

    ■ Although it does not really make sense, arrays are always TRUE, whether they are empty or not.

All built-in or user-defined functions can handle or return all those types (even arrays!).

Warnings about the NULL value

NULL and the array operator Reading an array element from a NULL value will immediately convert it into an array. An empty array of course, but no more an undefined variable. Changing this means big modifications in the NASL interpreter.

For example:

```
V = NULL;
# isnull(v)=TRUE and typeof(v)= "undef"
x = v[2];
# isnull(x)=TRUE and typeof(x)= "undef"
# But isnull(v)=FALSE and typeof(v)= "array"
```

NULL and isnull If you want to check if a variable is undefined, you have to used isnull(var). Testing the equality with the NULL constant (var == NULL) is not a good idea, as NULL will be converted to 0 or the empty string "" according to the type of the variable. This is necessary to ensure that variables are "automatically initialized" – changing this would probably break some existing scripts.

2.4 Operators

2.4.1 General operators

- **=** is the assignment operator.

  - x=42; puts 42 into the variable **x**. The previous value is forgotten.

  - x=y; copies the value of variable **y** into x. If **y** was undefined, **x** becomes undefined too.

- [ ] is the array index operator.

  - A variable cannot be atomic[6] and an array at the same time. If you changed the type, the previous value(s) is (are) lost.

  - However, this operator can be used to extract a character from a string: if **s = "abcde"**, then **s[2] = "c"**.

- In NASL1, this could be used to *change* the character too: you could write s[2] = "C"; and **s** became "**abCde**". This is no longer true; you have to use the **insstr** function and write something like s = insstr(s, "C", 2, 2); See **insstr**.

- y[1] = 42; makes an array out of **y** and puts 42 in the second element. If **y** was not an array, it's first undefined.

2.4.2 Arithmetics operators

Be aware that there is no strict rule on the integer size in NASL2. The interpretor implements them with the native "int" C type, which is 32 bit long on most systems, and maybe 64 bit long on a few one[7]. There is no overflow or underflow protection.

- \+ is the addition operator.

- – is the subtraction operator.

- * is the multiplication operator.

- / is the integer division operator. Please note that:

  - NASL2 does not support floating point operations.

  - Division by zero will return 0 instead of crashing the interpretor. How nice of us!

- % is the modulo. Once again, if the 2 operand is null, the interpretor will return 0 instead of crashing on SIGFPE.

- ** is the exponentiation or power function[8].

2.4.3 Nice C operators

NASL2 imported some nice operators from C:

- ++ is the pre-incrementation (++x) or post-incrementation (x++).

  ++x adds 1 to **x** and returns the result; x++ adds 1 to x but returns the previous value.

- –is the pre-decrementation (–x) or post-decrementation (x–).

- += –= *= /= %= have the same meaning as in C

e.g. x += y; is equivalent to x = x + y;but **x** is evaluated only once. This is important in expressions like a[i++] *= 2; where the index "i" is incremented only once.

- <<= and >>= also exist; we added >>>=

2.4.4 String operators

- \+ is the string concatenation. However, you should better use the **string** function.

- \- is the "string subtraction". It removes the first instance of a string inside another.
  For example **'abcd' - 'bc'** will give **'ad'**.

- [ ] extracts one character from the string, as explained before.

- >< is the "string match" operator. It looks for substrings inside a string.
  `'ab' >< 'xabcdz' is TRUE; 'ab' >< 'xxx' is FALSE.`

- >! < is the "string don't match" operator. It looks for substrings inside a string and returns the opposite as the previous operator.
  `'ab' >! < 'xabcdz' is FALSE; 'ab' >! < 'xxx' is TRUE.`

- = is the "regex match" operator. It is similar to a call to the internal function **ereg** but is quicker because the regular expression is compiled only once when the script is parsed
  `s ="[ab]*x+" is equivalent to ereg(string:s, pattern:"[ab]*x+", icase:1)`

- ! is the "regex don't match" operator. It gives the opposite result of the previous one[9].

2.4.5 Compare operators

- == is TRUE if both arguments are equals, FALSE otherwise.

- ! = is TRUE if both arguments are different, TRUE otherwise.

- > is the "greater than" operator.

- >= is the "greater than or equal" operator.

- **<** is the "lesser than" operator.
- **<=** is the "lesser than or equal" operator.

2.4.6 Logical operators

- **!** is the logical "not". TRUE if its argument is FALSE, FALSE other-wise.
- **&&** is the logical "and". Note that if the first argument is FALSE, the second is not evaluated.
- **||** is the logical "or". If the first argument is TRUE, the second is not evaluated.

2.4.7 Bit fields operators

- **~** is the arithmetic "not", the 1-complement
- **&** is the arithmetic "and".
- **|** is the arithmetic "or".
- **^** is the arithmetic "xor" (exclusive or).
- **<<** is the logical bit shift to the left.
- **>>** is the arithmetic / signed shift to the right[10].
- **>>>** is the logical / unsigned shift to the right[11].

In all shift operators, the count is on the right. i.e. x>>2 is equivalent to x/4 and x<<2 is x*4

2.4.8 Special behavior

- **break** can (but should not) be used to exit from a function or the script.
- In case its arguments have different types, + now tries very hard to do something smart, i.e. a string concatenation, then an integer addition. It prints a warning, though, because such automatic conversion is dangerous.
  - If one of its argument is undefined, + returns the other one.

- If one of its argument is a "pure string", the other argument is converted to a string, if necessary, and the result is a "pure string". "Impure string" are converted to pure string *without escape sequence interpretation*. i.e. **"AB\n"+'de'** gives **'AB\\nde'**, i.e. "AB", a backslash, then "nde".

- If one of its argument is an "impure string", the second argument is converted to string if necessary and the result is an "impure string". i.e. **"ABC"+2** gives **"ABC2".**

- If one of its argument is an integer, the other is converted to integer and the result is an integer.

- In any other case, NULL is returned.

- The "magical strings" from NASL1 have been removed. In NASL1, adding a string to an integer might give an integer if the string contained only digits.

- The minus operator follows the same type conversion rules as plus.

- Using unitialized variables is **bad**. However, to ensure that old scripts still work, the **NULL** undefined value will be into **0** or **""** according to the context (integer or string). That's why you have to use **isnull** to test if a variable is undefined. See "warnings about the NULL value" in 2.3.

2.5 Precedence

From the higher priority to the lower:

Operators	Associativity
++ --	None
**	Right
~ -(unary minus)	Left
!	Left
* / %	Left
+ -	Left
<< >> >>>	Left
&	Left
^	Left

Continued

Operators	Associativity
|	Left
<<= >>= == != < > =~ !~ >! <	
><	None
&&	Left
||	Left
= += -= *= /= %= <<= >>= >>>=	Right

2.6 Loops and control flow

2.6.1 Operators

- `for (expr1; cond; expr2) block;` is similar to the C operator and is equivalent to
  `expr1; while(cond) block; expr2;`
  A classical construction to count from 1 to 10 is:
  `for(i=1;i<=10;i++) display(i,'{\n');`

- `foreach var (array) block;` iterates all elements in an array. Note that *var* iterates through the *values* stored in the array, not the *indexes*. If you want that, just use: `foreach var (keys(array)) block;`

- `while (cond) block;` executes the block as long as the condition is TRUE. If the condition is FALSE, the block is never executed.

- `repeat block; until (cond);` executes the blocks as long as the condition is TRUE. The block is executed at least once.

- `break` breaks the current loop and jumps at its exit.
  If you are not inside a loop, the behavior is undefined[12].

- `continue`[13] jumps to the next step of the loop.
  If you are not inside a loop, the behavior is undefined.

- **`return`** returns a value from the current function.

2.6.2 Special behavior

2.7 Declarations

2.7.1 Variable declarations

NASL1 had only global variables. NASL2 uses global and local variables. Local variables are created in a function and stop existing as soon as the function returns. When the interpretor looks for a variable, it first searches in the current function context, then in the calling context (if any), etc., until it reaches the top level context that contains the global variables.

Normally, you do not need to declare a variable: either it exists, because you already used it in this context, or because a calling function used it, or it will be created in the current context. However, this may be dangerous in some cases:

1. if you want to write into a *global* variable from within a function and cannot be sure that the variable was created first in the top level context, or created as a local variable in a calling function context.

2. if you want to be sure that you are creating a brand new *local* variable and not overwriting a global variable with the same name.

So you can explicitly declare a variable:

- `local_var var;`

- `global_var var;`

If the variable already exists in the specified context, you will get an error message, but this will work!

2.7.2 Function declarations

- `function` **name (argname1, argname2) block;**

Note that the argument list may be empty, but if it is not, user-defined function parameters must be named[14]. Unnamed arguments may be used without being declared.

2.7.3 Retrieving function arguments

Inside a NASL function, named arguments are just accessed as any local variable. Unnamed arguments are implemented through the special array **__FCT_ANON_ARGS**. This variable will be NULL in interpretors below **NASL_LEVEL** 2180. You may put this at the start of scripts that need this function:

```
if (NASL_LEVEL < 2180) exit(0); # __FCT_ANON_ARGS is not implemented
```

Shell–like special variables **$1, $2**... or the **$*** array were introduced in NASL_LEVEL 2160, but they should not be used as they break the compatibility with older interpretors: the scripts cannot be parsed.

2.7.4 Calling functions

Here is an example with named arguments:

```
function fact(x)
{
 local_var i, f;
 f = 1;
 for (i = 1; i <= n; i ++) f *= i;
 return f;
}
display("3 !  = ", fact(x: 3), "\n");
```

And the same with unnamed arguments:

```
function fact()
{
 local_var i, f;
 f = 1;
 for (i = 1;  i <= $1;i ++) f *= i;
 return f;
}
display("3 !  = ", fact(3), "\n");
```

And another, mixing the two flavors:

```
function fact(prompt)
```

```
{
  local_var i, f;
  f = 1;
  for (i = 1; i <= $1; i ++)
  {
    f *= i;
    display(prompt, i, '!  = ', f, '\n');
  }
  return f;
}
n = fact(3, prompt: '> ');
```

3 The NASL2 library

3.1 Predefined constants

These constants are actually variables, i.e. you can modify their value in a script. If you really want to shoot you in the foot, that is...

- Booleans constants
    - **FALSE** = 0
    - **TRUE** = 1

- Plugin categories
    - **ACT_INIT**: the plugin just sets a few KB items (kinds of global variables for all plugins).
    - **ACT_SCANNER**: the plugin is a port scanner or something like it (e.g. ping).
    - **ACT_SETTINGS**: just like ACT_INIT, but run after the scanners, once we are sure that the host is alive (for performance).
    - **ACT_GATHER_INFO**: the plugin identifies services, gather data, parses banners, etc.
    - **ACT_ATTACK**: the plugin launches a soft attack, e.g. a web directory traversal.

- **ACT_MIXED_ATTACK**: the plugin launches an attach that might have dangerous side effects (crashing the service most of the time).

- **ACT_DESTRUCTIVE_ATTACK**: the plugin tries to destroy data[15] or launch some dangerous attack (e.g. testing a buffer overflow is likely to crash a vulnerable service).

- **ACT_DENIAL**: the plugin tries to crash a service.

- **ACT_KILL_HOST**: the plugin tries to crash the target host or disable it (e.g. saturate the CPU, kill some vital service…).

- **ACT_FLOOD**: the plugin tries to crash the target host or disable it by flooding it with incorrect packets or requests. It may saturate the network or kill some routing, switching or filtering device on the way.

- Network constants

  - Nessus "encapsulation"

  - **ENCAPS_IP** = 1; this is the "transport" value for a pure TCP socket.

  - **ENCAPS_SSLv23** = 2; this is the "transport" value for a SSL connection in compatibility mode. Note that the **find_service** plugin will never declare a port with this "encapsulation", but you may use it in a script.

  - **ENCAPS_SSLv2** = 3. The old SSL version which only supports server side certificates.

  - **ENCAPS_SSLv3** = 4. The new SSL version: it supports server and client side certificates, more ciphers, and fixes a few security holes.

  - **ENCAPS_TLSv1** = 5; TLSv1 is defined RFC 2246. Some people call it "SSL v3.1".

- Sockets options

  - **MSG_OOB**, a socket option used to send "out of band data".

- Raw sockets

  - **IPPROTO_ICMP** as defined in the system C include files.

- **IPPROTO_IGMP**

- **IPPROTO_IP**

- **IPPROTO_TCP**

- **IPPROTO_UDP**

- **pcap_timeout** = 5

- **TH_ACK** = 0x10. This TCP flag indicates that the packet contains a valid acknowledgment.

- **TH_FIN** = 0x01. This TCP flag indicates that the packet negotiates the end of the session.

- **TH_PUSH** = 0x08.

- **TH_RST** = 0x04. This TCP flag indicates that the connection was refused or "reset by peer".

- **TH_SYN** = 0x02. This belong to the initial handshake (connection opening).

- **TH_URG** = 0x20. This TCP flag indicates that the packet contains urgent data.

- Miscellaneous constants

  - **NULL** is the undefined value.

- Nessusd glue

  - **description** is set to **1** when **nessusd** parses the script the first time (to get its name, description, summary, etc.), then to **0** when it is run.

  - **COMMAND_LINE** is set to **0** when the script is run by **nessusd** or to **1** when it is run by the **nasl** standalone interpretor.

3.2 Built-in functions

Internal built-in functions can have unnamed and named arguments. Some use both types.

3.2.1 Knowledge base functions

This KB is used for inter-plugin communication.

- **set_kb_item** creates a new entry in the KB.
  It takes two named string arguments: **name** and **value**.
  Entering an item several times creates a list.

- **get_kb_item** retrieves an entry from the KB.
  It takes one unnamed string argument (the **name** of the KB item).
  If the item is a list, the plugin will fork and each child process will use a
  different value. Nessus remebers which child got which value: reading
  the same item a second time will not fork again!
  You should not call this function when some connections are open if
  you do not want to see several processes fighting to read or write on the
  same socket.

- **get_kb_list** retrieves multiple entire from the KB. It takes one unnamed
  string argument which may either designate a literal KB entry name, or
  a mask. The returned value is a "hash", i.e. an array with potentially
  duplicated indexes; because of this, you need to convert it with
  make_list() or use **foreach** to access each element (the **make_array**
  function allows you to create such hashes).

```
# Retrieves the list of all the web servers
webservers = get_kb_list("Services/www");
# Retrieves the list of all the services
services = get_kb_list("Services/*");
# Retrieves the whole KB
services = get_kb_list("*");
```

3.2.2 Report functions

Those functions send back information to the Nessus daemon.

- **scanner_status** reports the port scan progress (if the plugin is a port
  scanner!).
  It takes two named integer arguments:

  - **current**, the number of ports already scanned,

  - **total**, the full number of ports to be scanned.

- **security_note** reports a miscellaneous information.
  It either takes an unnamed integer argument (the port number), or a some of those named arguments:

  - **data** is the text report (the "description" by default).

  - **port** is the TCP or UDP port number of the service (or nothing if the bug concerns the whole machine, e.g. the IP stack configuration).

  - **proto** (or **protocol**) is the protocol ("**tcp**" by default; "**udp**" is the other value).

- **security_hole** reports a severe flaw.
  It either takes an unnamed integer argument (the port number), or a some of those named arguments:

  - **data** is the text report (the "description" by default).

  - **port** is the TCP or UDP port number of the vulnerable service (or nothing if the bug concerns the whole machine, e.g. the IP stack configuration).

  - **proto** (or **protocol**) is the protocol ("**tcp**" by default; "**udp**" is the other value).

- **security_warning** reports a mild flaw.

  It either takes an unnamed integer argument (the port number), or a some of those named arguments:

  - **data** is the text report (the "description" by default).

  - **port** is the TCP or UDP port number of the vulnerable service (or nothing if the bug concerns the whole machine, e.g. the IP stack configuration).

  - **proto** (or **protocol**) is the protocol ("**tcp**" by default; "**udp**" is the other value).

3.2.3 Description functions

All those functions but **script_get_preference** are only used in the "description part" of the plugin, i.e. the block that is run when the **description** variable is **1**.

They only make sense in the Nessus environment and have no effect when the plugin is run with the standalone **nasl** interpretor.

- **script_add_preference** adds an option to the plugin.
  It takes tree named arguments:

  - **name** is the option name. As it is displayed "as is" in the GUI, it usually ends with ":".

  - **type** is the option type. It may be:

    - **checkbox**

    - **entry**

    - **password**

    - **radio**

  - **value** is the default value ("yes" or "no" for checkboxes, a text string for "entries" or "passwords") except for "radios", where it is the list of options (separate the items with ";"). e.g.
    script_add_preference(name: " Reverse traversal", type: "radio", value: "none;Basic;Long URL");

- **script_bugtraq_id** sets the SecurityFocus "bid".
  It takes one or several unnamed integer arguments.

- **script_category** sets the "category" of the plugin.
  Usually, its unnamed integer argument is one of those pre-defined constants [16]:

  - **ACT_INIT**

  - **ACT_SCANNER**

  - **ACT_SETTINGS**

  - **ACT_GATHER_INFO**

  - **ACT_ATTACK**

  - **ACT_MIXED_ATTACK**

  - **ACT_DESTRUCTIVE_ATTACK**

  - **ACT_DENIAL**

  - **ACT_KILL_HOST**

- **script_copyright** sets the copyright string of the plugin (usually the author's name).
  It takes an unnamed string argument, or one or several named[17] arguments: **english**, **francais**, **deutsch**, **portuguese**.

- **script_cve_id** sets the CVE IDs of the flaws tested by the script.
  It takes any number of unnamed string arguments. They usually looks like "CVE-2002-042" or "CAN-2003-666".

- **script_dependencie** is the same function as **script_dependencies** (too many typos?).

- **script_dependencies** sets the lists of scripts that should be run before this one (if "optimize mode" is on).
  It takes any number of unnamed string arguments.

- **script_description** sets the "description" of the plugin.
  It takes an unnamed string argument, or one or several named arguments: **english**, **francais**, **deutsch**, **portuguese**. If the argument is unnamed, the default language is **english**.

- **script_exclude_keys** sets the list of "KB items" that must *not* be set to run this script in "optimize mode".
  It takes any number of unnamed string arguments.

- **script_family** sets the "family" of the plugin.
  It takes an unnamed string argument, or one or several named arguments: **english**, **francais**, **deutsch**, **portuguese**. If the argument is unnamed, the default language is **english**. There is no standardized family, but you should avoid inventing too many new ones. Here is a list:

english	francais
Backdoors	Backdoors
CGI abuses	Abus de CGI
CISCO	CISCO
Denial of Service	Déni de service
Finger abuses	Abus de finger
Firewalls	Firewalls
FTP	FTP
Gain a shell remotely	Obtenir un shell à distance

Continued

english	francais
Gain root remotely	Passer root à distance
General	General
Misc.	Divers
Netware	
NIS	
Ports scanners	Port scanners
Remote file access	Accès aux fichiers distants
RPC	RPC
Settings	Configuration
SMTP problems	Problèmes SMTP
SNMP	SNMP
Untested	Untested
Useless services	Services inutiles
Windows	Windows
Windows : User management	

- **script_get_preference** reads an option. It takes an unnamed string argument.
  Note that it might returns an empty string if you are running the script from the standalone NASL interpretor.

- **script_id** sets the script number[18]. It takes an unnamed integer argument.

- **script_name** sets the "name" of the plugin.
  It takes an unnamed string argument, or one or several named arguments: **english**, **francais**, **deutsch**, **portuguese**. If the argument is unnamed, the default language is **english**.

- **script_require_keys** sets the list of "KB items" that must be set to run this script in "optimize mode".
  It takes any number of unnamed string arguments.

- **script_require_ports** sets the list of TCP ports that must be open to run this script in "optimize mode".

It takes any number of unnamed integer or string arguments. e.g. **23** or **"Services/telnet"**.

- **script_require_udp_ports** sets the list of UDP ports that must be open to run this script in "optimize mode".
  It takes any number of unnamed integer arguments[19].

- **script_summary** sets the "short description" of the plugin.
  It takes an unnamed string argument, or one or several named arguments: **english**, **francais**, **deutsch**, **portuguese**. If the argument is unnamed, the default language is **english**.
  Each of its arguments should be a single line of text.

- **script_timeout** sets the default timeout of the plugin.
  It takes an unnamed integer argument. If it is **(–1)**, the timeout is infinite.

- **script_version** sets the "version" of the plugin.

  It takes an unnamed string argument[20].

3.2.4 Other "glue" functions

- **get_preference** takes an unnamed string argument and returns the "preference" value. This function is necessary to retrieve some server options. For example:

```
p = get_preference('port_range');    # returns something like
1-65535
```

3.2.5 Network functions

Note: the "socket" data type used by those functions is in fact an integer. However, you should not touch it and it may be turned into an opaque data type some day. In case of error, all those functions returns a value that can be interpreted as FALSE (most of the time NULL).

- **close** closes the socket given in its only unnamed argument.

- **end_denial** takes no argument and returns TRUE if the target host is still alive and FALSE if it is dead. You must have called **start_denial** before your test.

- **ftp_get_pasv_port** sends the "**PASV**" command on the open socket, parses the returned data and returns the chosen "passive" port. It takes one named argument: **socket**.

- **get_host_name** takes no argument and returns the target host name.

- **get_host_ip** takes no arguments and returns the target IP address.

- **get_host_open_port** takes no argument and returns an open TCP port on the target host. This function is used by tests that need to speak to the TCP/IP stack but not to a specific service.

- **get_port_transport** takes an unnamed integer (socket) argument and returns its "encapsulation."

- **get_port_state** takes an unnamed integer (TCP port number) and returns TRUE if it is open and FALSE otherwise. As some TCP ports may be in an unknown state because they were not scanned, the behavior of this function may be modified by the "consider unscanned ports as closed" global option. When this option is reset (the default), **get_port_state** will return TRUE on unknown ports; when it is set, **get_port_state** will return FALSE.

- **get_tcp_port_state** is a synonym for **get_port_state**.

- **get_udp_port_state** returns TRUE if the UDP port is open, FALSE otherwise (see **get_port_state** for comments). Note that UDP port scanning may be unreliable.

- **islocalhost** takes no argument and returns TRUE if the target host is the same as the attacking host, FALSE otherwise.

- **islocalnet** takes no argument and returns TRUE if the target host is on the same network as the attacking host, FALSE otherwise.

- **join_multicast_group** takes an string argument (an IP multicast address) and returns TRUE if it could join the multicast group. If the group was already joined, the function joins increments an internal counter.

- **leave_multicast_group** takes an string argument (an IP multicast address).

Note that if **join_multicast_group** was called several times, each call to **leave_multicast_cast** only decrements a counter; the group is left when it reaches 0.

- **open_priv_sock_tcp** opens a "privileged" TCP socket to the target host.
  It takes two named integer arguments:

  - **dport** is the destination port,

  - **sport** is the source port, which may be inferior to 1024.

- **open_priv_sock_udp** opens a "privileged" UDP socket to the target host.
  It takes two named integer arguments:

  - **dport** is the destination port,

  - **sport** is the source port, which may be inferior to 1024.

- **open_sock_tcp** opens a TCP socket to the target host[21].
  It takes an unnamed integer argument (the port number) and two optional named integer arguments:

  - **bufsz**, if you want to bufferize IO (this is disabled by default).

  This parameter has been added after Nessus 2.0.10.

  - **timeout**, if you want to change it from the default,

  - **transport**, to force Nessus a specific "transport". Its main use is to disable Nessus "auto SSL discovery" feature on dynamic ports (e.g. FTP data connections).

    The possible values for **transport** were explained in 3.1. They are:

    - **ENCAPS_IP**

    - **ENCAPS_SSLv23**

    - **ENCAPS_SSLv2**

    - **ENCAPS_SSLv3**

    - **ENCAPS_TLSv1**

- **open_sock_udp** opens a UDP socket to the target host. It takes an unnamed integer argument, the port number.

- **recv** receives data from a TCP or UDP socket.
  For a UDP socket, if it cannot read data, NASL will suppose that the last sent datagram was lost and will sent it again a couple of time. It takes at least two named arguments:

  - **socket** which was returned by **open_sock_tcp**, for example,

  - and **length**, the number of bytes that you want to read at most.

  recv may return before **length** bytes have been read: as soon as at least one byte has been received, the timeout is lowered to 1 second. If no data is received during that time, the function returns the already read data; otherwise, if the full initial timeout has not been reached, a 1 second timeout is re-armed and the script tries to receive more data from the socket. This special feature was implemented to get a good compromise between reliability and speed when Nessus talks to unknown or complex protocols. Two other optional named integer arguments can twist this behavior:

  - **min** is the minimum number of data that must be read in case the "magic read function" is activated and the timeout is lowered. By default this is **0**.

  - **timeout** can be changed from the default.

- **recv_line** receives data from **socket** and stops as soon as a *line feed* character has been read, **length** bytes have been read or the default timeout has been triggered.

- **send** sends data on a socket.
  Its named arguments are:

  - **socket,**

  - **data**, the data block. A string is expected here (pure or impure, this does not matter).

  - **length** is optional and will be the full data length if not set,

  - **option** is the flags for the send() system call. You should not use a raw numeric value here; the only interesting constant is **MSG_OOB**. See Sockets-options.

- **scanner_add_port** declares an open port to nessusd.
  It takes two named arguments and returns no value:

  - **port** is the port number,

  - **proto** is "**tcp**" or "**udp**".

- **scanner_get_port** walks through the list of open ports. It takes one unnamed integer argument, an index, and returns a port number or **0** when the end of the list if reached. A good way to use it is:

```
i = 0;
while (port = scanner_get_port(i++))
{
  do_something_with_port;
}
```

- **tcp_ping** launches a "TCP ping" against the target host, i.e. tries to open a TCP connection and sees if anything comes back (SYNACK or RST). The named integer argument **port** is not compulsory: if it is not set, **tcp_ping** will use an internal list of common ports[22] .

- **telnet_init** performs a telnet negotiation on an open socket [**RFC854/STD8**]. This function takes one unnamed argument (the open socket) and returns the data read (more or less the telnet dialog plus the banner).

- **this_host** takes no argument and returns the IP address of the current (attacking) machine.

- **this_host_name** takes no argument and returns the host name of the current (attacking) machine.

- **ftp_log_in** performs a FTP identification / authentication on an open socket. It returns TRUE if it could login successfully, FALSE otherwise (e.g. wrong password, or any network problem). It takes three named arguments:

  - **user** is the user name (it has *no* default value like "anonymous" or "ftp"),

  - **pass** is the password (again, no default value like the user e-mail address),

  - and **socket**.

- **start_denial** initializes some internal data structure for **end_denial**. It takes no argument and returns no value.

3.2.6 String manipulation functions

- **chomp** takes an unnamed string argument and removes any spaces at the end of it. "Space" means white space, vertical or horizontal tabulation, carriage return or line feed.

- **crap** returns a buffer of required length. This function is mainly used in buffer overflow tests. Its arguments are:
  - **length**, the size of the wanted buffer,
  - **data**, the pattern that will be repeated to fill the buffer. By default **'X'**.

- **display** takes an unlimited number of arguments, calls **string** on them, then displays them.
  It returns the number of output characters.
  Unprintable characters are replaced with ".".

- **egrep** looks for a pattern in a string, line by line and returns the concatenation of all lines that match. Its arguments are:
  - **icase,**
  - **pattern,**
  - **string**.

- **ereg** matches a string against a regular expression. It returns the first found pattern. Its arguments are:
  - **string,**
  - **multiline,** which is FALSE by default (string is truncated at the first "end of line"), and can be set to TRUE for multiline search.
  - **pattern** (standard extended POSIX regex, no PCRE for the moment!),
  - and **icase**, which is FALSE by default, and can be set to TRUE for case insensitive search.

- **ereg_replace** searches and replaces all the occurrences of a pattern inside a string. It returns the modified string, or the original string if the pattern did not match. Its arguments are:

  - **string**, the original string,

  - **pattern**, the pattern that should be matched,

  - **replace**, the replacement, which may contain escape sequences like **\1** to reference found sub-patterns. The index is the number of the opening parenthesis, as usual[23],

  - **icase**, the case insensitive flag.

- **eregmatch** searches for a pattern into a string and returns NULL if it did not match or an array of all found sub-patterns. There is at least one returned pattern, which is the part of the string that matched the whole pattern. For those used to Perl, the elements of the returned array are equivalent to **$0, $1, $2**...[24]. Its argument are

  - **icase,**

  - **pattern,**

  - **string.**

Note that all the regex functions work the same way. If you want to match from the beginning / end of your string (or your line, in the case of **egrep**), you'll have to use **^** or **$**. If you want to eliminate what's before or after a pattern with **ereg_replace**, you'll have to play with something like **^.*** or **.*$** and **\1**. You should read your (POSIX) system manual for details on regular expressions.

- **hex** converts its unnamed integer argument into the hexadecimal representation. It returns a string.

- **hexstr** takes one unnamed string argument and returns a string made of the hexadecimal representation of the ASCII codes of each input character. For example, **hexstr('aA\n')** returns **'61410a'**.

- **insstr** takes three or four unnamed arguments: a first string, a second string, a start index and an optional end index . Indexes starts at 0. The function replaces the declared slice in the first string by the second string, and returns the result. For example,

```
insstr('abcdefgh', 'xyz', 3, 5)
```

returns **'abcxyzgh'**.

- **int** converts its unnamed argument into an integer. If the argument is not a string, it returns **0**.

- **match** matches a string against a simple shell-like pattern and returns TRUE or FALSE. This function is less powerful than **ereg** but it is quicker and its interface is simple. Its arguments are:

  - **icase** if the match should be case insensitive.

  - **string** is the input string.

  - **pattern** is the searched pattern. The only wildcards are * (for any string, even empty) and **?** (for any character).

- **ord** takes one unnamed string argument and returns the (integer) ASCII code of the first character of the string.

- **raw_string** takes any number of unnamed arguments and returns a "pure" string resulting from these operations:

  - "Impure" strings are parsed and escaped sequences are interpreted[25].

  - Each integer is converted to the corresponding ASCII character[26].

  - Undefined variables are skipped[27].

  - Arrays are converted to some ASCII representation[28].

  - "Pure" strings are left as they were

  - And last but not least, the processing stops as soon as RAW_STR_LEN = 32768 have been entered. **string** does not have such a limitation.

- **str_replace** replaces any occurrence of a substring inside a bigger string and returns the modified string. Its arguments are:

  - **string** is the original string.

  - **find** is the sub-string that is looked for.

  - **replace** is the replacement sub-string.

  - **count** is optional; if set, **str_replace** stops after this number of occurences have been replaced and leave the rest of the string as it is.

- **string** takes any number of unnamed arguments and returns a "pure" string[29] resulting from these operations:
  - "Impure" strings are parsed and escaped sequences are interpreted.
  - Integer are converted to their ASCII representation (in decimal base). That's where it is different from **raw_string**.
  - Undefined variables are skipped[30].
  - Arrays are converted to some ASCII representation.
  - "Pure" strings are left as they were.

- **strcat** takes any number of unnamed arguments and returns a "pure" string resulting from these operations:
  - Integer are converted to their ASCII representation (in decimal base).
  - Undefined variables are skipped.
  - Arrays are converted to some ASCII representation[31].
  - "Pure" and "impure" strings are left as they were.

- **stridx** takes two or three unnamed arguments, looks for a substring inside a string (starting from the optional position) and returns its index (or -1 if not found or in case of error).
  - The first argument is the string (the haystack).
  - The second is the substring that is looked for (the needle)
  - The optional third argument is the starting position (by default **0**)
  - Note that the return value is not **NULL** if the substring was not found but **-1**.

- **strstr** takes two unnamed string arguments and searches the first occurrence of arg2 into arg1. It returns NULL if nothing was found, or the piece of arg2 from the first matching character till the end. For example **strstr('zabadz', 'ad')** returns **'adz'**.

- **split** splits a string into an array of "lines" or "sub strings". It takes an unnamed parameter (the input string), an optional **sep** string argument and an optional **keep** integer argument; it returns the array.

If **sep** is not set, **split** cuts the input strings into lines. A line is supposed to end with the single character **LF** or the sequence **CR LF**.
By default[32], the separator (whatever it is) will be included in the sub-strings or lines, unless **keep** is set top **0**

- **strlen** returns the length of the unnamed string argument. If the argument is not a string, you get an undefined result[33].

- **substr** takes two or three unnamed arguments: a string, a start index (counting from 0) and an optional end index (by default, the end). It returns the desired substring.
  For example, substr('abcde', 2) returns 'cde' and substr('abcde', 1, 3) returns 'bcd'.

- **tolower** converts its unnamed string argument to lower case.

- **toupper** converts its unnamed string argument to upper case.

3.2.7 HTTP functions

- **cgibin** takes no argument and returns the cgi-bin path elements. In fact the NASL interpretor forks and each process gets one value. This function should be considered as *deprecated* and **cgi_dirs()** should be used instead.

- **http_delete** formats an HTTP DELETE request for the server on the port. It will automatically handle the HTTP version and the basic or cookie based authentication. The arguments are **port** and **item** (the URL). **data** is not compulsory and probably useless in this function. It returns a string (the formatted request).

- **http_get** formats an HTTP GET request for the server on the port. It will automatically handle the HTTP version and the basic or cookie based authentication. The arguments are **port** and **item** (the URL). **data** is not compulsory and probably useless in this function. It returns a string (the formatted request).

- **http_close_socket** closes a socket. Currently, it is identical to **close** but this may change in the future.

- **http_head** formats an HTTP HEAD request for the server on the port. It will automatically handle the HTTP version and the basic or cookie based authentication. The arguments are **port** and **item** (the URL). **data** is not compulsory and probably useless in this function. It returns a string (the formatted request).

- **http_open_socket** opens a socket to the given port. Until Nessus 2.0.10, this functions is identical to **open_sock_tcp**; afterwards, it sets a 64K buffer for IO.

- **http_recv_headers** reads all HTTP headers on the given socket (unnamed integer argument). It stops at the first blank line and returns a string made of all headers, starting with the HTTP answer code.

- **http_post** formats an HTTP POST request for the server on the port. It will automatically handle the HTTP version and the basic or cookie based authentication. The arguments are **port**, **item** (the URL) and **data**. It returns a string (the formatted request).

- **http_put** formats an HTTP PUT request for the server on the port. It will automatically handle the HTTP version and the basic or cookie based authentication. The arguments are **port**, **item** (the URL) and **data**. It returns a string (the formatted request).

- **is_cgi_installed** tests if a CGI is found. If the path is relative (does not start with a slash), the CGI is search into the cgi-bin path. This functions returns the port of the web server where it was found (it will fork if there are several web servers); this magical behavior allows you to write very short plugins. For example:

```
if (port = cgi_installed("vuln.cgi")) security_warning(port);
```

The arguments are:

- **item**, for the CGI path,

- and **port**; by default, the function will look on all found web servers (i.e. read the KB entry **Services/www**).

3.2.8 Raw IP functions

All those functions work on blocks of data which are implemented as "pure strings". This means that you could change them with the string manipulation functions, but this is probably not very easy.

- **dump_ip_packet** dumps IP datagrams. It takes any number of unnamed (string) arguments and does not return anything.

- **dump_tcp_packet** dumps the TCP parts of datagrams. It takes any number of unnamed arguments.

- **dump_udp_packet** dumps the UDP parts of datagrams. It takes any number of unnamed arguments.

- **forge_icmp_packet** fills an IP datagram with ICMP data. Note that the **ip_p** field is not updated. It returns the modified IP datagram. Its arguments are:

  - **data** is the payload.

  - **icmp_cksum** is the checksum, computed by default.

  - **icmp_code** is the ICMP code.

  - **icmp_id** is the ICMP ID.

  - **icmp_seq** is the ICMP sequence number.

  - **icmp_type** is the ICMP type.

  - **ip** is the IP datagram that is updated.

  - **update_ip_len** is a flag (TRUE by default). If set, NASL will recompute the size field of the IP datagram.

- **forge_igmp_packet** fills an IP datagram with IGMP data. Note that the **ip_p** field is not updated. It returns the modified IP datagram. Its arguments are:

  - **code**

  - **data**

  - **group**

  - **ip** is the IP datagram that is updated. Note that the IGMP checksum is automatically computed.

  - **type**

  - **update_ip_len** is a flag (TRUE by default). If set, NASL will recompute the size field of the IP datagram.

- **forge_ip_packet** returns an IP datagram inside the block of data. The named argument are:

  - **data** is the payload.

  - **ip_hl** is the IP header length in 32 bits words. **5** by default.

  - **ip_id** is the datagram ID; by default, it is random.

  - **ip_len** is the length of the datagram. By default, it is **20** plus the length of the **data** field.

  - **ip_off** is the fragment offset in 64 bits words. By default, **0**.

  - **ip_p** is the IP protocol. **0** by default.

  - **ip_src** is the source address in ASCII. NASL will convert it into an integer in network order.

    Note that the function accepts an **ip_dst** argument but ignore it!

  - **ip_sum** is the packet header checksum. It will be computed by default.

  - **ip_tos** is the "type of service" field. **0** by default

  - **ip_ttl** is the "Time To Live". **64** by default.

  - **ip_v** is the IP version. **4** by default.

- **forge_tcp_packet** fills an IP datagram with TCP data. Note that the **ip_p** field is not updated. It returns the modified IP datagram. Its arguments are:

  - **data** is the TCP data payload.

  - **ip** is the IP datagram to be filled.

  - **th_ack** is the acknowledge number. NASL will convert it into network order if necessary.

  - **th_dport** is the destination port. NASL will convert it into network order if necessary.

  - **th_flags** are the TCP flags.

  - **th_off** is the size of the TCP header in 32 bits words. By default, **5**.

  - **th_seq** is the TCP sequence number. NASL will convert it into network order if necessary.

- **th_sport** is the source port. NASL will convert it into network order if necessary.

- **th_sum** is the TCP checksum. By default, the right value is computed.

- **th_urp** is the urgent pointer. **0** by default.

- **th_win** is the TCP window size. NASL will convert it into network order if necessary. **0** by default.

- **th_x2** is a reserved field and should probably be left unchanged.

- **update_ip_len** is a flag (TRUE by default). If set, NASL will recompute the size field of the IP datagram.

- **forge_udp_packet** fills an IP datagram with UDP data. Note that the **ip_p** field is not updated. It returns the modified IP datagram. Its arguments are:

- **data** is the payload.

- **ip** is the old datagram.

- **uh_dport** is the destination port. NASL will convert it into network order if necessary.

- **uh_sport** is the source port. NASL will convert it into network order if necessary.

- **uh_sum** is the UDP checksum. Although it is not compulsory, the right value is computed by default.

- **uh_ulen** is the data length. By default it is set to the length the **data** argument plus the size of the UDP header.

- **update_ip_len** is a flag (TRUE by default). If set, NASL will recompute the size field of the IP datagram.

- **get_icmp_element** returns an ICMP element from a IP datagram. It returns a data block or an integer, according to the type of the element. Its arguments are:

- **element** is the name of the TCP field (see **forge_tcp_packet**).

- **icmp** is the IP datagram (*not* the ICMP part only).

- **get_ip_element** extracts a field from a datagram. It returns an integer or a string, depending on the type of the element. It takes two named string arguments:

  - **element** is the name of the field, e.g. "**ip_len**" ou "**ip_src**". Note that "**ip_dst**" works here!

  - **ip** is the datagram or fragment.

- **get_tcp_element** returns a TCP element from a IP datagram. It returns a data block or an integer, according to the type of the element. Its arguments are:

  - **element** is the name of the TCP field (see **forge_tcp_packet**).

  - **tcp** is the IP datagram (*not* the TCP part only).

- **get_udp_element** returns an UDP element from a IP datagram. It returns a data block or an integer, according to the type of the element. Its arguments are:

  - **element** is the name of the UDP field (see **forge_udp_packet**).

  - **udp** is the IP datagram (*not* the UDP part only).

- **insert_ip_options** adds an IP option to the datagram and returns the modified datagram. Its arguments are:

  - **code** is the number of the option.

  - **length** is the length of the option data.

  - **ip** is the old datagram.

  - **value** is the option data.

- **pcap_next** listens to one packet and returns it. Its arguments are:

  - **interface** is the network interface name. By default, NASL will try to find the best one.

  - **pcap_filter** is the BPF filter. By default, it listens to everything.

  - **timeout** is **5** seconds by default.

- **set_ip_elements** modifies the fields of a datagram. The named argument **ip** is the datagram; the other arguments are the same as **forge_ip_packet**. Once again, **ip_dst** is ignored. It returns the new datagram.

- **set_tcp_elements** modifies the TCP fields of a datagram. The named argument **tcp** is the IP datagram; the other arguments are the same as **forge_tcp_packet**. It returns the new IP datagram.

- **set_udp_elements** modifies the UDP fields of a datagram. The named argument **udp** is the IP datagram; the other arguments are the same as **forge_udp_packet**. It returns the new IP datagram.

- **send_packet** sends a list of packets (passed as unnamed arguments) and listens to the answers. It returns a block made of all the sniffed "answers".

  - **length** is the length of each packet by default.

  - **pcap_active** is TRUE by default. Otherwise, NASL does not listen for the answers.

  - **pcap_filter** is the BPF filter. By default it is **"ip and (src host** target **and dst host** nessus_host**)"**.

  - **pcap_timeout** is **5** by default.

3.2.9 Cryptographic functions

They are only implemented if Nessus is linked with OpenSSL.

- **HMAC_DSS** takes two named string arguments (**data** and **key**) and returns the HMAC as a string.

- **HMAC_MD2** takes two named string arguments (**data** and **key**) and returns the HMAC as a string.

- **HMAC_MD4** takes two named string arguments (**data** and **key**) and returns the HMAC as a string.

- **HMAC_MD5** takes two named string arguments (**data** and **key**) and returns the HMAC as a string.

- **HMAC_RIPEMD160** takes two named string arguments (**data** and **key**) and returns the HMAC as a string.

- **HMAC_SHA** takes two named string arguments (**data** and **key**) and returns the HMAC as a string.

- **HMAC_SHA1** takes two named string arguments (**data** and **key**) and returns the HMAC as a string.

- **MD2** takes an unnamed string argument and returns the hash as a string.

- **MD4** takes an unnamed string argument and returns the hash as a string.

- **MD5** takes an unnamed string argument and returns the hash as a string.

- **RIPEMD160** takes an unnamed string argument and returns the hash as a string.

- **SHA** takes an unnamed string argument and returns the hash as a string.

- **SHA1** takes an unnamed string argument and returns the hash as a string.

3.2.10 Miscellaneous functions

- **defined_func** takes one unnamed string argument and returns TRUE if a function with this named is defined. Whether it is a user or a built-in function does not matter.

- **dump_ctxt** is a debugging function which is not very useful for end users. It does not take any argument.

- **func_has_arg** takes a first string arguments (the function name) and a second string or integer argument (the argument name or number). It returns TRUE if the function accepts this argument, FALSE otherwise.

- **func_named_args** takes one unnamed string argument (the function name) and returns an array of all named arguments.

- **func_unnamed_args** takes one unnamed string argument (the function name) and returns the number of unnamed arguments.

- **gettimeofday** takes no argument and returns the number of seconds and microseconds since January 1, 1970. The return value is a character string formatted like a floating point number: the seconds are on the left of the decimal point and the microseconds on the right, on six digits. For example: **"1067352015.030757"** means **1067352015** seconds and **30757** microseconds.

The string manipulation functions can be used to extract the two numbers. e.g. **v = split(value, sep:'.');** would convert it into an array of two elements.

- **isnull** takes one unnamed argument and returns TRUE if it is not initialized, and FALSE otherwise.
  Remember that most of the time, (x == NULL) will not give the same result as **isnull(x)**

- **make_array** takes any *even* number of unnamed arguments and returns an array made from them. Contrary to **make_list**, only "atomic" values are accepted. The first argument in each pair is the key (either an integer or a character string), the second is the value. For example, **v=make_array(1,'one', 'Two', 2);** is equivalent to **v[1]='one'; v['Two']=2; make_array** can return arrays with duplicated keys, that have to be converted with **make_list** or walked through with **foreach**

- **make_list** takes any number of unnamed arguments of any types and returns an array made from them. If an argument is an array, it is split into its elements (i.e. make_list does not create a multi-dimensional array); the "integer indexed" elements will be re-indexed but the order will be kept.
  e.g., this:

  ```
  v = make_list(0,-1,'two'); w = make_list('A', v);
  ```

  is equivalent to:

  ```
  v[0] = 0; v[1] = -1; v[2] = 'two';
  w[0] = 'A'; w[1] = 0; w[2] = -1; w[3] = 'two';
  ```

- **max_index** takes one unnamed array argument and returns the bigger integer index used plus 1.
  e.g., to add an element at the end of any array, you may write
  ```
  w[max_index(w)] = value;
  ```

- **safe_checks** takes no argument and returns the boolean value of the "safe checks" option.

Dangerous plugins which may crash the remote service are expected to change their behavior when "safe checks" is on. Usually, they just identify the service version (e.g. from the banner) and check if it is known as vulnerable.

In "safe checks" mode, plugins from the most dangerous "categories" (ACT_DESTRUCTIVE_ATTACK, ACK_DENIAL and ACT_KILL_HOST) are not launched. So you do not need to test the value of **safe_checks** in those scripts.

You shouldn't either write code like if (safe_checks()) exit(0);. If you do not want to run your test in this mode (e.g. because you do not know how to parse the banner), you should move your plugin to one of those "dangerous" categories, probably **ACT_DESTRUCTIVE_ATTACK**.

- **sleep** takes one unnamed integer argument and waits for this number of seconds.

- **type_of** returns the type of the argument. The return value is a string:
  - **"undef"** if the variable / argument is not initialized.
  - **"int"** if it is an integer.
  - **"string"** it if is an "impure string".
  - **"data"** if it is a "pure string".
  - **"unknown"** if the type is unknown, which means that you have found a bug in the interpretor!

- **usleep** takes one unnamed integer argument and waits for this number of microseconds.

- **unixtime** returns the current Unix time, i.e. the number of seconds since January 1, 1970.

3.2.11 "unsafe" functions

The following functions are only allowed in "trusted" signed scripts[34]. If they could run anywhere, a user could upload a script and run arbitrary root code or perform a denial of service against the Nessus server.

- **find_in_path** searches a command in **$PATH** and returns **TRUE** if found, or **FALSE** if not. It takes one string argument (the command name).

- **pread** launches a process, reads its whole output and returns it as a string. The arguments are:

  - **cmd** is the name of the program that will be run. If it is not an absolute path, the program will be searched in **$PATH**.

  - **argv** is an array of strings. Each string is an argument. Note that **argv[0]** is the name of the program (which may be different from **cmd**, but will be equal in most cases).

  - **cd** is a boolean, **FALSE** by default. If **TRUE**, Nessus changes its current directory to the directory where the command was found.

- **fread**[35] reads a file on the Nessus server. It takes one unnamed string argument (the file name) and returns the whole file content in a string variable or **NULL** if an error occurred.

3.3 NASL library

It is implemented through "include files". Some of the functions are not very interesting because they were not designed to be called directly: they are used by other functions in the ".inc" file.

3.3.1 dump.inc

- **dump** (ddata, dtitle)
  prints the optional title and dumps the data block to the standard output. This function is useful for debugging only.

- **hexdump** (ddata)
  dumps a data block into hexadecimal and returns the results (as a string).

3.3.2 ftp_func.inc

- **ftpclose** (socket)
  cleanly closes a FTP connection: sends "QUIT", waits for the answer and then closes the socket. This functions does not return any value.

- **get_ftp_banner** (port)
  returns the FTP banner that was stored in the KB under **"ftp/banner/ port_number"**. If the KB item is not present, the function connects to the FTP server, reads the banner, stores it into the KB and returns it.

- **ftp_recv_line** (socket)
  reads a line on the socket until the 4th character is different from "–". Useful to skip a long login banner.

3.3.3 http_func.inc

- **check_win_dir_trav** (port, url, quickcheck) connects to port and sends a HTTP GET request to the given **url**. You are supposed to try to access AUTOEXEC.BAT, BOOT.INI or WIN.INI
  If **quickcheck** is TRUE, the function returns TRUE if it gets a 200 (OK) answer.
  If **quickcheck** is FALSE, it looks for pattern in the answer; it will returns TRUE if it can find "ECHO", "SET", "export", "mode", "MODE", "doskey", "DOSKEY", "[boot loader]", "[fonts]", "[extensions]", "[mci extensions]", "[files]", "[Mail]", or "[operating systems]". You are supposed to set **quickcheck** if the server answers with clean 404 codes to requests to unknown pages, i.e. if "**www/no404/**port" is not set in the KB.

- **get_cgi_path** (port) returns the list of directories where the CGI might be installed. The list is a string where the items are separated with ":".
  WARNING: this function is not a good idea and may disappear in the future.

- **get_http_banner** (port) returns the HTTP banner that was stored in the KB under **"www/banner/**port_number"**. If the KB item is void, the function connects to the HTTP server, sends a GET request, and stores the result into the KB.

- **get_http_port** (default) reads the KB item **"Services/www"**, verifies that the port is open, that there is an HTTP server behind it, and returns it. Note that the function will fork if there are several web servers on the target machine.
  If the KB item is void, the **default** port is tested.
  If no HTTP port is found, *the script exits*.

- **http_is_dead** (port, retry)
  tries very hard to test if the web server is still alive even if there is a transparent or reverse proxy on the way. It sends a HTTP GET request for a random page (**/NessusTest**<rand>**.html**) and waits for the answer. The optional argument **retry** is the number of times it should wait (one second) and retry to open the socket to the remote service if this failed in the first time (by default, there is no retry).
  It returns TRUE if

  - the connection was refused, or

  - no valid HTTP answer was received, or

  - a 502 (bad gateway) or 503 (service unavailable) was received.

- **http_recv_body** (socket, headers, length)
  reads N bytes from the **socket**. N is defined like this:

  - If the **header** field is not defined, the function first calls **http_recv_headers**; the "Content-Length" field is extracted from the headers.

  - Note that the headers will not be returned, only the HTTP "body".

  - Then, if **length** is set

    - if content_length could be extracted from the headers, N = max(length, content_length)

    - otherwise, N = length

  - else if content_length could be extracted from the headers, N = content_length,

  - else N defaults to 8192 bytes.

- **http_recv** (socket, code)
  reads the HTTP headers and data from the socket and returns all this.
      This function is efficient because it just reads the right number of bytes without waiting for a network timeout. The code argument is optional. If you read the HTTP code (with **recv_line**), you have to put it into this argument[36].

- **http_recv_length** (socket, bodylength)
  reads the HTTP headers, then calls **http_recv_body** with length=bodylength, and returns the concatenated headers and body.

- **locate_cgi** (port, item)
  looks for a given CGI on a web server. It returns its path if it could be found, or NULL otherwise.
  WARNING: the implementation is wrong, so this function may disappear in the future.

- **php_ver_match** (banner, pattern)
  the function returns TRUE if the regex pattern matches a "Server:" ou "X-Powered-by:" line in the banner. A way to use this function is, for example:

  ```
  if (php_ver_match(banner:banner,
      pattern: ".*PHP/((3.*)--(4\.0.*)--(4\.1\.[01].*)) " ))
    security_hole(port);
  ```

- **cgi_dirs** ()
  returns an array containing all the directories that may have CGIs in it (by default /cgi-bin and /scripts). Several scripts try to augment this list (in particular *webmirror.nasl*).

3.3.4 http_keepalive.inc

Nessus 2.0.1 and newer support HTTP keep-alive connections, which avoid to re-open a socket for each request. This saves bandwidth and CPU cycles, especially through SSL/TLS. At this time, only the requests made from within the same plugin can be kept alive, however sharing one socket among multiple plugins could be done in the future. To work properly, this file must be included after **http_func.inc**.

- **http_keepalive_send_recv** (port, req)
  sends the request **req** to the remote web server listening on port **port** and returns the result of the request, or NULL if the connection could not be established. Internally, this function will automatically determine if the remote host supports Keep-Alive connections and will restore the connection if it was cut. **req** is a full HTTP request, as returned by **http_get()**.
  It is not recommended to send potentially destructive attacks on top of a kept-alive connection.

- **is_cgi_installed_ka** (port, item)
  acts the same way as **is_cgi_installed()** but on top of a kept-alive connection.

- **check_win_dir_traversal_ka** (port, url, quickcheck)
acts the same way as **check_win_dir_traversal()** but on top of a kept-alive connection.

3.3.5 misc_func.inc

- **register_service** (port, proto)
"registers" a service. Used values for the proto arguments are: **aos**, **bug-bear**, **DCE/**guid, **dns**, **lpd**, **uucp**, **irc**, **daytime**, **ftp**, **smtp**, **nntp**, **ssh**, **auth**, **finger**, **www**, **mldonkey-telnet**, **nessus**, **QMTP**, **radmin**, **RPC/**name, **portmapper**, **rsh**, **x11**, **xtel**, **xtelw**.
   In practice, this function defines two items in the KB:

  - **Known/tcp/**port = proto

  - **Services/**proto = port

   This may create a list if several servers are known on differents ports.

- **known_service** (port) returns TRUE if the service is known on the port, FALSE otherwise. Note that if the service was "registered" several times, **known_service** may fork. So the right way to use this function is to exit if it returns TRUE. For example:

  ```
  port = get_kb_item("Services/unknown");
  # This was set by find_service.nes but another plugin
  # may have identified the service. So:
  if (known_service(port: port)) exit(0);
  ```

- **get_unknown_banner** (port, dontfetch)
reads **unknown/banner/**port from the KB. If a value is found, it is returned. If no value is found and **dontfetch** is set, the function returns NULL. Otherwise the function connects to the port, tries to read a banner, stores it in the KB and returns it.

- **set_unknown_banner** (port, banner)
sets **unknown/banner/**port to **banner** in the KB.

- **get_service_banner**_line (service, port)
reads **Services/**service from the KB. If no value is found, uses the **port** parameter. It then reads service/**banner/**port from the KB; if it exists, it is returned. If not, the function connects to the port, reads one line and returns it, *but does not store it in the KB.*

Note that this function may fork.

- **get_rpc_port** (program, protocol)
  calls the portmapper and gets the port where the service specified by the parameters is located. **program** is a RPC number and **protocol** may be IPPROTO_TCP or IPPROTO_UDP. If the portmapper could not be reached or the service is down, the function returns **0**.

3.3.6 nfs_func.inc

NFS read and write functions are not defined yet. You can only mount a NFS share and inspect its contents.

- **mount** (soc, share)
  attempts to mount **share** (defined in **NFS/exportlist** in the KB). **soc** is a UDP socket opened to the remote mount daemon (mountd, rpc program#100005). This function returns NULL in case of failure, or a file handle (fid) in case of success.

- **umount** (soc, share)
  unmounts **share** – basically, this tells the remote mount daemon that we will stop using its services. **soc** is a UDP socket opened to the remote mount daemon.

- **readdir** (soc, fid)
  returns the content of the directory pointed by **fid**. **soc** is a UDP socket opened to the remote NFS daemon (nfsd, rpc program #100003). This function returns an array.

- **cwd** (soc, fid, dir)
  changes directories. **soc** is a UDP socket opened to the remote NFS daemon, **fid** is the current working directory and **dir** is the name of the directory we would like to change it. This function returns NULL on failure, or a handle (fid) to the directory we changed to.

3.3.7 smb_nt.inc

The SMB library provides a way to interact with Windows hosts using SMB, either on top of port 139 or on top of port 445. Since Microsoft protocol is barely documented, most if not all of these functions have been coded by packet analysis. Therefore, the name of the functions may vary compared to what you would find in Microsoft-Land.

The functions described here are both low-level and high-level. This a description of the SMB protocol (and DCE/RPC over SMB) is beyond the scope of this manual, we suggest you refer to the books listed in the bibliography if needed. The functions are defined in this guide in the order they are usually used :

Setting up an SMB session

- **smb_session_request** (soc, remote)
  pre-establishes a SMB session with the remote host. **soc** is a socket opened to port 139 or 445 if the remote host supports it. You must open the connect to the port pointed by the KB item **SMB/transport**, which is defined in the plugin *cifs445.nasl*. **remote** is the netbios name of the remote host (as stored in the KB item **SMB/name**, created in the plugin *netbios_name_get.nasl*). If the name is not defined you can try to use *****SMBSERVER** which is recognized by most SMB hosts. If the connection takes place on top of port 445, this function immediately returns as it is unnecessary in this case.

- **smb_neg_prot** (soc)
  negociates the protocol we will use to log into the remote host. This function asks for NTLMv1 authentication if possible, and returns a buffer suitable to be used with **smb_session_setup()**, which contains the authentication protocols the remote host supports. **soc** must be the socket opened to the remote SMB server, and a call to **smb_session_request()** has to be made before this function is called.

- **smb_session_setup** (soc, login, password, domain, prot)
  setups the SMB session to the remote host. It logs as **login** with the password **password**, in the domain **domain** (which can be NULL, in which case the function will log locally). This function returns a buffer suitable to use with the function **session_extract_uid()**, or NULL if the authentication failed. Internally, the function will use either cleartext or NTLMv1 authentication, depending on what the remote host supports and the options set by the user. **prot** is the buffer returned by the function **smb_neg_prot()**. **soc** must be the socket opened to the remote SMB server, and a call to **smb_neg_prot()** must have been made prior to calling this function. **smb_session_setup()** returns a buffer suitable to be used with **session_extract_uid()**.

- **session_extract_uid** (reply)
  extracts the user id from **reply**. It is used each time a new SMB call is made. It returns 0 if **smb_session_setup()** failed.

Connecting and reading from the remote shares

Each SMB host exports shares – virtual directories accessible from accross the network, usually containing files. The list of shares exported by a given host is written in **SMB/shares**, which is written to by *smb_enum_shares.nasl*.

- **smb_tconx** (soc, name, uid, share)
  connects to **share** (i.e.: "IPC$") on top of the socket **soc** connected to the smb host whose name is **name.** The option **uid** comes from the call to **session_extract_uid()**. This function returns a buffer suitable to be used with **tconx_extract_tid()**.

- **tconx_extract_tid** (reply)
  extracts the tree id from **reply**, which is a buffer returned by a call to **smb_tconx()**. It returns 0 if the call to **smb_tconx()** failed.

- **OpenAndX** (socket, uid, tid, file)
  opens **file** on the share pointed by **tid**, and returns a file id (fid) or NULL if the call failed (ie: file does not exist or can not be read).

- **ReadAndX** (socket, uid, tid, count, off)
  reads **count** bytes starting at offset **off** in the file **fid** and returns the content (or NULL if the call failed)

- **smb_get_file_size** (socket, uid, tid, fid)
  returns the size of the file pointed by **fid.**

Accessing the remote registry

- **smbntcreatex** (soc, uid, tid)
  this function creates a connection to the remote \winreg named pipe. It should be rewritten to support a fourth argument (pipename) but it is not the case at this time. **soc** is a socket connected to the remote SMB host, **uid** is our user id (obtained via **smb_session_setup()** and **session_extract_uid()**) and **tid** is pointing to the special share IPC$. This function returns a buffer suitable to be used with **smbntcreatex_extract_pipe()** or NULL if the called failed (ie: there is no \winreg named pipe).

- **smbntcreatex_extract_pipe** (reply)
  extracts the pipe id from the buffer returned by **smbntcreatex()**. It returns 0 if the call failed.

- **pipe_accessible_registry**(soc, uid, tid, pipe)
  what this function does is quite unclear. It should be called before continuing to explore the registry, just after **smbntcreatex()**. **pipe** is the integer returned by **smbntcreatex_extract_pipe()**.

- **registry_access_step_1**(soc, uid, tid, pipe)
  this function should be renamed registry_open_hklm (and will probably be). It opens HIVE_KEY_LOCAL_MACHINE and returns a buffer suitable to use with **registry_get_key()** and **registry_get_key_security()**.

- **registry_get_key** (soc, uid, tid, pipe, key, reply)
  opens the registry key "**key**" (as in "SOFTWARE\Microsoft\Windows NT") and returns a buffer suitable to use with **registry_get_item_dword()**, **registry_get_item_sz()**, or **registry_get_key_security()**. **reply** is the buffer returned by **registry_access_step_1()**. This function returns NULL if the key does not exist or is not accessible.

- **registry_get_item_sz** (soc, uid, tid, pipe, item, reply)
  returns the content of **item** in the currently opened key (designated by **reply**, which is a buffer returned by **registry_get_key()**). It returns a buffer which needs to be decoded with **registry_decode_sz()**. **item** must be a string key value. If **reply** is the reply to a call to **registry_get_key**(key:"SOFTWARE\Microsoft\Windows NT"), **item** could be equal to "CurrentVersion".

- **registry_decode_sz** (data)
  decodes the value returned by **registry_get_item_sz()** and returns a string containing the value, or NULL if the call to **registry_get_item_sz()** failed.

- **registry_get_item_dword** (soc, uid, tid, pipe, item, reply)
  returns the content of **item** in the currently opened key (designated by **reply**, which is a buffer returned by **registry_get_key()**). It returns a buffer which needs to be decoded with **registry_decode_dword()**. **item** must be an integer key value.

- **registry_decode_dword** (data)

decodes the value returned by **registry_get_item_dword()** and returns an integer containing the value, or NULL if the call to **registry_get_item_dword()** failed.

- **registry_get_key_security** (soc, uid, tid, pipe, reply) obtains the ACLs associated to the key opened with **registry_get_key()**. **reply** is the buffer returned by **registry_get_key()**. It returns a security descriptor which contains the ACLs and which has to be parsed manually. The function **registry_key_writeable_by_non_admin()** is a great example of usage for this.

- **registry_key_writeable_by_non_admin** (security_descriptor) decodes the buffer returned by **registry_get_key_security()** and returns TRUE if a user other than the owner of the key or a member of the administrator group can write to the key.

SAM access

- OpenPipeToSamr(soc, uid, tid)
- SamrConnect2(soc, tid, uid, pipe, name)
- _SamrEnumDomains(soc, uid, tid, pipe, samrhdl)
- SamrDom2Sid(soc, tid, uid, pipe, samrhdl, dom)
- SamrOpenDomain(soc, tid, uid, pipe, samrhdl, sid)
- SamrOpenBuiltin(soc, tid, uid, pipe, samrhdl)
- SamrLookupNames(soc, uid, tid, pipe, name, domhdl)
- SamrOpenUser(soc, uid, tid, pipe, samrhdl, rid)
- SamrQueryUserGroups(soc, uid, tid, pipe, usrhdl)
- SamrQueryUserInfo(soc, uid, tid, pipe, usrhdl)
- SamrQueryUserAliases(soc, uid, tid, pipe, usrhdl, sid, rid)

3.3.8 smtp_func.inc

- **smtp_send_socket** (socket, from, to, body) sends a SMTP message on an open socket and returns TRUE if the message for accepted for delivery, or FALSE if some problem occurred.

- **smtp_send_port** (port, from, to, body)
  opens a socket to **port**, sends a SMTP message, and closes the socket. It returns TRUE if the message for accepted for delivery, or FALSE if some problem occurred.

- **smtp_from_header** ()
  returns the default "From" address. If the KB item **SMTP/headers/from** is not set, the default address is "nessus@example.com".

- **smtp_to_header** ()
  returns the default "To" address. If the KB item **SMTP/headers/to** is not set, the default address is "postmaster@[1.2.3.4]" (where 1.2.3.4 is the target host IP).

- **get_smtp_banner** (port)
  reads the KB item **smtp/banner/**port and returns it, or if it is not set, connects to the port, reads the SMTP banner, stores it into the KB and returns it.

- **smtp_recv_banner** (socket)
  reads lines from the socket and returns the first line that does not started with "220-".

3.3.9   telnet.inc

- **get_telnet_banner** (port)
  reads **telnet/banner/**port from the KB and returns it. If no value is found, connects to the port, grabs the telnet banner, stores it into the KB and returns it.

- **set_telnet_banner** (port, banner)
  writes **banner** into the KB item **telnet/banner/**port

3.3.10   uddi.inc

- **create_uddi_xml** (ktype,path,key,name)
  formats a UDDI XML query, whatever this means.

4 Hacking your way inside the interpretor

4.1 How it works

4.1.1 The parser

The lexical analyzer   It is written directly in C because flex cannot generate C reentrant code[37]. That's why it is rather crude. Anyway, I was surprised to see that according to cachegrind, we do not lose much time in it.

The lexer entry point is the "mylex" function in nasl_grammar.y. The parser calls it; you are not supposed to do it. I mention it because that's where you can add "tokens".

The syntactic analyzer   It is written in Bison and you cannot compile it with Yacc, because we use the %pure_parser instruction. This generates a reentrant parser, allowing us to handle "includes" very simply[38]. While reading the source, the parser builds a "syntax tree".

The syntax tree   You can find a description of the "cell type" in nasl_tree.h. The only used data type is the tree_cell structure. Each cell maybe linked to children cells: from 0 (if it is a leaf) to 4 (if I remember correctly, only the "for" instruction uses this).

For example, this code:

```
x = y * 2;
f(arg1: x);
```

will become this tree:

```
NODE_INSTR_L
1: NODE_AFF
    1: NODE_VAR Val= "x"
    2: EXPR_MULT
        1: NODE_VAR Val= "y"
        2: CONST_INT Val=2
2: NODE_INSTR_L
    1: NODE_FUN_CALL Val= "f"
        1: NODE_ARG Val= "arg1"
            1: NODE_VAR Val= "x"
```

4.1.2 The interpretor

> To iterate is human, to recurse is divine.

The entry point is **nasl_exec**. This function takes two arguments (a "lexical context" and a "tree cell") and returns the result another "tree cell", the result of the evaluation of the a "tree cell" in the "context". To perform its job, **nasl_exec** calls itself again and again[39].

4.1.3 Memory management

Memory copy is expensive[40], memory allocation too. So I tried to avoid unnecessary duplications of "cells". That's why I implemented a poor man's garbage collector: each "cell" has a reference count. **ref_cell** increments it, and **deref_cell** decrements it. Once it reaches 0, the cell is freed[41].

To use, do not try to be smart, just follow a couple of simple rules:

- **nasl_exec** never tries to free its input argument.

- **nasl_exec** returns a value that is "referenced" (i.e. ref_count > 0). Once you have finished playing with it, you have to "dereference" it.

- Internal functions should return "referenced" cells.

4.1.4 Internal functions interfaces

Every internal function uses the same interface: it reads a "lexical context" on input and returns a "cell". The interface is described in details in the next paragraph.

The function name and NASL arguments are declared in **nasl_init.c**

4.2 Adding new internal functions

4.2.1 Interface

Every internal function has the same interface:

- it takes one input argument, a "lexical context". The NASL arguments are variables in the context, either "named" or "numbered". The context is chained to the calling context.

- and it returns a "tree cell". The returned cell should be "referenced" once; you shouldn't have to do anything as all the cell allocation functions set "ref_count" to 1.

- If you do not want to return a value, returns **FAKE_CELL**.

- If you want to return a serious error, returns **NULL**.

A simple example:

```
tree_cell*
my_test_function(lex_ctxt* lexic)
{
   fprintf(stderr, "My test function was called\n");
   /* let's look at the context */
   dump_ctxt(lexic);
   /* And return nothing (in NASL) */
   return FAKE_CELL;
}
```

4.2.2 Reading arguments

The arguments are stored as "named" or "numbered" variables in the context. This NASL code:

```
f(1, "TWO", a: 33, z: "three");
```

will create four variables in the context, two "numbered" and two "named":

- 0 -> 1

- 1 -> "TWO"

- a -> 33

- z -> "three"

To read those arguments, you can use one of those functions:

- char* **get_str_var_by_num** (lex_ctxt* lexic, int num)
  reads the variable and converts it to a string if necessary. Do not free the result and do not call the function twice in a row on a non-string variable[42] without copying the result somewhere, as the function returns a pointer to a static buffer in this case.
  If the variable is not initialized or cannot be converted to character, NULL is returned.

- int **get_int_var_by_num**(lex_ctxt* lexic, int num, int default_value)
  reads the variable and converts it to an integer if necessary.
  If the variable is not initialized or cannot be converted, the default value is returned.

- char* **get_str_local_var_by_num**(lex_ctxt* lexic, const char* name)
- int **get_int_local_var_by_num**(lex_ctxt* lexic, int num, int default_value)
- int get_local_var_size_by_name
- int get_var_size_by_num

4.2.3 Returning a value

Returning void is easy: just returns **FAKE_CELL** (which is currently defined as "**(void*)1**", but this might change). To return a value, you have to allocate a cell, reference it once (this is automatically done by all the alloc_* cell functions) and put data into it. Examples:

```
tree_cell     *retc;
char          *p;
/* return 42 */
retc = alloc_typed_cell(CONST_INT);
retc->x.i_val = 42;
return retc;
/* return "abcd" */
retc = alloc_typed_cell(CONST_DATA);
retc->x.size =4;
retc->x.str_val = p = emalloc(5);
strcpy(p, "abcd");
return retc;
```

4.2.4 Adding your function in nasl_init.c

Your function is not yet known to the NASL interpretor. You have to add it into **nasl_init.c**

4.2.5 Cave at

You should be careful not to open security holes with your new C functions. Here are examples of potentially dangerous system calls:

open   as it allows to read protected files if the argument is not properly checked (the Nessus daemon runs as root).

unlink   as it allows to delete protected files.

fork   as a malicious user may implement a fork bomb. More, it breaks the current model, where Nessus controls the son processes.

kill   as you might kill system processes if the arguments is not properly checked.

4.3 Adding new features to the grammar

4.3.1 caveat

First, if you do not know what "yacc" or "bison" do, how they do it and why, if you ignore what a lexical analyzer is, a regular expression or a LALR context-free grammar, a finite state machine or a stack automata, just *don't* touch the grammar.

This is important: the current grammar is clean. The precedence of every operator is clearly defined; the grammar has only one shift/reduce conflict, the classical "dangling else" ambiguity[43]. That's why there is an "**%expect 1**" directive. If you modify the grammar and add ambiguities, you are *not* supposed to solve them by increasing the expected number of conflicts. Do whatever is necessary (and clean) to remove them.

One last time: if you have never studied language theory and theoretical computer science, stop reading here!

4.3.2 Adding a new operator in the grammar

You will have to modify the lexical analyzer to recognize the token.

4.3.3 Adding a new type to the grammar

4.4 Checking the result

References

1. [RFC 821]SMTP protocol...

2. [RFC 854 / STD 8]Telnet protocol...

3. [RFC 1945]Hypertext Transfer Protocol – HTTP/1.0. T. Berners-Lee, R. Fielding, H. Frystyk. May 1996.

4. [RFC2246]The TLS Protocol Version 1.0. T. Dierks, C. Allen. January 1999.

5. [RFC2616]Hypertext Transfer Protocol – HTTP/1.1. R. Fielding, J. Gettys, J. Mogul, H. Frystyk, L. Masinter, P. Leach, T. Berners-Lee. June 1999.

6. [SSL v3]SSL 3.0 SPECIFICATION http://wp.netscape.com/eng/ssl3/

7. [SSL v3 (03/96)]http://wp.netscape.com/eng/ssl3/ The SSL Protocol Version 3.0 - Internet Draft - March 1996 (Expires 9/96) - Alan O. Freier, Netscape Communications; Philip Karlton, Netscape Communications, Paul C. Kocher, Independent Consultant.

8. [SSL v3 (11/96)]http://wp.netscape.com/eng/ssl3/draft302.txt The SSL Protocol Version 3.0 - November 18, 1996 - Alan O. Freier, Netscape Communications; Philip Karlton, Netscape Communications, Paul C. Kocher, Independent Consultant.

9. [DCE/RPC]DCE/RPC over SMB - Luke Kenneth Casson Leighton - Macmillan Technical Publishing - ISBN 1-57870-150-3.

Endnotes

1. They used to work in K&R C.

2. This is an heritage from NASL1, it would have been too complex to break it. The **string** function interprets escape sequences in "impure" strings and returns a "pure" string; it just copy "pure" strings without changing them. Note that **display** calls **string** before printing its argument on the standard output.

3. Much less than in C, but I don't think we need the octal representation, wide chars, etc. Note that the parser did not accept \0 in older NASL2 versions; and \x00 truncated the string before the nul character. This has been fixed.

    So... \n is the newline character, \t the horizontal tabulation, \v the vertical tabulation, \r line feed, \f form feed, \' the single quote, \" the double quote (just in case), and \x42 is "B", because its ASCII code is 0x42 (66 in hex).

4. Elements are numbered from 0, just like in C. Negative indexes are not supported (yet) and big values are not recommended as they would eat

memory. If you want such indexes, you should convert them into strings, so that they get hashed. I admit that this is neither clean nor efficient.

5. Like the Perl hashes. Hashes have a big inconvenient: they destroy the order of the data they store.

6. i.e. a "string" or an "integer", or even "null".

7. Yes, no more 16 bit systems! Who wants to port NASL2 to MS/DOS?

8. * * is Fortran syntax. Maybe some of you will regret the Basic syntax, but ^ is already used by the exclusive-or (xor) operator (C syntax).

9. In fact, there is a pathological case where both operator returns **NULL**: when the pattern could not be compiled. You will get an error when the pattern is parsed, then every time you try to execute the line.

10. The sign bit, if any, is propagated.

11. The sign bit is pushed to the right and replaced with zero.

12. Currently, it exits from the current function or the script. But you should not rely upon this behavior.

13. WARNING! This operator was introduced in Nessus 2.1.x; Nessus 2.0.x. cannot parse the script.

14. Unnamed arguments were introduced in NASL2.1.

15. By the way, there is only *one* plugin that really tries to destroy data. This is *http_methods.nasl*

16. Using an integer is definitely not a good idea, as new values may be inserted before the one you used. Actually, those values are not constants but initialized variables; changing their values in your script is a good way to shoot you in the foot.

17. If you want to use a full sentence like "this plugin was written by Foo Bar" which would be translated in French, "ce plugin a été écrit par Foo Bar".

18. Which should you use? Well, there is only one rule: two scripts must have two different IDs. Ff your script is integrated into the Nessus distribution, the maintainer will choose an unaffected number.

19. **find_service.nes** identifies TCP services and has no equivalent for UDP. So do not expect something like "Services/DNS" to returns a value different from 53.

20. Usually, it is set to "$Revision" which is updated by CVS.

21. In NASL, there is no way you can open connections to some specific host. This way, a NASL script cannot be trojaned.

22. 22 (SSH), 25 (SMTP), 53 (DNS), 110 (POP3), 113 (IDENT), 443 (HTTPS), 993 (IMAPS), 8080 (alt HTTP), 65534.

23. For example,

```
ereg_replace(string:'ZABCABD',pattern:'A([ABC]+)D',replace:'92921')
```

    will return **'ZBCAB'**.

24. For example,

```
v = eregmatch(string:'XYZ IADAOZOOH',pattern:'([AEIOU]+).*(Z.*H)');
```

    will set **v[0]='I'ADA OZOOH' v[1]='IA'**
    and **v[2]='ZOOH'**.

25. In NASL1, only the first character of the string was kept.

26. That's the only way to enter a null character into a string in older version of NASL2. Remember this if you want to be portable on old Nessus versions.

27. Old versions of Nessus 1.3 were badly designed and **string** stopped processing its arguments at the first undefined value. Other functions may suffer from this bug; do not hesitate to tell.

28. Which is not necessarily a good idea. Maybe we should expand them; the problem is hash elements are not ordered.

29. Note that its size is unlimited

30. Old versions of Nessus 1.3 were badly designed and **string** stopped processing its arguments at the first undefined value. Other functions may suffer from this bug; do not hesitate to tell.

31. Which is not necessarily a good idea. Maybe we should expand them; the problem is hash elements are not ordered.

32. The keep argument appeared in Nessus 2.0.2; older versions of the NASL library do not recognize it.

33. Most of the time, the "internal size" of the data, which might be 0 even if it is not true!

34. The command line interpretor trusts the script if the option –X is given. And the Nessus server trusts any script if **nasl_no_signature_check** is set to **yes** in **nessusd.conf**

35. This function appeared in Nessus 2.1.2. Previous version can emulte it with something like: x = pread(cmd: '/bin/cat', argv: '/etc/passwd');

36. In fact, **http_recv** only needs to know that the code was read, because **http_recv_header** may not work in this case. **http_recv** uses its own loop to read the remaining headers before the body.

37. It is able to generate reeentrant C++ code but we do not want to link Nessus with C++.

38. OK, a good preprocessor could do it. But the fact that include("file.inc"); is a simple instruction allows some interesting things, e.g.

    ```
    if (! defined_func("gizmo") include("gizmo_compat.inc");.
    ```

39. Although there are much quicker ways to interpret a language, walking along the syntax tree is simple. We know that we could run 10 times faster or even more by implementing a code generator and a Virtual Machine, but we do not need it yet. Maybe there will be a NASL3.

40. If you do not believe me, run a slow plugin like webmirror.nasl with cachegrind and look at the result.

41. And if it becomes negative, the interpretor aborts because this is a serious bug! In fact, the reference count becomes negative when the cell is "referenced" too many times (integer roll over).

42. i.e. integer or array.

43. In the construction "if (T1) if (T2) I1; else I2;" the "else" can be attached to the first or the second "if". All modern parsers attach it the second (= nearest) "if".

Utilizing Domain Credentials to Enhance Nessus Scans

Contributed by Ty Gast

Topics in this Appendix:

- **Account Creation and Configuration**

- **Manual Modifications**

- **Nessus Scan Configuration**

Overview

Nessus is often used to perform network-based assessments of Windows® domain computer systems. However, giving Nessus a little insider information can result in more thorough and accurate scans, and can allow "local" registry security checks to be conducted using a "remote" network scan. Specifically, Nessus can use a pre-configured domain username and password to access system registry settings that would not be accessible without the required credentials.

By default, remote registry access is typically only accessible to domain administrators. It is possible to create an account on a domain, give it domain administrator privileges, and configure Nessus to use that account when performing scans. However, this presents problems for both domain security and the scan results. It is undesirable to have more administrator accounts than absolutely necessary, so creating additional admin accounts just for the purpose of running scans may be unacceptable. During times when no scans are being conducted, individuals may attempt to use the domain admin account for purposes other than what was intended. While it is possible to disable accounts when not in use and enable them only when running scans, this can become burdensome from a management perspective.

Another shortcoming to using an account with full domain admin credentials is that scan results may not accurately reflect the true security posture of the target environment. For example, it may be difficult to detect improperly configured file shares on various domain servers because the Nessus scan using full domain admin privileges will have much more access than what a normal account would have. Domain admin accounts will typically be able to access most (if not all) of the shares in a domain, and this will be reflected in the Nessus results.

One approach to solving these problems is to create a domain account that has minimal domain privileges while still having enough access for Nessus to be able to perform remote registry checks. This paper explains the steps required to create an account that has the minimal amount of privileges while still providing Nessus with the access it needs to perform its scanning. It also covers the steps to configure Nessus to use the account information.

Account Creation and Configuration

All of the following steps need to be performed using a domain administrator account. First, a new global group called "Nessus Test Accounts" should be created on the domain. Nessus will be able to use any account members of this group for remote registry access. Next, a new domain account should be created called "nessustest". This account should not be a part of any other domain group other than the newly created "Nessus Test Accounts" group.

For Windows NT 4.0 systems and later, remote access to the registry is regulated by the permission on a single key within the registry. In other words, the remote access permissions mirror those that are present on the key. The key to be modified is:

```
HKEY_LOCAL_MACHINE\SYSTEM\CurrentControlSet\Control\SecurePipeServers\winreg
```

All Windows systems in the domain must have a change made to the permission of this local registry key to allow the newly created Nessus accounts to have remote access. For Windows NT 4.0 systems, this key may not exist and will need to be created before making the necessary permission changes. This is done as follows:

1. Use the registry editor and go to the key **HKEY_LOCAL_ MACHINE\SYSTEM\CurrentControlSet\Control**.

2. On the **Edit** menu click **Add Key** and enter: **SecurePipeServers** for the key name and **REG_SZ** for the class.

3. Go into the new key **SecurePipeServers**.

4. On the **Edit** menu click **Add Key** and enter: **winreg** for the key name and **REG_SZ** for the class.

5. Go into the new key **winreg**.

6. On the **Edit** menu click **Add Value** and enter: **Description** for the value name and **REG_SZ** for the data type.

7. Modify the new **Description** string value to be **Registry Server**.

If the key already exists these steps will not be necessary. Once the key is in place, the next step is to modify the permissions of the key. These modifications can be accomplished in many different ways.

Manual Modifications

Typically the most time consuming method would be to use the **regedt32** application to manually change the permissions on the key for every Windows machine in the domain.

1. Using **regedt32** connect to the computer system (if not running locally), navigate to the key, and select the **Permissions** option from the **Security** menu.

2. In the dialogue box click **Add...**, select the domain group **Nessus Test Accounts** from the list, and click **Add** followed by **OK**.

3. Click on **Advanced...**, highlight the newly created entry, and click on **View/Edit...**

4. In the **Apply onto:** drop down box select **This key only**, click **OK**, then click **OK** again.

The resulting new entry will appear not to have any permissions whatsoever. The checkboxes beside **Read** and **Full Control** will be unchecked. However, clicking on **Advanced...** will show that the group now has **Read** permission for **This key only**, which will equate to the **Nessus Test Accounts** group having remote read permission for accessing the registry. The actual dialogue box will be similar to the following screenshot (Figure B.1):

Figure B.1 Command Line Modifications

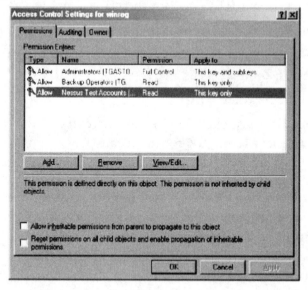

Another more efficient means to accomplish the same task would be to use a command line tool to script the changes remotely. One such tool is SetACL, available from http://setacl.sourceforge.net/. This provides a command line interface to changing many permissions settings, not just for the registry but for files and directories as well. SetACL can be used to change the registry permission settings in the following manner:

```
setacl -on "MACHINE\SYSTEM\CurrentControlSet\Control\SecurePipeServers\winreg" -
ot reg -actn ace -ace "n:DOMAIN\GROUPNAME;p:read;m:grant;w:dacl;i:np"
```

When performing this remotely, the *machine name* can precede the key designation, as shown in the following screen shot (Figure B.2):

Figure B.2 Modifications Using User Logon Scripts

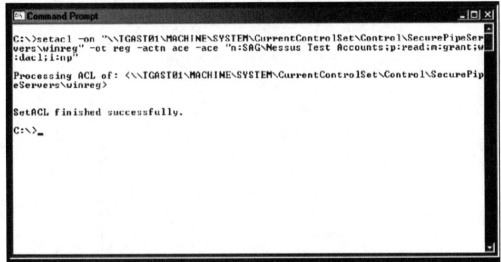

Another possible method would be to use a Windows domain logon script to automatically make the necessary changes when someone logs into the domain. It would be necessary to write a script that can handle all of the potential issues, such as different operating systems, missing keys and mapping drives to have access to the necessary tools. That effort is outside the scope of this document and is left to the reader to accomplish.

Once all of the systems on the domain have had the necessary registry permissions put in place, a Nessus scan can use the created accounts to gain access during a network scan. Configuring Nessus to use the account credentials is relatively simple, either by using the graphical interface or modifying the ".nessusrc" file directly.

Nessus Scan Configuration

Setting up the Nessus client to use domain credentials via the graphical interface is very straightforward and can be applied to any existing scan configuration. Once all the other settings for the scan are entered, navigate to the "Prefs" tab. Scrolling down will show the "Login configurations" section where username/password pairs are entered for various services, as shown here (Figure B.3):

Figure B.3 "Login configurations" Section

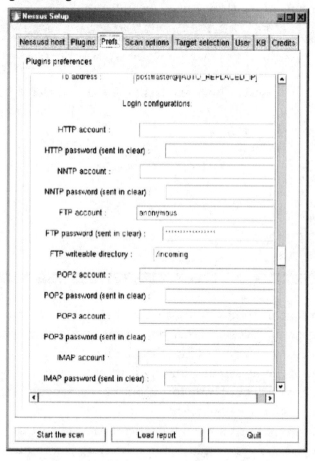

Scroll down to locate where the SMB username and password are listed. This is the location where the domain credentials for the "nessustest" account will be entered, as shown here (Figure B.4):

Figure B.4 "nessustest" Account will be Entered

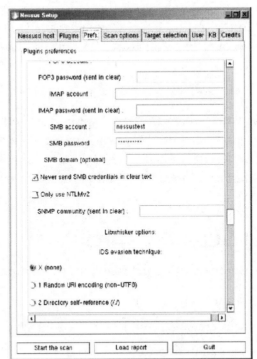

Once the scan starts, all security checks that require remote access to the registry will be able to use those credentials.

In additional to using the GUI, the Nessus configuration file ".nessusrc" can also be manually modified to use domain credentials. Using a text editor, navigate down to the preferences section, which is framed by the lines:

```
begin(PLUGINS_PREFS)
.
   {preference settings here}.
.
end(PLUGIN_PREFS)
```

This section of the configuration file holds all the individual settings for the various plugin preferences, including any username/password settings. Within this preferences section find the entries for the SMB account information, which includes the following two lines:

```
Login configurations[entry]:SMB account : =
Login configurations[password]:SMB password : =
```

If these lines do not exist they can be added manually. Appending the respective username and password information at the end of these lines will make the information available to the plugins. The following example lines show the setup using the "nessustest" account (with a password of "changem3") created previously.

```
Login configurations[entry]:SMB account : = nessustest
Login configurations[password]:SMB password : = changem3
```

Note that the password information is stored in plain text, which may pose a security issue in some environments. However, given the limitations that have been placed on the "nessustest" account, the exposure is much more limited than if an actual domain administrator account and password were used in the configuration file for the testing.

Comparing Scan Results

Three different scans were run using the following configurations:

- **Scan 1** No domain credentials used
- **Scan 2** Domain credentials with registry read rights
- **Scan 3** Domain administrator credentials

The differences in scan accuracy between the three scans are easily seen in the results output.

Comparing Scan 1 with Scan 2

Scan 2 was able to perform many more localized checks using the domain credentials provided. These additional checks included registry-related findings, some examples of which included:

- Determining which Service Pack was installed on the target
- Permission settings and values for critical registry keys
- Vulnerabilities related to Internet Explorer
- Services running on the target
- A list of shares available

Obviously the additional access allowed Nessus to gain a better picture of the security implemented on the target system.

Comparing Scan 2 with Scan 3

All of the potential vulnerabilities and findings discovered by Scan 2 were also discovered during Scan 3. However, Scan 3 had some results that were misleading as to the true security condition of the target system. Specifically, Scan 3 results indicated that all file shares on the target were accessible. This is misleading in that using a domain administrator account gave Nessus the level access that would allow any share to be accessed. The credentials used in Scan 2 would only identify those shares that were truly open to remote access from the network.

Conclusion

The comparisons show a marked improvement in scanning results when using the special created account with remote registry access, even over those scans run under the domain administrator privileges. Conducting internal Nessus scans across corporate networks may not provide the truest assessment of security unless domain credentials are used. Creating an account with the necessary access, while not providing the complete and total access that domain admin privileges provide, increases the accuracy of testing while minimizing the impact to local domain security.

One last consideration for choosing to create the special account instead of using domain administrator credentials has to deal with the potential for some plugins to damage target systems. Specifically, it could prove disastrous if a Nessus plugin that has not been thoroughly tested were given full domain admin privileges. The potential for data to be corrupted or deleted exists, and putting complete trust in plugins to appropriately handle full domain admin privileges may be asking for trouble. In the interest of obtaining the most complete security picture for an environment, using the specially created account bridges the gap between too much access and enough to get a clearer view of the security situation.

Index

GNU GENERAL PUBLIC LICENSE

Version 2, June 1991

Copyright (C) 1989, 1991 Free Software Foundation, Inc.

59 Temple Place - Suite 330, Boston, MA 02111-1307, USA

Everyone is permitted to copy and distribute verbatim copies
of this license document, but changing it is not allowed.

Preamble

The licenses for most software are designed to take away your freedom to share and change it. By contrast, the GNU General Public License is intended to guarantee your freedom to share and change free software—to make sure the software is free for all its users. This General Public License applies to most of the Free Software Foundation's software and to any other program whose authors commit to using it. (Some other Free Software Foundation software is covered by the GNU Library General Public License instead.) You can apply it to your programs, too.

When we speak of free software, we are referring to freedom, not price. Our General Public Licenses are designed to make sure that you have the freedom to distribute copies of free software (and charge for this service if you wish), that you receive source code or can get it if you want it, that you can change the software or use pieces of it in new free programs; and that you know you can do these things.

To protect your rights, we need to make restrictions that forbid anyone to deny you these rights or to ask you to surrender the rights. These restrictions translate to certain responsibilities for you if you distribute copies of the software, or if you modify it.

For example, if you distribute copies of such a program, whether gratis or for a fee, you must give the recipients all the rights that you have. You must make sure that they, too, receive or can get the source code. And you must show them these terms so they know their rights.

We protect your rights with two steps: (1) copyright the software, and (2) offer you this license which gives you legal permission to copy, distribute and/or modify the software.

Also, for each author's protection and ours, we want to make certain that everyone understands that there is no warranty for this free software. If the software is modified by someone else and passed on, we want its recipients to know that what they have is not the original, so that any problems introduced by others will not reflect on the original authors' reputations.

Finally, any free program is threatened constantly by software patents. We wish to avoid the danger that redistributors of a free program will individually obtain patent licenses, in effect making the program proprietary. To prevent this, we have made it clear that any patent must be licensed for everyone's free use or not licensed at all.

The precise terms and conditions for copying, distribution and modification follow.

TERMS AND CONDITIONS FOR COPYING, DISTRIBUTION AND MODIFICATION

0. This License applies to any program or other work which contains a notice placed by the copyright holder saying it may be distributed under the terms of this General Public License. The "Program", below, refers to any such program or work, and a "work based on the Program" means either the Program or any derivative work under copyright law: that is to say, a work containing the Program or a portion of it, either verbatim or with modifications and/or translated into another language. (Hereinafter, translation is included without limitation in the term "modification".) Each licensee is addressed as "you".

Activities other than copying, distribution and modification are not covered by this License; they are outside its scope. The act of running the Program is not restricted, and the output from the Program is covered only if its contents constitute a work based on the Program (independent of having been made by running the Program). Whether that is true depends on what the Program does.

1. You may copy and distribute verbatim copies of the Program's source code as you receive it, in any medium, provided that you conspicuously and appropriately publish on each copy an appropriate copyright notice and disclaimer of warranty; keep intact all the notices that refer to this License and to the absence of any warranty; and give any other recipients of the Program a copy of this License along with the Program.

You may charge a fee for the physical act of transferring a copy, and you may at your option offer warranty protection in exchange for a fee.

2. You may modify your copy or copies of the Program or any portion of it, thus forming a work based on the Program, and copy and distribute such modifications or work under the terms of Section 1 above, provided that you also meet all of these conditions:

a) You must cause the modified files to carry prominent notices stating that you changed the files and the date of any change.

b) You must cause any work that you distribute or publish, that in whole or in part contains or is derived from the Program or any part thereof, to be licensed as a whole at no charge to all third parties under the terms of this License.

c) If the modified program normally reads commands interactively when run, you must cause it, when started running for such interactive use in the most ordinary way, to print or display an announcement including an appropriate copyright notice and a notice that there is no warranty (or else, saying that you provide a warranty) and that users may redistribute the program under these conditions, and telling the user how to view a copy of this License. (Exception: if the Program itself is interactive but does not normally print such an announcement, your work based on the Program is not required to print an announcement.)

These requirements apply to the modified work as a whole. If identifiable sections of that work are not derived from the Program, and can be reasonably considered independent and separate works in themselves, then this License, and its terms, do not apply to those sections when you distribute them as separate works. But when you distribute the same sections as part of a whole which is a work based on the Program, the distribution of the whole must be on the terms of this License, whose permissions for other licensees extend to the entire whole, and thus to each and every part regardless of who wrote it.

Thus, it is not the intent of this section to claim rights or contest your rights to work written entirely by you; rather, the intent is to exercise the right to control the distribution of derivative or collective works based on the Program.

In addition, mere aggregation of another work not based on the Program with the Program (or with a work based on the Program) on a volume of a storage or distribution medium does not bring the other work under the scope of this License.

3. You may copy and distribute the Program (or a work based on it, under Section 2) in object code or executable form under the terms of Sections 1 and 2 above provided that you also do one of the following:

a) Accompany it with the complete corresponding machine-readable source code, which must be distributed under the terms of Sections 1 and 2 above on a medium customarily used for software interchange; or,

b) Accompany it with a written offer, valid for at least three years, to give any third party, for a charge no more than your cost of physically performing source distribution, a complete machine-readable copy of the corresponding source code, to be distributed under the terms of Sections 1 and 2 above on a medium customarily used for software interchange; or,

c) Accompany it with the information you received as to the offer to distribute corresponding source code. (This alternative is allowed only for noncommercial distribution and only if you received the program in object code or executable form with such an offer, in accord with Subsection b above.)

The source code for a work means the preferred form of the work for making modifications to it. For an executable work, complete source code means all the source code for all modules it contains, plus any associated interface definition files, plus the scripts used to control compilation and installation of the executable. However, as a special exception, the source code distributed need not include anything that is normally distributed (in either source or binary form) with the major components (compiler, kernel, and so on) of the operating system on which the executable runs, unless that component itself accompanies the executable.

If distribution of executable or object code is made by offering access to copy from a designated place, then offering equivalent access to copy the source code from the same place counts as distribution of the source code, even though third parties are not compelled to copy the source along with the object code.

4. You may not copy, modify, sublicense, or distribute the Program except as expressly provided under this License. Any attempt otherwise to copy, modify, sublicense or distribute the Program is void, and will automatically terminate your rights under this License. However, parties who have received copies, or rights, from you under this License will not have their licenses terminated so long as such parties remain in full compliance.

5. You are not required to accept this License, since you have not signed it. However, nothing else grants you permission to modify or distribute the Program or its derivative works. These actions are prohibited by law if you do not accept this License. Therefore, by modifying or distributing the Program (or any work based on the Program), you indicate your acceptance of this License to do so, and all its terms and conditions for copying, distributing or modifying the Program or works based on it.

6. Each time you redistribute the Program (or any work based on the Program), the recipient automatically receives a license from the original licensor to copy, distribute or modify the Program subject to these terms and conditions. You may not impose any further restrictions on the recipients' exercise of the rights granted herein. You are not responsible for enforcing compliance by third parties to this License.

7. If, as a consequence of a court judgment or allegation of patent infringement or for any other reason (not limited to patent issues), conditions are imposed on you (whether by court order, agreement or otherwise) that contradict the conditions of this License, they do not excuse you from the conditions of this License. If you cannot distribute so as to satisfy simultaneously your obligations under this License and any other pertinent obligations, then as a consequence you may not distribute the Program at all. For example, if a patent license would not permit royalty-free redistribution of the Program by all those who receive copies directly or indirectly through you, then the only way you could satisfy both it and this License would be to refrain entirely from distribution of the Program.

If any portion of this section is held invalid or unenforceable under any particular circumstance, the balance of the section is intended to apply and the section as a whole is intended to apply in other circumstances.

It is not the purpose of this section to induce you to infringe any patents or other property right claims or to contest validity of any such claims; this section has the sole purpose of protecting the integrity of the free software distribution system, which is implemented by public license practices. Many people have made generous contributions to the wide range of software distributed through that system in reliance on consistent application of that system; it is up to the author/donor to decide if he or she is willing to distribute software through any other system and a licensee cannot impose that choice.

This section is intended to make thoroughly clear what is believed to be a consequence of the rest of this License.

8. If the distribution and/or use of the Program is restricted in certain countries either by patents or by copyrighted interfaces, the original copyright holder who places the Program under this License may add an explicit geographical distribution limitation excluding those countries, so that distribution is permitted only in or among countries not thus excluded. In such case, this License incorporates the limitation as if written in the body of this License.

9. The Free Software Foundation may publish revised and/or new versions of the General Public License from time to time. Such new versions will be similar in spirit to the present version, but may differ in detail to address new problems or concerns.

Each version is given a distinguishing version number. If the Program specifies a version number of this License which applies to it and "any later version", you have the option of following the terms and conditions either of that version or of any later version published by the Free Software Foundation. If the Program does not specify a version number of this License, you may choose any version ever published by the Free Software Foundation.

10. If you wish to incorporate parts of the Program into other free programs whose distribution conditions are different, write to the author to ask for permission. For software which is copyrighted by the Free Software Foundation, write to the Free Software Foundation; we sometimes make exceptions for this. Our decision will be guided by the two goals of preserving the free status of all derivatives of our free software and of promoting the sharing and reuse of software generally.

NO WARRANTY

11. BECAUSE THE PROGRAM IS LICENSED FREE OF CHARGE, THERE IS NO WARRANTY FOR THE PROGRAM, TO THE EXTENT PERMITTED BY APPLICABLE LAW. EXCEPT WHEN OTHERWISE STATED IN WRITING THE COPYRIGHT HOLDERS AND/OR OTHER PARTIES PROVIDE THE PROGRAM "AS IS" WITHOUT WARRANTY OF ANY KIND, EITHER EXPRESSED OR IMPLIED, INCLUDING, BUT NOT LIMITED TO, THE IMPLIED WARRANTIES OF MERCHANTABILITY AND FITNESS FOR A PARTICULAR PURPOSE. THE ENTIRE RISK AS TO THE QUALITY AND PERFORMANCE OF THE PROGRAM IS WITH YOU. SHOULD THE PROGRAM PROVE DEFECTIVE, YOU ASSUME THE COST OF ALL NECESSARY SERVICING, REPAIR OR CORRECTION.

12. IN NO EVENT UNLESS REQUIRED BY APPLICABLE LAW OR AGREED TO IN WRITING WILL ANY COPYRIGHT HOLDER, OR ANY OTHER PARTY WHO MAY MODIFY AND/OR REDISTRIBUTE THE PROGRAM AS PERMITTED ABOVE, BE LIABLE TO YOU FOR DAMAGES, INCLUDING ANY GENERAL, SPECIAL, INCIDENTAL OR CONSEQUENTIAL DAMAGES ARISING OUT OF THE USE OR INABILITY TO USE THE PROGRAM (INCLUDING BUT NOT LIMITED TO LOSS OF DATA OR DATA BEING RENDERED INACCURATE OR LOSSES SUSTAINED BY YOU OR THIRD PARTIES OR A FAILURE OF THE PROGRAM TO OPERATE WITH ANY OTHER PROGRAMS), EVEN IF SUCH HOLDER OR OTHER PARTY HAS BEEN ADVISED OF THE POSSIBILITY OF SUCH DAMAGES.

END OF TERMS AND CONDITIONS

How to Apply These Terms to Your New Programs

If you develop a new program, and you want it to be of the greatest possible use to the public, the best way to achieve this is to make it free software which everyone can redistribute and change under these terms.

To do so, attach the following notices to the program. It is safest to attach them to the start of each source file to most effectively convey the exclusion of warranty; and each file should have at least the "copyright" line and a pointer to where the full notice is found.

one line to give the program's name and an idea of what it does.

Copyright (C) *yyyy name of author*

This program is free software; you can redistribute it and/or
modify it under the terms of the GNU General Public License
as published by the Free Software Foundation; either version 2
of the License, or (at your option) any later version.

This program is distributed in the hope that it will be useful,
but WITHOUT ANY WARRANTY; without even the implied warranty of
MERCHANTABILITY or FITNESS FOR A PARTICULAR PURPOSE. See the
GNU General Public License for more details.

You should have received a copy of the GNU General Public License
along with this program; if not, write to the Free Software
Foundation, Inc., 59 Temple Place - Suite 330, Boston, MA 02111-1307, USA.

Also add information on how to contact you by electronic and paper mail.

If the program is interactive, make it output a short notice like this when it starts in an interactive mode:

Gnomovision version 69, Copyright (C) *year name of author*

Gnomovision comes with ABSOLUTELY NO WARRANTY; for details

type `show w'. This is free software, and you are welcome

to redistribute it under certain conditions; type `show c'

for details.

The hypothetical commands 'show w' and 'show c' should show the appropriate parts of the General Public License. Of course, the commands you use may be called something other than 'show w' and 'show c'; they could even be mouse-clicks or menu items—whatever suits your program.

You should also get your employer (if you work as a programmer) or your school, if any, to sign a "copyright disclaimer" for the program, if necessary. Here is a sample; alter the names:

Yoyodyne, Inc., hereby disclaims all copyright

interest in the program `Gnomovision'

(which makes passes at compilers) written

by James Hacker.

signature of Ty Coon, 1 April 1989

Ty Coon, President of Vice

This General Public License does not permit incorporating your program into proprietary programs. If your program is a subroutine library, you may consider it more useful to permit linking proprietary applications with the library. If this is what you want to do, use the GNU Library General Public License instead of this License.

SYNGRESS PUBLISHING LICENSE AGREEMENT

THIS PRODUCT (THE "PRODUCT") CONTAINS PROPRIETARY SOFTWARE, DATA AND INFORMATION (INCLUDING DOCUMENTATION) OWNED BY SYNGRESS PUBLISHING, INC. ("SYNGRESS") AND ITS LICENSORS. YOUR RIGHT TO USE THE PRODUCT IS GOVERNED BY THE TERMS AND CONDITIONS OF THIS AGREEMENT.

LICENSE: Throughout this License Agreement, "you" shall mean either the individual or the entity whose agent opens this package. You are granted a limited, non-exclusive and non-transferable license to use the Product subject to the following terms:

(i) If you have licensed a single user version of the Product, the Product may only be used on a single computer (i.e., a single CPU). If you licensed and paid the fee applicable to a local area network or wide area network version of the Product, you are subject to the terms of the following subparagraph (ii).

(ii) If you have licensed a local area network version, you may use the Product on unlimited workstations located in one single building selected by you that is served by such local area network. If you have licensed a wide area network version, you may use the Product on unlimited workstations located in multiple buildings on the same site selected by you that is served by such wide area network; provided, however, that any building will not be considered located in the same site if it is more than five (5) miles away from any building included in such site. In addition, you may only use a local area or wide area network version of the Product on one single server. If you wish to use the Product on more than one server, you must obtain written authorization from Syngress and pay additional fees.

(iii) You may make one copy of the Product for back-up purposes only and you must maintain an accurate record as to the location of the back-up at all times.

PROPRIETARY RIGHTS; RESTRICTIONS ON USE AND TRANSFER: All rights (including patent and copyright) in and to the Product are owned by Syngress and its licensors. You are the owner of the enclosed disc on which the Product is recorded. You may not use, copy, decompile, disassemble, reverse engineer, modify, reproduce, create derivative works, transmit, distribute, sublicense, store in a database or retrieval system of any kind, rent or transfer the Product, or any portion thereof, in any form or by any means (including electronically or otherwise) except as expressly provided for in this License Agreement. You must reproduce the copyright notices, trademark notices, legends and logos of Syngress and its licensors that appear on the Product on the back-up copy of the Product which you are permitted to make hereunder. All rights in the Product not expressly granted herein are reserved by Syngress and its licensors.

TERM: This License Agreement is effective until terminated. It will terminate if you fail to comply with any term or condition of this License Agreement. Upon termination, you are obligated to return to Syngress the Product together with all copies thereof and to purge and destroy all copies of the Product included in any and all systems, servers and facilities.

DISCLAIMER OF WARRANTY: THE PRODUCT AND THE BACK-UP COPY OF THE PRODUCT ARE LICENSED "AS IS". SYNGRESS, ITS LICENSORS AND THE AUTHORS MAKE NO WARRANTIES, EXPRESS OR IMPLIED, AS TO RESULTS TO BE OBTAINED BY ANY PERSON OR ENTITY FROM USE OF THE PRODUCT AND/OR ANY INFORMATION OR DATA INCLUDED THEREIN. SYNGRESS, ITS LICENSORS AND THE AUTHORS MAKE NO EXPRESS OR IMPLIED WARRANTIES OF MERCHANTABILITY OR FITNESS FOR A PARTICULAR PURPOSE OR USE WITH RESPECT TO THE PRODUCT AND/OR ANY INFORMATION OR DATA INCLUDED THEREIN. IN ADDITION, SYNGRESS, ITS LICENSORS AND THE AUTHORS MAKE NO WARRANTY REGARDING THE ACCURACY, ADEQUACY OR COMPLETENESS OF THE PRODUCT AND/OR ANY INFORMATION OR DATA INCLUDED THEREIN. NEITHER SYNGRESS, ANY OF ITS LICENSORS, NOR THE AUTHORS WARRANT THAT THE FUNCTIONS CONTAINED IN THE PRODUCT WILL MEET YOUR REQUIREMENTS OR THAT THE OPERATION OF THE PRODUCT WILL BE UNINTERRUPTED OR ERROR FREE. YOU ASSUME THE ENTIRE RISK WITH RESPECT TO THE QUALITY AND PERFORMANCE OF THE PRODUCT.

LIMITED WARRANTY FOR DISC: To the original licensee only, Syngress warrants that the enclosed disc on which the Product is recorded is free from defects in materials and workmanship under normal use and service for a period of ninety (90) days from the date of purchase. In the event of a defect in the disc covered by the foregoing warranty, Syngress will replace the disc.

LIMITATION OF LIABILITY: NEITHER SYNGRESS, ITS LICENSORS NOR THE AUTHORS SHALL BE LIABLE FOR ANY INDIRECT, INCIDENTAL, SPECIAL, PUNITIVE, CONSEQUENTIAL OR SIMILAR DAMAGES, SUCH AS BUT NOT LIMITED TO, LOSS OF ANTICIPATED PROFITS OR BENEFITS, RESULTING FROM THE USE OR INABILITY TO USE THE PRODUCT EVEN IF ANY OF THEM HAS BEEN ADVISED OF THE POSSIBILITY OF SUCH DAMAGES. THIS LIMITATION OF LIABILITY SHALL APPLY TO ANY CLAIM OR CAUSE WHATSOEVER WHETHER SUCH CLAIM OR CAUSE ARISES IN CONTRACT, TORT, OR OTHERWISE. Some states do not allow the exclusion or limitation of indirect, special or consequential damages, so the above limitation may not apply to you.

U.S. GOVERNMENT RESTRICTED RIGHTS. If the Product is acquired by or for the U.S. Government then it is provided with Restricted Rights. Use, duplication or disclosure by the U.S. Government is subject to the restrictions set forth in FAR 52.227-19. The contractor/manufacturer is Syngress Publishing, Inc. at 800 Hingham Street, Rockland, MA 02370.

GENERAL: This License Agreement constitutes the entire agreement between the parties relating to the Product. The terms of any Purchase Order shall have no effect on the terms of this License Agreement. Failure of Syngress to insist at any time on strict compliance with this License Agreement shall not constitute a waiver of any rights under this License Agreement. This License Agreement shall be construed and governed in accordance with the laws of the Commonwealth of Massachusetts. If any provision of this License Agreement is held to be contrary to law, that provision will be enforced to the maximum extent permissible and the remaining provisions will remain in full force and effect.

*If you do not agree, please return this product to the place of purchase for a refund.

Syngress: *The Definition of a Serious Security Library*

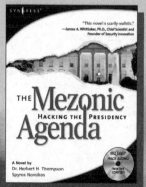